LYLE

What's It Worth?

Anthony Curtis

A PERIGEE BOOK

Perigee Books
are published by
The Berkley Publishing Group
200 Madison Avenue
New York, NY 10016

Copyright © 1995 by Lyle Publications
All rights reserved. This book, or parts thereof,
may not be reproduced in any form without permission.
Published simultaneously in Canada

ISBN 0-399-51937-8
First edition: June 1995

Cover design by Pat Smythe

Printed in the United States of America
5   6   7   8   9   10

This book is printed on acid-free paper.
∞

LYLE

What's It Worth?

Most Perigee Books are available at special quantity discounts for bulk purchases for sales promotions, premiums, fund-raising or educational use. Special books, or book excerpts, can also be created to fit specific needs.

For details, write: Special Markets, The Berkley Publishing Group, 200 Madison Avenue, New York, New York 10016.

What's It Worth?

Once upon a time, collecting (we're not talking Federal furniture or Storr silver here) was a strictly amateur game, indulged in by elderly eccentrics or schoolkids practising to become elderly eccentrics. Whatever the object of their passion it was likely to be collected strictly for its own sake and not for the likelihood of its bringing in a cool million or two.

But now all that is changing. Maybe it's the speed at which life is moving nowadays, with new technology creating new materials and new tastes every other week, or maybe it's a reaction to the feeling of impermanence created by our throwaway society, but it seems everyone is jumping on the collecting bandwagon. And the rationale of collecting is changing subtly too. There is no doubt that we live in an increasingly materialistic age, when the question 'What's it Worth?' is asked ever more often.

The question is to some extent still a vexed one. On the one hand, you collect things which you like for their own sake, and with which you like to be surrounded. On the other hand, especially if you're paying considerable sums to acquire them, it's good, even vital to know that they will hold or appreciate in value and that, in extremis, you could sell them at a nice little profit.

This aspect matters more, of course, if, as seems increasingly to be the case, potentially large sums are involved. For example, if you collect, say, soup can labels which come free with the product, then you probably think more about the items themselves than making a fortune out of them. If, on the other hand, you're an arctophilist (teddy bear collector), in the present climate you'll want to know if your much loved teddy bear could be worth $1,000, $50,000 or even $150,000 – the staggering sum which 'Teddy Girl', a 1904 Steiff cinnamon center-seam teddy fetched at auction recently.

And the range of things which merit the question 'What's it Worth?' is expanding all the time as more and more people come into the game. For popularity quite as much as rarity plays a determining role when establishing value. If enough people wake up to the attractions of the above-mentioned soup can labels, then the amateur (in the narrow sense of the word) collector could, willy-nilly, find himself sitting on a fortune. Take the 1930s radio, for example, which sold for over $26,000 recently. It made instant headlines, and suddenly the market in period radios has really taken off, for success in such fields seems to be instantly newsworthy and thereafter almost self-perpetuating.

The other development of the past few years is that we're not just talking potential works of art here, or at least items where the attractiveness of the design is paramount. Collectors now are latching onto the most banal and practical items of the sort which are most likely of all to be consigned to garage, attic, or even the local garbage dump – old toasters, hair dryers, gas cookers, sewing machines and even lawn mowers have become so popular as collectibles and attracted so wide a following that even the major auction houses are adopting them as regulars. For when sewing machines and typewriters (of the write type, so to speak!) are known to sell for more than $25,000, it's not surprising that people sit up and take notice.

In this book, you'll find chapter and verse on the sort of items, both the mainstream and the decidedly offbeat, which are nevertheless worth substantial sums. Each is fully identified and illustrated to give you all the basic information you need to recognise them when you see them in your local flea market or garage sale. This book, too, will provide you with an invaluable insight into the type of stars which could be tipped to rise next in the collecting firmament, and about which it is well worth asking the question 'What's It Worth?'

ACKNOWLEDGEMENTS

AB Stockholms Auktionsverk, Box 16256, 103 25 Stockholm, Sweden

Academy Auctioneers, Northcote House, Northcote Avenue, Ealing, London W5 3UR

Allen & Harris, St Johns Place, Whiteladies Road, Clifton, Bristol

Jean Claude Anaf, Lyon Brotteaux, 13 bis place Jules Ferry, 69456 Lyon, France

Anderson & Garland, Marlborough House, Marlborough Crescent, Newcastle upon Tyne NE1 4EE

The Auction Galleries, Mount Rd., Tweedmouth, Berwick on Tweed

Auction Team Köln, Postfach 50 11 68, D-5000 Köln 50 Germany

Auktionshaus Arnold, Bleichstr. 42, 6000 Frankfurt a/M, Germany

Bearnes, Rainbow, Avenue Road, Torquay TQ2 5TG

Biddle & Webb, Ladywood Middleway, Birmingham B16 0PP

Bigwood, The Old School, Tiddington, Stratford upon Avon

Black Horse Agencies, Locke & England, 18 Guy Street, Leamington Spa

Boardman Fine Art Auctioneers, Station Road Corner, Haverhill, Suffolk CB9 0EY

Bonhams, Montpelier Street, Knightsbridge, London SW7 1HH

Bonhams Chelsea, 65–69 Lots Road, London SW10 0RN

Bonhams West Country, Dowell Street, Honiton, Devon

Bosleys, 42 West Street, Marlow, Bucks SL7 1NB

Bristol Auction Rooms, St Johns Place, Apsley Road, Clifton, Bristol BS8 2ST

Butterfield & Butterfield, 220 San Bruno Avenue, San Francisco CA 94103, USA

Butterfield & Butterfield, 7601 Sunset Boulevard, Los Angeles CA 90046, USA

Canterbury Auction Galleries, 40 Station Road West, Canterbury CT2 8AN

Christie's (International) SA, 8 place de la Taconnerie, 1204 Genève, Switzerland

Christie's Monaco, S.A.M, Park Palace 98000 Monte Carlo, Monaco

Christie's Scotland, 164–166 Bath Street Glasgow G2 4TG

Christie's South Kensington Ltd., 85 Old Brompton Road, London SW7 3LD

Christie's, 8 King Street, London SW1Y 6QT

Christie's East, 219 East 67th Street, New York, NY 10021, USA

Christie's, 502 Park Avenue, New York, NY 10022, USA

Christie's, Cornelis Schuytstraat 57, 1071 JG Amsterdam, Netherlands

Christie's SA Roma, 114 Piazza Navona, 00186 Rome, Italy

Christie's Swire, 2804–6 Alexandra House, 16–20 Chater Road, Hong Kong

Christie's Australia Pty Ltd., 1 Darling Street, South Yarra, Victoria 3141, Australia

Cooper Hirst Auctions, The Granary Saleroom, Victoria Road, Chelmsford, Essex CM2 6LH

Dee, Atkinson & Harrison, The Exchange Saleroom, Driffield, Nth Humberside YO25 7LJ

Diamond Mills & Co., 117 Hamilton Road, Felixstowe, Suffolk

David Dockree Fine Art, 224 Moss Lane, Bramhall, Stockport SK7 1BD

William Doyle Galleries, 175 East 87th Street, New York, NY 10128, USA

Dreweatt Neate, Donnington Priory, Donnington, Berkshire.

Hy. Duke & Son, 40 South Street, Dorchester, Dorset

Du Mouchelles Art Galleries Co., 409 E. Jefferson Avenue, Detroit, Michigan 48226, USA

WHAT'S IT WORTH?

Sala de Artes y Subastas Durán, Serrano 12, 28001 Madrid, Spain

Eldred's, Box 796, E. Dennis, MA 02641, USA

R H Ellis & Sons, 44/46 High St., Worthing, BN11 1LL

Fellows & Son, Augusta House, 19 Augusta Street, Hockley, Birmingham

Finarte, 20121 Milano, Piazzetta Bossi 4, Italy

Peter Francis, 19 King Street, Carmarthen, Dyfed

Fraser Pinney's, 8290 Devonshire, Montreal, Quebec, Canada H4P 2PZ

Galerie Koller, Rämistr. 8, CH 8024 Zürich, Switzerland

Galerie Moderne, 3 rue du Parnasse, 1040 Bruxelles, Belgium

Geering & Colyer (Black Horse Agencies) Highgate, Hawkhurst, Kent

Glerum Auctioneers, Westeinde 12, 2512 HD's Gravenhage, Netherlands

Graves Son & Pilcher, 71 Church Road, Hove, East Sussex, BN3 2GL

Greenslade Hunt, Magdalene House, Church Square, Taunton, Somerset, TA1 1SB

Peter Günnemann, Ehrenberg Str. 57, 2000 Hamburg 50, Germany

Hampton's Fine Art, 93 High Street, Godalming, Surrey

Hanseatisches Auktionshaus für Historica, Neuer Wall 57, 2000 Hamburg 36, Germany

William Hardie Ltd., 141 West Regent Street, Glasgow G2 2SG

Andrew Hartley Fine Arts, Victoria Hall, Little Lane, Ilkely

Hauswedell & Nolte, D-2000 Hamburg 13, Pöseldorfer Weg 1, Germany

Giles Haywood, The Auction House, St John's Road, Stourbridge, West Midlands, DY8 1EW

Muir Hewitt, Halifax Antiques Centre, Queens Road/Gibbet Street, Halifax HX1 4LR

Hobbs & Chambers, 'At the Sign of the Bell', Market Place, Cirencester, Glos

Hotel de Ventes Horta, 390 Chaussée de Waterloo (Ma Campagne), 1060 Bruxelles, Belgium

Jacobs & Hunt, Lavant Street, Petersfield, Hants. GU33 3EF

P Herholdt Jensens Auktioner, Rundforbivej 188, 2850 Nerum, Denmark

Kennedy & Wolfenden, 218 Lisburn Rd, Belfast BT9 6GD

G A Key, Aylsham Saleroom, 8 Market Place, Aylsham, Norfolk, NR11 6EH

Kunsthaus am Museum, Drususgasse 1–5, 5000 Köln 1, Germany

Kunsthaus Lempertz, Neumarkt 3, 5000 Köln 1, Germany

W.H. Lane & Son, 64 Morrab Road, Penzance, Cornwall, TR18 2QT

Langlois Ltd., Westaway Rooms, Don Street, St Helier, Channel Islands

Lawrence Butler Fine Art Salerooms, Marine Walk, Hythe, Kent, CT21 5AJ

Lawrence Fine Art, South Street, Crewkerne, Somerset TA18 8AB

Lawrence's Fine Art Auctioneers, Norfolk House, 80 High Street, Bletchingley, Surrey

David Lay, The Penzance Auction House, Alverton, Penzance, Cornwall TA18 4KE

Lots Road Chelsea Auction Galleries, 71 Lots Road, Chelsea, London SW10 0RN

Morphets, 4–6 Albert Street, Harrogate, North Yorks HG1 1JL

D M Nesbit & Co, 7 Clarendon Road, Southsea, Hants PO5 2ED

John Nicholson, 1 Crossways Court, Fernhurst, Haslemere, Surrey GU27 3EP

Onslow's, Metrostore, Townmead Road, London SW6 2RZ

Outhwaite & Litherland, Kingsley Galleries, Fontenoy Street, Liverpool, Merseyside L3 2BE

J R Parkinson Son & Hamer Auctions, The Auction Rooms, Rochdale, Bury, Lancs

Phillips Manchester, Trinity House, 114 Northenden Road, Sale, Manchester M33 3HD

Phillips Son & Neale SA, 10 rue des Chaudronniers, 1204 Genève, Switzerland

Phillips West Two, 10 Salem Road, London W2 4BL

Phillips, 11 Bayle Parade, Folkestone, Kent CT20 1SQ

Phillips, 49 London Road, Sevenoaks, Kent TN13 1UU

Phillips, 65 George Street, Edinburgh EH2 2JL

Phillips, Blenstock House, 7 Blenheim Street, New Bond Street, London W1Y 0AS

Phillips Marylebone, Hayes Place, Lisson Grove, London NW1 6UA

Phillips, New House, 150 Christleton Road, Chester CH3 5TD

Riddetts, Richmond Hill, Bournemouth

Ritchie's, 429 Richmond Street East, Toronto, Canada M5A 1R1

Derek Roberts Antiques, 24–25 Shipbourne Road, Tonbridge, Kent TN10 3DN

Russell, Baldwin & Bright, The Fine Art Saleroom, Ryelands Road, Leominster HR6 8JG

Schrager Auction Galleries, 2915 N Sherman Boulevard, PO Box 10390, Milwaukee WI 53210, USA

Selkirk's, 4166 Olive Street, St Louis, Missouri 63108, USA

Skinner Inc., Bolton Gallery, Route 117, Bolton MA, USA

Sotheby's, 34–35 New Bond Street, London W1A 2AA

Sotheby's, 1334 York Avenue, New York NY 10021

Sotheby's, 112 George Street, Edinburgh EH2 2LH

Sotheby's, Summers Place, Billingshurst, West Sussex RH14 9AD

Sotheby's Monaco, BP 45, 98001 Monte Carlo

Southgate Auction Rooms, 55 High St, Southgate, London N14 6LD

Henry Spencer, 20 The Square, Retford, Notts. DN22 6BX

Stride & Son, Southdown House, St John's St., Chichester, Sussex

G E Sworder & Son, Northgate End Salerooms, 15 Northgate End, Bishop Stortford, Herts

Taviner's of Bristol, Prewett Street, Redcliffe, Bristol BS1 6PB

Tennants, Harmby Road, Leyburn, Yorkshire

Thomson Roddick & Laurie, 24 Lowther Street, Carlisle

Venator & Hanstein, Cäcilienstr. 48, 5000 Köln 1, Germany

Wallis & Wallis, West Street Auction Galleries, West Street, Lewes, E. Sussex BN7 2NJ

Ward & Morris, Stuart House, 18 Gloucester Road, Ross on Wye HR9 5BN

Warren & Wignall Ltd, The Mill, Earnshaw Bridge, Leyland Lane, Leyland PR5 3PH

Dominique Watine-Arnault, 11 rue François 1er, 75008 Paris, France

Wells Cundall Nationwide Anglia, Staffordshire House, 27 Flowergate, Whitby YO21 3AX

Woltons, 6 Whiting Street, Bury St Edmunds, Suffolk IP33 1PB

Peter Wilson, Victoria Gallery, Market Street, Nantwich, Cheshire CW5 5DG

Woolley & Wallis, The Castle Auction Mart, Salisbury, Wilts SP1 3SU

CONTENTS

ADDING MACHINES

A Curta Type II four-function sliding cylinder calculator, the smallest ever built, by Curt Herzstark, 1948.
(Auction Team Köln)
$540

An early German Archimedes Model C tiered platen adding machine with ten inputs, by Reinhold Poethig, Glashuette/Sachsen, 1912. (Auction Team Koeln)
$1,284

An Exact (Addi 7) rare export version of the Addi 7 (Lipsia) adding machine, with original box, 1930. (Auction Team Koeln)
$164

A mechanical Brandt Automatic Cashier money changer with full keyboard, 1921.
(Auction Team Köln)
$170

The famous Swiss Millionaer adding machine, made by Hans W. Egli, Zurich, in fine wooden box with purpose made sloping wooden desk, 1895. (Auction Team Koeln)
$3,852

A Curta Type 1 calculator, sectioned for display with separate components, in fitted green case, by Contina, Liechtenstein.
(Christie's)
$1,187

A Thatcher's rotary calculator by Keuffel & Esser, New York, with instructions on baseboard and mahogany case, 24in. wide.
(Christie's)
$1,036

A Brical calculator, with five scales and windows for L.S.D., in plush lined case, 7in. wide.
(Christie's S. Ken)
$216

A Millionaire calculator by Hans W. Egli, with brass bed, facility for addition, subtracting, division and multiplication, 25½in. wide.
(Christie's)
$1,079

A carved and painted pine and gesso 'pig' butcher's trade sign, American, 20th century, carved in the round, length 30in.
(Sotheby's) $3,450

A painted composition and zinc Indian scout cigar store figure, W. Demuth & Co., 501 Broadway, New York, circa 1870, 77in. high.
(Sotheby's) $26,400

A 1920's metal-body hanging advertising sign in the shape of a film box with hanging panel and mounted bracket.
(Christie's) $285

An advertising clock for Busch Light Beer, 110v electric, unused and in original packing with operating instructions, 35cm. diameter.
(Auction Team Köln)
                               $117

A painted wooden and wrought-iron barber shop trade sign, American, 19th century, with three shaped panels inscribed *Ladies Barber and Gents* in red letters on blue and white grounds, 35½in. wide.
(Christie's) $1,650

A good ammunition display board, the center with the trade mark of Nobel Industries Ltd. encompassed by a circle of cartridges and a further circle of brass cased ammunition, 79 x 64cm.
(Phillips) $3,111

An Ever Ready Safety Razor advertising clock, made of wood with American 8 day movement, the price of 12 blades on the pendulum.
(Auction Team Köln)
                             $2,064

An Elgin advertising display, a driver standing cranking his vintage car before an Elgin billboard on which lights flash on and off, clock attachment above, 42cm. high, circa 1920.
(Auction Team Köln)
                               $195

K. Kunik, West Germany, a 16mm. red-body Mickey Mouse camera with paper Mickey laid on to shaped metal advertising stand.
(Christie's) $388

An amusing carved and painted pine circus advertising figure of a zebra, Cole Brothers Circus, Indiana, circa 1920, height 59in. (Sotheby's) $5,175

A carved and painted pine fish trade sign, American, late 19th/early 20th century, the solid, boxy fish with open jaws and carved fin, length 32in. (Sotheby's) $4,313

Gilt zinc apothecary trade sign, America, 19th century, 40in. high. (Skinner) $468

Fill Your Sump From The Castrol Pump, pictorial printed tinplate, 46 x 34cm. (Onslow's) $432

A painted sheet-iron blacksmith sign, American, late 19th/early 20th century, painted black, 36in. high. (Sotheby's) $2,310

A Coca Cola neon advertising clock with second hand and surrounding neon tube with typical Coco Cola Stop Sign symbol, in green hammered casing, 40 x 39cm, 1942. (Auction Team Köln) $463

A glazed wall display cabinet of I. Sorby 'Punch' Brand Tools, including hand and tenon saw, 43^1/2 x 39in. (Christie's) $3,350

An amusing carved and painted pine circus advertising figure of a tiger, Cole Brothers Circus, Indiana, circa 1920, height 59in. (Sotheby's) $4,313

Victorian six-drawer spool cabinet by J. P. Coates, paneled ends, flanking columns, 20^1/2in. high. (Eldred's) $385

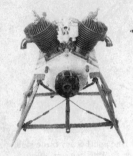

An extremely rare Anzani full-sized V-twin aero engine, crankcase No. 5435, with starting handle and chain drive. (Christie's)　　　　$3,052

A detailed flying scale model of the Curtis Owl with wooden airframe, working elevators, rudder ailerons and flaps, finished in USAAF camouflage, wingspan 82in. (Christie's)　　　　$760

A rare model 5-cylinder radial spark-ignition aluminium aero engine, with air-cooled cylinders, push-rod operated valves, carburettor, inlet pipes and exhaust stubs, 5in. (Christie's)　　　　$1,119

A four-bladed laminated mahogany aircraft propeller, the boss stamped *G64N51, D2366P3340, T28096 LH, 200HP, HISPANO SUIZA, SE5,* 94in. diameter. (Christie's)　　　　$1,260

A gilt-bronze medallion, the obverse embossed with a pilot's head and shoulders, in flying dress, embossed *Lindbergh Medal of the Congress of the United States of America, Act May 4 1928*, 2³/₄in. diameter. (Christie's)　　　　$145

A brown flying-jacket of the Irvin thermally-insulated type (the zip fasteners at the wrists possibly replaced). (Christie's S. Ken)　　　　$676

A World War II German airman's watch in gray painted case, the matt gray dial with luminous hands and Arabic numerals.　　　　$1,200

A detailed static display model of the Sopwith Pup, the cockpit with flying and engine controls, windscreen, machine gun, 9-cylinder rotary engine, propeller, undercarriage and other details, 9¹/₂in. long. (Christie's)　　　　$543

A leatherette and silk lined correspondence folder, the cover embossed in gilt *Graf Zeppelin*, with a pictorial representation of LZ 127, 17¹/₂in. wide opened. (Christie's)　　　　$1,043

A handpainted pottery mug, decorated with an F-86 Sabre, the crest of 18 Fighter Bomber Wing and lettered *'N.C.O. Open Mess'*, 4in. high.
(Christie's) $81

A fine and detailed flying scale model of the Bucker Bu131 Jungmann with fabric covered wooden airframe with working control surfaces, finished in Luftwaffe markings and camouflage, wingspan 72in.
(Christie's) $1,260

A USAAF issue silk lined leather flying jacket, size 30, the back decorated with an F86 Saber surrounded by stars.
(Christie's) $369

An R.A.F. 2nd World War period sector clock, the dial sectors in colors with R.A.F. crest, 17$\frac{1}{4}$in. diameter overall.
(Christie's) $3,476

A control column handgrip from a Bf-109 with armament at ptt switches, with plaque embossed *'Bauart: Argus Motoren G.M.B.H. Hersteller: Original Bruhn'*, 10$\frac{1}{4}$in. high.
(Christie's) $651

A bronze medallion commemorating the Montgolfier brothers' ascent, with molded signature *N. Galteaux*, 1$\frac{5}{8}$in. diameter.
(Christie's) $304

A gong formed from a Monosopape rotary engine, cylinder suspended above a mahogany mount, carved from a propeller boss, 20in.
(Christie's) $224

A Supermarine Spitfire blind flying panel, comprising air speed indicator, artificial horizon, climb and descent indicator, 14in. wide.
(Christie's) $869

A menu card, The Graf Zeppelin over New York from the first Europe Pan-American flight, issued by the Louis Sherry Hotel N.Y., 1929.
(Christie's) $478

A late 19th century Italian alabaster bust of Galileo, unsigned, 14in. high. (Christie's) **$2,081**

A 17th century Flemish alabaster relief panel of the Flight into Egypt, in the background soldiers carry out Herod's Edict, $6^1/_2$ x 9in. (Christie's S. Ken) **$1,995**

'Il Spinario', an alabaster figure after the Antique, the seated boy leaning over to draw a thorn from his foot, $17^5/_8$in. high. (Christie's East) **$880**

A pair of late 19th century Italian alabaster seated putti, one reading an alphabet book, the other writing *Canova*, 43cm. and 41cm. high. (Christie's London) **$3,500**

An Italian carved alabaster figure group of the birth of Venus by Fliaccini, circa 1880, inscribed *Prof. H. Fliaccini, Florence*, $23^1/_2$in. high. (Christie's East) **$11,000**

A pair of Italian alabaster and brass urns, the gadrooned body with two handles and centered by a bacchic mask on a pinched socle and stepped square base, late 18th century, $18^3/_4$in. high. (Christie's) **$5,634**

An Italian alabaster group of lovers, by F. Vichi, shown embracing, stylized clouds behind, signed, late 19th/20th century, 20in. wide. (Christie's) **$4,250**

A pair of Italian alabaster ewers with zoomorphic spouts and exotic bird handles with stop-fluted baluster bodies, late 19th century, $33^1/_4$in. high. (Christie's) **$2,275**

A 19th century alabaster bust of a young lady in pre-Raphaelite headdress, signed E. Fiaschi, 50in. high. (Sworders) **$1,500**

One of a pair of late 19th century French alabaster and ormolu mounted urns, the covers with pineapple finials, 18in. high. (Christie's)
(Two) $1,500

A sculpted alabaster model of a snarling lion with inset glass eyes, its head turned to dexter, on a naturalistic rocky base, 22in. long. (Christie's S. Ken.) $900

One of a pair of carved alabaster and ormolu mounted figural wall brackets, each in the form of satyrs holding twin cornucopiae branches, 32cm. wide. (Phillips)(Two) $3,363

A Greek alabaster figure of a maiden, shown standing beside a well, her robe falling loosely from one shoulder, holding a ewer attached to a rope in her right hand, late 19th century, 23¹/₄in. high. (Christie's) $1,899

Two early 17th century alabaster sculptures in high relief of the Crucifixion and the Compassion of Christ, the figures still with traces of gilding, monogramed *IDH*, Malines, 24 x 19cm. (Finarte) $12,988

An Italian white alabaster figure of a young boy playing a flute, his shirt tied with a bow and wearing knee-length breeches, on a circular base, second half 19th century, 24¹/₄in. high. (Christie's) $3,188

Polychrome alabaster group of the Nativity, Venice, 17th century, 44 x 42cm. (Finarte) $11,290

A 19th century alabaster tazza, with a molded rim raised on a turned base, the wreath carved loop handles with lion mask terminals, 14in. wide. (Christie's S. Ken.) $1,100

A painted and molded composition bust portrait of George Washington, American, 20th century, height 23¹/₄in. (Sotheby's) $1,035

A three drum coin operated Rotomat amusement machine. (Auction Team Köln)

$501

A Jokers Wild poker dice coin machine for 5 cent pieces by the Von Star Amusement Co., Columbia SC, USA, circa 1930. (Auction Team Köln)

$405

Your Horoscope amusement machine 'Is this Your Lucky Day?', made in the U.K., circa 1930. (Costa/Bates)

$270

A coin operated Rotomat Super Krone wall-hanging amusement machine by Günter Wulff Apparatebau, Berlin, in working order, circa 1970. (Auction Team Köln)

$77

A German 3 drum Omega amusement machine with four peppermint roll dispensers and three brake buttons, by Max Jentzsch & Meerz, Leipzig, restored and in working order, circa 1931. (Auction Team Köln)

$578

A Fayre Win pinball amusement machine, set for old one penny pieces, in working order, American, circa 1930. (Auction Team Köln)

$463

A Bryans Quadmatic Allwin, having two Elevenses Allwins, a seven cup Allwin and a U-Win Allwin with one large U-shaped winning cup, 66in. high. (Bonhams)

$853

A Yankee Trade Stimulator cigarette promoting amusement machine for Wings shop counters, a five-drum machine for 1 cent coins. (Auction Team Köln)

$254

A Mill's Stars three-drum amusement machine with jackpot, set for 5 cent pieces, with key and coins, circa 1958, unrestored, in full working order. (Auction Team Köln)

$1,389

American coin operated Baseball Machine pinball machine set for US 1 cent pieces, circa 1935.
(Auction Team Köln)
$463

Film Star Gum Vender, made in Belgium, circa 1950.
(Costa/Bates) $225

An early 20th century coin operated 'Playball' game with eight winning shots, 71cm. high.
(Spencer's) $300

The Governor, a three drum amusement machine by Jennings, USA, with original key, set for US 10 cent pieces, original condition, 1964.
(Auction Team Köln)
$1,158

'Egg laying hen' early stamped metal vending machine made by C F Schulze & Co Berlin. The hen sits on an oval basket and on insertion of 10pfg in her comb and turning of the handle a 12 part container for 59 eggs is moved so that an 'egg' (containing confectionery) is laid. Fully operational, circa 1900. (Auction Team Köln)
$4,725

'British Beauties Bureau' amusement machine made in the U.K., circa 1900.
(Costa/Bates) $2,700

'Clairvoyance' amusement machine 'The Secrets of Clairvoyance and Mesmerism', made in the U.K. by Illusion Machines, circa 1890.
(Costa/Bates) $3,600

A late Victorian cast-iron platform weighing machine, labeled *Salter 1897*, to weigh 24 stone, with elaborate all over decoration, approx. 66in. high.
(Bonhams) $1,876

'Automatic Doctor' vending machine 'For the convenience of visitors' made by the Allied Chemical Co. Ltd., 1930's.
(Costa/Bates) $450

A fine Etruscan full-bodied handled olpe with trefoil lip and spur red handle, 7¼in. high.
(Bonhams) $477

An ancient near Eastern terracotta chariot, in the form of a ram, circa 2nd Millennium B.C., 6³/₄in.
(Bonhams) $2,122

A Roman style metallic gray terracotta comic actor's mask, wearing the skin of Herakles, 3¹/₂in.
(Bonhams) $238

A pottery seated 'Mother Goddess' figurine, her arms curved beneath prominent breasts, 3¹/₂in., Tel-Halaf, 6th Millennium B.C.
(Bonhams) $2,612

An Egyptian limestone relief fragment with the cartouches of the Pharoah Ptolemy V, 205–180 B.C., 11 x 9¹/₂in.
(Bonhams) $986

A buff pottery near Eastern twin-handled tripod vessel, with painted umber decoration of four armed warriors, early 1st Millennium B.C., 5¹/₂in. high.
(Bonhams) $445

A North Iranian sea-green glazed deep cylindrical pottery beaker, with horizontal lug handles and five yellow wheel-sunbursts around the exterior, 4in. high.
(Bonhams) $286

An Apulian red-figure volute krater, with white painted masks instead of volutes on the handles, Greek, South Italy, 4th century B.C., 24¹/₂in.
(Bonhams) $6,530

A white limestone plaque with strongly modeled figure of the dwarf god Bes in high relief, Roman Egypt, 1st-2nd century A.D., 7³/₄in. high.
(Bonhams) $731

A finely detailed wooden panel mummy portrait of a young woman with open eyed gaze and wearing a thin loop chain necklace, Roman Egypt, 2nd-3rd century A.D., 10½in. high. (Bonhams) $2,600

A bronze figure of a prancing horse with head held high and mane flying back, 6.3cm. high, 1st–2nd century A.D. (Phillips) $563

Mochica figural pottery vessel, circa 200–500 A.D., the rectangular base surmounted by a fierce looking human head, having long fangs, 8¾in. high. (Butterfield & Butterfield) $715

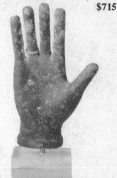

Jalisco kneeling pottery female figure, circa 150 B.C.–250 A.D., the short bent legs covered by a skirt and supporting a massive torso, 11½in. high. (Butterfield & Butterfield) $220

Mayan polychrome pottery cylinder vase, circa 550–950 A.D., painted allover in a repeat panel pattern of bat face profiles, 8in. high. (Butterfield & Butterfield) $770

A Roman heavy bronze hollow votive hand, with extended fingers, and a late Roman thin gold ring, 3rd-4th century A.D., 5¾in. high. (Bonhams) $3,700

An Apulian black-glazed hydria decorated with the draped standing figure of a winged Nike, early 4th century B.C., 11¾in. high. (Bonhams) $4,000

Veracruz seated pottery figure, circa 550–950 A.D., with legs crossed and hands to the knees, 14½in. high. (Butterfield & Butterfield) $1,980

A large Apulian black-glazed bell krater with red-figure decoration of a seated nude female gazing into a mirror, Greek South Italy, late 4th century B.C., 12½in. (Bonhams) $2,000

A carved and stained-wood relief in the manner of Grinling Gibbons, with a spindle-galleried rope-twist basket issuing scrolling foliage, 19th century, 17in. high.
(Christie's) $3,011

An unusual and rare molded copper canopy corbel, Clinton and Russell, New York, circa 1900, in Renaissance style, height 33in.
(Sotheby's) $2,645

One of a set of three carved sandstone capitals, the octagonal tops above deeply carved foliate and floral middle sections, 23¹/₂in. wide.
(Christie's) (Three) $740

A Coade stone keystone, 'The Laughing Philosopher', of tapering form, the leering face shown bearded and wearing the floppy turban, the base signed *Coade London, 1790*, late 18th century, 13in. wide at top.
(Christie's) $2,834

A pair of Vicenza stone fruit baskets and a pair of pineapple finials, the baskets: 17¹/₂in., the finials: 25in. high.
(Christie's) $1,293

One of a pair of reconstituted stone gate pier finials, each sphere of two sections, on circular socle and square base, 40in. high.
(Christie's) (Two) $1,110

A Japanese granite lantern, with pagoda top, the pierced octagonal shaft decorated with raised carved naturalistic scenes on stepped base, 69in. high.
(Christie's) $2,374

Early World War II Phoney War period propaganda urinal with Swastika and open mouthed pictures of Hitler, Goering and Mussolini, makers' stamp for Twyfords Ltd.
(Bosley's) $1,080

One of a pair of sandstone 'flambeau' gate pier finials, each with stylized frond decoration tops, on square chamfered base, 19th century, 20in. wide.
(Christie's) (Two) $317

The Grocers' Company Coade stone camel, with a roped bale, standing beside rockwork, on an oval base signed *COADE--99*, late 18th century, 53in. wide.
(Christie's) $25,300

A stone keystone, carved with a bearded mask, 19th century, 13½in. wide, 17¾in. high.
(Christie's) $483

One of a pair of cast-iron gargoyles, each formed of two sections, with grotesque features and outstretched wings, late 19th century, 20in. high.
(Christie's)   (Two) $639

One of a pair of brown glazed terracotta chimney pots, the 'crown' tops above octagonal shafts and square spreading bases, 37½in. high.
(Christie's)   (Two) $102

A pair of carved stone sphinxes, each with an elaborate tasseled headdress and saddles by a raised floral ornament band, 24in. high.
(Christie's) $2,009

Leaded glass scenic window, cathedral arched panel arranged as a copy of the waterfall window designed by Tiffany Studios, 100in. high, 36in. wide.
(Skinner) $5,750

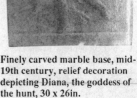

A carved stone plinth of Baroque design, each side carved with inset panels depicting foliate motifs, 25in. high.
(Christie's) $733

A pair of Vicenza stone sea-horses, each carved riding on the 'waves' with scaled fish-like tail, on a rectangular base, 20th century, 31½in. wide.
(Christie's) $1,518

Finely carved marble base, mid-19th century, relief decoration depicting Diana, the goddess of the hunt, 30 x 26in.
(Eldred's) $825

A clockwork nodding cobbler figure, French, circa 1915, the seated figure with black painted composition head and well defined features, 17¼in. high.
(Sotheby's) $1,128

A Martin painted tinplate and fabric 'Le Pianiste', with musical mechanism, 5in. wide.
(Christie's) $783

A Michel Bertrand musical automaton of a clown acrobat, after a Gustave Vichy design and using many original Vichy parts, 20th century, 37in. high.
(Sotheby's) $15,617

A Renou musical automaton of a magic baker, French, circa 1900, the Jumeau head stamped in red *DÉPOSÉ TÊTE JUMEAU B^TE S.G.D.G.*, with open mouth and upper teeth, 17in. high.
(Sotheby's) $6,941

A Gustave Vichy musical automaton of Pierrot serenading the moon, French, circa 1890, the painted papier-mâché crescent moon with rolling brown glass eye and articulated lower jaw, 21in. high.
(Sotheby's) $41,646

A singing bird automaton, French, last quarter 19th century, the glass case containing a tree with silk leaves and flowers and a total of seven birds and two large beetles.
(Tennants) $1,767

A late 19th century French musical automaton diorama, the double sided display depicting Summer and Winter scenes, 22½in. high.
(Bearne's) $626

An automaton of two blacksmiths, probably German, circa 1900, the two figures stand hammering a horseshoe upon an anvil with the forge and bellows beyond, 14½in. high.
(Tennants) $1,488

A good French twin singing bird automaton, the brass wire domed cage containing a bird on a perch, with a companion below, 22in. high overall, second half 19th century.
(Tennants) $3,348

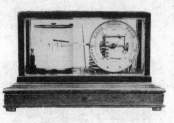

An oxidized and lacquered brass aneroid barometer signed *J. Goldschmid a Zurich*, with internal scale, 6in. wide.
(Christie's) $756

A lacquered brass barograph/barometer, unsigned, with recording drum, key, mechanism, ink bottle, ink needle, and circular weather indicator, 14¹/₄in. wide.
(Christie's) $1,735

An early Improved pocket barometer, signed *T. Cooke York*, with ivorine dial, 9³/₄in. long.
(Christie's) $239

A pocket aneroid altitude barometer, thermometer and compass, French, dated 1901, unsigned with 'open' silvered dial, 5cm diameter.
(Bonham's) $184

A Victorian perpetual calendar mantel clock, with white enamel dial enclosing a roundel with visible anchor escapement, flanked by a perpetual calendar dial and a white enamel barometer/thermometer dial, 21in. wide.
(Christie's) $1,519

A late 19th century desk barometer, the white circular dial with aneroid movement in cut glass surround with four ormolu supports, 9in. high.
(Christie's) $795

A Victorian Tunbridgeware parquetry columnar-compass inscribed *J. Barton, Tonbridge Wells*, on a molded socle and square plinth base, 5¹/₄in. high.
(Christie's) $567

A good 19th century self recording aneroid barometer/timepiece by J. H. Steward, London, the timepiece with black Roman numerals to the circular silvered dial, 71cm. wide.
(Spencer's) $2,499

A French giltwood barometer, the paper dial signed in ink *Scatino, Opticien, Boulevarde St. Martini, à Paris*, 2ft. 8in. high.
(Bonhams) $990

BASKETS

Nantucket basket, Nantucket Island, Massachusetts, early 20th century, with swing handle, incised base, 5in. high. (Skinner) **$605**

Four Shaker splint baskets, 11 to 22in. wide. (Skinner) **$2,860**

A fine cut-tin reticulated basket filled with an assortment of painted stone fruit, American, 19th century, height 10in. (Sotheby's) **$2,300**

An unusual woven splint oval basket, American, late 19th/early 20th century, the tightly woven basket in Nantucket-style with scalloped rim, height 9 1/2in. (Sotheby's) **$1,265**

A mahogany and cane newspaper basket, designed by Sir Edwin Lutyens, with carved 'rope' decoration and cane panels, 81cm. wide. (Christie's) **$7,876**

Lightship basket, Nantucket Island, Massachusetts, early 20th century, with swing handle, 8in. high. (Skinner) **$1,100**

Nantucket basket, signed *Stanley Roop*, Nantucket Island, Massachusetts, cover with carved ivory plaque of a dolphin, 8in. high. (Skinner) **$1,100**

A wooden basket, American, 19th century, circular with finger molding and handle for carrying, stamped on the lid and bottom *J. DYER*, 13 1/4in. diameter. (Christie's) **$110**

A woven splint basket, American, late 19th century, with square base and circular rim with stationary split ash handle, diameter 15in. (Sotheby's) **$173**

A woven splint and ash potato-stamp decorated basket, Eastern Woodland Indian Tribes of the Iroquois Nation, early 20th century, 6¹/₂in. high. (Sotheby's)   **$633**

Shahsavan egg basket, Northwest Persia, early 20th century, stepped polygons in blue, ivory, aubergine, gold and blue-green on the red field, 6in. wide. (Skinner)   **$495**

A potato stamp-decorated woven splint single-handled basket, Eastern Woodland Indian Tribes of the Iroquois Nation, early 20th century, 9¹/₂in. wide. (Sotheby's)   **$403**

A rare miniature potato-stamp decorated woven splint covered basket, Eastern Woodland Indian Tribes of the Iroquois Nation, late 19th century, 3in. high. (Sotheby's)   **$690**

One of a pair of mahogany octagonal waste paper baskets each with molded top above pierced gothic fretwork, 13¹/₄in. high. (Christie's)   **$6,776**

A fine potato-stamp decorated woven splint covered basket, initialed *JHS*, Eastern Woodland Indian Tribes of the Iroquois Nation, late 19th century, 9¹/₂in. high. (Sotheby's)   **$2,875**

A rare potato-stamp decorated single-handled woven splint covered basket, attributed to *JHS*, Eastern Woodland Tribes of the Iroquois Nation, late 19th century, 8in. high. (Sotheby's)   **$2,588**

A fine potato-stamp decorated woven splint open basket, Eastern Woodland Indian Tribes of the Iroquois Nation, early 20th century, 4¹/₂in. high. (Sotheby's)   **$748**

A fine potato-stamp decorated woven splint basket, Eastern Woodland Indian Tribes of the Iroquois Nation, early 20th century, 4³/₄in. high. (Sotheby's)   **$575**

A Regency blue john and bronze mounted urn, the ovoid body raised on an acanthine chased square tapering plinth, 12in. high overall.
(Christie's) $1,500

A brass-mounted Derbyshire bluejohn and alabaster wall bracket, the plateau with cast-leaf chased border, late 18th/early 19th century, 10½in. wide.
(Christie's) $6,545

A Derbyshire bluejohn ovoid urn, the riveted, reeded body with lotus leaf cast finial, on square carrara marble base, late 18th century, 12¼in. high, overall.
(Christie's) $1,348

A pair of George III ormolu-mounted blue john twin-branch candelabra by Matthew Boulton, each with removable stepped turned fluted domed foliate finial issuing stylized Greek-key pattern scrolled acanthus-cast branches, 12in. wide.
(Christie's) $75,735

A large Derbyshire bluejohn urn, the 'fine vein' body with gadrooned top and pineapple finial, the carrara marble and black slate stand with flaming torch amidst foliage, late 18th century, 20in. high.
(Christie's) $12,513

A pair of George III ormolu-mounted blue john cassolettes by Matthew Boulton, each with domed reversible top with acanthus finial and guilloche frieze enclosing a nozzle, 7½in. high.
(Christie's) $15,989

A 19th century blue john urn, mounted on a fleur-de-pêche marble plinth, 10¾in. high.
(Bonhams) $1,800

A pair of George III turned blue john ovoid urns, with stepped surmounts and cylindrical socles, 7¼in. high.
(Christie's) $1,050

A fine George III blue john urn of large size with heavily veined body of good color, 13in. high.
(Bonhams) $3,000

A Derbyshire fluorspar or 'bluejohn' goblet on knopped stem and circular foot, 17cm. high.
(Phillips) $3,382

A pair of English bluejohn urns each with stepped turned finial and on turned socle, 19th century, 13½in. high.
(Christie's) $6,195

A bluejohn cup with circular tapering body on ring-turned tapering shaft and spreading circular base, 6½in. high.
(Christie's) $3,203

A pair of Derbyshire fluorspar or 'bluejohn' obelisks, raised on alabaster and black slate mounted plinths, 42cm. high.
(Phillips) $6,408

A George III ormolu and bluejohn candelabrum by Matthew Boulton, the ovoid body mounted with herms issuing from acanthus foliage, 20¼in. high, 23in. wide. (Christie's) $79,464

A pair of 19th century Derbyshire fluorspar or 'bluejohn' urns with fruiting cone finial, on spreading brass foot and square plinth, 21cm. high.
(Phillips) $2,544

A Derbyshire fluorspar campana-shaped urn, on black slate and gray marble stepped square base, 19th century, 13¾in. high.
(Christie's) $925

A Derbyshire fluorspar or 'bluejohn' turned cup raised on a fluted stem and domed foot, 11cm. diameter.
(Phillips) $641

A George III ormolu-mounted bluejohn perfume burner attributed to Matthew Boulton, the circular top with pierced beaded collar, lacking cover, 7in. high.
(Christie's) $4,145

An English brass-mounted fruitwood box, 19th century, in the form of a lady's purse, 8½in. high
(Christie's) **$4,830**

A rare Chippendale walnut spice chest, Pennsylvania, late 18th century, the door opening to an arrangement of fifteen small drawers fitted with brass pulls, 15¼in. wide.
(Sotheby's) **$9,900**

A painted and decorated shopkeeper's bag sorter, American, late 19th century, 16in. high.
(Christie's) **$863**

An Indo-Portuguese hardwood and ivory inlaid cabinet, geometrically inlaid all-over with a lozenge design, the fall front opening to reveal eight small drawers and a deeper central drawer, 18¼in. wide.
(Christie's S. Ken) **$4,433**

A brown oak letter box either by George Bullock or George Morant, banded overall in holly, first half 19th century, 8¾in. wide.
(Christie's) **$588**

A Momoyama period small rectangular wood coffer and domed cover decorated with panels of mandarin orange trees, magnolia and cherry in gold lacquer, late 16th century, 23 x 13.2 x 15.6cm. high.
(Christie's) **$13,002**

An unusual paint decorated apple box, mid 19th century, and a miscellaneous group of painted stone fruit, early 20th century, approximately 20 pieces.
(Sotheby's) **$4,025**

A mid-Victorian oak miniature hall postbox, the domed top with arcaded panels above a ring-turned shaft centered by a hinged flap inscribed *letters*, 14¾in. high.
(Christie's) **$4,209**

A rectangular maroon lacquered salmon fly reservoir with approx. twenty-one fully dressed gut eyed salmon flies.
(Bonham's) **$849**

BOXES

A Victorian burr walnut and foliate cut brass mounted liqueur casket in the form of a writing slope, with four decanters and a set of twelve cordial glasses, 15in. wide.
(Christie's S. Ken) $964

A 17th century Dutch painted box of oblong form with sliding carved lid, with pierced arched hanging backplate, 36cm. high.
(Phillips) $540

George IV rosewood letter box, circa 1825, gilt bronze finial, rectangular form, open turned spindle sides, 7³/₈in. high.
(Skinner Inc.) $1,200

An Austro-Hungarian ormolu-mounted blue-painted tôle and cast-iron strongbox, the serpentine base with double eagle-headed key escutcheon, depicting the arms of the Holy Roman Empire, mid-18th century, 37in. wide.
(Christie's) $71,148

An important Swiss necessaire with singing bird automaton and twin musical movements, by Frères Rochat, Geneva, circa 1825, the implements with restricted warranty mark for gold, Paris, 1819–1839.
(Christie's) $175, 230

A rare Spanish damascened jewel casket (arqueta), by Plácido Zuloaga of Eibar, dated 1876, the domed coffer with gilt and silvered Moorish decorations on bun feet, the lockplate signed, 21cm. wide.
(Sotheby's) $1,503

A late 17th/early 18th century kingwood veneered and brass bound coffret, the hinged lid and front with radiating veneers, probably Dutch, 39cm. wide.
(Phillips) $2,226

An aventurine lacquer powder box, French, circa 1790, circular, inset with a colorful 3-dimensional collage of the 'Fédération du 14 juillet 1790', leather-lined, 6.5cm. diameter.
(Sotheby's) $1,354

A James II oak spice box, opening to reveal an interior fitted with four variously sized drawers, 14¹/₂in. wide.
(Christie's) $1,996

An extremely fine and rare paint decorated basswood domed top document box, probably Albany, New York State, early 19th century, 12in wide.
(Sotheby's) $29,900

An unusual stenciled and painted 'Theorem' box, American, probably New England, mid 19th century, with hinged lid opening to a compartmented interior with slide, 9³/₄in. wide.
(Sotheby's) $2,200

William IV Sterling and fabric jewel casket by Robert Garrard, London, 1838, the domed green velvet top secured at the edge by dentilated silver border above the lid framing, 6³/₄in. wide.
(Butterfield & Butterfield) $2,750

A painted and decorated pine bride's ribbon box, probably Continental, late 18th/early 19th century, decorated on the top with the figures of an amorous couple, 19¹/₄in. long.
(Sotheby's) $3,300

Gothic style champlevé enamel casket, late 19th century, the corners with female therms, raised on four C-scroll, fruit, and mask-cast feet, 15³/₄in. wide.
(Butterfield & Butterfield) $3,300

A Chippendale brass-mounted mahogany serpentine-front letter box, probably American, circa 1785, the sloped lid opening to a divided well, 13in. high.
(Sotheby's) $1,430

An Anglo-Indian Vizagapatam ebony and ivory games board in the form of two volumes, 19th century, 18¹/₄in. wide.
(Christie's) $1,953

A cherry and mahogany cigar box designed by David Joel, with three bar curved chrome handles, the top with medallion inlaid with *RJWP* monogram, 50cm. wide.
(Christie's) $766

A fine mahogany ballot box, circa 1840, with yes and no drawers with ivory plaques, 12in. high.
(Sotheby's) $8,496

A rare William and Mary oblong silver-mounted shagreen instrument case, the elaborate hinges and lock plate engraved with stylized flowers and pierced with kidney-shaped motifs, circa 1695.
(Christie's) $5,653

A rare paint decorated bentwood oval Shaker sugar box, a Maine Shaker community, circa 1835, 13¾in. long.
(Sotheby's) $4,025

An 18th century German marquetry box with hinged, beveled top inset with a mirror to the reverse, the whole inlaid with panels of griffins, birds and mythological animals, 1ft. 8½in.
(Phillips) $1,752

A pine pipe box, American, dated 1723, with upswept cresting centered by a flowerhead above a rectangular box with shaped top carved with a flowerhead, 12½in. high.
(Christie's) $1,980

A pair of Regency japanned chestnut urns of tapering form, the navette section lids with spire finial, 32cm. high.
(Phillips) $1,602

An Indian teak revolving cigar cabinet carved with foliage and scrolling tendrils, the stand with cabriole legs joined by an undertier, 26in. square.
(Bearne's) $396

A South Staffordshire cylindrical enamel taper-box, the deep blue ground body with color flower cartouches, circa 1770, 2½ in. diam.
(Christie's) $619

A Victorian lace box of plain rectangular form veneered in burr walnut and with elaborate brass hinges and mounts, 21in. wide, mid-19th century.
(Bearne's) $1,504

Baltimore and Ohio railroad wallpaper covered hat box, dated Newburyport June 7, 1833, 16in. wide.
(Skinner) $11,000

ANIMALS

A patinated bronze model of a hound branded *W*, on naturalistic base, signed *P. J. Mene*, 1843, 9¼in. wide. (Christie's) **$703**

A 19th century French gilt bronze and plated encrier, modeled with sheep on a rocky promontory, signed *J. Moigniez*, 12in. wide. (Christie's S. Ken) **$602**

A bronze figure of a walking lion, cast from a model by Antoine Louis Barye, French, late 19th century, 9in. high. (Christie's) **$1,150**

A 19th century animalier bronze figure of a mountain goat, incised J. Moigniez, 26cm. high. (Phillips) **$1,100**

Two rare French bronze models of hares, entitled *'Chasse fermée'* and *'Chasse ouverte'*, cast from models by Jules Moigniez, mid 19th century, 11½in. high. (Christie's) **$9,207**

A 19th century animalier bronze figure of a chamois, incised J. Moigniez, 24cm. high. (Phillips) **$750**

A late 19th century Viennese cold painted bronze figure of a North American buffalo, 7½in. high. (Christie's S. Ken) **$1,441**

One of a pair of bronze deer with brown patina, 34½in. high. (Christie's) **$3,500**

A late 19th century French bronze model of a lioness carrying a cub in her mouth, cast from a model by A. N. Cain, 61 x 84cm.(Christie's) **$5,000**

A French bronze group of a pointer and a retriever, cast from a model by Pierre-Jules Mêne, the two hounds pointing a partridge, 19th century, 8³/₄in. high.
(Christie's) $2,739

Late 19th century bronze model of a rhinoceros on marble stand, 48cm. long.
(Christie's) $5,500

A large bronze model of a hare, signed on the base Hisatoshi, 27cm. long.
(Christie's) $2,250

A late 19th century French bronze figure of a crouching field mouse, the naturalistic white marble base signed *Valton*, 4¹/₂in. high, overall.
(Christie's S. Ken) $429

A pair of cast bronze figures of well-groomed hunting dogs, seated and alert, hand finished brownish-green patina, 24in. high.
(Selkirk's) $1,800

A French bronze model of a stag, cast from a model by Pierre-Jules Mêne, standing on a rocky outcrop, second half 19th century, 23³/₈in. high.
(Christie's) $4,706

A fine French bronze model of a walking bull, cast from a model by Isidore Bonheur, head alert and raised, and tail curled forward, on naturalistic base, 19th century, 15¹/₈in. high.
(Christie's) $7,775

A bronze model of a goat, on a naturalistic base, signed *P. J. Mene*, 5¹/₂in. wide.
(Christie's) $1,087

A good mid-19th century bronze group of a bloodhound studying the slow traverse of a tortoise, cast from a model by Henri-Alfred-Marie Jaccquemart, 7¹/₈in. wide.
(Christie's S. Ken)
                        $2,106

ANIMALS

A French bronze figure of a Fribourg milking cow, cast from a model by Isidore Bonheur, standing on a sloping rockwork base, late 19th century, 11¼ x 13⅝ in.
(Christie's) $2,046

'Middle White Sow: Wharfdale Royal Lady', A gilt-bronze figure, cast from a model by Herbert Haseltine, American, late 19th/early 20th century, 5¼ in. high.
(Christie's) $16,100

A French bronze model of a walking bear, cast from a model by Isidore Bonheur, striding forward, on naturalistic ground strewn with the bones of his last meal, 19th century, 5⅛ in. high.
(Christie's) $5,227

French patinated bronze figure of a bulldog cast after a model by Valton, circa 1900, the excited dog with snarling barking face, 18¼ in. high.
(Butterfield & Butterfield)
$2,750

A pair of bronze models of seated rats holding chestnuts, signed on the bases, Shosai chu, Meiji period, approx. 17cm. long. (Christie's)
$2,000

A 19th century large cold painted Austrian bronze inkstand modeled as a group of a bear fending off two attacking hounds, 15in. high.
(Christie's) $7,500

An oriental gilt bronze figure of a seated monkey, shown seated with head slightly raised and holding a ball on his raised left knee, 9¾ in. high.
(Christie's) $3,680

A French bronze group of an Indian elephant mounted by a mahout crushing a tiger, cast from a model by Antoine-Louis Barye, the mahout lightly clad in a cloak and wearing a turban, mid-19th century, 11in. high.
(Christie's) $12,685

A late 19th century bronze model of the Farnese Bull, after Giambologna, shown with his left foreleg raised, on a rectangular base, 9in. high.
(Christie's S. Ken)
$2,217

BIRDS

A bronze group of two crows perched on a tree stump, Meiji period, 58.5cm. high. (Christie's)

$3,875

A bronzed and parcel-gilt Napoleonic eagle with outstretched wings and clutching a ribbon-tied laurel wreath, 19th century, 38½in. wingspan. (Christie's)

$3,762

A 19th century French animalier bronze figure of a cockerel, the naturalistic oval base signed *P.J. Mêne*, 5in. high, overall. (Christie's)

$895

A bronze koro modeled as an egret, engraved detail and gilded eyes, the base formed as breaking waves, late 19th century, 12.5cm. high. (Christie's)

$3,678

A pair of large bronze models of standing geese, 58cm. and 78cm. high. (Christie's)

$2,350

French bronze figure of a pheasant, late 19th century, after Jules Moigniez, cast life-sized, 27½in. high. (Robt. W. Skinner Inc.)

$1,200

A French bronze model of a reeve, cast from a model by Jules Moigniez, shown with a berry in its beak, its wings partially splayed, signed, 19th century, 9¼in. high. (Christie's)

$1,535

A fine French silvered bronze group of a cockerel and hen, cast from a model by Auguste Nicolas Cain, the cockerel rampant on a basket overflowing with vegetables and straw, signed *CAIN SC* and engraved *CHRISTOPHLE & CIE*, second half 19th century, 8¼in. high. (Christie's)

$2,831

'Peacocks', a cold-painted bronze group cast from a model by A. Kéléty, of two stylized peacocks with polychrome cold-painted decoration, 42.5cm. high. (Christie's)

$2,455

BUSTS

A bronze bust cast from a model by Charles Vyse, of an Army Officer, on a tapering square section stepped base, circa 1918, 34.5cm. high.
(Christie's) $861

A 19th century French bronze head of a child, 'Bebe Endormi', cast from a model by Aime-Jules Dalou, 19cm. high. (Christie's) $4,000

Paul Jean Baptiste Gasq, French (1860–1944), cast bronze figure, allegorical female bust on a red marble plinth, 24in. high. (Selkirk's) $1,500

An English bronze bust of 'La Boulonnaise', cast from a model Aimé-Jules Dalou, wearing traditional hooded cloak fastened at the neck with a decorative clasp, 19th century, 18¼in. high.
(Christie's) $1,863

A pair of French bronze busts of bacchantes, after Clodion, the female bacchante with a decolleté revealing her breasts, the male wearing a goatskin tunic, 19th century, 10⅝in. high.
(Christie's) $2,046

A French parcel-gilt bronze bust of a young woman, cast from a model by Eugène Laurent, shown wearing a hat, tied with a bow, signed E. Laurent, on a circular spreading socle and square plinth, 22in. high.
(Christie's) $5,667

A bronze bust of Cendrillon, cast from a model by Emmanuele Villanis, shown wearing a scarf, on square shaped socle, circa 1895, 12in. high.
(Christie's) $2,125

Early 20th century bronze bust of Woman, signed Wigglesworth, stamped Gorham Co. Founders, 13¾in. high. (Robt. W. Skinner Inc.) $900

A French bronze bust of Shakespeare, shown wearing contemporary dress, stamped and numbered on the reverse F. Barbedienne Fondeur 109, late 19th century, 27¼in. high.
(Christie's) $1,594

A Victorian bronze bust of a gentleman, after J.B. Carpeaux, on a square-shaped socle base, 7¼ in. high, with a white marble plinth below.
(Christie's S. Ken) $931

Emile Corillan Guillemin, French, (1841–1907), cast metal figure, 'What a Fly', signed in metal, 29in. high.
(Selkirk's) $4,000

An Italian bust of Plato, after the Antique, the hair, beard and tunic finely chiseled, attributed to the Chiurazzi foundry, early 19th century, 10½ in. high.
(Christie's) $2,046

An Italian bronze bust of a gentleman, cast from a model by Giuseppe Renda, shown with a large moustache, on molded socle, late 19th century, 19¾ in. high.
(Christie's) $2,374

A pair of bronzed resin busts of Charles Stewart Rolls and Frederick Henry Royce, 8½ in. high.
(Christie's) $1,210

A magnificent 19th century French bronze parcel gilt and enameled bust of La Juive d'Alger, by Charles-Henri-Joseph Cordier, signed and dated *Cordier 1863*. (Christie's London) $301,070

A 19th century French bronze bust of Napoleon as Emperor, wearing cocked hat, signed and dated *P. Colombo, 1885*, 14in. high, overall.
(Christie's) $2,500

A late 19th century English bronze mask of Mary Swainson, cast from a model by Alphonse Legros, 30cm. high.
(Christie's London) $2,325

A bronze bust of Dalila, cast from a model by Emmanuele Villanis, shown wearing a shawl, signed on a naturalistic socle, circa 1890, 12½ in. high.
(Christie's) $2,125

EQUESTRIAN

A 19th century Russian bronze group, cast from a model by A. Gratchev, of a soldier on horseback, a lance in his right hand, on a naturalistic base, 11¾in. high.
(Christie's S. Ken) **$1,773**

A bronze figure of a stallion, cast from a model by Jules Moigniez, French, 19th century, 13in. high.
(Christie's) **$1,725**

A 19th century equestrian bronze group of the uniformed Wellington, astride Copenhagen, on a naturalistic rectangular base, 14in. high, overall.
(Christie's S. Ken) **$1,104**

A bronze group of a Cossack on horseback, shown with his left hand raised to his brow and turning to his rear, a lance to his right hand, indistinctly signed, 10in. high.
(Christie's S. Ken) **$887**

A French bronze and parcel gilt group entitled *'Chasseur Persan au Guepard'*, cast from a model by Alfred Dubucand, the seated hunter in elaborate costume, a seated panther by his side, signed, late 19th century, 17½in. wide.
(Christie's) **$9,740**

A 19th century Russian bronze group, cast from a model by A. Gratchev, of a Murid tribesman on horseback with a maiden, his horse negotiating a steep incline, 13½in. high.
(Christie's S. Ken) **$1,108**

A 19th century French bronze group of a fallen Amazonian warrior holding the reins of her attentive steed, signed *GECHTER*, circa 1840, 15¼in. wide.
(Christie's) **$2,800**

An Italian bronze equestrian portrait of Wellington, cast from a model by Carlo Marochetti, the general shown seated upon his favourite horse Copenhagen, 19th century, 17in. high.
(Christie's) **$2,191**

An English bronze figure of a cowboy on horseback, cast from a model by Walter Winans, the horse jumping over a tree trunk, late 19th century, 15¾in. high.
(Christie's) **$3,312**

EQUESTRIAN

A large French bronze group of a racehorse with jockey up, entitled *'Le grand jockey'*, cast from a model by Isidore Bonheur, circa 1860s, 37½ in. high.
(Christie's) $30,690

A German bronze sculpture of a horse by Hans Lindl, 1885, 40cm. high.
(Arnold) $824

Lord Kitchener by Sydney March, 1915, inscribed *Sydney March, Elkington & Co.*, 1915, bronze, mid brown patination, 18½ in. high.
(Sotheby's) $7,672

A bronze group of a horse and dog, cast from a model by Maximilien-Louis Fiot, the horse shown standing, his head bowed looking at the seated dog, signed by the foundry *Susse Frs Edts Paris*, 14¾ in. high, 23¼ in. long.
(Christie's S. Ken) $5,541

A French bronze group of two stallions, cast from a model by Jules Moigniez, on naturalistic oval base, circa 1860, 13⅛ x 16½ in.
(Christie's) $6,138

A late 19th century bronze group of a man kneeling at prayer on a rug, cast from a model by M. Bouger, shown with his shoes removed, a saddled and reined horse at his side, 6¾ in. wide.
(Christie's S. Ken) $1,441

A French bronze equestrian group of Louis XIV, cast from a model of Baron François-Joseph Bosio, signed *Baron Bosio*, mid 19th century, 17¾ in. high.
(Christie's) $3,069

A German bronze group of two rearing horses, the two stallions standing adjacent to each other, their forelegs raised and their heads turned down, 19th century, 13 in. high.
(Christie's) $4,792

An Austrian bronze equestrian group of a nude Indian woman on horseback, cast from a model by F. Mazura, with elaborate coiffure, the horse with his head bowed down, 18½ in. wide.
(Christie's) $5,140

FIGURES

A fine bronze of a young boy, in running pose, 21½in. high, the base signed *J. Injalbert*.
(Canterbury) $653

A pair of French bronze figures of Neapolitan dancers, cast from models by Francisque Joseph Duret, both youths lightly clad, mid 19th century, 17in. high.
(Christie's) $2,864

A Continental cold painted bronze figure of an Arab carpet seller, 7in. high.
(Christie's) $1,059

A pair of gilt-bronze allegorical groups of Summer and Winter, French, third quarter 19th century, Summer holding a sprig of flowers, Winter drawing around her heavy folds of drapery, 80cm. high, and 81cm. high.
(Sotheby's) $8,018

An amusing German bronze group, cast from a model by Gustav Adolf Daumiller, as two naked children, the girl carrying a bouquet, 54.5cm. high. (Phillips London)
                    $4,500

A pair of 19th century French bronze groups, after the Antique, of Boreas, the North Wind, carrying off Proserpine; and another of Pluto, God of the Underworld, claiming Ceres's daughter, Oreithyia, inscribed *Girardot*, 18½in. high, overall.
(Christie's S. Ken)
                    $4,432

An early 20th century French bronze statuette of a naked woman, known as 'La Verite Meconnue', after Aime Jules Dalou, 22.5cm. high.
(Christie's) $2,000

A pair of French bronze figures of soldiers, cast from models by Albert-Ernest Carrier-Belleuse, each in full Renaissance armor, late 19th century, 16¾in. high.
(Christie's) $2,656

A 19th century bronze and parcel gilt figure of a water goddess, shown seated, her hair tied with a band of bullrushes and foliage, 7in. high.
(Christie's S. Ken) $1,219

FIGURES

'The Star', a gilt bronze and ivory figure, cast and carved from a model by Philippe, of a young woman, stepping forward and raising arms, 52.5cm. high. (Christie's) $10,098

Pair of bronze figures of Harlequin and Columbine, after Alfred Richard, France, late 19th century, 23in. high. (Skinner Inc.) $2,500

Georg Kolbe, German (1877–1947), bronze, Crouching Girl 1925, golden brown patina, signed with monogram, 11¼in. high. (Selkirk's) $9,250

A pair of French bronze figures, depicting Venus and Cupid, each shown partially clad, both standing by a tree trunk on naturalistic bases inscribed *SEVRES*, on circular stepped black marble feet, 12¾in. high. (Christie's) $1,727

A rare pair of French bronze figures of the Neapolitan fisher boy and girl, cast from models by Jean Baptiste Carpeaux, he crouching down, holding a conch shell, she with plaited hair, seated on a basket of fish, 39in. and 35½in. high. (Christie's) $94,019

A pair of 19th century French bronzes, cast from a model by Jean Louis Gregoire, each depicting an allegorical maiden, in flowing dress, a cherub at her feet, 16¼in. high. (Christie's S. Ken) $4,211

An Art Deco bronze sculpture, of a lady kneeling, one arm resting on her knee, the other outstretched, mounted on a black and white marble base, 36cm. high. (Christie's) $1,053

Pair of patinated bronze figures of a Harlequin and Columbine, cast after models by Paul Dubois, 32¾in. high. (Butterfield & Butterfield) $7,150

A French silvered and parcel-gilt bronze of Penelope, cast from a model by Pierre-Jules Cavelier, seated on a curved chair covered with a tiger skin and cushion, 19th century, 9⅞in. high. (Christie's) $9,207

A Georgian brass-mounted mahogany plate bucket of conventional form with swing handle and slatted sides, 14in. high.
(Bearne's) $1,377

A pair of late Victorian black-painted and parcel-gilt leather fire-buckets each with later loop handle and green-painted interior, 12in. high.
(Christie's) $420

A small mahogany brass bound bucket of oval shape with three brass bands, brass liner and swing handle, 9in. high.
(Lawrence Fine Art) $517

An early 19th century brass bound mahogany peat bucket of oval form, with brass swing handle and liner, 34cm. high.
(Phillips) $783

A pair of George III Irish brass-bound mahogany plate buckets, each with a brass swing handle above a spirally-turned body, 24½in. high.
(Christie's) $12,547

A George III mahogany plate bucket with brass rim and swing handle, vertical pierced pale sides, 11¾in. diameter.
(Lawrence) $1,475

A fine painted pine and sheet-iron bucket, Joseph Lehn, Lititz, Pennsylvania, circa 1860, bound with three sheet-iron bands painted with a running rosebud motif, height 9¼in.
(Sotheby's) $4,025

A pair of painted leather fire buckets, Newport, Rhode Island, 1843, 12¼in. high.
(Christie's) $1,200

A George III mahogany octagonal plate pail with brass swing handle above a narrow brass band and with vertical pierced sides, 12¾in. high.
(Tennants) $2,232

A Regency brass-bound mahogany peat-bucket of tapering form with removable zinc liner, 14¾in. wide. (Christie's) **$2,455**

A pair of painted fire buckets, signed and dated *Wiscasset Fire Society, 1801, Chas. Weeks, 1882*, each 11⅜in. high. (Christie's) **$2,530**

A mid 19th century Dutch cherrywood bucket with brass swing handle and liner, 16in. high. (Andrew Hartley) **$977**

A brass-bound mahogany bucket, with gadrooned rim , the sides with lion-mask and ring-handles, 13¾in. high. (Christie's) **$2,093**

A pair of Dutch fruitwood and ebonized buckets of ripple turned tapering outline, each with brass liner, 19th century, 14in. high. (Christie's London) **$2,325**

A mahogany plate-bucket, with replaced brass liner and brass-bound pierced slatted tapering body mounted with tamed lion-mask handles and on replaced claw-and-ball feet, 14½in. high. (Christie's) **$1,014**

A painted and decorated leather fire bucket, New England, 1806, decorated with oval reserve, with draped figure of Mercury, 12¾in. high. (Robt. W. Skinner Inc.) **$27,000**

A pair of Irish George III mahogany and brass-bound plate buckets of ribbed tapering cylindrical form, with brass swing handles, 15in. diameter. (Christie's) **$9,741**

A George III brass-bound mahogany bucket of tapering form with later copper liner, 15in. diameter. (Christie's) **$3,212**

A 45 x 107mm. Stereo Mentor camera no. 12444 with a pair of Carl Zeiss Jena Tessar f/4.5 9cm. lenses, three double darkslides and a Mentor filmpack, in maker's leather case.
(Christie's) $424

A 4.5 x 6cm. baby Deckrullo camera no. 641700 with a Carl Zeiss Jena Tessar f/2.7 8cm. lens no. 659881 and twelve single metal slides, in maker's leather case.
(Christie's) $873

A 35mm. Sept camera with a Roussel, Paris Stylor f/3.5 50mm. lens no. 42725 and three Sept film cassettes, in maker's fitted leather case.
(Christie's) $458

C. P. Stirn, Germany, a 4 inch diameter Concealed Vest No. 1 camera no. 7158 with lens and front panel engraved *Patentees Agents J. Robinson & Sons*.
(Christie's) $1,247

Thomas Sutton/A. Ross, London, a 10 x 5¹/₂ inch mahogany-body Sutton Panoramic camera with lacquered brass fittings, rear focusing screw, top-mounted locking screw.
(Christie's) $45,903

A 4.5 x 6cm. Ermanox camera no. 1185290 with an Ernemann Anastigmat Ernostar f/2 10cm. lens no. 150548, film pack adapter and single metal side, in maker's leather case.
(Christie's) $1,559

A 35mm. Mecaflex camera no. A-288 with Type-R-Seroa Anastigmat 4mm. f/3.5 lens, in maker's case.
(Christie's) $938

S. J. Levi & Co., London, a quarter-plate The Pullman detective camera with tan leather covered body and a brass bound lens in a rolled blind shutter.
(Christie's) $1,247

J. Lancaster & Son, Birmingham, a 1¹/₂ x 2 inch Improved-pattern patent watch camera with nickel-plated body.
(Christie's) $21,186

A 35mm. walnut-body cinematographic camera/projector no. 130 with brass-body direct vision finder, a walnut film magazine, maker's plate *Cinématographe, Auguste et Louis Lumière*.
(Christie's) $23,901

A 6 x 13cm. Heidoscop camera no. 9596 with a Carl Zeiss Jena Sucher-Triplet f/4.2 7.5cm. viewing lens no. 714362, in maker's fitted case.
(Christie's) $790

A quarter-plate brass and mahogany tailboard camera with a brass bound Ross, London 5 x 4 Rapid Symmetrical lens no. 34554, Waterhouse stops, double darkslide and plaque *Newton & Co.*
(Christie's) $624

Marion & Co., London, a post card horizontal tropical Soho reflex camera no. 3399 with polished teak body, brass binding, red leather viewing hood and bellows.
(Christie's) $2,772

Eastman Kodak Co., Rochester, NY, a 120-rollfilm cardboard-body George Washington Kodak camera with blue star-patterned body covering, the front section with center-set waistlevel viewfinder.
(Christie's) $29,029

A 120-rollfilm tele-Rolleiflex camera no. S.2303308 with light meter, a Heidosmat f/4 135mm. viewing lens no. 2719888 and a Carl Zeiss Sonnar f/4 135mm. taking lens, in maker's ever ready case.
(Christie's) $1,663

A 35mm. Leica R4 camera no. 1608360 with a Leitz Summicron-R f/2 50mm. lens no. 3083797, in maker's ever ready case.
(Christie's) $830

A 5 x 3¹/₂mm. decoratively engraved camera disguised as a finger ring with Russian marks on back section.
(Christie's S. Ken) $22,143

A 35mm. chrome Nikon F camera no. 6732600 with a Nikon Motordrive F36 unit no. 87071.
(Christie's) $624

Eastman Kodak Co., Rochester, NY, a 127-rollfilm blue-colored 'flash pattern' Kodak Petite camera with original blue colored bellows.
(Christie's) $490

A 4.5 x 6cm. Monocular disguised camera with reflecting viewfinder, magazine back and a H. Roussell Stylor f/6.3 25mm lens.
(Christie's) $2,452

A 35mm. Peggy I camera no. M.165/3 with a Carl Zeiss Jena Tessar f/3.5 5cm. lens no. 1292504 in a Compur shutter, in maker's leather ever ready case.
(Christie's) $447

A 35mm. black Leica M4 camera no. 1207276 with a Leitz Summicron f/2 50mm. lens no. 2340225 and 12585 lenshood.
(Christie's) $2,079

A Compur Leica I(b) camera No. 6056 with dial-set Compur shutter No. 348126 and Leitz Elmar f/3.5 50mm. lens.
(Christie's) $9,378

A 35mm. Weltini camera with a Leitz Elmar 5cm. f/3.5 lens in a rimset Compur Rapid shutter, in maker's leather ever ready case.
(Christie's) $290

A 35mm. black Nikon SP camera 6219041 with a Nippon Kogaku W-Nikkor f/2.5 3.5cm. lens no. 244179 and related accessories.
(Christie's) $1,767

A Leica I(c) Luxus camera No. 48419 with gilt finished body, red skin covered body and a matched gilt barrel Leitz Elmar f/3.5 50mm. lens.
(Christie's) $51,150

Zeiss Ikon, Germany, a 35mm. Nettax 538/24 camera no. A.47738 with a Carl Zeiss Jena Tessar f/2.8 5cm. lens no. 1551159, in maker's leather ever ready case.
(Christie's) $790

A half-plate tropical Vaido camera model B with polished teak and brass bound body, tan leather bellows and viewing hood.
(Christie's) $1,752

C. P. Goerz, Germany, a 45 x 107mm. Photo-Stereo-Binocle camera no. 233 with two sets of rotating lenses, in maker's fitted case.
(Christie's) $2,079

Eastman Dry Plate & Film Co., Rochester, NY, a rollfilm No. 1 Kodak camera no. 13199 with winding key, shutter, lens and felt lens plug.
(Christie's) $2,978

Nippon Kogaku, Japan, a 35mm. chrome Nikon S2 camera no. 6147510 with a Nippon-Kogaku Nikkor-S.C f/1.4 5cm. lens no. 359858.
(Christie's) $1,081

A rollfilm tropical The King's Own De Luxe Model B camera no. B.407 with polished teak body, brass binding.
(Christie's) $1,489

A Leitz Canada black-dial Leica 72 (18 x 24) camera No. 357430, film speed reminder dial and with a Leitz Elmar 5cm. f/3.5 lens No. 806594.
(Christie's) $23,870

A 35mm. Witness camera no. 5010 with a Dallmeyer Super-Six anastigmat f/1.9 2 inch lens no. 383472, lenshood, guarantee sheet and original instruction booklet.
(Christie's) $2,079

A Ticka watch pocket camera with swinging viewfinder lens and lens cap, in slip case, in maker's box, and a Wynne's Infallible Exposure meter in maker's tin.
(Christie's) $1,143

A 35mm. 'no name' Contax camera no. 6306372 with a Carl Zeiss Sonnar f/2 50mm. lens no. 1733933, in maker's leather ever ready case.
(Christie's) $1,340

A 35mm. black Leicaflex SL2 camera no. 1424093.
(Christie's) $790

A Leica Flex SLII black with 50mm. F2 Summicron R lens.
(Spencer's) $907

A 35mm. black paint Nikon S3M camera no. 6600056 with a Nikon Nikkor-H f/2 5cm. lens.
(Christie's) $45,545

Asahi Optical Co., Japan, a 35mm. Asahiflex IIb camera no. 79334 with an Asahi-Kogaku Takumar f/2.4 58mm. lens no. 88310, in maker's ever ready case.
(Christie's) $541

A 9 x 12cm. Universal Juwel 275/7 camera no. P.90770 with a Carl Zeiss, Jena Tessar f/4.5 15cm. lens.
(Christie's) $841

A 35mm. black-paint Nikon S3M camera no. 6600090 with rear-mounted sliding viewfinder frame adjuster.
(Christie's) $32,407

J. Waite, Cheltenham, an 8 x 4¹/₂in. mahogany-body stereoscopic sliding box camera with removable focusing screen, pair of brass bound rack and pinion focusing lenses.
(Christie's) $11,415

A 6 x 9cm. tropical Minex camera Folding Model no. 8090 with polished teak body, tan leather focusing hood and bellows.
(Christie's) $10,718

A. Adams and Co., London, a quarter-plate De Luxe hand camera with red-leather covered body, 18 carat gold fittings hallmarked *London, 1901*, the majority with finely-chased foliate decoration.
(Christie's) $60,588

A quarter-plate fifteen-lens Royal Mail Copying camera by W. Butcher and Sons, London stamped 15 with polished mahogany body and brass fittings.
(Christie's S. Ken) $1,720

A Thornton Pickard brass mounted mahogany cased 'Ruby' camera, with black leather bellows, together with a shutter and spare set of shutter blinds.
(Henry Spencer) $876

A 6.5 x 9cm. Sigriste jumelle camera with polished teak body, leather panels body covering metal fittings, adjustable sportsfinder.
(Christie's S. Ken)

$8,200

The Griffiths Camera Co. Ltd., a double quarter-plate boxform falling plate camera with shutter, wheel stops, independent plate changing mechanisms, and maker's label.
(Christie's) $623

Scovill & Adams, New York, a 5 x 4in. book camera, stamped 2, the exterior modeled as three books with marbled leaves and gilt stamped titles, French, Latin, Shadows.
(Christie's) $18,755

Houghton Lrd., London, a 5 x 4in. mahogany and brass Sanderson field camera, in fitted leather case, a wood tripod in canvas case.
(Christie's) $897

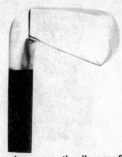

A malacca cane, the silver snuff box handle in the form of a golf club.
(Christie's S. Ken) $1,004

A cane handle by Tiffany & Co., New York, circa 1900, formed as a bird's head above a barrel-shaped collar, 4in. wide, 2oz. 10dwt.
(Christie's) $550

A St. Cloud dolphin-shaped cane-handle with an iron-red mouth and eyes and blue, yellow and green head and fins, circa 1740, 8.5cm. high.
(Christie's) $2,988

A walking stick with silver collar, the ivory handle carved with the heads of two reined horses.
(Christie's S. Ken) $350

A pair of 19th century walking canes, the carved nut grips modeled with grimacing and smiling infants.
(Christie's S. Ken) $301

A malacca walking stick, the white metal handle modeled with a figure of a young woman kneeling amidst reeds.
(Christie's S. Ken) $900

A 19th century bamboo walking cane, the carved nut grip modeled in the form of a bulldog's head, collar stamped *BRIGG.*
(Christie's S. Ken) $381

A gold-mounted walking cane, the handle of tao form, one end engraved with a crest, the other tapering to a sea-monster's head, circa 1760, 34in. long.
(Christie's) $4,500

A 19th century French boxwood walking cane, the grip carved with the head and neck of a swan, stamped *BROT PALAIS-ROYAL.*
(Christie's S. Ken) $903

A chromium-plated Minerva,
circa 1935, 6in. high.
(Christie's)   **$445**

René Lalique, mascot, 'Cinq
Chevaux', after 1925, clear
glass, wood mount, 6¹/₂in. high.
(Sotheby's)   **$5,702**

A nickel-plated bulldog wearing
goggles, 3¹/₂in. high.
(Christie's)   **$355**

A car mascot in the form of a
cross-legged Pierrot playing a
mandolin, the face and hands in
simulated ivory, mounted on a
radiator cap, 4¹/₂in. high.
(Christie's)   **$1,210**

A nickel-plated Radial Aero
Engine, the rotating propeler
stamped *Robt. Beney & Co*, 5in.
high.
(Christie's)   **$603**

A monkey mascot, with an
elongated mouth, brass, circa
1920, mounted on a brass base,
4in. high.
(Christie's)   **$239**

Grenouille, a Lalique glass car
mascot, modeled as a small
frog in crouched position, 6cm.
high, signed *R. Lalique, France,*
(Phillips London)
                    $19,560

'Saint-Christophe', a Lalique
glass Car Mascot of disc shape,
intaglio-molded on the reverse,
11.5cm. high.
(Phillips)   **$1,500**

Hirondelle, a Lalique glass car
mascot, molded as a swallow
perched on a circular base,
14.8cm. high. (Phillips London)
                     $2,325

A Red Ashay clear glass devil (slightly chipped), 5½in. high. (Christie's London) **$450**

Darel, Indian head Mohican, circa 1930, chromium-plated bronze, mounted on wooden base, 4³/₄in. high. (Christie's) **$391**

Tete de Belier, a Lalique glass ram's head, on chromium plated mount (base repaired), 4in. high. (Christie's London) **$9,000**

A silvered bronze wind spirit, the crouching female figure with flowing hair and cloak, signed *Guiraud Riviere*, 7½in. high. (Christie's London) **$5,400**

A bronze showroom display of a graceful winged speed goddess, with hair streaming in the wind, her base inscribed *Susse Frs. Ed. Paris, Cire Perdue*, and signed *Ch. Soudant*, 21¼in. high. (Christie's London) **$7,500**

A bronze nickel-plated head of a retriever carrying a pheasant, signed on the collar *Ch. Paillet*, 3³/₄in. high. (Christie's) **$319**

A brass circus elephant standing on its two front legs with trunk raised, 7¹/₂in. long. (Christie's) **$470**

'Tête d'Aigle', a Lalique mascot, the clear and satin-finished glass molded in the form of an eagle's head, 11cm. high. (Christie's) **$2,726**

'Grande Libellule', a Lalique glass car mascot, modeled as a large dragonfly resting on a circular base, 21cm. high. (Phillips) **$7,000**

A carved second row Dentzel jumper, circa 1908, in the Philadelphia style, with original dappled body paint, 52in. wide. (Sotheby's) $8,250

Carved and painted rooster carousel figure, attributed to Coquereau and Marechal, France, circa 1900, 51in. high. (Skinner Inc.) $3,300

Carved and painted outside row prancer, Rederich Heyn, Germany, circa 1900, 55½in. high. (Skinner Inc.) $2,200

Center row carousel horse, circa 1900, 47in. long, carved by Herschel Speilman, peg construction, on brass pole. (Du Mouchelles) $2,250

An unusual pair of carved pine miniature carousel horses, Muller-style, American, late 19th/early 20th century, carved in the round, overall height 13½in. (Butterfield & Butterfield) $3,850

Carved polychrome horse carousel figure, America, late 19th century, old repaint, 37in. high. (Skinner) $1,650

A carved and painted wood 'Prancer' carousel horse, Looff or Dentzel, New York or Philadelphia, circa 1895, 62in. long. (Sotheby's) $6,900

A fine carved and painted pine outside row carousel horse jumper, Gustav Dentzel & Co., Philadelphia, circa 1880. (Sotheby's) $14,950

A fine carved and painted pine outside row standing carousel horse, Gustav Dentzel & Co., Germantown, Philadelphia, circa 1895. (Sotheby's) $23,000

Carved and painted carousel
bull, late 19th/early 20th
century, the full body with horns
and sweeping tail in a running
position, 39in. long.
(Butterfield & Butterfield)
$1,760

A carved wood zebra, Jumper,
the figure with short carved
mane and looped tail, 43in. long.
(Christie's East) $11,000

Carved and painted elephany
carousel figure, attributed to
Bayol, France, circa 1920, 25in.
high.
(Skinner Inc.) $1,925

A carved wood stork, the figure
in a striding pose with deeply
carved feathers, saddle with a
baby at cantle and blanket, 67in.
high.
(Christie's East) $25,300

A German carved wood pig,
Jumper, by Friedrich, Heyn,
circa 1900, the figure with a
sweet expressive face and
wagging tongue, 29½ in. long.
(Christie's East) $935

A rare carved carousel frog,
Herschell-Spillman Co., North
Tonawanda, New York, circa
1914, 42in. long.
(Sotheby's) $19,800

A French carved wood nodding
head donkey, Gustave Bayol of
Angers, circa 1885, the figure
with carved short mane, saddle
and tail, 49in. long.
(Christie's East) $6,050

A carved wood leaping frog, the
figure with whimsical
expression, carved saddle vest
and bow tie, 41in. long.
(Christie's East) $15,400

A carved and painted wooden
carousel horse, with mane to
right, hole for pole and iron
strengthening straps, circa 1900.
(Christie's) $471

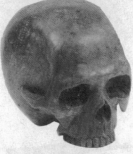

Italian polychrome wooden panel, 18th century, shaped and decorated as a heraldic crest, 72in. high.
(Skinner Inc.) $1,900

A carved wood skull, 7½in. high.
(Christie's S. Ken) $676

A boxwood model of the takarabune with detachable models of the Seven Gods of Good Fortune and their various attributes on deck, unsigned, late 19th century, 48cm. long.
(Christie's) $6,068

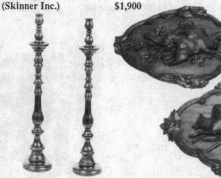

A pair of late 19th century stained beech candlesticks, the turned knopped columns with wide circular drip pans, 52¾in. high.
(Christie's S. Ken) $1,323

A pair of 19th century Black Forest relief carved panels, carved with hunting trophies of dead game and weapons surrounded by branches and foliage, 34in. wide.
(Bearne's) $971

A pair of mid 19th century fruitwood candle stands, the wide drip pans supported on barley twist columns with spreading circular bases, 36½in. high.
(Christie's S. Ken) $1,730

A carved pine doll's head, possibly mid-Atlantic, circa 1800-1820, depicting the bust of a young girl, with fully articulated face and collar of dress, long hair and shoulders, 13¼in. high.
(Christie's) $1,265

A painted pine parcheesi game board, American, 19th century, painted in tones of red, green and black, 19¼ x 19¼in.
(Sotheby's) $1,430

Venetian baroque parcel-gilt, carved, and polychromed wood crest, early 18th century, the top half with a spread-winged eagle on yellow ground above craggy white peaks, 5ft. 3¾in. high.
(Butterfield & Butterfield) $4,950

Humorous inlaid wood study of a kappa, Meiji period, the mythical creature shown with one foot caught in the ivory-inlaid mouth of a giant clam shell, 1¼in. long.
(Butterfield & Butterfield)
$978

A French giltwod wall applique with pierced ribbon-tied cresting suspending an overturned basket of flowers, a cage with billing birds and crossed garden tools, 29 x 23in.
(Christie's)
$3,762

A prisoner-of-war 'Coco-de-mer' table ornament, early 19th century, elaborately carved with scrolling foliage and the coat-of-arms of Great Britain, 19½in.
(Christie's)
$2,070

Dutch painted, carved and parcel giltwood sled, 18th century, of boat shape, the front carved with two griffin's head finials, height 37in.
(Butterfield & Butterfield)
$3,738

A pair of Japanese bamboo vases, each of cylindrical form, carved in low relief with figures in a garden setting, 22in. high.
(Spencer's)
$895

Boxwood animal study, 19th century, signed *Yoshinobu*, featuring two frogs with black-inlaid eyes, the baby perching tentatively on its mother's back, 1¾in. long.
(Butterfield & Butterfield)
$518

Peter Schumann, dated 1820, a speckled and checkerboard **Distelfink** with red bird and flowers, a watercolor Fraktur drawing, 5½ by 3⅝in.
(Sotheby's)
$12,650

An unusual painted pine checkerboard, American, late 19th century, the playing surface with brown and red squares within black and red borders, 15¼ x 15¼in.
(Sotheby's)
$1,725

An early 19th century pin cushion designed as a crown of turned wood, inscribed *King George the fourth crowned July 19 1821*.
(Phillips)
$202

ANIMALS

A Victorian treen tobacco jar, carved in the form of a boxer dog's head, with inset eyes and leather collar, 6in. high.
(Christie's) $895

Two carved oak figures of recumbent dogs, one short and the other long-haired, 33in. and 32in. long.
(Christie's) $10,908

A Black Forest umbrella stand in the form of a standing bear with glass eyes and open mouth.
(Bearne's) $1,673

A Bavarian stained oak seat in the form of a bear with outstretched arms, late 19th century, 51in. wide.
(Christie's S. Ken) $2,949

A pair of Austrian carved wood models of a cow and bull, attributed to Franz Egg, both on naturalistically carved ground, numbers and the name *Egg* inscribed, late 19th century.
(Christie's) $3,542

A Swiss carved softwood model of a begging dog, on a molded naturalistic base stamped *BERGEN & CO INTERLAKEN*, late 19th/early 20th century, 31½in. high.
(Christie's) $14,107

A painted wooden hollow standing horse, American, circa 1850/90, 49in. long, possibly used as a harness-maker's sign.
(Christie's) $4,500

Camel carousel figure, possibly New York State, 19th century, the stylized carved and painted figure of a camel with hemp tail and fringed leather and canvas saddle, 48in. wide.
(Robt. W. Skinner Inc.) $10,000

A carved walnut bull's-head, American, 19th century, with tapering horns, groove carved eyes, nostrils and mouth with carved applied ears, 11in. high.
(Christie's) $2,420

BIRDS

Carved and painted kingfisher, America, late 19th century, 20in. high.
(Skinner) $825

A carved and painted rooster and hen, Wilhelm Schimmel (1817-1890), Carlisle County, Pennsylvania, carved in the round, the larger of the two painted yellow with black details, 5in. high and 3¹/₂in. high.
(Christie's) $5,520

A decorative carved and painted preening yellowleg, A. Elmer Crowell, East Harwich, Massachusetts, 1862-1952, 14in. high.
(Christie's) $9,000

Two carved and painted eaglets, Wilhelm Schimmel (1817-1890), Carlisle County, Pennsylvania, each carved in the round with fully articulated eyes, beak and folded wings, 5in. high; 4³/₄in high.
(Christie's) $1,035

Carved and painted perched eagle, America, 19th century, 24¹/₂in. high.
(Skinner) $5,225

Pair of carved and giltwood eagles, American, second half 19th century, each with wings spread, standing on a ball on a brown-painted octagonal base, height 21in.
(Butterfield & Butterfield) $3,450

An unusual carved and painted pine and sheet-metal American eagle birdhouse, made by E. G. James, Mingo County, West Virginia, circa 1920, height 53in.
(Sotheby's) $8,050

A carved and painted oversized canvas back drake decoy, Wisconsin, with original red, black and white paint, leather thong, glass eye, 18in. long.
(Sotheby's) $5,463

A fine carved, painted and gessoed American eagle, Wilhelm Schimmel, Cumberland Valley, Pennsylvania, circa 1880, wingspan 22¹/₂in.
(Sotheby's) $38,500

BLACKAMOORS

CARVED WOOD

A pair of Venetian polychrome blackamoors, the boy, holding a dished plate, 38 and 39½in. high, 19th century.
(Christie's) $10,626

An interesting and impressive 18th century Venetian carved wood figure of a crouching blackamoor as an occasional table, 82cm. high. (Henry Spencer) $3,500

A pair of Venetian painted and gilded blackamoor stands, each in the form of a negro boy doing a handstand, 31in. high.
(Christie's) $27,000

A pair of polychrome-painted Venetian blackamoor torchères, each with a boy holding a torchère with a glass shade, 19th century, 69in. high.
(Christie's) $34,672

A pair of Italian 'blackamoor' tables, probably Florence, circa 1880, each octagonal top supported on the feet of a jester performing a handstand, in carved and stained fruitwood, 85.5cm. high.
(Sotheby's) $6,682

A pair of large polychrome blackamoor torchères, Italian, 19th century, each formed as a young boy with feathered turban raised on a tripartite cushioned tabouret, 77½in. high.
(Christie's East) $9,900

Two Venetian parcel gilt, polychrome and ebonized blackamoor torchères, each wearing a turban and a costume tied at the waist, 62¼in. high.
(Christie's S. Ken) $8,866

A Victorian walnut occasional table, labeled Plucknett & Steevens, Cabinet Makers & Upholsterers, Warwick & Leamington, 28in. high.
(Christie's) $1,500

Pair of Venetian parcel-gilt and polychromed blackamoor monkeys on pedestals, late 18th/early 19th century, each figure depicted wearing a perruque, 4ft. 6in. high.
(Butterfield & Butterfield) $33,000

BRACKETS

A Regency mahogany clock bracket with later mottled brown marble top and five-part scrolled support, 14½in. wide. (Christie's) **$5,452**

A pair of Italian walnut baroque style figural brackets each in the form of a winged cherub holding aloft a tazza, 29in. high. (Christie's) **$1,902**

One of a pair of Continental baroque style parcel-gilt and gray painted carved wood corner wall brackets, 19th century, 19½in. wide. (Butterfield & Butterfield) (Two) **$1,980**

A fine pair of George III giltwood wall brackets, with beaded moldings on acanthus leaf carved spreading supports and guilloche ornament below with foliate pendants, 1ft. 9in. x 1ft. 4in. (Phillips) **$10,812**

A fine William III limewood and giltwood bracket, in the manner of Daniel Marot, hung with lambrequin ornament supported on central palmette and flanked by putti heads, 1ft. 9in. high. (Phillips) **$4,452**

A pair of figured maple hanging shelves, American, early 19th century, each in the shape of a lyre with a shelf and pierced stars below, 18¼in. high. (Christie's) **$4,370**

A pair of Continental giltwood and gesso wall brackets, the serpentine platform supported on a pierced tapering cartouche molded with foliate scrolls and flowers, 10¼in. across. (Phillips) **$1,168**

A pair of Federal gilt wall brackets, American, circa 1790, each tapered shelf above a tapering gadrooned support and scrolled sides, 13¾in. high. (Christie's) **$34,500**

One of a pair of giltwood wall brackets, with lotus-carved frieze above a tapering stiff-leaf-carved body and fruiting finial, 10½in. high. (Christie's) **$3,872**

CARVED WOOD

A carved and painted figural whirligig, American, 19th century, the upright figure in marching position with black military or police hat, 22in. high.
(Christie's) **$1,725**

An exceptionally finely carved pair of life-size wooden figures representing Grenadiers of circa 1801–08, possibly those of the Royal East India Company Volunteers, with bearskin caps, 78in. high.
(Christie's) **$14,685**

A carved and painted whirligig, Pennsylvania, probably late 19th/early 20th century, the standing figure of a man in top hat and suit painted black and green, 12½in. high.
(Christie's) **$1,150**

Large gilt and polychrome decorated wooden figure of a Buddhist Abbot, Meiji period, depicting Shinran shonin wearing monastic robes partially covered by a gilt brocade kesa, 25⅛in. high.
(Butterfield & Butterfield) **$1,265**

French carved and polychromed wood tailor's trade sign, circa 1900, the tailor depicted in shirtsleeves, waistcoat and trousers wearing gold spectacles beneath bushy brows, 22½in. high.
(Butterfield & Butterfield) **$660**

Fine wood study of a skeleton and Oni, late 19th century, signed *Shoko*, the macabre composition combining a well-articulated skeleton who stands with arms grasping the shoulders of a kneeling demon, 2½in. high.
(Butterfield & Butterfield) **$3,163**

A very rare wood articulated human figure, the tall rectangular torso hollowed out to provide a compartment beneath a removable chest cover, 4th–6th century AD, 168cm. long.
(Christie's) **$20,976**

Pair of German baroque parcel-gilt and polychromed wood figures of putti, 18th century, each seated figure carved with wavy brown hair wearing a gilt cloth about his loins, 17½in. high.
(Butterfield & Butterfield) **$3,025**

A carved walnut figure of a couple, Pennsylvania, 19th century, the fully carved-in-the-round figures depicted holding hands and possibly dressed in Mennonite garb, 10¼in. high.
(Christie's) **$230**

Carved and painted 'Dewey Boy' whirligig, America, circa 1900, 12in. high.
(Skinner) $935

A pair of Flemish carved oak putti, with short curling hair, some drapery around their hips, late 17th century, 21½in. high.
(Christie's) $2,310

A painted wood figure of a worshipping Chinaman with glass eyes, wearing a green cloak with polychrome floral decoration, 19th century, 21in. wide.
(Christie's) $2,798

An early 16th century Flemish oak group of the Flagellation, guild mark of Antwerp, 7in. high, mounted on a later shaped oak base.
(Christie's S. Ken) $2,217

A painted cherrywood and gesso group of a couple dancing, 'Tango', 36in. high, by Elie Nadelman.
(Christie's) $2,860,000

Good wood inlaid study of a horse and groom, Taisho Period, signed (Mu)tei (Tomin), the groom shown washing down a spirited steed whose front legs are perched in a low water tub, 1¾in. high.
(Butterfield & Butterfield) $920

Fine polychromed wood figure of a Rakhan, early Edo period, the disciple of Buddha, constructed in the joined block technique covered with gesso and polychrome pigments, 20½in. high.
(Butterfield & Butterfield) $9,200

Two carved and painted figural children, American, circa 1900, depicting a young African-American boy and girl, the boy carrying a watermelon, 5in. high.
(Christie's) $539

Good boxwood and ivory inlaid figural Study of Three Long Lived Men, late 19th century, signed Chikusai, comprising Urashima accompanied by a minogame, Takeuchi no Sukune and Miura no Osuke, 1⅜in. high.
(Butterfield & Butterfield) $1,093

MASKS

An Egyptian Anthropoid wood mask, 18cm. high, Ptolemaic Period.
(Phillips) **$350**

A substantial gilded cartonnage mummy head-dress with long lappet wig, winged scarabeus and sun disk above forehead, late period, 20½in. high. (Bonhams) **$12,000**

A 19th century lacquered wood mask of Ayagiri, 4.6cm. high. (Christie's) **$1,500**

Carved and painted counter figure, probably New York City, late 19th century, the stylised head of a bearded Turk wearing a turban, 19½in. high. (Robt. W. Skinner Inc.) **$2,500**

Pair of carved mahogany wall plaques, late 19th century, each in the form of an Indian, 20in. high.
(Skinner) **$1,760**

An Egyptian fragmentary painted cartonnage mummy mask of a child, late period, after 600 B.C., 7½in.
(Bonhams) **$979**

Egyptian wood mummy mask, late period, large form, traces of white and black pigment decoration over a natural ground, 18½in. high.
(Skinner) **$660**

A brightly colored cartonnage mummy mask, with a deep lappet wig, Late Ptolemaic, 2nd–1st century B.C., 13in. high.
(Bonhams) **$3,410**

Dan wood mask, Liberia, the oval face with eye slits opening from almond-shaped orbs, the projecting mouth bristling with sharp curved teeth, 10½in. high. (Butterfield & Butterfield) **$550**

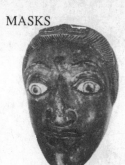

Antique lacquered painted and carved Plah-noh mask, good facial detail, 7in., oriental, 18th/19th century. (G.A. Key) **$45**

Baule wood mask, Ivory Coast, the heart-shaped face bearing protruding slit eyes, elongated nose and tiny mouth, 14in. high. (Butterfield & Butterfield) **$1,650**

A 19th century painted wood No mask of Kumasaka, signed Deme Eiman, 20.6cm. high. (Christie's) **$900**

Northwest coast portrait mask of polychrome carved and incised cedar, collected pre 1884, 10½in. high. (Robt. W. Skinner Inc.) **$25,000**

Northwest coast hawk mask of polychromed alder wood, 9½in. high, 8in. wide. (Skinner Inc.) **$41,000**

A gilded and painted Ptolemaic cartonnage mask with a deep lappet wig, Ptolemaic, 300–30 B.C., 13¾in. high. (Bonhams) **$1,007**

A Yoruba wood helmet mask for the Gelede festival, the smiling face with numerous exposed teeth and black and red rimmed pierced eyes, 41.5cm. high. (Phillips) **$493**

A giltwood No Mask of a demon, his face with grimacing expression, inlaid glass eyes, 8¼in., Meiji period. (Bonhams) **$998**

A Yoruba wood head-dress for the Egungun Society, egungun solde, the sharp-featured face with three horizontal scarifications on the cheeks and vertical ones on the brow, 28.5cm. high. (Phillips) **$114**

VESSELS

Austrian carved fruitwood goblet, 19th century, attributed to Schwanthaler, depicting the four seasons, 12½in. high. (Skinner) $385

Scandinavian carved and painted wood beer bowl, 19th century, the red-painted oval bowl with two handles carved in the shape of horse's heads, 16¼in. long. (Butterfield & Butterfield) $825

A 14in. Georgian carved wooden toby jug figure of a seated auctioneer holding a gavel, in the form of a money box. (R.H. Ellis) $4,800

A good late 17th century Norwegian birchwood tankard, the lid carved GT.KL, two coats of arms surmounted by doves and 1693, 7¼in. high. (Woolley & Wallis) $87,500

Two wooden tankards, 18th century, each tapering cylindrical bound with hoops, the larger 9in. high. (Christie's) $1,760

A good Norwegian burr-wood peg tankard, the cover, handle and feet carved with heraldic lions, late 18th/early 19th century, 9in. high. (Bearne's) $1,324

A James I pearwood armorial standing cup with circular slightly-tapering body with four panels divided by twin-pilasters with heart-filled spandrels, the panels incised with the royal coat-of-arms, lacking cover, 9½in. high. (Christie's) $15,074

A mahogany cheese coaster of dished outline, the scrolled division and frieze edged with chainlink above rockwork and acanthus-carved frieze, 20¼in. wide. (Christie's) $3,098

A late Elizabeth I pearwood cup and cover with circular slightly-domed cover surmounted by a stepped turned finial carved with ogee-leaves and surrounded by a band carved with a lion, a unicorn, a dove and an antelope, 10¾in. high. (Christie's) $16,959

A Berlin National Model 442X cash register with florid Art Nouveau decoration on the bronze casing, 1911. (Auction Team Koeln) **$1,800**

A German National Model 642S cash register on wooden base with four control levers, decorated in the Art Nouveau style, circa 1910. (Auction Team Koeln) **$1,100**

A National cash register for Dutch currency, circa 1900. (Auction Team Koeln) **$1,100**

An early National Model 8 cash register for Dutch currency, *N. J. Creyghton* inscribed on the ornate casing, circa 1900. (Auction Team Koeln) **$1,150**

A very decorative mahogany cash register by G. H. Glenhill & Sons Ltd., Halifax, Serial No. 79.103, circa 1885. (Auction Team Koeln) **$900**

A richly decorated National Model 44 plated cash register for German currency up to 4.95 marks, Serial No. 255960, circa 1900. (Auction Team Koeln) **$400**

National Model 345 cash register, with extensively decorated nickel housing, prices in English currency, receipt dispenser, marble cover plate, circa 1920. (Auction Team Köln) **$378**

A National Model 313 cash register for German currency up to 2.95 marks, of narrow construction, Serial No. 690.423, circa 1910. (Auction Team Koeln) **$400**

A National Model 442X cash register with richly decorated nickel casing with crank, for German currency to 99.99 marks and receipt dispenser, circa 1908. (Auction Team Koeln) **$1,200**

Quezal two-tier chandelier, designed by Martin Boch, five elongated bell-form opal, green and gold pulled feather shades, 46in. high.
(Skinner) $4,125

Daum Art glass chandelier, three-socket ceiling light with oval gilt metal drop supporting orange and amethyst glass bell shades, 20in. high.
(Skinner) $605

Chandelier with Tiffany acorn shades, suspended from elaborate metal cased light bowl with cast butterflies, women and Art Nouveau floral elements.
(Skinner) $5,170

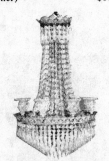

Baroque style gilt-metal twelve-light chandelier, 19th century, the fluted baluster-form shaft applied with gilt-bronze foliate-and-scroll-and-therm-cast mounts, 42in. high.
(Butterfield & Butterfield)
                             $4,950

An ormolu and cut-glass eight-light chandelier with foliate corona hung with icicle drops above a cascade of faceted circular drops, basically early 19th century, 33in. high.
(Christie's) $6,098

An Empire ormolu ten-light chandelier with flaming finial and spreading shaft cast with lotus leaves above a band of bees and cornucopia garlanded with laurel wreaths and anthemia, 41in. wide.
(Christie's) $75,845

A late 19th century Murano glass chandelier, with gilt heightened and white enameled tulip shaped sconces and storm shades, 37in. high.
(Christie's S. Ken) $1,628

A William IV ormolu and bronze twenty-one light chandelier with foliate corona hung with later pierced chains, above a pine-cone boss, 44in. high.
(Christie's) $23,958

Steuben three light chandelier, rib molded trumpet form gold Aurene shades affixed to vasiform hanger, total height 22½in.
(Skinner) $715

AGATE

CHINA

A Staffordshire solid agate tea
canister, marbled in gray, brown
and cream below a lead glaze,
12.5cm.
(Phillips) $1,280

A Staffordshire solid-agate
pectin-shell molded teapot and
cover, circa 1760, with dolphin
handle, lion finial and serpent
spout, 5¹/₂in. high.
(Christie's) $6,600

A Staffordshire saltglaze solid-
agate model of a seated cat,
circa 1745, in dark-brown and
buff clays with blue ears and
splashed in blue, 4in. high.
(Christie's) $4,950

ARITA

An Arita blue and white charger
painted with a central roundel
enclosing the letters *V.O.C.*,
surrounded by two Ho-o birds,
late 17th century, 14¹/₂in.
diameter.
(Christie's) $22,500

An Arita blue and white vase
decorated with three shaped
panels containing peonies
among rockwork, divided by
lotus sprays, late 17th century,
41.5cm. high.
(Christie's) $13,475

An Arita blue and white tureen
and cover decorated with six
shaped panels depicting sprays
of peony and chrysanthemum
among rockwork, late 17th
century, 31cm. diameter.
(Christie's) $12,000

BASALT

Wedgwood basalt figure
"Nymph at Well", England,
circa 1840, modeled as a female
figure holding a shell, 11in. high.
(Skinner Inc.) $1,045

A pair of Wedgwood and
Bentley black basalt urn-shaped
vases and covers, the latter with
Sybil finials, 28cm. high.
(Phillips) $4,500

'Bull', a Wedgwood black basalt
figure designed by John
Skeaping, impressed factory
marks and facsimile signature,
5¹/₄in. high.
(Christie's) $941

BELLEEK

A Belleek vase modeled as a nautilus shell upheld on coral branches above a circular-section base, Second Period, black printed mark, 8³/₄in. high. (Christie's) $399

A Belleek porcelain three strand circular basket and cover, the finial formed as a large spray of flowers, buds and leaves including a rose, shamrock and daisy, early 20th century, 10in. diameter. (Christie's) $2,159

A First Period Belleek shaped circular tray from a 'Chinese' pattern tea-service, molded in relief with a dragon chasing a pearl, printed black mark and registration lozenge for 1872, 15¹/₄in. diameter. (Christie's) $1,101

BENNINGTON

A Rockingham flint enamel hot water urn, Bennington, Vermont, 1849, baluster-form, with domed faceted cover with acorn finial, 21in. high. (Christie's) $9,200

A flint enamel poodle, Lyman Fenton & Company, Bennington, Vermont, 1849-1858, with fruit basket in mouth, applied coleslaw mane and ears, 8¹/₄in. high. (Christie's) $2,070

A flint enamel pitcher and washbowl, Lyman Fenton & Company, Bennington, Vermont, 1849-1858, the pitcher with ribbed body and circular faceted foot and squared handle, 12¹/₂in. high. (Christie's) $2,070

BERLIN

A Berlin figure of a putto emblematic of Plenty standing holding a gilt spirally molded cornucopia of fruit, blue scepter marks, 19th century, 7½in. high. (Christie's S. Ken) $300

A very good Berlin porcelain plaque, depicting courtiers in a garden setting, possibly Mary Antoinette, 13³/₄in. diameter. (John Nicholson) $4,500

A Berlin rectangular plaque painted by R. Dittrich with a portrait of Ruth in the cornfields, impressed KPM and scepter marks, 19¹/₄ x 11³/₄in. (Christie's) $9,500

BÖTTGER

CHINA

A Böttger white bust of an infant modeled by Paul Heermann with his head turned to his left and with curls around the hairline, circa 1719, 13cm. high.
(Christie's) $28,934

A baluster teapot and cover, the curved spout with molded bearded mask terminal enriched in Böttger luster, circa 1730, 14cm. high.
(Christie's) $27,720

A Böttger pagoda, circa 1715, seated, his right hand resting on his raised knee, with black hair, eyebrows and eyes, his robe in Böttger luster reserved with black foliage, 3¹/₄in. high.
(Christie's) $10,925

BOW

Two Bow figures of a youth and companion, he standing before a tree-stump playing the bagpipes, his companion holding a posy, circa 1760, 15cm. high.
(Christie's) $2,817

A pair of rare Bow models of small green parrots perched on flower-encrusted cross boughs, the green plumage with black markings and orange patches on the wings, 11.4cm.
(Phillips) $2,720

An extremely rare pair of Bow white 'Lisard candlesticks' after Chinese Fukien originals, 18.5cm. high.
(Phillips) $3,360

CANTON

Pair of Canton Blue and White Tea Caddies, China, mid 19th century, hexagonal shape, with lids, 6in. high.
(Skinner Inc) $5,750

A giltmetal-mounted Canton famille rose bowl, the bowl polychrome decorated to the interior and exterior with reserves of flowers, birds and butterflies and figures, the bowl mid-19th century, 16¹/₂in. high.
(Christie's) $6,198

A pair of unusual Canton vases, applied with writhing dragons below an everted rim, the body brightly painted with processions, 63.5cm. high.
(Bearne's) $1,500

CARDEW

An earthenware cider jar by Michael Cardew, the top half with green slip drawn through to brown, Winchcombe Pottery seals, 14½in. high.
(Bonhams) $568

An earthenware open bowl by Michael Cardew, with trailed dark brown slip over a vivid green and ocher glaze, circa 1930, 13¾in. diameter.
(Bonhams) $2,202

An early earthenware Winchcombe jug by Michael Cardew, with a band of painted swirls, ocher and brown, 9in. high.
(Bonhams) $587

CARLTON

A Carlton Ware ginger jar and cover, covered in a mottled blue glaze, with gilt and polychrome enamel decoration of a heron in flight, 26cm. high.
(Christie's) $766

A pair of Carlton Ware book ends, each modeled with a Britannia figure standing with shield and serpent against a triangular back, 18.5cm. high.
(Christie's) $184

A Carlton Ware ovoid ginger jar and cover, printed and painted in colors and gilt with exotic trees on a blue spotted ground, 28cm. high.
(Christie's) $435

CASTEL DURANTE

A Castel Durante majolica dish decorated with a portrait of a warrior and inscribed *Gallafrone*, circa 1520, 8¾in. diameter.
(Christie's) $46,838

A Casteldurante squat drug jar painted with the naked Fortune arising from the waves on the back of a dolphin, circa 1580, 23.5cm. wide. (Christie's London) $27,280

An interesting small Castel Durante dish with sunken center painted with a coat of arms of a standing figure of a negro inscribed *V: Sapes: Forts*, 17cm. diameter.
(Phillips) $850

CAUGHLEY

Caughley porcelain dessert dish of square form, decorated with a blue weir pattern, circa 1790, 8in. wide.
(G. A. Key) **$361**

Caughley porcelain milk jug, leaf molded with blue and white floral patterns and mask lip, English, late 18th century.
(G. A. Key) **$240**

A Caughley fable-decorated plate painted in shades of gray with the fable of the Wolf & Crane, titled to the reverse, circa 1795, 8¹/₄in. diameter.
(Christie's) **$759**

CHANTILLY

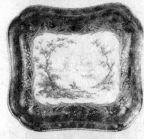

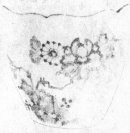

A 1870s Chantilly dish with gros bleu ground and a central gilt cartouche depicting, in puce, a chateau by a lakeside, 24cm. across.
(Phillips) **$456**

A pair of Chantilly white wolves naturalistically modeled seated on their haunches looking to left and right, with ferocious looking teeth, pricked ears, long curly coats and bushy tails forming the bases, circa 1740, 21cm. high.
(Christie's) **$17,000**

A Chantilly 'Kakiemon' lobed beaker painted with stylized magnolia and chrysanthemum branches issuing from rockwork, circa 1745, 2¹/₄in. high.
(Christie's) **$783**

CHELSEA

One of a pair of Chelsea finger bowls painted in colors with flower sprays and scattered springs including a striped tulip and rose, 7.5cm. high.
(Phillips) **$2,380**

A Chelsea teaplant coffee-pot, with spirally-molded brightly colored teaplants, 1745–49, 13.5cm. high.
(Christie's) **$8,200**

A Chelsea 'Hans Sloane' botanical soup-plate painted in a vibrant palette with a spray of magnolia and with scattered butterflies and insects, circa 1756, 23.5cm. diameter.
(Christie's) **$12,953**

CHELSEA KERAMIC

Chelsea Keramic Art Works
double handled vase,
Massachusetts, circa 1885, blue-
green and brown glaze, 6¼in.
high.
(Skinner Inc.) $200

Chelsea Keramic Art Works
slipper, Massachusetts, circa
1885, mottled olive green and
brown glaze, 6in. long.
(Skinner Inc.) $300

Chelsea Keramic Art Works
elephant vase, Hugh C.
Robertson, circa 1880, angular
'metal shape' octagonal body
with applied elephant head
handles, 6½in. high.
(Skinner) $495

CLARICE CLIFF

A 'Bizarre' grotesque mask
designed by Ron Birks, painted
in orange, red, yellow and black,
30cm. long.
(Christie's) $1,851

'Age of Jazz' a 'Bizarre' table
decoration of two musicians in
full evening dress playing piano
and banjo, naturalistically
painted, on rectangular base,
14.5cm. high.
(Christie's) $7,069

A 'Bizarre' single-handled Lotus
jug in the 'Luxor' pattern,
painted in orange, green,
lavender and blue between
yellow borders, 30cm. high.
(Christie's) $2,020

COALPORT

An interesting Coalport
commemorative racing cup and
cover for the St. George Races,
painted with two horses coming
up neck-and-neck to the winning
post, 28cm.
(Phillips) $1,928

A remarkable Coalport trompe
l'oeil plate decorated in London
in red, brown, gold and
platinum luster, on solid gilt
ground, 23.5cm.
(Phillips) $1,200

A Coalport tapering cylindrical
vase, the richly gilt handles
surmounted by lion's heads,
painted by E. Ball with a river
landscape titled *Loch Stark*,
circa 1900, 5in. high.
(Christie's) $522

COOPER, SUSIE

A Susie Cooper oviform jug painted with overlapping geometric shapes in shades of yellow, brown, gray and black, 12cm. high.
(Christie's) $185

A pair of Susie Cooper slender ovoid vases in the 'Moon and Mountain' pattern, painted in colors, 22.5cm. high.
(Christie's) $2,188

A Susie Cooper Crown Works plate, painted in silver luster with stylized tulips, with lime green border, 28cm. diameter.
(Christie's) $251

COPER, HANS

A magnificent spade form by Hans Coper, the buff body with inlaid horizontal and spiraling lines, the whole surface varied in tones, circa 1972, 13³/₄in. high.
(Bonhams) $17,433

A handsome sack form by Hans Coper, with wide brown disk rim on circular neck, the buff body accentuated with brown texturing, circa 1974, 9³/₄in. high.
(Bonhams) $16,515

A wonderful oval cup form by Hans Coper, the upper part mottled with dark brown and deep orange, the cup mounted on a cylindrical base which rises to a point, circa 1972, 6¹/₄in. high.
(Bonhams) $27,525

CREAMWARE

A Staffordshire creamware arbor group, circa 1765, modeled as a couple in a covered arbor splashed in ocher, brown and green, 6in. high.
(Christie's) $71,500

A Staffordshire creamware satyr mask cup, circa 1780, with loop handle splashed in brown, green and ocher, on a flaring foot, 4¹/₂in. high.
(Christie's) $368

A Wedgwood creamware oviform teapot and cover painted in the manner of David Rhodes with vertical bands of stylized ornament, circa 1768, 14cm. high.
(Christie's) $3,347

DE MORGAN

A Craven Dunhill yellow luster charger decorated with a design by William De Morgan, 38cm. diameter.
(Christie's) $1,380

A William De Morgan two-handled vase, Merton Abbey Period, circa 1882–1888, painted with peacocks and Iznik flowers bordered with fish on a blue scale ground, 13³/₈in. high.
(Sotheby's) $6,820

A William De Morgan 'Rose trellis' tile, painted with two yellow, brown and red flowers, 15.2cm. square, and three similar.
(Bonhams) $517

DEDHAM

Dedham Pottery experimental vase, Massachusetts, late 19th/early 20th century, executed by Hugh C. Robertson, 6in. high.
(Skinner Inc.) $350

Dedham pottery cat plate, early 20th century, stamped, 9in. diameter.
(Skinner Inc.) $4,840

Dedham Pottery Stein, Massachusetts, early 20th century, rabbit pattern, impressed and ink stamped marks, 5¹/₄in. high.
(Skinner Inc.) $225

DELFT

A London delft blue and white royal portrait shallow circular dish painted with bust portraits of King William III and Queen Mary, circa 1690, 25cm. diameter.
(Christie's) $4,726

A Lambeth delft blue and white posset-pot and cover, circa 1690, decorated in the 'Transitional' style with Chinamen seated in landscapes, 6³/₄in. high.
(Christie's) $6,600

An English delft farmhouse plate painted in yellow, red and blue with a cockerel amongst sponged manganese trees, blue line rim, 21cm. diameter.
(Phillips) $1,530

DELLA ROBBIA

A Della Robbia twin-handled vase decorated by Liz Wilkins, with incised and slip decoration of daffodils framed within leafy border, 40.5cm. high.
(Christie's)   **$886**

A Della Robbia terracotta vase, incised with stylized flowers and foliage painted in brown, green and yellow, dated *1896*, 23cm. high.
(Christie's)   **$251**

A Della Robbia twin-handled terracotta vase by John Shirley, decorated on both sides with confronted peacocks, dated *1898*, 41.5cm. high.
(Christie's)   **$1,421**

DERBY

An important Derby Royal Presentation gum container modeled as a circular turret raised on the backs of four gilded elephants, 14.5cm. high.
(Phillips)   **$3,675**

A pair of Derby figures of a boy with a Macaroni dog and a girl with a cat, on pierced scrolling bases, early 19th century, 6¹/₄in. high.
(Christie's)   **$1,393**

A Derby trout's head stirrup-cup naturally modeled and colored, the rim reserved and inscribed in gilt *THE ANGLER'S DELIGHT*, circa 1800, 10.5cm. high.
(Christie's)   **$1,969**

DERUTA

A Deruta Armorial dish painted in the center with a shield with a wide band in ocher on a dark **blue ground, 38cm.**
(Phillips)   **$6,175**

A Deruta maiolica wet-drug jar painted in colors with a plain banner on a ground of grotteschi and foliage, 8¹/₄in. high.
(Christie's)   **$1,362**

A Deruta blue and gold lustered dish, the center painted with a winged mythical beast with the naked torso of a woman and the lower part of a hoofed monster with a divided tail, circa 1525, 43cm. diameter.
(Christie's)   **$55,132**

DOCCIA

CHINA

A Doccia globular teapot and cover from the Isola Marana service, the branch handle with leaf terminals, circa 1749, 18cm. wide.
(Christie's) $36,047

A pair of Doccia figures of Harlequin and Columbine from the Commedia dell'Arte, in black masks and iron-red and yellow checkered theatrical costumes, circa 1770, 12.5cm. high.
(Christie's) $13,150

A Doccia giltmetal-mounted oval snuff-box con basso relievo istoriato, the cover with Mars and Venus before a ruin and Time in flight above, circa 1750, 8cm. wide.
(Christie's) $4,066

DOULTON

A large and good Doulton Lambeth biscuit barrel by Hannah Barlow, incised with a band of horses, impressed mark and dated *1883*, 7¹/₄in. high.
(John Nicholson) $802

A good pair of Doulton Lambeth vases and covers by Hannah Barlow, incised with a band of lions, 13in. high.
(John Nicholson) $2,332

Royal Doulton porcelain plate, hand painted, signed *D. Demsberry*, 10¹/₂in. diameter.
(Peter Wilson) $158

DRESDEN

A Dresden porcelain figure group modeled as a courting couple, the gentleman embracing the lady from behind as a young man looks on, circa 1900, 12¹/₂in. high.
(Christie's) $2,274

An impressive pair of Dresden Helena Wolfsohn porcelain large vases and covers, of ovoid form, painted in colors with courtiers and peasants seated in open landscapes, 50cm. high.
(Spencer's) $1,538

A Dresden center-piece formed as a young man and a woman wearing striped and flowered 18th century-style rustic dress, playing hide-and-seek around a tree, circa 1880, 28¹/₂in. high.
(Christie's) $2,815

FAIRYLAND LUSTER

A fine and rare Wedgwood Fairyland luster 'Ghostly Wood' ginger jar and cover, designed by Daisy Makeig-Jones, 12³/₄in. high.
(Bonhams) $24,667

A pair of Wedgwood Fairyland luster 'Torches' vases, printed in gold and painted on the exterior in Flame Fairyland tones with 'Torches', 28.5cm. high.
(Phillips) $3,500

A Wedgwood Fairyland luster oviform vase, painted with three panels of fairies, elves and birds before river landscapes, 8¹/₂in. high.
(Christie's) $1,378

FAMILLE ROSE

A Chinese porcelain famille rose warming-pot and cover, late 19th century, fitted with a removable inner dish, decorated on the sides with figures at leisure and in garden settings, 6¹/₂in. diam.
(Christie's) $690

A pair of famille rose blue-ground double-gourd vases, iron-red Qianlong seal marks, Daoguang, each raised on a flaring foot and surmounted by a tall neck with a floral rim, 8¾in. high.
(Christie's) $7,111

A fine and very rare famille rose celadon-ground molded lobed vase, underglaze-blue Qianlong seal mark and of the period, the slightly-flattened gourd-shaped vase with splayed foot and flaring neck, 14¹/₄in. high.
(Christie's) $384,028

FULPER

Fulper pottery double handled vase, Flemington, New Jersey, circa 1915–25, no. 575, glossy green and eggplant glaze, impressed vertical mark, 6³/₄in. high.
(Skinner Inc.) $225

Fulper pottery buttress vases with glossy streaked glaze in muted green and metallic brown flambé, 8in. high.
(Skinner Inc.) $1,100

Fulper Pottery urn, Flemington, New Jersey, circa 1915, cucumber green crystalline glaze, vertical ink mark, 13in. high.
(Skinner Inc.) $1,700

GARDNER

A Gardner biscuit group of two peasant children cracking Easter eggs, both in tunics and breeches, on a rectangular base, 16cm.
(Phillips) $731

A Gardner biscuit figure of a mother holding a child wrapped in gray cloth, the woman standing barefoot dressed in gray and blue, 25cm.
(Phillips) $447

A Gardner biscuit figure of a peasant, reputedly Tolstoy, seated on logs and wearing a pink tunic, pale blue breeches and boots, 17cm.
(Phillips) $528

GOLDSCHEIDER

A Goldscheider polychrome painted pottery figure, from a model by Dakon, of a young girl, emerging from a blue hat box, 16cm. high.
(Christie's) $1,683

An amusing Goldscheider painted group modeled as three young black boys each wearing short trousers, 56.5cm. high.
(Phillips) $2,400

A Goldscheider polychrome painted pottery figure, from a model by Lorenzl, of a dancer, in high stepping pose with shawl draped behind, 37cm. high.
(Christie's) $1,094

GRUEBY

Grueby pottery vase, Ruth Erickson, circa 1905, impressed mark and incised artist's cipher, 16⅜in. high.
(Skinner) $29,900

Navy blue Grueby pottery vase, Boston, circa 1910, impressed and artist initialed (glaze imperfection and bubble bursts), 5½in. high.
(Skinner Inc.) $1,900

Grueby pottery vase, Boston, circa 1905, partial paper label and artists monogram *JE* (minor nicks), 12in. high.
(Skinner Inc.) $2,300

HAMADA

A stoneware teapot by Shoji Hamada, with floral decoration, orange, buff and brown, circa 1942, 7in. wide.
(Bonhams) **$514**

A stoneware square dish by Shoji Hamada, kaki, the upper surface with resist stepped cross pattern, 10¹/₂in. square.
(Bonhams) **$2,840**

An important stoneware cut sided bottle by Shoji Hamada, tenmoku glaze over red body, circa 1951, 11in. high.
(Bonhams) **$5,995**

HÖCHST

A Höchst group 'Der Chinesische Kaiser', circa 1765, formed as a majestic figure in gilt and turquoise crown, a figure in pink-striped gray dress and pink trousers making obeisance, 14in. high.
(Christie's) **$36,800**

A Höchst pug dog naturally modeled and seated on his haunches to the right and scratching his chin, circa 1755, 10cm. high.
(Christie's) **$4,435**

A Höchst group of the fortune-teller modeled by Simon Feilner, as a gallant standing beside his seated companion while a bearded fortune-teller examines her hand, iron-red wheel mark, circa 1755, 17cm. high. (Christie's) **$8,797**

IMARI

A Japanese Imari vase and cover, 19th century, painted overall in underglaze blue, copper red, green enamel and gilt, 23¹/₈in. high.
(Christie's) **$3,450**

A large Imari fluted dish decorated with a central medallion of three gambolling karashishi among scrolling peony flowers, 19th century, 64.3cm diam.
(Christie's) **$1,760**

An Imari model of a potter standing at his wheel making a large vase decorated with mythical birds in flight among foliage, 19th century, 20cm high.
(Christie's) **$791**

JONES, GEORGE

A George Jones majolica cheese-dish and cylindrical cover molded to simulate a barrel with yellow bands entwined with blossoming bramble leaves, circa 1873, 11¼in. high. (Christie's) $1,122

A George Jones majolica punch-bowl modeled as Mr. Punch lying on his back, being crushed beneath the weight of a large bowl, the surface molded and colored to stimulate orange-rind, circa 1874. (Christie's) $4,750

A George Jones model of a camel, partially glazed on a dark-brown parian body, supported on a cluster of green leaves with two turquoise saddle-bags bound with gilt and black cord suspended from its back, circa 1868, 8½in. high. (Christie's) $2,072

KAKIEMON

A rare Kakiemon oviform ewer of Islamic form, decorated in iron-red, green, aubergine, yellow and black enamels and molded in low relief, late 17th/early 18th century, 30cm. high. (Christie's) $15,180

A pair of Kakiemon cockerels, vividly decorated in iron-red, green, blue, yellow and black enamels, late 17th/early 18th century, mounted on wood stands, 28cm. high. (Christie's) $99,693

A Kakiemon vase and cover, the shoulder with geometric and foliate designs including hanabishi, the domed cover with flattened knop finial, late 17th century, 32.5cm. high. (Christie's) $64,750

KANGXI

A Chinese porcelain vase decorated in underglaze blue and overglaze polychrome enamel colors, 6¾in. high. Kangxi 1675–1690. (Tennants) $1,004

A blue and white jardinière, Kangxi, painted to the exterior with The Three Friends, pine, prunus and bamboo below a band of key pattern, 17in. diameter. (Christie's) $1,419

A fine blue and white cup, encircled Kangxi six-character mark, finely penciled to the exterior with a continuous mountainous landscape and huts obscured behind willow, 3in. high. (Christie's) $43,750

CHINA

KINKOZAN

A Kinkozan vase decorated with detailed figurative scenes, divided by scattered brocade designs, stamped *Kinkozan zo*, late 19th century, 27cm. high. (Christie's) $4,514

Fine Kinkozan Satsuma vase, 19th century, signed *Dai Nihon*, tapering globular form, reserves of eight immortals and samurai, 15in. high. (Skinner Inc.) $9,500

A Kinkozan vase decorated with numerous revelers, the shoulder with a band of brocade designs, signed and sealed *Kinkozan sei* and *Masayasu*, 17.4cm. high. (Christie's) $3,950

LEACH

A St. Ives stoneware vase by Bernard Leach, with incised decoration, covered in a thick matt pale yellow green glaze running and pooling at the foot, circa 1960, 34.2cm. high. (Christie's) $2,871

A fine stoneware charger by Bernard Leach, the cream glazed ground with wax-resist decoration of a bird in flight, the rim with diagonal bands, 36.5cm. diameter. (Christie's) $16,434

A superb stoneware vase by Bernard Leach, with incised mountain design, glazed brown above gray, 9^{1}/$_{2}$in. high. (Bonhams) $10,093

LENCI

A Lenci polychrome ceramic figure of a mermaid and her baby astride a giant turtle, painted in shades of green and brown, 12¾in. high. (Christie's S. Ken) $2,150

A Lenci bust of a father and baby, the sleekly groomed, dark-haired man clasping and kissing a rosy-cheeked, fair-haired and somewhat reluctant baby, 18cm. high. (Phillips) $1,244

A Lenci polychrome painted pottery figure of a young woman wearing a short black dress, relaxing with her feet up in a floral patterned armchair, 25cm. high. (Christie's) $2,356

LINTHORPE

A Linthorpe goat's-head vase, designed by Dr. Christopher Dresser, double gourd shape, decorated with four goats' heads, 28cm. high.
(Christie's) $5,933

A Linthorpe vase, designed by Dr. Christopher Dresser, the gourd-shaped body with double angular spout and curved carrying-bar, streaked glaze of green and brown.
(Christie's) $2,046

A Linthorpe vase, designed by Dr. Christopher Dresser, glazed in streaky pale and dark green, with molded maze patterns and linear designs, 22.5cm. high.
(Christie's) $982

LIVERPOOL

Liverpool creamware pitcher, England, circa 1790, black transfer printed with Boston Fusilier (McCauley 251) enhanced with red, yellow and blue enamels, 11½in. high.
(Skinner) $5,225

Liverpool transfer-printed creamware masonic large jug, probably Herculaneum, early 19th century, 13in. high.
(Butterfield & Butterfield) $1,500

Liverpool transfer-printed creamware jug, circa 1800, transfer-printed in black on one side with a three-masted ship flying the American flag, 10¾in. high.
(Butterfield & Butterfield) $1,200

LONGTON HALL

A Longton Hall cream jug molded with vine leaves, the twisted stems as a handle, 7.7cm. high, late 18th century.
(Bearne's) $2,025

A Longton Hall figure of a seated flower seller on a rococo scroll base, 4⅞in. high.
(Bonhams) $375

A Longton Hall two-handled oviform vase painted with loose bouquets, flower-sprays and scattered foliage, circa 1755, 23cm. high.
(Christie's) $1,276

LUDWIGSBURG

CHINA

A pair of Ludwigsburg miniature masked figures from the Carnival de Venise series after models by Johann Jakob Louis, circa 1765, 6.8cm. high. (Christie's) **$13,518**

A Ludwigsburg figure of a lady with a musical score, modeled by P. F. Lejeune, scantily clothed in a white blouse, circa 1770, 13.5cm. high. (Christie's) **$1,200**

A pair of Ludwigsburg figures of a gallant and companion modeled by Franz Anton Pustelli, circa 1760, 13cm. high. (Christie's) **$5,710**

MARBLEHEAD

Marblehead Pottery decorated vase, Arthur Baggs, 1913, hand-thrown cylinder with subtle repeating decoration of five conventionalized tree clusters, 9³/₄in. high. (Skinner) **$5,500**

Marblehead Pottery decorated vase, Marblehead, Massachusetts, early 20th century, with incised and painted repeating design of flowers, 3³/₄in. high. (Skinner Inc.) $2,000

Marblehead Pottery decorated vase, Massachusetts, early 20th century, with design of alternating elongated trees, 6³/₈in. high. (Skinner Inc.) $1,200

MARTINWARE

A Martin Brothers grotesque character jig, modeled either side with a humorous face, covered in a brown to orange glaze, dated *1899*, 7in. high. (Christie's) **$1,725**

A rare Martin Brothers triple bird group of 'Two's company, three's none', circa 1906, modeled as a central, complacently smirking male bird with his wings about two females, 7¹/₂in. high. (Sotheby's) $14,492

A Martin Brothers vase, with incised floral decoration, covered in a matt brown glaze with painted brown, green, white and blue, dated *1887*, 20.1cm. high. (Christie's) **$985**

CHINA

MEISSEN

A pair of late Meissen vases, finely painted with panels of Venus and Cupid after Boucher, 53cm. high.
(Phillips) $10,400

A Meissen circular tureen and cover with crisply molded fish handles and finial enriched in purple and iron-red and with gilt supports, circa 1728, 29.8cm. wide.
(Christie's) $55,440

Two unusual late Meissen models of Bolognese hounds, their faces, ears and patches of their coats picked out in brown, 26cm.
(Phillips) $3,451

MING

A very fine Ming-style blue and white moon flask, Qianlong seal mark and of the period, painted to each side in rich cobalt-blue with eight petals, 19^{1}/$_{4}$in. high.
(Christie's) $192,519

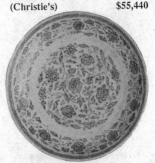

A fine Ming-style yellow and green-glazed blue and white dish, encircled Yongzheng six-character mark and of the period, 10^{5}/$_{8}$in. diameter.
(Christie's) $99,355

An early Ming blue and white small jar painted with a band of four blooming lotus flowers on a continuous leafy vine below closed flower buds, 13cm. high.
(Christie's) $44,000

MINTON

A pair of Minton figures of the Coachee and Easy Johnny with nodding heads, circa 1860, 7^{1}/$_{2}$in. high.
(Christie's) $1,223

A Minton majolica lamp base modeled as a boy and a girl putto scantily clad in manganese drapes tied in ocher, date code for 1872, 13^{3}/$_{4}$in. high.
(Christie's) $1,990

A pair of Minton pâte-sur-pâte vases, circa 1872–1894, decorated by L. Birks, with birds perched on bullrushes reserved on a blue ground, 10in. high.
(Sotheby's) $3,069

MOORCROFT

A Moorcroft Eventide pattern two handled vase, with green piped decoration of tall trees before distant mountains, covered in an amber, green, crimson and inky blue glaze, circa 1925, 21.2cm. high. (Christie's London) **$3,500**

A Moorcroft Eventide Landscape pattern dish, with green piped decoration of trees in hilly landscape, covered in amber, crimson, green and blue glaze, circa 1925, 27.5cm. diam. (Christie's London) **$2,000**

A Moorcroft Cornflower pattern three handled cylindrical vase, with white piped decoration of cornflowers, covered in a yellow, blue and green glaze against a cream ground, 19cm. high. (Christie's London) **$2,250**

MORAVIAN

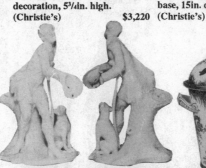

A Moravian brown-glazed fish flask, Salem or Bethabara, North Carolina, early to mid-19th century, the full-bodied holloware form molded in the shape of a fish, 4¾in. long. (Christie's) **$4,830**

A Moravian green-glazed ring flask, Salem or Bethabara, North California, early 19th century, the circular holloware form with double-reeded ring decoration, 5¾in. high. (Christie's) **$3,220**

A Moravian brown-glazed bowl, Salem or Bethabara, North Carolina, 19th century, the circular form with double reeded edge, on plain circular base, 15in. diam. (Christie's) **$460**

NYMPHENBURG

A Nymphenburg figure of Cupid as Vulcan from the series of Ovidian Gods modeled by Franz Anton Bustelli, circa 1757, 11cm. high. (Christie's) **$9,012**

A Nymphenburg white figure of a beggar modeled by Franz Anton Bustelli, wearing tattered clothes, in a contra-posto pose holding out an empty tattered hat in his right hand, circa 1760, 17cm. high. (Christie's) **$39,380**

A Nymphenburg two-handled tapering oval pail and domed cover in the Frankenthal style, with a striped multiple leaf finial, circa 1860, 20¾in. high. (Christie's) **$7,771**

CHINA

PARIS

A Paris porcelain cabinet cup painted with a female gardener with a watering can, 19th century.
(Christie's) $246

A pair of Paris biscuit busts of a bacchante and satyr, after Clodion, modeled leering over opposing shoulders, both wearing vine wreaths heavy with grapes, 9½in. high.
(Christie's) $805

A Paris porcelain inkstand, painted with bouquets of flowers and applied with a seated model of a hound, blue mark for Jacob Petit, 19th century.
(Christie's) $665

PAUL REVERE

Paul Revere Pottery decorated tea tile, Boston, Massachusetts, early 20th century, with central decoration of a cottage, 5¾in. diameter.
(Skinner Inc.) $375

Paul Revere Pottery decorated vase, Boston, Massachusetts, early 20th century, with incised and painted band of tree design, 8½in. high.
(Skinner Inc.) $2,300

Paul Revere Pottery Saturday Evening Girl tile, incised Boston street scene, colored pink, blue, brown, white and gray with black outlines, 3¾ x 3¾in.
(Skinner) $385

PEARLWARE

A pearlware model of Obadiah Sherratt type of The Flight into Egypt, the Virgin Mary modeled seated on a donkey, circa 1820, 7¾in. high.
(Christie's) $626

Two pearlware figures emblematic of Hope and Charity modeled as women, circa 1820, 8in. high.
(Christie's) $500

A rare Staffordshire pearlware ale bench group with figures of a lady and gentleman seated in yellow chairs and drinking, 21cm. high.
(Phillips) $3,520

CHINA

PETIT

A pair of Jacob Petit oviform ewers, painted with panels of figures and flowers, the handles molded with flowers, blue *J.P.* mark circa 1850, 14in. high. (Christie's) **$1,077**

A Jacob Petit porcelain inkstand painted with flowers on an emerald green and gilt ground, circa 1840. (Duran, Madrid) **$1,391**

A Jacob Petit garniture of a clock and a pair of candlesticks all moulded with rococo scrolls, shells and leaf motifs, 39.5cm. (Phillips) **$1,683**

POOLE POTTERY

A pottery oviform jug, shape no. 304, painted by Marjorie Batt with bluebirds and foliage in typical colors, impressed *CSA Ltd* mark, 5in. high. (Christie's S. Ken) **$400**

A terracotta plate painted by Anne Hatchard with a green spotted leaping gazelle amongst fruiting vines, impressed *CSA* mark, 12in. diam. (Christie's S. Ken) **$1,500**

A Poole Pottery baluster vase painted by Ruth Pavely with a design attributed to Truda Carter, impressed C.S.A. mark, painted rhebus, impressed 947, 11¾in. high. (Christie's S. Ken) **$1,400**

PRATTWARE

A creamware model of an owl, circa 1785, of Pratt type, with alert expression and incised **plumage and splashed in ocher,** green and brown spots, 5½in. high. (Christie's) **$5,280**

Pair of Prattware figures of Elijah and the Widow of Zarephath, England, late 18th century, 9½in. high. (Skinner Inc.) **$660**

A Prattware cider jug, circa 1880, molded with exotic barnyard fowl within an oval reserve edged with stiff leaf-tips, 7¾in. high. (Christie's) **$1,430**

91

QIANLONG

A fine robin's-egg-glazed oviform vase, impressed Qianlong seal mark and of the period, covered overall with a mottled glaze of turquoise and rich blue tone, 9¼in. high, box.
(Christie's) $24,179

A rare large famille rose kneeling boy pillow, Qianlong, the plump infant crouching on all fours with a smiling face raised to the left and his feet in the air, 15in. long.
(Christie's) $39,000

A fine celadon-glazed molded vase, Meiping, impressed Qianlong seal mark and of the period, relief-moulded on the body with sprays of the sanduo, fruiting peach, finger citrus and pomegranate, 9in. high.
(Christie's) $36,903

ROCKINGHAM

A Rockingham dated claret-ground cylindrical mug, painted with a horse with jockey up, inscribed in gilt *First Year of WATH RACES, MDCCCXXXI*, 1831, 13cm. high.
(Christie's) $7,482

A pair of Rockingham porcelain small spill vases, each decorated with a continuous scene of a spoonbill and other birds, 3¼in. high, circa 1830.
(Tennants) $3,726

An important Rockingham Royal Service plate, from the service made for William IV, the light blue border gilt with oak leaves with acorns, 24cm.
(Phillips) $5,760

ROOKWOOD

Rookwood Pottery wax resist vase, Cincinnati, Ohio, 1928, executed by Elizabeth Neave Lingenfelter Lincoln (1892–1931), 11in. high.
(Skinner Inc.) $300

Rookwood pottery scenic plaque, 'The End of Winter', Cincinnati, Ohio, 1918, original frame, 12¼in. x 9¼in.
(Skinner Inc.) $2,800

Rookwood pottery scenic vellum vase, Cincinnati, 1913, decorated with landscape scene in gray-blue on shaded yellow to peach background, 13⅝in. high.
(Skinner Inc) $2,000

ROYAL DUX

Pair of Royal Dux porcelain figural vases, late 19th century, mid Eastern couple standing beside palm trees, 36in. high. (Skinner Inc.) $715

A Royal Dux bisque porcelain Art Nouveau style flower holder, as a maiden draped in a brown robe seated upon a rocky outcrop, 27cm. high. (Spencer's) $856

A pair of Royal Dux figures of a near eastern desert dweller and fishergirl, both wearing green and apricot rustic dress, pink triangle pad mark, 20th century, 24¼in. high. (Christie's) $1,425

ROZENBURG

Earthenware vase with basket handle, by J.L. Verhoog, manufactured at the Hague by Rozenburg, date-coded 1898, 13in. high. (Skinner Inc.) $1,600

Unusual pair of Rozenburg pottery vases, the Hague, date coded 1898, decorated with polychrome floral and dragon motif on brown ground, 9½in. high. (Skinner Inc.) $1,300

Rozenburg thistle wall plate, the Hague, date coded 1898, hand painted with stylized thistle flowers in earthy tones brown, rust and lavender-gray, 10¾in. diameter. (Skinner Inc.) $700

RUSKIN

A Ruskin high-fired stoneware vase, the oatmeal ground clouded with green and speckled with irregular areas of purple and blue, 1915, 21.cm. high. (Christie's) $2,134

A Ruskin high-fired egg-shell stoneware bowl, with dark mottled red glaze clouding to green and purple towards the foot, 21cm. diameter. (Christie's) $2,134

A Ruskin high-fired stoneware vase, pale ground mottled overall in purples and greens fragmented with random 'snake-skin' patterning, 1914, 32.3cm. high. (Christie's) $3,201

CHINA

SALTGLAZE

A Staffordshire saltglaze solid-agate model of a cat, circa 1750, modeled to the right with brown and buff clays, brown slip eyes and splashed with blue on the ears and back, 5in. high.
(Christie's) $1,610

A Staffordshire saltglaze Jacobite quatrefoil teapot and cover, circa 1760, enameled in colors with Charles II in the branches above the shells, 5¼in. high.
(Christie's) $8,250

A Staffordshire saltglaze arbor group, circa 1760, modeled as a couple seated beneath an arbor, his hands on her bare knee, 6in. high.
(Christie's) $60,500

SAMSON

A French gilt-bronze mounted vase with cover, Napoléon III, by Sampson of Paris, circa 1870, 52cm. high.
(Sotheby's) $9,620

A pair of Samson models of Bolognese hounds, after Meissen originals, each modeled seated with gray or brown markings, 9in. high, the largest.
(Christie's) $2,645

Samson porcelain teapot and cover with fluted molded body, domed lid, shaped handle and spout.
(G. A. Key) $131

SATSUMA

A large reticulated koro and pierced domed cover modeled as a kiku head with upright square handles, 14½in. high.
(Christie's) $13,800

19th century Satsuma porcelain figure of a boy playing a drum, his gilded robe richly decorated in black, red, white and blue, 38cm. high.
(Finarte) $5,726

Satsuma globular-shaped vase, Japan, mid to late 19th century, gilt and enamel decorated scenes of warriors within bamboo framed panels, 8½in. high.
(Skinner Inc.) $1,900

SAVONA

A Savona syrup jar named for *Sy. Rosato. Semce* in blue on a banner on a ground of scattered stylized flowers, circa 1700, 8³/₄in. high.
(Christie's) $809

A Savona blue and white circular stand, the well painted with a bird in flight above fortified buildings within a border of figures and animals in landscape, 18th century, 9in. diameter.
(Christie's) $913

A Savona blue and white oviform wet-drug jar, titled in manganese *S. de Pharfara* between bands of foliage, circa 1720, 7³/₄in. high.
(Christie's) $548

SÈVRES

A pair of Sèvres biscuit figures of Spring and Autumn, possibly modeled by Flaconet, she with incised *F* mark.
(Phillips) $1,020

A gilt-metal-mounted Sèvres-pattern vase of broad and squat form, the body painted with figures wearing 18th century dress at a marriage banquet, late 19th century, 28¹/₂in. high.
(Christie's) $8,217

A pair of Sèvres-style gilt-metal mounted oviform vases and covers, each painted with a Watteauesque scene of couples in 18th century dress, the covers with pineapple finials, 19th century, 12¹/₄in. high.
(Christie's) $1,505

SLIP DECORATED

A rare slip-decorated redware pie plate, Pennsylvania, 19th century, of circular form with crimped edge, 12¹/₈in. diameter.
(Sotheby's) $1,955

A rare slip-decorated glazed redware large pie plate, Pennsylvania, 19th century, the interior with yellow slip inscription *G. W. Rhoads Dealer in Dry goods groceries & cc also Schwitzer Kase*, diameter 13¹/₂in.
(Sotheby's) $3,738

A very fine and rare slip-decorated redware charger, New England, 19th century, with the inscription *Temperance, Health, Wealth*, 13³/₄in. diameter.
(Sotheby's) $19,550

SLIPWARE

A Staffordshire slipware press-molded dated 'Man within the Cumpas' charger by Samuel Malkin, 1726, 35cm. diameter.
(Christie's) $14,680

A Staffordshire slipware documentary thistle-shaped tankard, dated 1679, with initials *'IT LT 1679'* above combed decoration, 3¼in. high.
(Christie's) $9,200

A Staffordshire slipware dish, second quarter 18th century, the center with a four-petaled brown flower with blue edging, 15¾in. diameter.
(Christie's) $11,000

SPODE

A Spode lavender-ground potpourri-vase and pierced cover with gilt dragon handles and finial, painted with shells and seaweed, circa 1825, 21cm. high.
(Christie's) $3,275

A rare pair of Spode tapersticks, brightly decorated with the popular Japan pattern, No. 967, on circular bases, 3⅛in. high.
(Bonhams) $640

A Spode miniature watering-can painted in an Imari palette with flower-sprays within shaped gilt cartouches, circa 1815, 10cm. high.
(Christie's) $1,436

STAFFORDSHIRE

An early Staffordshire pottery group of a shepherd sitting on a rocky outcrop, playing a flute, his companion standing at his side, 25cm.
(Bearne's) $687

A Staffordshire pearlware cow creamer and stopper with a pink lustered border, a milkmaid seated to one side, 14cm.
(Phillips) $898

A remarkable Staffordshire slipware owl jug and cover, the head lifting off to form a drinking cup, the body molded in buff colored clay, 23cm.
(Phillips) $33,660

CHINA

TANG

A large painted pottery horse standing foursquare on a rectangular base, the saddle draped with a knotted cloth falling in folds above a striped saddle blanket, Tang Dynasty, 41cm. high.
(Christie's) $5,600

A red painted pottery standing horse and a groom, the horse with plain saddle and brick-red painted body, the groom with clenched wrists and looking upwards, Tang Dynasty, the groom 28cm. high.
(Christie's) $9,845

A rare brown-glazed ewer of ovoid shape on a short foot, surmounted by a slightly tapered cylindrical neck applied with a molded loop handle and short cabriole spout, Tang Dynasty, 13.5cm. high.
(Christie's) $2,685

TECO

Teco pottery vase with four handles, Terra Cotta, Illinois, circa 1910, squat, impressed twice, 6½in. high. (Skinner Inc.) $1,300

Teco floor vase, Gates Potteries, Terra Cotta, Illinois, circa 1906, green glazed with rolled rim continuing into four squared vertical strap handles, 20⁵/₈in. high.
(Skinner) $7,150

Teco pottery wall pocket, green matt glaze on hanging vase with angular top over molded roundel, 5¼in. wide.
(Skinner Inc.) $385

THURINGIAN

A Thuringian figure of a lady, possibly Wallendorf, holding her black apron in one hand, wearing a lace collar, a red bodice and a floral skirt, 13cm.
(Phillips) $825

A pair of Thuringian figures of a shepherd and shepherdess, he in a long coat, she in a black and red hat, white bodice with a purple edge, circa 1770, 14cm. high.
(Christie's) $2,166

A Thuringian pear-shaped coffee-pot and cover with scroll handle and shell-molded spout, one side painted with a huntsman and companion and a hound, circa 1770, 24.5cm. high.
(Christie's) $8,446

CHINA

URBINO

An Urbino istoriato dated documentary large circular dish painted by Francesco Xanto Avelli da Rovigo with The Rape of Helen, 1535, 46.5cm. diameter.
(Christie's) $73,852

A finely painted Urbino istoriato dish, by Francesco Xanto Avelli da Rovigo, signed and dated 1532, and lustered probably at Gubbio, 26cm.
(Phillips) $22,330

An Urbino istoriato dish, painted with a standing figure of Venus with Cupid beside her, a central figure of Jupiter holding a thunderbolt and with his eagle at his side, 26.5cm.
(Phillips) $10,556

VAN BRIGGLE

Van Briggle pottery vase, caramel glaze with moss green mottling, inscribed mark and 1913, 6in. high.
(Skinner) $467

A Rookwood pottery basket, by artist Artus Van Briggle, decorated in slip underglaze with blossoms, berries and leaves, 6½in. high. (Robt. W. Skinner Inc.) $700

Van Briggle Pottery vase, Colorado Springs, circa 1904, with molded floral design yellow and ocher semi-matte glaze, 8½in. high.
(Skinner Inc.) $850

VENICE

A Venice wet drug jar, painted with a profile bust portrait of a soldier in blue helmet, under the spout, 21.5cm.
(Phillips) $1,319

A Venice large cylindrical albarello, the berettino ground named in gothic script for *Sandali•R•* on a scrolling ribbon surrounded by scrolling flowering foliage, circa 1580, 30.5cm. high.
(Christie's) $5,174

A Venice drug bottle, painted on one side with a head and shoulders portrait of a man wearing blue tunic and hat, 22cm.
(Phillips) $5,278

VIENNA

A Vienna figure of a dwarf 'Die Walper Hollriglin' modeled by J. L. C. Lück, advancing, her arms outstretched and her mouth open, circa 1755, 11cm. high. (Christie's) $18,925

CHINA

Extremely fine pair of Continental porcelain vases, bearing the Vienna beehive mark, 18$\frac{1}{2}$in. high, early 19th century. (G.A. Key) $4,779

A Vienna pear-shaped hot-water jug, painted on one side with two hearts tied with ribbon to a tree above the inscription *Toujours en vigueur*, 7$\frac{1}{2}$in. high. (Christie's) $804

VINCENNES

A Vincennes large pot-pourri vase and a cover, the shoulders with puce and gilt foliage scrolls with harebells suspending sprays of flowers, between seven pierced holes molded with gilt cartouches, circa 1752, 32cm. high. (Phillips) $34,500

A Vincennes tureen, cover and stand of oval form, gilt with panels of birds in flight within scrolling gilt cartouches, 25.5cm. wide. (Phillips) $7,820

A Vincennes bleu celeste two-handled vase (vase Duplessis à fleurs) of campana form with elaborate foliage-scroll handles, each side painted with bouquets of flowers and fruit within cartouches, circa 1755, 15cm. high. (Christie's) $13,196

WEDGWOOD

A Wedgwood black and white solid jasper copy of the Portland or Barberini vase by Thomas Lovatt, of conventional type, the base with Paris wearing the Phrygian cap, circa 1880, 26cm. high. (Christie's) $1,871

A garniture of two Wedgwood crocus pots and covers and a small flower vase each colored in cream and brown, with relief molded cream ribbon-tied swags, 14cm. to 16cm. (Phillips) $460

A Wedgwood gilt-copper mounted blue and white jasper octagonal scent-bottle, circa 1790, decorated with two putti dancing beneath a tree, 2$\frac{5}{8}$in. high. (Christie's) $1,495

WEMYSS

A Wemyss 'Bute' vase, circa 1900, painted with pink roses, impressed and script marks, 19cm.
(Sotheby's) $567

A Wemyss Ware three-handled loving cup painted with sweet-peas, two impressed Wemyss marks, 9^1/$_2$in. high.
(Christie's) $810

A rare Wemyss jar and cover, circa 1900, painted with a band of strawberries above a leaf border, the cover painted with strawberries, impressed mark, 17cm.
(Sotheby's) $1,327

WESTERWALD

A Westerwald globular jug glazed in blue and manganese and molded with a royal equestrian portrait medallion, circa 1690, 28cm. high.
(Christie's) $2,367

A Westerwald stoneware spirit-barrel of ribbed form, the blue ground incised with bands of scrolling stylized foliage, the ends with winged cherubs' heads and flowers, 18th century, 33cm. long.
(Christie's) $1,530

A Westerwald desk-set modeled as two gallants in incised perukes, their companion holding a shallow circular container and wearing a pleated dress, early 18th century, 23cm. high.
(Christie's) $5,544

WORCESTER

A Worcester partridge tureen and cover sitting on a rest, with natural colored plumage in shades of brown, red and black, the head in red, 14.5cm.
(Phillips) $2,639

A Worcester small baluster mug with grooved loop handle, painted with a loose bouquet and scattered flowers, circa 1760, 8.5cm. high.
(Christie's) $886

A Royal Worcester 'Aesthetic' teapot and cover, circa 1882, polychrome decorated in 'greenery yallery' colors, 6^1/$_8$in. high.
(Sotheby's) $3,410

A 35mm. Newman and Sinclair cinematographic camera no. 395 with polished duraluminium body, a Ross, London patent Xpres 1¹/₂ inch f/1.9 lens.
(Christie's S. Ken) $810

A 35mm. Kinarri 35 cinematographic camera by Arnold & Richter, Munich, Germany, with an Arrinar f/2.7 35mm. lens.
(Christie's S. Ken) $5,262

A 35mm. hand-cranked, wood-body Superb cine camera with brass fittings, crank and two internal film holders.
(Christie's S. Ken) $615

A 35mm. Empire No. 3 cinematograph camera with polished mahogany body, brass binding and footage indicator. Manufactured by W. Butcher & Sons Ltd., in maker's fitted leather case.
(Christie's S. Ken) $2,347

A 35mm. mahogany cased cinematographic camera by Alfred and Darling and Co., with metal binding strips and a Williamson-pattern cinematographic tripod.
(Christie's S. Ken) $567

Thornton-Pickard Mfg. Co. Ltd., Altrincham, a 16mm. black-crackle finished Ruby cinematographic camera with direct vision finder, the film gate stamped, 39, a Dallmeyer 1 inch f/1.9 lens no. 121480 and front panel marked *The Ruby*.
(Christie's) $936

H. Ernemann, Dresden, a 17¹/₂mm. hand-cranked Kino I cinematographic camera stamped 99 with hand-crank, removable direct finder and rack and pinion focusing.
(Christie's) $4,574

A 35mm. Ensign cinematograph camera no. 128 with black leather covered body, brass fittings, hand-crank and an Aldis-Ensign Anastigmat 2 inch f/3.1 lens.
(Christie's S. Ken) $1,107

A 16mm. RCA Sound cinematographic camera Type PR–25 No. 1156 with a Taylor-Hobson Cooke Cinema 1 inch f/3.5 lens, in maker's fitted leather case.
(Christie's) $1,271

An interesting mid 18th century chiming verge lantern clock by Markwick Markham, London, playing tunes on the quarters upon four bells, 15¹/₂in. high.
(Tennants) $5,220

A gilt brass combination timepiece aneroid barometer and thermometer, the timepiece with platform lever escapement, 11in. high.
(Lawrence Fine Art) $854

A rosewood and mother of pearl inlaid drop dial timepiece, W. Nerilger, Brighton, circa 1870, 11in., signed *W. Nerilger, Brighton*, 21in. high.
(Bonhams) $608

A late Federal pillar-and-scroll mahogany shelf clock, labeled by Seth Thomas, Eli Terry Patent, Plymouth, Connecticut, circa 1820, eglomisé panel with a central medallion and village scene, 29in. high.
(Christie's) $1,725

An Empire ormolu and marble striking mantel clock with green marble base on toupie feet, a lady seated in a bergère reading at a draped table on paw feet with oil lamp atop, signed *Leroy & Fils Hgers. du Roi A Paris No. 1065*, 12³/₄in. high.
(Christie's) $4,023

A Regency mahogany bracket clock in rectangular-shaped case, with stepped chamfered top, ring handles and pierced scalloped side frets, twin-chain fusée movement, 16¹/₂in. high.
(Christie's S. Ken) $2,213

An unusual 19th century Austrian miniature porcelain timepiece, the shaped case decorated with flowers on paw feet, signed *Doker, in Wien*, 55mm. high.
(Phillips) $828

A Japanese gilt-brass and padouk wood striking mantle clock of standard form with four baluster pillar movement, 5¹/₄in. high.
(Christie's) $3,234

A brass skeleton clock with passing strike, English, circa 1875, 5¹/₄in. enamel chapter ring with Roman numeral, the single fusée movement with half dead beat escapement, 18in. high.
(Bonhams) $730

An ormolu and porcelain French mantel clock, the shaped case decorated with swags and foliage and surmounted by two doves, 11in. high.
(Phillips) $792

A French ormolu and bronze cartel clock of Louis XVI style, 19th Century, signed *Bagues Freres Fabrts de Bronzes, Paris*, 32¹/in. high.
(Christie's) $3,542

Empire ormolu mantel clock, 19th century, circular dial inscribed *Manneville Rue St. Honore a Paris*, 18¹/2in. high.
(Skinner Inc.) $3,000

A rare quarter chiming lantern clock, the going train with verge escapement and later pendulum suspension, signed *D. Lesturgeon, London*, circa 1700, 7in. wide.
(Christie's New York)
                              $2,860

A good French gilt-bronze mantel clock, Napoléon III, circa 1870, the case cast with four cherubs, the base now malachite-veneered, the dial signed *Denière Fᵗ de Bronzes à Paris*, 63cm. high.
(Sotheby's) $10,356

A fine chased gilt grande sonnerie carriage clock with moon phase, calendar, thermometer and winding indicator, the movement stamped *H.L.* in lozenge punch, circa 1860, 8in. high.
(Christie's New York)
                              $22,000

An 18th century Continental thirty-hour wall clock, the shaped pierced painted dial with single hand, the posted frame movement with verge escapement.
(Phillips) $1,890

A Regency mahogany wall timepiece, the silvered engraved dial signed *Edw. Tutet London*, Roman and Arabic chapters, 15³/₄in. diameter.
(Christie's) $1,293

A Royal Worcester clock case, colored in ivory and gold and encrusted with flowers, containing a French circular eight-day striking movement, 29cm., date code for 1887.
(Phillips) $1,421

A German oak and walnut cased desk clock with calendar automaton, the 8-day movement with half hour striking on a gong, circa 1890, 51cm. high. (Auction Team Köln) $2,623

An attractive late 19th century French black slate mantel clock/ perpetual calendar/aneroid barometer, 18in. high. (Spencer's) $1,485

An ivory and 9ct. gold carriage clock, French/English, 1914, 1$\frac{1}{4}$in. enamel dial with Roman numerals, 3$\frac{1}{2}$in. (Bonhams) $750

A 19th century brass double-dialed barometer and timepiece in the form of a ship's wheel surmounted by a gimbaled compass, signed *La Fontaine Opticien*, 11$\frac{1}{2}$in. high. (Christie's S. Ken) $2,213

Hand painted, floral decorated Ansonia porcelain desk clock, signed *La Savoie von F M, Bonn, Germany*, the American 8 day movement striking the half hours on a gong, 29cm. high, circa 1900. (Auction Team Köln) $300

A Regency ormolu and marble mantel timepiece, the case on milled bun feet supporting the rectangular white marble base applied with a ribbon-tied fruiting swag, signed *Webster London*, 8in. high. (Christie's) $2,461

Gothic Revival ebonized wood and brass bracket clock, Handley & Moore, London, late 18th century, painted metal face, time and strike movement, with pendulum, 16$\frac{1}{2}$in. high. (Skinner) $1,100

A 19th century French white marble, ormolu and bronze mantel clock, surmounted by two naked putti, signed *Aubanel & Rochat, A. Paris*, 1ft. 6in. high. (Phillips) $810

An 18th century ebonized bracket clock, the 17cm. square brass dial inscribed *Jonathan Lowndes, Pall Mall, London*, 16in. high. (Spencer's) $3,900

A mid Victorian gilt-metal strut timepiece, the case designed in the form of card suits, the frame as a diamond engraved with foliage, 7½in. high.
(Christie's) $11,652

Patinated bronze double face clock, the drum shaped case encircled by ropework, set on a simple square base, 25in. high.
(William Doyle Galleries) $2,415

Unusual Japanese desk clock in brass with decorative carved back plate and striking bell to top, complete with hardwood stand.
(G. A. Key) $962

A Black Forest carved wood striking cuckoo clock of standard form, the dial with Roman chapter ring, pierced bone hands, a cuckoo and seated boy appearing on the hour behind shutters, 30in. high.
(Christie's) $1,714

An attractive 19th century French gilt metal mantel clock by Le Roy & Fils of Paris, housed in a fluted horizontal cylindrical drum surmounted by a garland of flowers, a naked putto seated to the side, 35cm. high.
(Spencer's) $2,719

An ormolu and marble mantel timepiece, French, second half 19th century, 3½in. enamel dial, movement now electric but retains original striking lever movement by T. Martin & Co., 12in.
(Bonhams) $900

A mahogany drop-dial timepiece, Dutton Fleet St. London, Victorian, 1852, 12in. silvered dial with engraved Roman numerals and Royal Cypher, in mahogany case, 18in.
(Bonhams) $1,500

An attractive 19th century French porcelain mantel clock, backplate inscribed *Dupont a Paris*, in a lancet shaped case with foliate sheathed column stiles, 32.5cm. high.
(Spencer's) $882

A Regency mahogany striking bracket clock, the case in the Egyptian taste on foliate carved feet and with brass-lined and shaped recessed panel to the front flanked by bronze Egyptian caryatids, 20in. high.
(Christie's) $3,427

A silver, cloisonné and russet iron tripod koro, the body decorated with two shaped and pierced panels with a ho-o bird among paulownia and a karashishi among peonies, late 19th century, 12cm. high.
(Christie's) $10,120

A cloisonné enamel and gilt-bronze recumbent mythical lion, the rich black body set with white, yellow, turquoise and iron-red details, 18th century, 18cm. long.
(Christie's) $4,332

A cloisonné enamel box and cover of hexagonal form, the cover decorated with a cockatoo perched on a maple branch, signed 12.5cm.
(Hy. Duke & Son)
$21,000

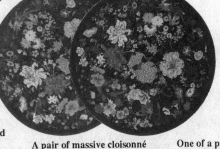

Fine Canton enamel tripod censer and cover, Qianlong mark and period, painted with lotus flowers interwoven with leafy tendrils and assorted flowers bracketed by a stylized plantain leaf and a ruyi-lappet band, 8½in. high.
(Butterfield & Butterfield)
$3,575

A pair of massive cloisonné chargers decorated in vibrant colored enamels and various thicknesses of wire, with dense profusions of flowers and foliage, late 19th century, 92.5cm. diameter.
(Christie's) $19,250

One of a pair of gilt-bronze and polychrome cloisonné enamel vases, raised with an all over design of peonies and foliate scrolls, and with two panels of assorted vases in a scrolling dragon border, 26in. high.
(Christie's) (Two)
$1,900

A pair of cloisonné vases decorated in various colored enamels and thicknesses of wire depicting alternate panels of ducks, egrets amongst reeds and Mount Fuji, Gonda Hirosuke, late 19th century, 41cm. high.
(Christie's) $5,460

One of a pair of cloisonné and gilt-bronze horses and riders, the riders seated on saddle cloths, wearing long cloaks and wide brimmed hats, 12½in. high, 19th century.
(Bonhams)(Two) $7,460

A massive pair of Japanese cloisonné vases, the bodies decorated with four red-capped cranes and birds amidst flowering branches, 53¼in. overall.
(Woolley & Wallis)
$11,770

A fine large cloisonné enamel and gilt-rectangular baluster vase and cover, all decorated with turquoise and enriched with gilt key-pattern cloisons, Qianlong, 53cm. high.
(Christie's) $11,814

A pair of cloisonné enamel turquoise-ground standing duck vessels, their plumage detailed in wire, Qianlong/Jiaqing, 21.5cm. long.
(Christie's) $7,482

A fine and large cloisonné enamel baluster vase with gilt-bronze handles surmounted with monster masks, Qianlong, 61cm. high.
(Christie's) $11,362

A Hayashi kodenji cloisonné vase decorated in various colored enamels and thicknesses of silver wire on a deep blue ground with sparrows, signed *Nagoya Hayashi saku*, late 19th century, 31.5cm. high.
(Christie's) $8,085

A pair of Japanese cloisonné vases, each finely decorated with birds amongst wisteria on a bamboo trellis, 7¼in. high.
(Bearne's) $946

One of a pair of gilt-bronze and polychrome cloisonné enamel vases, each of baluster form, with two bordered panels depicting birds, butterflies and spring flowers, 20¾in. high.
(Christie's)   (Two) $2,090

A cloisonné vase decorated in various colored enamels and thicknesses of gold and silver wire in the Namikawa style with a ho-o bird and a dragon, late 19th century, 15.5cm. high.
(Christie's) $1,223

A cloisonné enamel censer, decorated with prunus and petals on a cracked-ice ground above a band of lotus panels above the pedestal foot, incised Qianlong four-character seal mark, 20cm. wide.
(Christie's) $8,536

A Namikawa Sosuke vase of baluster form finely worked in silver wire and musen-jippo with a magpie in plum blossom, signed *Sosuke*, late 19th century, 29.5cm. high.
(Christie's) $86,526

A Dinanderie brass alms dish embossed with the Paschal lamb, with everted rim and geometric decoration, 16in. diameter.
(Christie's) $586

A Victorian copper cheese-vat, the molded rim and swollen circular body with carrying-handles to sides, 42½in. diameter.
(Christie's) $3,450

Large copper cauldron with metal swing handle and lid, stamped *Paul, Bury*, Victorian period, 18in.
(G. A. Key) $248

A brass lantern in the form of a pierced owl, a hinged opening to one side, late 19th/early 20th century, 13in. high.
(Christie's) $5,634

Four brass Standard Measures by DeGrave Short and Fanner London.
(Christie's S. Ken) $1,062

A Victorian cast brass plaque depicting an embossed classical head, with beveled edge, 9in. x 6½in.
(Phillips) $45

A South German brass alms dish, the well repoussé with Adam and Eve beneath the Tree of Knowledge, 14¾in. diameter.
(Bonhams) $1,045

A Flemish brass oval jardinière with beaded rim, the sides with repoussé decoration of a bed of flowerheads, with lion-mask ring-handles, on paw feet, 19th century, 17½in. wide.
(Christie's) $2,789

An Artificers Guild hammered brass bowl designed by Edward Spencer, supported on six-shaped feet with pierced openwork decoration of stylized foliage, 19.7cm. high.
(Christie's) $1,244

A mid 19th century brass tavern tobacco box with central carrying handle flanked by two lidded compartments.
(Phillips) $369

Copper and brass kettle, burner and stand, 19th century.
(G.A. Key) $90

Gebelein hammered copper bowl, circa 1915, repeating foliate band with copper finish rim and stepped disk base, 8¹/₂in. diameter.
(Skinner) $330

A brass bucket, with a swing handle and incised ribbing, 9¹/₂in. diameter.
(Lawrence) $607

A pair of Georgian brass candlesticks, 18th century, each with cylindrical stem with a low drip cup, 8in. high.
(Christie's) $4,400

A George III brass samovar with circular ribbed lid and foliate finial, with scrolled bone handles on a plinth base and bun feet, 17in. high.
(Christie's) $792

An inlaid hammered copper vase by Paul Mergier, with inlaid white-metal decoration of leaping antelope amid foliage, with inlaid signature *P. Mergier*, 30cm. high.
(Christie's) $2,920

A Wiener Werkstätte brass five-piece coffee service, designed by Josef Hoffmann, each piece stamped with designer's monogram, *Made in Austria*, 22.6cm. height of coffee pot.
(Christie's) $7,656

John Pearson repoussé copper candle sconce, England, circa 1895, incised marks, 15¹/₂in. long.
(Skinner) $632

An early Victorian brass doorstop, in the form of opposing entwined dolphins, with ring handle to the top, 8¹/₂in. high.
(Christie's) **$964**

A yellow copper collection plate with a central repoussé medallion surrounded by inscriptions, 17th century German.
(Galerie Moderne) **$1,058**

A mid-Victorian brass helmet coal-scuttle with rosewood handles, with a horse's head and fleur-de-lys pressed mark, 49.5cm. deep.
(Christie's) **$457**

One of a handsome pair of gilt metal pedestals, with tapered columns headed by bacchic masks and cast with intricate acanthus scrolls, 45in. high.
(Bonhams)
(Two) **$5,157**

Three brass candlesticks, early 18th century, with short faceted tapering stems above a circular stem over a circular dish drip pan, 6¹/₂in. high.
(Christie's) **$2,860**

Jarvie brass three-branch candelabra, circa 1905, three removable trumpet bobeches supported by coiling arms mounted on central shaft, 10¹/₄in. high.
(Skinner) **$1,210**

A Benham & Froud copper coffee-pot designed by Dr. Christopher Dresser, globular form with tapering cylindrical neck and hinged cover, circa 1884, 22cm. high.
(Christie's) **$1,378**

Pair of North African brass and ivory-inlaid large urns, early 20th century, inlaid with various star and geometric motifs, raised on a spreading circular base, 42¹/₂in. tall.
(Butterfield & Butterfield) **$2,750**

A Dutch brass and copper jardinière, the open circular top above bombé sides with lion-mask and ring-handles, on studded plinth base, 20¹/₄in. high.
(Christie's) **$2,274**

A 19th century copper milk churn from Trafalgar Dairies Ltd. Devon Port, 20½in. high. (Phillips) $210

A brass folding fan-shaped spark guard, 39½in. wide. (Christie's) $789

A pair of Regency brass candlesticks, early 19th century, each anthemion-cast nozzle over a circular tapering shaft, 12¾in. high. (Christie's) $4,600

A Glasgow style copper wall sconce, rectangular, with repoussé decoration of peacocks amid stylized honesty, 36.5cm. high. (Christie's) $479

A fine pair of 19th century copper log boxes with brass fittings, 17in. high. (Phillips) $465

Early 19th century copper samovar of squat circular form with bone handles, brass tap, stemmed to a rectangular base, 15in. high. (G.A. Key) $630

One of a pair of 18th century Dutch embossed copper wall sconces, decorated with two seated cherubs above an oval shield, with scrolling upswept arms, 31cm. wide. (Phillips) (Two) $1,260

W.M.F. brass coffee set, Germany, circa 1910, Wuerttembergische Metal Fabrik, wicker covered handles with maufacturer's mark. (Skinner Inc.) $500

Art Nouveau copper fire screen, England, circa 1900, framed in wrought iron, central ceramic insert with blue glaze, unsigned, 28½in. high. (Skinner) $330

Gustav Stickley copper serving tray, no. 274 variant, circa 1907, wide rim with riveted handles and hammered finish, 16⁷/₈in. diameter.
(Skinner) $550

A brass jardinière with rounded rectangular top above a trellis-etched slightly tapering body flanked by lion-masks, on claw-and-ball feet, 19th century, 28¹/₄in. wide.
(Christie's) $3,584

A 17th century style brass alms dish of Nuremberg type, the center raised with the figures of Adam and Eve, 16¹/₂in. diameter.
(Christie's) $1,350

Talwin Morris, two embossed brass finger plates each with a central motif of a heart imposed on a stylized foliate grid of blooming and budding roses, circa 1893, 11 x 5in.
(Christie's) $650

A very fine gilt-copper pear-shaped ewer and cover, 16th century, probably circa 1550, modeled after a near eastern metalwork shape, relief cast with petal-shaped panels at either side depicting dignitaries, 11⁷/₈in. high.
(Christie's) $31,226

A matched pair of Charles X gilt brass curtain ties, of oval form with hinged clasp, having continuous stamped florette decoration, 22cm. and 23cm.
(Phillips) $713

A Regency brass kettle-on-stand, the shaped carrying-handle of reeded ebony, the ovoid kettle with domed stepped lid, on foliate cabriole legs and pad feet, 18¹/₂in. high.
(Christie's) $1,195

A pair of W. A. S. Benson chamber sticks, copper and brass, each on flared stepped base with curved up-turned handles, the sconce in the form of a lotus flower, 13.8cm. high.
(Christie's) $383

A Siebe, Gorman & Co. brass and copper diver's helmet, 50cm. high, and a 1916 Admiralty Diving manual.
(Bearne's) $2,025

Copper jelly mold in the form of a turret castle, stamped *F.M.18*, 6¹/₂in. tall, English, 19th century.
(G. A. Key) $180

A Perry, Son & Co. copper hot water jug designed by Dr. Christopher Dresser, with angled spout and loop handle, 19cm. high.
(Christie's) $1,083

Hammered copper fruit cooler, probably Austria, circa 1905, with geometric detail, raised on four cut-out and stepped feet, 15in. high.
(Skinner Inc.) $275

A pair of Georgian brass candlesticks, second quarter, 19th century, each with molded flaring bobèche and turned stem with push-up mechanism over a beaded baluster, 8¹/₂in. high.
(Christie's) $462

Brass Art Nouveau ashtray from the Orient Express, with a female head in relief, design after Alphonse Mucha, circa 1900.
(Auction Team Köln)
                               $179

A pair of massive late Victorian brass ewers of highly ornamental form, on circular bases, 35in. high.
(Christie's) $2,834

Large Georgian brass footman on cabriole front legs with carrying handles.
(G. A. Key) $530

Large brass helmet shaped coal scuttle, together with shovel, turned wooden handles, 20in. wide.
(G.A. Key) $409

A brass jardinière with rounded rectangular open top above a studded frieze, the sides with lion-mask and ring-handles, on paw feet, 19th century, 26¹/₂in. wide.
(Christie's) $2,731

A Thomason brass-barreled corkscrew decorated with fruiting vines and with turned bone handle, no brush. (Christie's S. Ken) $820

A good example of a James Heeley's bronzed double lever corkscrew by Weir, marked with a catalog no. 428. (Christie's S. Ken) $750

Early 19th century variant of Thomason's double action corkscrew with elliptical brass turning handle and helical worm. (Christie's) $1,500

A bone handled King's Screw corkscrew with brass barrel, metal winding handle and fine wire helix. (Christie's S. Ken) $375

A Victorian engine-turned silver gilt traveling set comprising sandwich box and pair of roundlets with corkscrew and railway carriage key. London 1869. (Graves Son & Pilcher Fine Arts) $2,325

A signed Lunds King's pattern with silvered patent tablet, lacking 2 of 3 bottle grips. (Graves Son & Pilcher Fine Arts) $375

A Thomason 1802 patent corkscrew with brass barrel and wire helix, a brass Royal coat of arms affixed to the case. (Christie's S. Ken) $375

A Gay Nineties folding corkscrew modeled as a pair of lady's stockinged legs. (Christie's S. Ken) $450

A Hull's presto patent screw with solid brass thin barrel and rosewood handle with pusher. (Graves Son & Pilcher Fine Arts) $750

A Charles Hull's 1864 Royal Club corkscrew, with brass tablet fixed, bearing traces of bronze paint.
(Christie's S. Ken) **$1,325**

An unusual simple corkscrew, the electroplated handle formed as two opposing fish, bearing Victorian diamond registration marks.
(Christie's S. Ken) **$860**

A Thomason corkscrew, the brass barrel embossed with vine decoration and with turned bone handle, brush lacking.
(Christie's S. Ken) **$720**

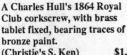

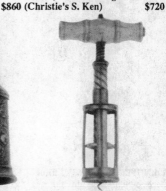

A brass-barreled King's Screw corkscrew with turned bone handle and side handle, brush deficient.
(Christie's S. Ken) **$548**

A Thomason patent corkscrew with bone handle, the brass barrel cast with vines, damaged.
(Christie's S. Ken) **$358**

A Thomason open barrel cork screw with turned bone handle, the barrel top marked: *Edward's Compound, Ne Plus Ultra, Thomason's Patent.*
(Christie's S. Ken) **$739**

'Amor', a German figural folding corkscrew, formed as a Bakelite soldier and his lady, circa 1900, height closed 2¾in. (Christie's) **$600**

A rotary eclipse bar corkscrew, in brass, with steel helical worm and wood side handle. (Christie's) **$800**

A German novelty erotic folding corkscrew, the bone handles carved in the form of a scantily-clad woman.
(Christie's) **$1,100**

An open robe of chintz printed with exotic scrolling flowers in red, blue and purple, circa 1780. (Christie's) **$29,123**

A Jeanne Lanvin embroidered evening jacket, Paris, autumn-winter, 1925–26, with large woven satin label. (Sotheby's) **$625**

A gown of ivory satin, printed with undulating bands of pink columbines against seagreen and lilac heart shaped leaves. (Christie's) **$7,788**

A mid 19th century lady's three piece gown of taupe silk, the slightly trained full skirt lavishly trimmed with shades of brown velour and silk fringe, circa 1855. (Phillips) **$1,362**

A nightshirt of fine linen reputed to have belonged to H.M. King Charles I, the deep square collar and the cuffs trimmed with lace, English, second quarter of the 17th century. (Christie's) **$2,000**

A open robe, with sack back, and petticoat of yellow silk woven with silvery white sprays of honeysuckle and roses, English, circa 1760. (Christie's S. Ken) **$26,598**

A Royal Company of Archers uniform comprising a coat of tartan trimmed with green braid, mid 18th century. (Christie's) **$17,138**

A late 19th century Han Chinese lady's padded jacket of red satin silk, bordered in pale yellow to the neck, sides and hem, circa 1890. (Phillips) **$589**

A gentleman's suit of pale green silk with a figured pin stripe, faced and lined with pink silk, 1770s. (Christie's) **$5,960**

A dress of blue and white striped satin, the cuffs and front trimmed with ivory satin and blue satin ribbons, with pleated train, late 1870's. (Christie's) $412

A doublet of black wool with small ball buttons possibly made of horsehair, early 17th century. (Christie's) $7,378

A rare child's linen suit comprising chemise and pantaloons, early 19th century. (Christie's) $792

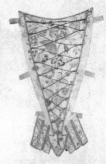

A pen and ink design for a 'rabat' collar of Venetian Gros Point de Venise lace, executed on vellum, circa 1675. (Christie's S. Ken) $3,990

A mid 19th century Chinese coat of silk and gold thread K'o-ssu, the midnight blue ground designed with archaic characters. (Phillips) $4,500

A stomacher of ivory silk, embroidered in colored silks, gilt and silver gilt threads, with a pattern of trailing naturalistic flowers and leaves, early 18th century. (Christie's S. Ken) $1,592

A sack-backed open robe and petticoat of pink silk brocaded with sprays of orange and pink flowers, circa 1755–60. (Christie's) $13,530

A gentleman's sleeved waistcoat of linen, the borders worked with exotic leaves in corded and knotted work, with small ball-shaped self-embroidered buttons to the hem, circa 1690. (Christie's S. Ken) $4,246

An evening coat of deep brown wool, the vermilion velvet collar heavily embroidered with gilt leather flowers, labeled *Schiaparelli, London*, 1937. (Christie's) $8,635

117

GLOVES

COSTUME

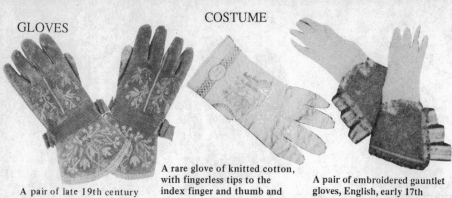

A pair of late 19th century
American Woodlands Indian
gauntlets of brown leather,
probably Cree.
(Phillips) $750

A rare glove of knitted cotton,
with fingerless tips to the
index finger and thumb and
worked with pots of flowers at
the knuckles, early 18th
century. (Christie's S. Ken)
$375

A pair of embroidered gauntlet
gloves, English, early 17th
century, of white kid leather,
embroidered in raised work gold
purl wire, 13¼in. long overall.
(Sotheby's) $1,215

A pair of white kid gloves
with deep cuffs of white
satin embroidered in silver
thread and sequins, mid
17th century. (Christie's)
$4,500

A pair of mid 19th century
North American Eastern
Woodlands Indian gloves of
light brown leather, lined,
probably Cree.
(Phillips) $300

A pair of gloves of pale
cream chamois leather, engraved under the thumb, F.
Bull & Co., Jan 4th 1791,
and a single glove of darker
color. (Christie's) $450

A pair of kid gloves, the cuffs of
pink silk embroidered in gold
thread and sequins and edged
with gold lace, early 17th
century.
(Christie's) $2,441

A lady's glove of white kid,
the deep cuff of ivory satin
lined with pink silk, early
17th century.
(Christie's) $450

A pair of kid gloves, the ivory
silk gauntlets embroidered in
colored silks, gilt threads and
spangles, English, circa 1610.
(Christie's) $2,524

WAISTCOATS

An early 19th century gentleman's waistcoat of ivory satin with fine colored silk embroidery to the high front and pocket flaps.
(Phillips) $350

An embroidered vest and pair of embroidered shoes, 18th century, the vest with floral sprays on ivory silk. (Robt. W. Skinner Inc.) $900

A fine double-breasted waistcoat of pale blue satin with an overlay of net worked with black velvet dots and sequins, circa 1790.
(Christie's S. Ken) $1,773

A gentleman's waistcoat of ivory satin, woven à disposition with chocolate cut and ciselé velvet floral border and pockets, 1740s.
(Christie's) $695

A lady's waistcoat of white cotton quilted in white silk and embroidered in yellow and red wools, English, circa 1730.
(Christie's) $4,500

A Sioux buckskin waistcoat, the entire surface sewn with beads, the front panels decorated with representational geometric designs in blue, red, yellow and green.
(Phillips) $2,220

A late 17th century lady's waistcoat of undyed linen embroidered with colored silks and designed with flower sprays and birds, altered, circa 1680's.
(Phillips) $6,500

A Chinese court vest of midnight blue silk, embroidered in colored silks and couched gilt thread, with a civil rank badge on the back and front embroidered with the fourth-rank goose, fringed.
(Christie's) $675

Gentleman's embroidered silk waistcoat, circa 1820, embroidered with silk threads, chenille yarns and ribbon in shades of blue, yellow, taupe.
(Skinner) $468

A mahogany and marquetry decanter box, the interior divided into four compartments each with cut-glass decanter, 8in. wide.
(Christie's) $792

A Victorian brass-inlaid ebony tantalus, inlaid overall with stylized floral trelliswork, on turned bun feet, 12¹/₂in. wide.
(Christie's) $1,847

A traveling decanter set, the case of plain rectangular form veneered in pollard oak, bound in cut-brass, 12¹/₄in. wide, mid-19th century. $1,466

A Dutch mahogany tantalus with checkered bandings and domed hinged top enclosing a later fitted interior for stationery, circa 1800, 9¹/₄in. wide.
(Christie's) $708

An Alpine carved beech liqueur box, Swiss or German, circa 1880, the hinged lid carved with a setter, with glazed sides divided by rusticated columns, 43cm. high.
(Sotheby's) $4,176

An Italian ivory-inlaid ebony and walnut double-domed decanter-box with twin octagonal finials above a paneled frieze with ripple moldings, late 17th century, 15in high.
(Christie's) $2,302

Early two-tiered traveling liquor case, oak with original red paint geometric design, the lower section with twenty rectangular decanters with stoppers, Spain, 1790–1810.
(Skinner Inc.) $2,200

A 19th century boulle and rosewood decanter box, holding four cut-glass decanters, decorated with gilt floral sprays, six similar glasses and five others, 13in. wide.
(Bonhams) $1,242

Napoleon III boulle liqueur case, third quarter 19th century, the top lifting and the sides opening to an interior with a removeable tray fitted with four fluted square decanters and fourteen faceted liqueurs, 13¹/₂in. wide.
(Butterfield & Butterfield) $3,300

A Heubach Koppelsdorf painted black bisque doll, German, circa 1926, with open mouth and two lower teeth, fixed brown glass eyes, and five piece composition body, 16in. high.
(Sotheby's) $612

A Bru Jeune pressed bisque doll, French, circa 1885, with open/closed mouth showing white between lips, together with a trunk in red, banded and studded, 15in. high.
(Sotheby's) $8,745

An 'H' pressed bisque doll, French, circa 1880, impressed 2/0 H, with open/closed mouth, fixed blue glass eyes, and jointed wood and composition body, 15in. high.
(Sotheby's) $73,458

A DEP bisque musical doll, French, circa 1900, with open mouth and upper teeth, fixed blue glass eyes, and jointed wood and composition body, 18in. high.
(Sotheby's) $1,749

A rare Lenci pressed felt 'Bersagliere' soldier doll, Italian, circa 1920, with painted face and brown eyes, in original Lenci box.
(Sotheby's) $1,399

Bisque boy, incised A.B.G. 1322/1, brushed stroked hair, intaglio eyes, open/closed mouth with teeth, papier mâché body, 12in. high.
(Butterfield & Butterfield)
$413

A fine Casimir Bru circle and dot pressed bisque doll, French, circa 1875, in eau-de-nil brocaded satin dress with aubergine satin edging and silk bows, 20½in. high.
(Sotheby's) $24,486

An S.F.B.J. bisque character doll, French, circa 1910, with auburn real hair wig and jointed wood and composition toddler body in white dress edged in orange, 18in. high.
(Sotheby's) $1,049

A fine large Bru Jeune pressed bisque doll, French, circa 1875, with open/closed mouth, dimple in chin, large blue glass paperweight eyes with well painted lashes, 35½in. high.
(Sotheby's) $26,235

A mulatto Simon & Halbig 1358, bisque head character doll, German, circa 1890, with weighted brown glass eyes, open mouth, 15½in. high.
(Bonhams) $3,726

A Rohmer shoulder-china fashion doll and her trunk, French, circa 1865, with closed mouth, fixed blue glass eyes, together with her trunk of studded black rexine, 13¾in. high.
(Sotheby's) $2,623

A Bruno Schmidt bisque Oriental doll, German, circa 1905, with open mouth and upper teeth, weighted brown glass eyes, and jointed wood and composition body, 13¾in. high.
(Sotheby's) $1,049

A Bru pressed bisque bébé, French, circa 1880, with open/closed mouth and simulated tongue, in checked pink, brown and beige silk dress and broderie-anglaise bonnet, 15¾in. high.
(Sotheby's) $19,239

A French fashionable doll with trunk and trousseau, the bisque swivel-head with closed mouth, fixed pale blue eyes, 15½in. high, impressed 2, by Gaultier with body by Gesland.
(Christie's) $18,997

A Lenci pressed felt girl doll, Italian, 1930's, with painted features, brown eyes glancing left, with stitched ears, light brown mohair wig, 17in. high.
(Bonhams) $543

Käthe Kruse boy doll, painted cloth head, sewn-on head and wide-hipped cloth body, sewn movable arms, original clothing, circa 1925, 43cm. long.
(Auction Team Köln) $1,852

An Armand Marseille/ Koppelsdorf bisque socket head character doll, with blonde mohair wig, painted features, closing blue glass eyes with eyelashes, 48cm. tall.
(Spencer's) $333

A Huret shoulder-china doll, French, circa 1860, with closed mouth, painted blue eyes, blonde lambswool wig over cork pate and jointed wood body, 17¼in. high.
(Sotheby's) $7,171

A bisque-headed character doll with open/closed mouth, blue intaglio eyes, 10½in. high, impressed with Heubach sunburst.
(Christie's) $607

A rare bisque-headed character doll, with open/closed mouth, blue sleeping eyes, deeply molded features, white gown and underwear, 15in. high, impressed *1428 9*, by Simon & Halbig.
(Christie's) $2,797

A Kestner 168 bisque head girl doll, German, circa 1890, with weighted blue glass eyes, open mouth, four upper teeth, 23in. high.
(Bonhams) $699

A fine J.D. Kestner bisque head 'Googly' eyed character doll, with brown hair wig, weighted blue eyes and closed 'watermelon' mouth, 16in. high.
(Bonhams) $6,650

A Bähr & Pröschild bisque Oriental doll, German, circa 1888, with closed mouth, fixed black glass eyes, with wooden composition body in original green and polychrome patterned dress, 13¼in. high.
(Sotheby's) $1,836

Felt boy, no visible marks, painted features on felt face, mohair wig, fully jointed, cloth body with felt limbs, 15in. high.
(Butterfield & Butterfield) $248

A fine pale pressed bisque Jumeau portrait doll, French, circa 1875, with blonde curly mohair wig over cork pate and the eight ball jointed wood and composition body with straight wrists, 24½in. high.
(Sotheby's) $20,988

A bisque-headed character doll, with closed pouty mouth, painted features, fair mohair wig, and jointed wood and composition toddler body, 13in. high.
(Christie's) $2,178

An S.F.B.J. black bisque character doll, French, circa 1910, with jointed wood and composition body in striped velvet trousers and rust velvet waistcoat over cream shirt, 13¾in. high.
(Sotheby's) $1,662

A Kestner bisque head character baby boy doll with sleeping and swiveling brown glass eyes and open mouth, 30in. high.
(Andrew Hartley) $1,884

A Simon and Halbig bisque and socket head character baby doll, with cropped mid brown wig, painted features, and flirty brown glass eyes, 40cm. tall.
(Spencer's) $599

A Jumeau triste pressed bisque doll, French, circa 1875, in apricot silk dress with embroidered white muslin overdress and pintucked cotton petticoats, 28in. high.
(Sotheby's) $8,745

Bisque bébé with paperweight eyes, closed mouth, and human hair wig, kid body with label, 24in. high.
(Butterfield & Butterfield) $23,100

A pair of rare Kestner 'Max and Moritz' all bisque character dolls, German, circa 1913, designed by Wilhelm Busch, 6¼in. high.
(Bonhams) $4,968

A bisque-headed bébé, with open/closed mouth, fixed blue eyes, bisque shoulder-plate and arms, 19in. high, impressed *Bru Jne 6*, circa 1880.
(Christie's) $26,103

A bisque-headed bébé, with closed mouth, brown yeux fibres, pierced applied ears, blonde mohair wig, 21½in. high, impressed *Deposé Jumeau 11*.
(Christie's) $6,563

An A. Thuillier pressed bisque doll, French, circa 1875, with open/closed mouth, fixed blue glass paperweight eyes, and jointed wood and composition body, 13½in. high.
(Sotheby's) $22,737

Bähr and Proschild type bisque head doll with wooden jointed arms and legs, painted features with open mouth and six upper teeth.
(Eldred's) $275

A gallows mousetrap with two holes, 1920. (Auction Team Koeln) **$30**

A South German polished steel door lock and key, shooting one bolt, engraved with scrolls and grotesque beasts, 17th/18th century, 12½in. wide. (Christie's) **$1,733**

A large Danish three part coffee grinder by Schroder & Jorgensen Eff, Copenhagen, circa 1950. (Auction Team Koeln) **$45**

A painted wooden storage barrel, New England, early 19th century, fastened with buttonhole laps, painted with original red paint, 20½in. high. (Sotheby's) **$633**

An Irish brass-mounted rosewood door lock plate, late 18th century, and another similar, 15in. wide. (Christie's) **$1,540**

A rare oversized turned and paint decorated treenware covered jar, Midwestern, probably Ohio, early 19th century, 14in. high. (Sotheby's) **$2,875**

A Fletcher Russell 'Celebrity' copper disk hot water heater with bracket, circa 1905. (Christie's) **$107**

Sailor-made pin cushion/spool stand, late 19th century, two tiers constructed of exotic woods with carved ivory fittings, 10in. high. (Skinner) **$715**

The Boye Needle Co. 'Needles & Shuttles', 1910, a circular magazine with numerous wooden tubes for needles and bobbins. (Auction Team Koeln) **$165**

Calor electric heater with light blue Art Nouveau ceramic front and 3 stage bakelite control, 48 x 40cm., circa 1920.
(Auction Team Köln)   **$141**

A Bernhardiner nutcracker of cast iron in the form of a dog, on a chromed base.
(Auction Team Köln)   **$85**

A George III copper plate warmer, of cylindrical helmet shape, on three cabriole feet, 20in. high.
(Lawrence)   **$729**

The first ever hot air fan with 2 stroke hot air motor driven by a copper petroleum lamp, on a richly decorated cast metal tripod stand with 2 wooden carrying handles, 113cm. high, only known example, circa 1860.
(Auction Team Köln)
$4,173

A Regency mahogany birdcage with spindle-filled domed top, front and sides with ivory finials, the solid back with flap, 17¼in. high.
(Christie's)   **$3,900**

A richly decorated cast metal Agrippina mangel, with the arms of Cologne and peacock feathers on both supports, stamped *HK & Co* circa 1880.
(Auction Team Koeln)
$450

An unusual automatic butter slicer by Strite-Anderson Mfg. Co., Minneapolis, with enameled base, circa 1920.
(Auction Team Köln)   **$139**

A green-painted wheelbarrow, the trapezoidal form with rounded sides, the outside painted with a running horse and *G.B. Tufts*, with tapering down-turned handle, chamfered tapering stops, and a central red painted front wheel, 51½in. long.
(Christie's)   **$2,860**

Coffee percolator, copper, boiler with decorated base complete with sieve equipment, petroleum burner and jug, circa 1880.
(Auction Team Köln)   **$220**

A Peugeot & Cie coffee mill, cast iron with wooden drawer without front lid, 30cm. high, circa 1900.
(Auction Team Köln) $86

A South German polished steel door lock and key, shooting one bolt, embellished with engraved foliage and applied rosettes, 17th/18th century, 10³/₄in. wide.
(Christie's) $1,636

A Fitzgerald Model 430 electric fan, gold-brown, with designer stand, circa 1955.
(Auction Team Köln) $85

A Mistral chromium plated electric coffee grinder, circa 1958. (Auction Team Koeln) $45

A set of Dutch oak egg shelves, the arched back carved with *K I H ANNO 1723*, the front and sides decorated with chip carving with two arched pierced doors, first quarter 18th century, Friesian, 13in. wide.
(Christie's) $1,716

Gustav Stickley wastebasket, no. 94, circa 1910, thirteen vertical slats attached to interior iron rings, unsigned, 14in. high.
(Skinner) $990

An Original Edison Hotpoint Automatic percolator, plated housing, possibly unused, with original 110v flex, 1924.
(Auction Team Köln) $154

A very rare and fine mechanical steel and ivory chain-saw, signed *Heine of Wurzburg*, with blued steel and gilt-brass fittings, the chain operated by a toothed cog wound by a handle of serpentine form, overall length 14in.
(Christie's) $35,574

Yellow cast samovar with original tray, circa 1880, 56cm. high.
(Auction Team Köln) $77

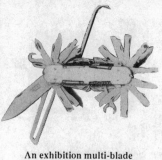

Crescent electric fire on a cast Art Nouveau base, circa 1920. (Auction Team Köln) $109

An exhibition multi-blade pocket knife with ninety-six blades and mother-of-pearl scales, marked *Hoffritz N.Y. Germany* and *Stainless*, 4³/₄in. long (folded). (Christie's) $2,603

An American automatic mouse trap with guillotine action, circa 1905. (Auction Team Köln) $77

US patent model A. C. Carey knitting machine, a demonstration model for the patent application of 18.4.1865, with copy of the patent. (Auction Team Köln) $463

An English brass brazier, first quarter 18th century, fitted with a mesh support above a conforming engraved vessel fitted with a sinuous handle, on bun feet, 8¹/₂in. high. (Christie's) $2,415

A de Maelzel metronome by Seth Thomas Clocks, Thomastown CT, in mahogany casing and with spring wound drive. (Auction Team Köln) $93

An early General Electric fan in an unusually decorative 'Industry-Design', detachable, motor with rotor, circa 1925. (Auction Team Köln) $131

A small fruit and wine must press, circa 1900. (Auction Team Koeln) $60

Original Miele butter machine, complete wooden barrel construction with original wooden lid, circa 1900. (Auction Team Köln) $118

128

A Wimshurst-pattern electrostatic plate machine, with six segmented glass contra-rotating plates, copper brushes and brass conductor combs, 27in. wide.
(Christie's) $5,482

A rare Henly's universal discharger, by J. Newman Lisle Street London, twin glass insulator pillars, rods and table with ivory center platform, 15in. wide.
(Christie's) $597

An unusually large electrostatic barrel machine, unsigned, possibly by Edward Nairne, with mahogany and fruitwood frame, 33¹/₂in. wide.
(Christie's) $979

A rare set of five aurora-borealis discharge tubes, signed *J. King & Son, 2 Clare Street, Bristol*, with lacquered brass caps and spheres in fitted pine case, 28¹/₂in. long.
(Christie's) $2,154

A unique collection of one hundred and twenty three Geissler tubes, of various patterns, designs, and sizes, including liquid filled 'Multi-Twist', 'Spiral', 'Multi-Bulb', 'Catherine-Wheel', 'Grecian-Urn', 'Trumpet', 'Raspberry' and other types many of tinted glass, 1883.
(Christie's) $33,286

An oxidized and lacquered brass 'Hendersons' rapid traverser, by E. T. Newton & Son, with 10 inch diameter, in fitted mahogany case with maker's trade label inside lid, 12in. wide.
(Christie's) $882

A most impressive and rare Crookes' 'Windmill' tube, containing a glass formed windmill with mica sails, the display demonstrates vividly the mechanical properties of electrons, 12¹/₂in. high.
(Christie's) $4,895

A late 19th century two-plate 'Wimshurst'-pattern electrostatic induction machine, unsigned, driven by leather belts, 21in.
(Christie's) $648

A rare 19th century Italian electromagnetic terrella stamped on the walnut base *Marcellino in Alessandria Marcellino*, with two conductors on baluster turned support, 14¹/₄in. high.
(Christie's) $2,216

A Staffordshire enamel snuff box of rectangular shape and with turquoise ground, the cover painted with a lady and gentleman in the park of a country house, 7.5cm. (Phillips) **$2,639**

A gin bari enamel bowl worked in repoussé with goldfish on a punched silver ground, silver mounts, Meiji period (1868–1912), 7.5cm. high. (Christie's) **$823**

A South Staffordshire rectangular enamel snuff-box, the cover painted with a couple strolling in a landscape, circa 1765, 3^1/$_8$in. long. (Christie's) **$1,089**

A pair of 19th century French enamel and ormolu cassolettes, the pink ground painted with figures and animals in landscapes, 8in. high. (Christie's S. Ken) **$1,030**

A Viennese table casket of ivory and enamel, with a central finial of St. George slaying the dragon, the whole set with polychrome enamel plaques of allegorical figures, 19th century, 17cm. high x 15cm. wide. (Lawrence Fine Art) **$4,659**

A pair of rare South Staffordshire enamel spirally fluted candlesticks, painted overall with flowers on a white ground, gilt-metal mounts, circa 1760, 10in. high. (Christie's) **$8,316**

A South Staffordshire enamel pink ground traveling writing case, the cover painted with a shepherd and shepherdess by a river with buildings in the background, circa 1765, 2^3/$_4$in. wide. (Christie's) **$3,960**

A 19th century Viennese enamel bulbous ewer and stand, the ewer with bear's head lid with silver and raised enamel collar, 10in. high; the matching stand of ovoid, lobed outline, 9^3/$_4$in. wide. (Christie's S. Ken) **$10,196**

A fine enameled and gilt bowl, Jules Barbe, probably for Thomas Webb and Sons, Stourbridge, late 19th century, painted with large flowers against an acid-finished reserve, 8^1/$_4$in. diameter. (Sotheby's) **$2,898**

A Staffordshire enamel oval patch box with a pink base, the white cover inscribed *Love constitutes the Value* within a jeweled border, 4.5cm. wide. (Phillips) $578

A 19th century Viennese enamel and ormolu mounted model of a coach, the pink ground painted with reserves of figures in landscapes, 8in. long. (Christie's) $2,574

Plique à jour bowl, 20th century, decorated overall with leafy blossoms in translucent colors on a white-flecked light green glass ground, 4⁷/₈in. diameter. (Butterfield & Butterfield) $770

An antique Viennese enamel vase featuring six finely executed oval allegorical reserves on a gold background with polychrome scrolling foliage, 19th century, 14in. high. (Selkirk's) $6,500

Louis XVI style onyx and champlevé enamel three-piece table garniture, circa 1900, each decorated en suite with an enameled band around the amber streaked cream body, 17¹/₂in. high. (Butterfield & Butterfield) $5,500

Viennese enamel and gilt-bronze ewer, circa 1900, the slender ovoid body with a shaped flaring mouth and the domical base all painted in polychrome with mythological figural scenes, 8in. high. (Butterfield & Butterfield) $2,200

A 19th century French enamel and gilt metal mounted box and cover, the pink ground painted with figures in landscapes, 4³/₄ in. wide. (Christie's S. Ken) $815

A fine south Staffordshire rectangular blue ground enamel tea caddy, the cover painted with three herdsmen and their cattle by a river, circa 1770, 8¹/₂in. long. (Christie's) $31,680

A very attractive Staffordshire enamel writing box, painted with a lady seated playing a lute and a man standing at her side playing a violin, 8.5cm. wide. (Phillips) $850

The Royal Family of Great Britain, a
lithographic fan on paper for which
Duvelleroy won a silver medal in 1849, 11in., in
Duvelleroy box.
(Christie's S. Ken) $1,271

A lace fan, the Chantilly lace leaf worked with
putti and flowers, the blonde tortoiseshell
sticks carved and pierced with putti, 13in.,
circa 1885, in box by Tiffany & Co., London.
(Christie's S. Ken) $2,429

A fine fan, the leaf painted with an elegant
lady and putti fishing, signed M. Rodigue, the
ivory sticks carved, pierced and painted with
putti, 14in., circa 1890.
(Christie's S. Ken) $2,429

A fine fan, the leaf painted with The Birth of
Venus in bright colors, the verso painted with
sprigs of flowers and fruit, with ivory sticks,
10in., Italian, circa 1690.
(Christie's S. Ken) $5,060

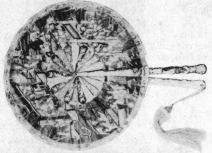

A Canton cockade fan, the leaf painted with
figures, with ivory faces and silk clothes, the
verso painted with flowers and birds, 16in.
diameter including handle, circa 1840.
(Christie's S. Ken) $2,429

The Twentieth birthday of Le Grand Dauphin,
a rare unmounted fan leaf painted in
bodycolor with Louis XIV, seated beside the
Queen, Marie Therese, 11in. x 21in., French,
circa 1681.
(Christie's S. Ken) $20,240

An early 18th century Flemish fan, portraying
the scene of Jupiter appearing in a shower of
gold coins to Danae reclining on a cushion,
28cm. long, circa 1720.
(Phillips) $1,415

A fine fan, the leaf painted with nymphs and
putti, signed in red *J. Calamatta 1870* verso
signed *Alexandre*, the mother of pearl sticks
finely carved and pierced.
(Christie's S. Ken) $8,906

Les Cuisines Républicaine de 1795.96 ... &c., a printed fan, the leaf with an engraving of street vendors and their clients, French, 9¼in.
(Christie's) $547

A fan, the leaf painted with Maria Leszczynska, daughter of King Stanislas of Poland, arriving at Versailles to meet Louis XV before their marriage in 1725, 10in., French, circa 1750.
(Christie's) $20,715

A fan, the black gauze leaf painted with circus scenes, signed *Donzel*, with ebony stick, the guardsticks carved with clowns with ivory heads and hands, 12½in., circa 1890.
(Christie's) $743

A fan, the silk leaf painted with an elegant family in a park, two portrait miniatures, and putti holding escutcheons with monograms *C.B.* or *G.B.*, 10in., circa 1775.
(Christie's) $2,542

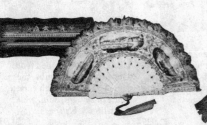

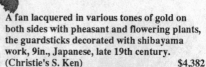

A mid-19th century Mandarin fan, originally made for export, having ivory sticks and guards densely carved with figures in a garden setting, 28cm. long, with tassel and white feather trim, Canton, circa 1860's.
(Phillips) $1,132

A fan lacquered in various tones of gold on both sides with pheasant and flowering plants, the guardsticks decorated with shibayama work, 9in., Japanese, late 19th century.
(Christie's S. Ken) $4,382

A pierced ivory brisé fan, painted with a circular vignette of a scene from a novel, and carved with smaller vignettes, 9½in., English, circa 1790.
(Christie's) $1,564

A fine fan, the lace leaf of Brussels point de gaze with three shaped silk insertions painted with elegant figures, signed *F. Houghton*, 14in., circa 1885.
(Christie's) $5,439

A classical cast-iron stove, stamped *Rice and Miller*, circa 1820-1840, the square classical facade surmounted at either corner by a ring-turned brass ball, 26in. wide.
(Christie's) $4,830

A Regency brass-mounted steel and cast-iron fire-grate, the design attributed to George Bullock, of sarcophagus form and with channeled scrolled back-plate and barred-grate, 34in. wide.
(Christie's) $21,976

A George III steel basket grate, the sparred front above a fretwork carved frieze, the later Regency backplate with foliate scrolled cresting centered by a foliate cast laurel wreath, 42in. wide.
(Christie's) $6,791

A Regency brass-mounted polished steel and cast-iron fire-grate in the style of George Bullock, the basket with turned rails and pyramid finials, 40$\frac{1}{2}$in. wide.
(Christie's) $7,128

An Adam style brass and cast iron fire grate, the barred serpentine front above a pierced frieze flanked by square tapering uprights, 28$\frac{1}{4}$in.
(Christie's S. Ken)
                        $2,035

A Regency cast iron and steel hearth grate, the railed front flanked by scroll jambs, the shaped backplate with raised foliate ornament, 36in. wide.
(Christie's S. Ken)
                        $1,933

An early George III cast-iron and seamed brass basket grate, with pierced fretwork apron, on turned baluster supports and square bases, 29$\frac{1}{2}$in. wide.
(Christie's) $4,792

A Regency cast iron fire grate, with gilt outlined double scroll back, with cable decoration and on paw supports, 96cm. wide.
(Allen & Harris) $3,939

A fine Neo Classical style steel and cast iron serpentine fronted fire grate, the polished and engraved steel façade of waisted outline, surmounted by acanthus chased urns, 43in. wide.
(Christie's S. Ken)
                        $9,158

A fine George III brass basket grate of serpentine section, having pierced apron with continuous husk, scroll and acanthus motifs, with central basket flanked by urn finials, 92cm. wide.
(Phillips) $8,750

A Victorian iron and brass fire grate, the bowed front with pierced fret flanked by stylized lion monopodiae standards, 26in. wide. (Christie's S. Ken) $1,500

A Regency cast iron and ormolu mounted fire grate, in the manner of George Bullock, with applied palmette motifs, on paw feet, 36in. wide.
(Christie's) $7,145

A George III paktong and steel basket-grate with serpentine railed basket and lift-off front, 32¹/₂in. wide.
(Christie's) $40,887

One of a pair of brass cast iron fireplace insets, the frieze and uprights with applied figures of amorini emblamatic of the arts within panels of trophies and foliage, basically Victorian, 40 x 39¼in. (Christie's S. Ken) $5,500

A steel basket-grate of serpentine outline, the frieze pierced with fluting on engraved tapering supports, late 18th century, 30in. wide.
(Christie's) $2,531

A Victorian cast iron fire grate, the 'U' shaped basket with railed serpentine front, the apron raised with figures of caryatid putti, griffins, masks and foliage, 36¹/₂in. wide.
(Christie's) $1,222

A Georgian iron and brass fire grate, the rectangular railed front flanked by applied oval bats' wing paterae above a pierced fret, 31in. wide.
(Christie's S. Ken) $2,100

A 19th century Dutch polished steel fire grate, the barred front and sides above a fret pierced frieze, the tapering standards with urn finials, 29in. wide.
(Christie's) $4,702

A brass, polished steel and cast-iron fire grate, the railed serpentine basket above a fret-pierced frieze with applied oval paterae, 30¼in. wide.
(Christie's) $6,160

An oval brass-mounted, polished steel fire grate, of brazier form, the pierced basket on waisted socle, the stepped square plinth with lamb head masks, 29in. wide.
(Christie's) $5,775

A cast-iron and polished steel fire grate, the railed front above a fret-pierced frieze with stylized anthemion motifs, late 18th century, 28½in. wide.
(Christie's) $3,080

A late Victorian brass and steel grate of Adam style, with arched back cast with interlaced laurel swags above a half-fan medallion, the pierced bow-fronted basket filled with waved sunburst, late 19th century, 36in. wide.
(Christie's) $3,029

A George III steel firegrate of large size and serpentine form, the basket with three horizontal bars flanked by two columnar supports crowned by urn finials, later framing and backplate, 43in. wide.
(Christie's) $4,567

A brass, steel and cast-iron fire grate, the railed frieze flanked by bulbous knopped standards with urn finials, on square bases, with conforming central support, late 17th/early 18th century, 35in. wide.
(Christie's) $3,850

A brass, polished steel and cast-iron fire grate, the railed front above a pierced frieze with engraved birds, trees and foliage, 19th century, 27½in. wide.
(Christie's) $5,583

A brass-mounted cast-iron fire grate, of Louis XVI style, the pierced basket above a riband laurel leaf frieze, the cylindrical uprights with chased harebells and pineapple finials, 28in. wide.
(Christie's) $3,160

A polished steel and cast-iron fire grate, of Chippendale style, the railed serpentine front above a pierced and engraved frieze, on stepped plinths, 19th century, 29¼in. wide.
(Christie's) $3,658

A George II cast-iron and polished steel fire grate, the railed basket surmounted by elongated knopped urn finials, 37½in. wide.
(Christie's) $2,888

An Irish gun metal, polished steel and cast-iron register grate, the railed front with urn finials above a pierced frieze with engraved oval paterae and foliage, late 18th century, 36¼in. wide.
(Christie's) $4,235

A brass, steel and cast-iron fire grate, by Thomas Elsley, the railed serpentine front above a fret-pierced frieze with incised plaque, 19th century, 32in. wide.
(Christie's) $8,085

A polished steel, gun metal and cast-iron fire grate, the basket with Chinese style fret rails, the pierced frieze flanked by column uprights with shaped urn finials, late 18th/19th century, 28¼in. wide.
(Christie's) $3,080

A polished steel and cast-iron fire grate, of George III style, the railed serpentine basket above a frieze pierced and engraved with birds, urns and scrolling foliage, 19th century, 30in. wide.
(Christie's) $1,251

An alloy fire grate, the railed serpentine basket above a pierced and beaded frieze with engraved urns and swags, the square tapering uprights with urn finials, early 19th century, 37½in. wide.
(Christie's) $3,658

A brass, polished steel and cast-iron fire grate, the railed serpentine basket above a fret-pierced frieze, flanked by square tapering uprights with urn finials, 36in. wide.
(Christie's) $5,390

A cast-iron fire grate, the backplate decorated in relief with a flaming urn flanked by foliate scrolls, early 19th century, 36in. wide.
(Christie's) $1,059

A modern brass, steel and cast-iron fire grate, the railed serpentine basket above a pierced frieze centered by an oval patera, on a stepped square plinth, 30¼in. wide.
(Christie's) $674

United Firemen's Insurance
Company, Philadelphia,
Pennsylvania, USA, cast iron,
oval, raised steam fire engine
in high relief, circa 1877.
(Phillips) $2,250

Rare lead firemark of the
Suffolk & General Country
Amicable Insurance Office,
Bury & Ipswich, 6½in. wide.
                             $1,500

Edinburgh Friendly Insurance,
lead, the shaped panel raised
with clasped hands, policy no.
8769. (Phillips) $450

Copper, raised with a standing
figure of King Alfred, 'West
of England' raised around,
'Exeter' raised on panel below.
(Phillips) $275

Church of England Life and
Fire Assurance, copper, circular, arms of the Church
raised on convexed center.
(Phillips) $450

Kent Insurance, copper,
raised horse forcene on octagonal panel 'Invicta' raised on
small panel above.
(Phillips) $700

Dundee Assurance, lead,
raised arms of the city,
impressed policy no. 3294.
(Phillips) $1,450

Edinburgh Friendly Assurance,
heavy lead, policy no. 1805
pierced through panel below.
(Phillips) $2,000

Rare lead firemark of the
Kent Fire Insurance Company,
Maidstone, with horse in
relief, 6½in. wide. $1,100

Liverpool Fire Office, lead, liver bird and torse raised on circular section, 'Liverpool' raised on panel below and impressed with policy no. 426. (Phillips) $1,500

Union Fire Office, lead, four clasped hands, with 'Union' raised on panel above, policy no. 27617. (Phillips) $1,100

Lead, open portcullis with Prince of Wales' feathers above, policy no. 36044 on panel below. (Phillips) $600

Lead, clasped hands, small cuffs, with open crown above, policy no. 76444 on panel below. (Phillips) $550

Lead, impressed portcullis with Prince of Wales' feathers above, policy no. 53252 on panel below. (Phillips) $450

London Assurance, lead, seated figure of Britannia with shield, spear and harp, policy no. 36327 on panel below. (Phillips) $700

Royal Exchange Assurance, lead, raised Royal Exchange building, policy no. 570 on panel below, issued circa 1721. (Phillips) $7,500

The General Insurance Company of Ireland, lead, square, raised phoenix, torse and borders. (Phillips) $550

Hibernian Fire Insurance, lead, Irish harp raised on oval with raised border, with open crown above. (Phillips) $750

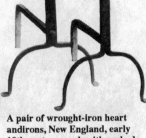

A pair of brass-mounted cast-iron fire dogs, of 'Haddon Hall' type, the uprights with pierced circular plaques with tulips and other flowers, 19th century, 12³/₄in. wide.
(Christie's) $2,503

Pair of Louis XVI style bronze chenets, 19th century, 16¹/₂in. long.
(Skinner) $1,320

A pair of wrought-iron heart andirons, New England, early 19th century, each with arched supports ending in penny feet, 16³/₈in. high.
(Sotheby's) $2,530

A set of three Regency steel and brass fire-irons, each with faceted finial, comprising: a poker, a pair of tongs and a shovel with pierced splayed dished pan with central rose, the poker 29¹/₂in. long.
(Christie's) $1,436

A pair of ormolu chenets, each cast with confronting C-scrolls and acanthus and surmounted by a young hurdy-gurdy player and his female companion, 15in. wide.
(Christie's) $1,542

A set of three George IV ormolu and gilt-steel fire-irons, each with fruiting finial, comprising: a poker, a pair of tongs and a shovel with pierced pan, the poker 29in. long.
(Christie's) $2,197

A knight-in-armor fire-iron set, with poker, tongs and brush, all held by a figure of a knight-in-armor, 35in. high.
(Christie's) $1,094

A pair of Louis XVI ormolu chenets, each with a putto and a dog on a plinth-shaped base with two pine-cone finials, 14¹/₂in. wide.
(Christie's) $6,950

A pair of silver plated andirons, 19th century, of baluster form with urn finials and leaf cast scroll feet, 2ft. 9in. high.
(Sotheby's) $9,772

A set of early 18th century English brass and steel fire irons, comprising: poker, shovel and tongs, 62cm. to 66cm. long. (Phillips) $1,460

A pair of Louis XVI ormolu and bronze chenets with recumbent lions upon draped shaped rectangular plinths with pine-cone finials, 15¾in. wide. (Christie's) $10,835

A set of George III brass fire-irons comprising: a pair of tongs, a shovel with engraved pierced pan and a poker, 30in. long. (Christie's) $7,430

A set of three Regency ormolu and steel fire-irons, comprising: a shovel, a pair of tongs and a poker, 30½in. long. (Christie's) $2,920

A pair of early Louis XV ormolu chenets of scrolled outline, cast with C- and S-scroll rockwork, supporting a rearing lion, 15in. wide. (Christie's) $18,700

A set of Victorian brass fire-irons each with faceted finial, comprising: tongs, poker and a pierced shovel, 29½in. long. (Christie's) $2,376

A set of three Regency brass fire-irons comprising: a pair of tongs, a shovel and a poker, each with turned shaft and octagonal finial, 29in. long. (Christie's) $2,335

A pair of Transitional ormolu chenets, each with a seated dog, probably Iñes and Mimi, the pet dogs of Madame de Pompadour, 9¾in. high. (Christie's) $8,976

A Harlequin set of George III steel fire-irons, each with engraved vase-shaped finial, comprising: tongs, a poker and a shovel, 30in. long. (Christie's) $1,386

141

Federal carved mantel, possibly Salem, Massachusetts, circa 1800, 73½in. wide. (Skinner) $1,320

A George III carved white marble chimneypiece, the fluted frieze centered by a tablet carved with three trophies in relief and flanked by twin-handled urns, 5ft. 8in. wide. (Phillips) $16,814

A pine and marble chimneypiece, of George III style, with a breakfront shelf with a molded edge, above a foliate-carved frieze, with verde antico marble ingrounds, the grate late 18th/19th century, the chimneypiece 32¼in. wide. (Christie's) $1,829

An 18th century white marble chimney piece, the rectangular breakfront shelf above a fluted frieze centered by a tablet carved with an allegory of music, the angles both surmounted by musical figures, above figures and motifs emblematic of Spring, 73¼ in. wide. (Christie's) $40,700

A George II Siena, jasper and statuary marble chimneypiece, attributed to Sir Henry Cheere, Bt., the conjoined Ionic columns supporting the entablature embellished with a flower head to each end, centred by a projecting bas-relief carved tablet of a pastoral scene, circa 1755, 79½in. wide. (Christie's) $40,480

A fine George III carved statuary marble and Spanish brocatelle chimneypiece, the frieze of arcaded form with husk spandrels, centered by palmette motif, the carved central tablet depicting 'The Marriage of Cupid and Psyche', circa 1775, 64in. wide. (Christie's) $32,868

A George II style pine fire surround, the pedimented shelf above acanthus leaf carved border with plain central tablet, the scrolled jambs carved with flower heads and bell husks, 60in. wide. (Christie's) $814

Italian neoclassical parcel-gilt and painted mantel, last quarter 18th century, the rectangular outstepped white faux marble shelf over a faux Siena marble frieze carved with a gilt foliate vine centered by a mask, 8ft. 4½in. wide. (Butterfield & Butterfield) $16,500

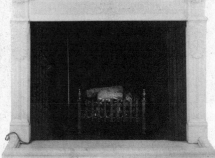

A 19th century variegated white marble fire surround of Louis XVI design, the rectangular breakfront shelf above a frieze carved with foliate arabesques centered by an oval with a monogram of *MA*, 60½in. wide. (Christie's) $6,919

An 18th century statuary white marble and siena chimney piece, the rectangular breakfront shelf above a plain siena frieze with central tablet carved with an oval medallion depicting a classical female figure, flanked at either side by floral wreaths with ribbon tie crestings, 72in. wide. (Christie's) $40,700

A George III jeweled, grained, ebonized and composition chimneypiece, with molded rectangular inverted-breakfront cornice decorated with acanthus above a tablet decorated with an urn flanked by volutes, 78in. x 63in. (Christie's) $3,098

A late Georgian pine and carved walnut mounted chimney piece, the rectangular breakfront shelf above a fluted frieze carved with central tablet supporting a medallion carved with blind Justice flanked by flaming torchères, 68½in. wide.(Christie's) $11,193

An Empire style gilt-metal-mounted mahogany fireplace and matching over-mantel mirror, the mirror with molded cornice and frieze with central female mask, 63in. wide.
(Christie's) $1,996

A white-painted, parcel-gilt carved wood chimneypiece, in the Kentian style, the breakfront shelf with an elaborately carved edge, above a frieze, centered by a mask, 66¼in. wide.
(Christie's) $8,663

A George II carved pine chimneypiece, with an inverted breakfront shelf with egg-and-dart molded edge, the frieze centered by two eagle heads and scrolling foliage, 67in. wide.
(Christie's) $13,943

A carved statuary marble chimneypiece, the breakfront shelf with a molded, acanthus-carved edge, the frieze centered by a mask flanked by drapery swags, 78in. wide.
(Christie's) $53,900

An early Victorian chinoiserie decorated Mason's ironstone chimneypiece, polychrome and gilt-decorated overall on a blue ground, with shaped inset panels of flower and pavilion landscapes, 62¾in. wide.
(Christie's) $17,325

An Irish George III statuary marble and scagliola chimneypiece, in the manner of Pietro Bossi, the breakfront shelf above a frieze decorated with ribbon-tied trophies, late 18th century, 73¾in. wide.
(Christie's) $50,050

ARMOIRES

This large cupboard, which consists basically of one or two long doors with one or more drawers in the interior or under, originated in 16th century France. *Armoire* is simply the French word for a cupboard or wardrobe. The armoire was treated monumentally by Boulle and his studio, and as a piece of furniture it is generally characterized by the solidity and massiveness of its appearance. It survived into the early Regency period, but all but disappeared thereafter as rooms became smaller.

A South German marriage armoire with fruitwood and ebonized inlay, on bracket feet 193cm. wide.
(Arnold) $4,118

A good 17th century Dutch oak armoire, the upper part with deep molded cornice, the frieze with three carved lions heads, 59in. wide.
(Canterbury) $3,900

Louis XV transitional pickled oak armoire, the cavetto cornice over triple panel sides and a pair of wire mesh double panel doors well carved with plumes, 4ft. 10in. wide.
(Butterfield & Butterfield) $9,900

An ormolu-mounted and brass-inlaid ebony and tortoiseshell boulle armoire with waved arched breakfront cornice above a pair of shaped glazed doors, part early 18th century, 72in. wide.
(Christie's) $26,000

A Louis XV style ormolu-mounted tulipwood and marquetry armoire, late 19th century, with a molded cornice above two paneled doors inset with medallions and inlaid with birds of paradise, 64$\frac{1}{2}$in. wide.
(Christie's) $19,550

An antique Italian rococo Venetian green painted wood armadio with silver-gilt highlights, 18th century, 7ft. 6in. wide.
(Selkirk's) $7,500

A chestnut and walnut armoire, Alsace Lorraine, Louis XV, circa 1750, the domed cornice above a pair of doors with cartouche shaped inlay and carving, 170cm. wide.
(Sotheby's) $4,087

A 17th century Flemish oak armoire, the projecting molded cornice above a frieze carved with scrolling foliage, on massive bun feet, 79in. wide.
(Bearne's) $3,956

BEDS

The earliest beds, of a form that would be recognised and accepted today, date from the 16th century – in Britain, anyway. Before that time the most important feature of the rich man's bed was the drapery, often of velvet or silk intricately embroidered with hunting or hawking scenes, which was suspended from the ceiling by means of rings.

This drapery would enclose a simply constructed oak framework of such crude design and make that it was rarely considered worth taking when the family moved house. The framework was usually made with holes drilled through ends and sides, a length of rope being threaded through the holes to form an open-mesh base on which would be supported a rush-work pallet and a couple of feather mattresses. Coverings would include sheets, often of silk, blankets and an embroidered bedspread probably trimmed with fur.

The poor man's bed was more often than not a heap of leaves or straw laid in a shallow box – and the most important feature as far as he was concerned was whether or not the leaves were dry.

Up and coming families, rich enough to afford large coffers, would sleep on these, the lids made more hospitable by means of straw palliasses.

Once the idea of beds caught on, however, the family bed soon became the most important item of furniture in the household. One of the best extant examples of this is the Great Bed of Ware, made in 1595, which was a massive ten feet eight inches wide.

Gustav Stickley double bed, circa 1907, no.. 923, tapering vertical posts centering five wide slats, signed, 57½in. wide. (Skinner Inc.) $3,300

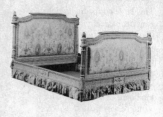

A green-painted tester bed, of Louis XVI style, with padded head, foot ends and domed tester covered in ivory and blue chintz, 70in. wide. (Christie's) $5,132

Italian baroque carved giltwood tester bed, composed of late 17th century and later elements, the spirally twisted endposts carved in high relief with fruiting vines, 5ft. 9in. wide. (Butterfield & Butterfield) $2,475

One of a pair of Louis XV style mounted mahogany beds, late 19th century, attributed to François Linke, each with a cartouche-shaped ormolu-molded headboard centering a rocaille, all on cabriole legs with scrolling sabots, 50in. wide. (Christie's)
(Two) $21,850

A George IV gray-painted double bed in the Gothic taste, the headboard surmounted by a red-painted and parcel-gilt Viscount's coronet, the front post bases joined by a paneled footboard with molded toprail, 85in. wide. (Christie's) $10,988

An Edwardian mahogany and marquetry double bedstead, the crossbanded and line-inlaid headboard and footboard each with scrolling foliage and bellflowers around a central urn, 65in. wide. (Christie's) $3,684

BEDS

Art Nouveau marquetry bed,
France, early 20th century,
headboard and footboard inlaid
with floral designs and carved
tendrils, 54in. wide.
(Skinner Inc.) $1,300

An oak single bed, the paneled
headboard carved with lozenges
enclosing stylized flowerheads,
partly 17th century, 42in. wide.
(Christie's) $2,087

An Empire ormolu mounted
mahogany lit bateau, each of
the paneled ends with a
rounded toprail and with box
spring and mattress.
(Christie's) $3,150

A George III green, buff, red
and blue painted four post bed,
the arched canopy decorated
with panels of flowers and
beading, extensively restored
and redecorated, 79in. wide.
(Christie's) $37,650

**An unusual paint decorated
bedstead, Pennsylvania or Ohio,
mid 19th century, the tall
shaped headboard flanked by
block and baluster-turned
headposts, 53in. wide.**
(Sotheby's)   **$7,188**

A mahogany four-post bed with
pale green-painted arched
canopy and two reeded baluster
columns, part early 19th
century, 58in. wide.
(Christie's) $5,328

A Federal birchwood and maple
four-post bedstead, New
England, circa 1810, on tapered
feet, with tester.
(Sotheby's) $5,750

An early Victorian oak half-
tester bed with fluted pointed
arched rear supports by a
central panel and supporting a
crenellated canopy, 90in. long.
(Christie's) $1,594

An oak tester bed, the paneled
headboard inlaid with bog-oak
and fruitwood, possibly
Lancashire, mid 17th century
and later, 83 x 64in.
(Christie's) $13,596

BEDS

Italian baroque style carved walnut posted bed, the massive cylindrical posts carved with three bands of vertical acanthus, 6ft. 9in. long.
(Butterfield & Butterfield)
$4,950

An oak bed, the footboard with two rectangular relief panels of lozenges flanked by carved caryatid panels, basically 17th century, 84in. long.
(Christie's) $4,145

A classical mahogany bedstead, Duncan Phyfe, New York, 1815–1833, the paneled head and foot boards with cylindrical crest rails, 58³/₄in. wide.
(Christie's) $11,500

A double bed, the headboard with a broken arch centered by two cherubs, the footboard inlaid with a marquetry arched panel of festive dancing cherubs, 68in. wide.
(Christie's) $5,313

A fine paint decorated cannon-ball bedstead, probably Eastern Connecticut, circa 1840, the whole exuberantly sponge-painted with patterns of red dots on a yellow-gold ground, 54¹/₄in. wide.
(Sotheby's) $4,600

One of a pair of North African Moorish ivory-inlaid walnut and parquetry beds, late 19th century, each with an arched rectangular paneled headboard crested by finials, on bun feet with similarly paneled rails, 53¹/₄in. wide.
(Christie's) $16,100

Italian Empire carved and painted pine daybed, first quarter 19th century, with paneled scrolled ends, the sides of the headboard each carved in relief with a recumbent leopard-headed sphinx, 5ft, 7¹/₂in. long.
(Butterfield & Butterfield)
$2,750

A rare red-painted cherrywood and pine, child's bedstead, American, first half 19th century, has full set of cotton crocheted hangings, width 36in.
(Sotheby's) $2,990

A French gilt-metal-mounted kingwood, rosewood and marquetry bed, the arched footboard and headboard above inlaid foliate quarter-veneered panels joined by shaped side rails, late 19th century, 62in. wide.
(Christie's) $2,870

BOOKCASES

Most early bookcases were designed by architects and made to fit a particular wall as the house was built. Fortunately for us, furniture designers such as Chippendale, Hepplewhite and the Adams, designed bookcases in sections in order that they might be moved into and out of houses.

Chippendale was among the first designers to build bookcases as separate units and it is clear that the architectural feeling of existing designs had some influence on the manner in which his were styled.

There were any number of open bookshelves designed at the end of the 18th century and such is their practicality that they have remained popular ever since.

The Georgian variety, elegantly tall and narrow with nicely graduated shelves, are made or mahogany, rosewood or satinwood, often japanned black or green and decorated with painted scenes or brass inlay. Some have cupboards or drawers in the base and they are supported on a variety of feet: bracket, scroll, claw, turned or with a shaped apron.

The revolving bookcase is the ideal piece of furniture for the idle bibliophile or for the family which lacks the wall space necessary for the more conventional methods of book display and storage.

Made in significant quantities between 1880 and 1920, many were given as free gifts by fast talking sales representatives, who offered them as inducements to potential purchasers of the innumerable home educator or encyclopaedia volumes in vogue at the time.

A late Victorian oak breakfront bookcase, with molded fluted cornice above four glazed doors, and four arched paneled doors, 74in. wide.
(Christie's) $2,861

An early Victorian walnut and tulipwood-banded bookcase, with molded cornice above a pair of glazed doors, on plinth base, 52in. wide.
(Christie's) $4,562

A Regency mahogany breakfront bookcase in six sections with molded **rectangular cornice, the angles with antifixes filled with paterae, above four glazed doors with arcaded glazing bars, 115in. wide.** (Christie's) $33,660

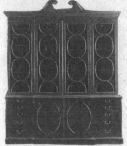

A George III mahogany breakfront bookcase with pierced swan-neck pediment terminated by floral patera upon a trelliswork ground, on a molded breakfront plinth, 95in. wide.
(Christie's) $41,124

A George III style mahogany breakfront bookcase, the dentil-molded and drop-pendant cornice above four astragal glazed doors on plinth base, 86in. wide.
(Christie's) $2,737

A Regency brass inlaid ebony and ebonized open bookcase **attributed to George Oakley, the triangular pediment inlaid with an elongated anthemion, on** plinth base, 54in. wide.
(Christie's) $15,629

149

BOOKCASES

A very fine Federal inlaid mahogany breakfront bookcase, Salem, Massachusetts, circa 1800, in two parts, on tapering legs, 5ft. 7³/₄in. wide.
(Sotheby's) $126,500

A late George III mahogany secrétaire breakfront bookcase, with molded cornice above two pairs of geometrically-glazed doors, on splayed bracket feet, 120¹/₄in. wide.
(Christie's) $22,874

A late Victorian mahogany breakfront bookcase, with molded cornice above four arched glazed doors flanked by applied scrolling foliate uprights, 95in. wide.
(Christie's) $8,752

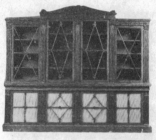

A Louis XIV ormolu-mounted boulle and ebony bibliothèque, the molded cornice with egg-and-dart ornament, the frieze with foliage, above a pair of double glazed paneled doors, early 19th century, 61in. wide.
(Christie's) $14,025

A Regency bronze-mounted and part-bronzed mahogany bookcase, the breakfront central stepped section, above a pair of glazed doors, and a further pair of doors, the straight-fronted base with rectangular top, 122¹/₄in. wide.
(Christie's) $131,565

A modern pine bookcase, of George III style, with breakfront stiff leaf egg-and-dart and dentil-molded cornice above a fluted frieze (parts of carving 18th century), 90in. wide.
(Christie's) $6,160

A Scottish oak bookcase, in two parts, rectangular overhung top above glazed folding cupboard doors, enclosing adjustable shelves, 128cm. wide.
(Christie's) $1,487

An early Victorian mahogany breakfront bookcase with molded bolection cornice and pediment above a frieze applied with the letters *XYZ*, 129in. wide.
(Christie's) $23,232

An early 20th century banded mahogany circular revolving bookstand, the radially-veneered top centered by a small inlaid florette motif, 34¹/₂in. high.
(Tennants) $1,105

BUREAU BOOKCASES

The introduction, at the end of the 17th century, of higher ceilings encouraged the development of taller items of furniture and one of the most successful adaptations of existing designs to the new fashion was the bureau bookcase, which entailed quite simply the placing of a cabinet on top of the already popular sloping front bureau.

The earliest Queen Anne bureau cabinets had paneled doors to the upper section, often containing Vauxhall mirror glass, which enclosed a multitude of small drawers and pigeon holes.

Since bureau bookcase carcasses tend to be very similar, the pattern made by the glazing bars is a good aid to establishing the date of a piece. Unfortunately, however, it is not infallible, since many of the designs were used throughout the different periods.

Broadly, however, in the late 17th century, the glazing was of plain rectangles secured with putty behind substantial, half round moldings. In the 1740's, the glass was mounted in a wavy frame and the establishment of mahogany soon after meant that, by the 1750's, the glazing bars could be finer and more decorative – usually forming 13 divisions or shaped in the fashion of Gothic church windows.

At the end of the 18th century, Hepplewhite introduced diamond glazing and also flowing curves and polygonal shapes, often enriched with foliate designs, in the glazing of his furniture. Sheraton too, used similar forms, often enhanced by their super-impositions on pleated silks.

Small painted poplar secretary desk, possibly Western New York, circa 1850, 35in. wide. (Skinner) $2,750

A mid 18th century Austrian fruitwood inlaid bureau cabinet on bun feet, 106cm. wide. (Finarte) $4,982

A George I figured walnut double-domed bureau-cabinet with molded cornice, lacking **finials, above a pair of arched mirror-glazed doors, each with** later beveled plate cut with stylized triple-leaf, 43¹/₂in. wide. (Christie's) $141,550

A small faded walnut veneered bureau bookcase, in George I style, with herringbone banding, central candleslide to the frieze, the front with two short and three long oak lined drawers, on bracket feet, 35in. overall. (Woolley & Wallis) $15,600

An unusual Edwardian mahogany inlaid bureau bookcase, the breakfront cornice with checker inlaid frieze, **126cm. wide.** (Phillips) $3,298

A Dutch East Indies (Sri Lanka) kaliatur and calamander brass mounted bureau cabinet, the molded arched cornice above two glazed doors, 18th century, 57in. wide. (Christie's) $3,550

BUREAU BOOKCASES

A Victorian mahogany cylinder bureau bookcase, the ogee molded cornice above a pair of arched glazed doors.
(Bonhams) **$3,110**

A Biedermeier mahogany bureau bookcase, with arched pediment above a pair of glazed doors and two short drawers, second quarter 19th century, 40in. wide.
(Christie's) **$4,497**

A George II figured walnut veneered bureau bookcase, the top with cavetto molded frieze, on fret bracket feet, 3ft. 2in. wide.
(Woolley & Wallis) **$8,400**

A George I walnut, crossbanded and feather strung bureau cabinet of small size, the upper part with a molded cornice and fitted with adjustable shelves, the lower centered by a recessed arch, inlaid sunburst, on bracket feet, 2ft. 9in. wide.
(Phillips) **$31,860**

A South German walnut, fruitwood and marquetry bureau cabinet, the bowed top fitted with two drawers, above a paneled cupboard door inlaid with panel of musicians and surrounded by nine serpentine drawers, 19th century, 46in. wide.
(Christie's) **$18,573**

A good 18th century mahogany cylinder-top bureau bookcase, the upper part with molded dentil cornice, fitted with a pair of astragal glazed doors, each door with two oval center panels, 39in. wide.
(Canterbury) **$7,155**

A good George III mahogany Irish bureau bookcase, with glazed doors enclosing eight pigeon holes and three shelves, on a carved base with claw feet, 3ft. 7in. wide.
(John Nicholson) **$3,645**

Italian Provincial neoclassical walnut bureau cabinet, late 18th century, the upper part with a shallow cavetto cornice over double-fielded panel doors, width 47³/₄in.
(Butterfield & Butterfield) **$5,175**

A Queen Anne desk-and-bookcase, Caribbean, possibly Jamaica or Bermuda, 1740-1760, the upper section with molded rounded arch pediment above paneled arched doors, 41³/₄in. wide.
(Christie's) **$5,750**

BUREAUX

The writing desk was born in the monasteries of the Middle Ages, originally as a small, Gothic style oak box with a sloping lid hinged at the back like old fashioned school desk tops.

As time passed and men of letters increased their output, the writing box grew and was made a permanent fixture in the copying rooms of the monasteries, being built upon a stand, usually high enough to be used by a man standing or seated on a high stool.

Later, the hinges of the lid were moved from the back to the front, allowing the lid to fall forward on supports and form a writing platform in the open position. The practice on the Continent was the cover this area with a 'burel' or russet cloth, probably named from the Latin *burrus* (red), the color of the dye used in its manufacture. It is doubtless from here that we gain the word bureau, though the connotations of the word have changed somewhat since it was first coined.

The bureau remained little more than a box on a stand until the close of the 17th century when it was married to a chest of drawers for obvious practical reasons. From that time onward, there have been few changes in the design beyond relatively small stylistic alterations which were reflections of the changing tastes of the fashionable rather than modifications dictated by practical usage.

Most reproductions of this period are of plain mahogany enhanced with a boxwood string inlay and a conch shell in the center of the bureau flap.

Chippendale mahogany slant-top desk, Massachusetts, circa 1790, brasses appear to be original, old refinish, 40in. wide. (Skinner) $4,400

A Dutch walnut, burr walnut and marquetry bureau inlaid overall with scrolling foliage and flowerheads, the rectangular top and hinged flap enclosing a fitted interior with slide, the reverse inlaid with dice, a candle and a pipe, 52in. wide. (Christie's) $20,587

Chippendale cherry and tiger maple slant lid desk, Connecticut, late 18th century, the two-tiered interior with a fan-carved central drawer, 36in. wide. (Skinner) $3,850

A rare Federal carved and paint decorated pine slant front desk, New England, early 19th century, 36in. wide. (Sotheby's) $34,500

A Chippendale walnut slant-front desk, Pennsylvania, 1760–1780, the rectangular hinged lid opening to a fitted interior above a case fitted with thumb-molded graduated long drawers, on ogee bracket feet, 41½in. wide. (Christie's) $7,150

Portuguese rococo style serpentine-fronted padouk slant-front desk, 19th century, raised on a projecting coved ebony base on compressed ball feet, 37in. wide. (Butterfield & Butterfield) $2,200

BUREAUX

A French red lacquer secrétaire en pente, Paris, circa 1850, in the Louis XV style of Dubois, the fall-front with a fitted interior including a well on cabriole legs, 100cm. wide.
(Sotheby's) $7,517

A George III oak bureau having fitted interior of pigeon holes and drawers with two secret drawers, on bracket feet.
(Russell, Baldwin & Bright) $2,220

A South German walnut and inlaid bureau, 18th century, with three drawers in the serpentine frieze and above a slope front inlaid with rectangular panel, 49in. wide.
(Lawrence Fine Art)
$4,805

An early 19th century Dutch mahogany and marquetry bombé cylinder bureau all over inlaid with flower stems and sprays within scrolling strapwork borders, 4ft. 5in. wide.
(Phillips) $9,735

A painted and chinoiserie-decorated bureau, decorated overall with courtly figures within a landscape of trees and padogas, the sloping fall enclosing fitted interior, 30in. wide.
(Christie's) $1,615

Italian baroque inlaid walnut bureau, Verona, circa 1720, the sloping fall enclosing a well and a fitted interior, the serpentine case fitted with three long banded drawers, length 45¼in.
(Butterfield & Butterfield)
$24,150

A walnut and feather-banded bureau with rectangular top and hinged slope above a fitted interior with three graduated drawers below, on later bun feet, early 18th century, 39in. wide.
(Christie's S. Ken)
$5,541

A George III mahogany bureau with rosewood banded fall enclosing a fitted interior above two short and three long drawers on ogee bracket feet, 43in. wide.
(Christie's) $3,115

A walnut bureau, the hinged flap enclosing a fitted interior with drawers and pigeon-holes above four long graduated drawers, on bracket feet, early 18th century, 36in. wide.
(Christie's S. Ken)
$5,541

BUREAUX

A Victorian lady's walnut cylinder bureau with a fitted interior.
(Greenslades)   **$2,008**

A Chinese export padouk wood bureau, the rectangular top and hinged slope enclosing a fitted interior with well, mid 18th century, 37$\frac{1}{4}$in. wide.
(Christie's)   **$2,517**

A lady's 19th century French figured walnut bureau with three quarters gallery above a concave fail-front, 2ft. 8in. wide.
(Riddetts)   **$1,316**

Dutch Neoclassical walnut and marquetry cylinder bureau, second quarter 19th century, scalloped apron on square tapering supports, 34$\frac{1}{2}$in. wide.
(Butterfield & Butterfield)   **$3,025**

A Japanese Export ebonized and marquetry cylinder bureau, last quarter 19th century, with a rectangular molded cornice above a superstructure fitted with pigeonholes, 45$\frac{3}{4}$in. wide.
(Christie's East)   **$9,900**

An early 19th century Dutch mahogany and floral marquetry cylinder bombé bureau inlaid with flowers and foliage heightened in mother-of-pearl and harewood, on open bracket feet, 4ft. 1$\frac{1}{2}$in. wide.
(Phillips)   **$9,735**

An 18th century Lombard walnut veneered bureau, the three drawers and fall front ebony banded, on splayed scroll feet, 115cm. wide.
(Finarte)   **$80,044**

A William and Mary stained burr-elm bureau attributed to Coxed and Woster, inlaid overall with pewter lines and crossbanded with kingwood, on bracket feet, 26in. wide.
(Christie's)   **$15,246**

An Edwardian inlaid mahogany bureau, with crossbanded sloping fall enclosing a fitted interior above four crossbanded long drawers on bracket feet, 40$\frac{1}{2}$in. wide.
(Christie's)   **$2,033**

CABINETS

Cabinets, as pieces of furniture, saw their British beginnings in the 17th century, when, designed basically for either specialized storage or display, they were introduced by craftsmen imported from the continent.

It was during the 18th and 19th centuries, however, that cabinets began to achieve a certain importance when they served to meet the needs of a nation obsessed with learning. Everybody, it would seem, began to collect things: coins, shells, fossils, ores, mineral samples, china – and what was the point of amassing vast collections of these wonders without having the means of displaying them for the enjoyment of family and admiring friends?

Cabinets, then, became indispensable, and although most of the earlier examples were imported from Europe, a few were actually made in Britain.

Handles can be a useful pointer to the age of a piece of furniture, though not infallible, for they were continually swapped around or replaced.

Earliest handles were brass drop loops which were held on to the backplates with brass or iron wire or, after 1700, by the heads of nutted bolts. The heavier brass loop handles began to be used in 1735, and each bolt head is mounted on a separate backplate.

Pierced backplates date from about 1720 and continued to be used, with the addition of ornamental key escutcheons, until about 1750, when sunken escutcheons began to be used.

A William IV amboyna and parcel-gilt side cabinet, the central paneled doors filled with pierced fretwork flanked by a pair of glazed doors enclosing purple velvet-lined shelves, on a plinth base, 72in. wide.
(Christie's) $7,524

A fine and rare French walnut amboyna side cabinet, Napoléon III, by Winckelsen of Paris, in Louis XVI manner, the rouge griotte marble top above a frieze drawer above a pair of glazed silk-lined doors enclosing a veneered interior, on toupie feet, 102cm. wide.
(Sotheby's) $20,045

A good kingwood meuble d'appui, by Henri Dasson of Paris, dated *1888*, the brêche violette marble top above two drawers, doors inlaid with cube parquetry, 132cm. wide.
(Sotheby's) $11,359

An English pietre dure side cabinet, Victorian, London, circa 1855, the door with an oval hardstone panel flanked by glazed convex doors divided by columns, the whole ebony-veneered, 173cm. wide.
(Sotheby's) $4,009

A Milanese ivory-inlaid ebony and marquetry cabinet, the inlaid frieze fitted with an arched paneled door engraved with an ivory-inlaid figure of Venus, the base with a cupboard door inlaid with a panel of Venus resting on a cloud, 19th century, 62½in. wide.
(Christie's) $45,276

A late Victorian inlaid ebonized, thuya wood and gilt-metal-mounted dwarf side cabinet, the raised breakfront center section with ledge back and arched glazed doors, on shaped plinth base, 60in. wide.
(Christie's) $1,945

CABINETS

A Regency rosewood, lacquer and black and gilt-japanned side cabinet, the concave-sided shaped rectangular three-quarter-galleried top above a pair of chicken-wire doors with pink silk-lining, 51in. wide.
(Christie's) $24,875

A pair of Italian walnut cabinets-on-stand, the platform base fitted with drawers, on angled paw feet, adapted in the 19th century from 17th century cassones, 55in. wide.
(Christie's) $3,455

A French marble topped side cabinet, by Linke of Paris, circa 1910, with a brèche violette marble top above a drawer, on cabriole legs, 110cm. wide.
(Sotheby's) $4,510

A French kingwood side cabinet, Napoléon III, Paris, circa 1855, in Louis XV manner, with a serpentine breccia marble top above a door lacquered with a Japanese-style hunting scene, 89cm. wide.
(Sotheby's) $4,343

A Napoléon III ormolu and porcelain-mounted tulipwood and rosewood side cabinet, with a removeable canted rectangular top enclosing a jardinière above a conforming paneled case inset with porcelain plaques depicting bouquets, 60¹/₂in. wide.
(Christie's) $17,250

One of two French or Belgian giltmetal-mounted thuya, ebonized, marquetry and parquetry side cabinets, each with inverted breakfront white marble top, last quarter 19th century, 33¹/₂in. wide.
(Christie's) $7,900

An Edwardian satinwood and painted side cabinet inlaid overall with kingwood, the D-shaped top painted with fan-shaped demi-lune within a ribbon-tied foliate border, on turned tapering legs carved with lotus leaves, 48in. wide.
(Christie's) $6,547

A rare Egyptian Revival painted music cabinet on stand, circa 1920, carved and painted with Egyptian courtiers, the music rack with five divisions, with brass hinges and locks, 121cm. high.
(Sotheby's) $5,011

A George III mahogany satinwood and burr-elm marquetry side cabinet with concave-fronted shaped rectangular top above a pair of trelliswork concave-fronted doors, 45¹/₄in. wide.
(Christie's) $63,651

CABINETS

A George IV rosewood breakfront dwarf side cabinet with central frieze drawer and four paneled doors, on plinth base, 52¹/₂in. wide. (Christie's) **$4,223**

Late 19th century rosewood coal compactiom with marquetry inlays, having raised shelf of serpentine form, 15in. wide. (G. A. Key) **$234**

A walnut marquetry side cabinet, possibly London, circa 1860, with an ogee mirrored door flanked by arched glazed doors inlaid with foliate marquetry, 5ft. 11in. wide. (Sotheby's) **$5,115**

A good French porcelain mounted side cabinet, by Sormani of Paris, circa 1875, in Louis XVI manner, flanked by eight short drawers veneered in amboyna with tulipwood and kingwood bandings, porcelain plaque signed *F. Bellanger*, 81.5cm. wide. (Sotheby's) **$34,134**

A pair of Napoléon III ormolu-mounted tulipwood and marquetry side cabinets, late 19th century, with doors centrally mounted with a silvered-bronze plaque depicting classical maidens, on shaped bracket feet, 37¹/₂in. wide. (Christie's) **$25,300**

A Scottish Arts and Crafts stained beech and brass-mounted cabinet, with central embossed and brass plaque in the style of Margaret MacDonald Mackintosh, the base fitted with a further hinged flap, 40in. wide. (Christie's) **$2,020**

A black-lacquer and chinoiserie-decorated side cabinet, the rectangular top above a pair of doors on bun feet, mid 19th century, 39in. wide. (Christie's) **$2,702**

A mid Victorian walnut floral marquetry and ormolu-mounted side cabinet with inlaid glazed paneled door flanked by female mask mounts, 31in. wide. (Christie's) **$2,879**

A 19th century breakfront side cabinet, veneered in burr yew banded in ebony with ivory marquetry penwork, circa 1870, 3ft. 10¹/₂in. (Woolley & Wallis) **$4,510**

CANTERBURYS

Originally designed to hold sheet music, this particular item could just as well have been called the Archbishop since, according to Sheraton, it was named after the Archbishop of Canterbury, who was among the first to place an order for one. Most of the original, late 18th century, varieties were rectangular in shape and were made with a drawer in the base.

Regency canterburys are of mahogany or rosewood; the later Victorian examples are generally of burr walnut with flamboyantly fretted partitions or barley twist supports.

An early Victorian rosewood canterbury, the foliate laurel slatted three division rectangular top, 18¹/₂in. wide.
(Christie's S. Ken) $2,000

A Regency rosewood canterbury with four lyre-shaped divisions, on turned legs with brass castors, 22¹/₄in. wide.
(Bearne's) $1,192

A Regency mahogany four division canterbury, the slatted divisions with curved top rails with two drawers below, 1ft. 5¹/₂in.
(Phillips) $3,828

A rare Federal mahogany canterbury, Boston or New York, circa 1815, the four turned uprights centering scrolled transverses, 20in. wide.
(Sotheby's) $3,025

A William IV rosewood canterbury with three C-scroll and leaf carved divisions, on turned legs, brass toes and castors, 21¹/₂in.
(Hy. Duke & Son) $1,400

A mahogany gothic canterbury, the dished rectangular top with gothic arches, paneled pillar-angles, five divisions and a scrolled carrying handle, 19th century, 19¹/₂in. wide.
(Christie's) $2,834

A Victorian inlaid walnut combined games table and canterbury, on baluster-turned supports with slatted spindle-turned canterbury below, 33in. wide.
(Christie's) $1,456

A mahogany and brass-mounted three division canterbury, with slatted dividers and finials to each corner, with scrolling ribbed handles, on tapering feet, 23¹/₂in. wide.
(Christie's) $803

DINING CHAIRS

The Hepplewhite style is renowned for its flowing curves, shield, oval and heart-shaped backs and straight lines broken by carved or painted wheat ears and corn husks, all of which Hepplewhite adapted from the work of Robert Adam, the distinguished architect/designer and published in his famous guide: *The Cabinet Maker and Upholsterer*.

Another distinctive Hepplewhite design incorporated the three feathers crest of the Prince of Wales in the backs of chairs.

Though his designs have much in common with those of Hepplewhite, Thomas Sheraton (1751–1806), a drawing master from Stockton on Tees, much preferred straight lines to the curves favored by Hepplewhite, his chairs achieving their feminine delicacy with their fine turning and slender frames.

Sheraton served his apprenticeship as a cabinet maker but he never actually manufactured furniture himself, concentrating on creating designs which he published in his *Cabinet Maker's and Upholsterer's Drawing Book (1791–1794)*.

Thomas Chippendale designed and made furniture for the wealthy in his premises in St. Martin's Lane, London, establishing styles of his own rather than copying and adapting those of others. Like Sheraton and Hepplewhite, Chippendale published his designs, which were used by cabinet makers throughout the country, with the result that a considerable number of 'Chippendale' chairs were produced in a variety of qualities and a medley of styles.

Two of a set of four George III mahogany dining chairs, the oval backs carved and pierced with floret filled wheel splats.
(Phillips)   (Four) $900

A rare ebonized oak 'ladder back' chair, designed by Charles Rennie Mackintosh for the Willow Tearooms, 1903.
(Christie's) $25,875

Two of a set of six classical mahogany gondola chairs, Duncan Phyfe, New York, circa 1833, each with an arched crest rail, on cabriole legs, 18¹/₂in. wide.
(Christie's)
          (Six) $23,000

One of a set of twelve Federal maple side-chairs, New York, 1790–1810, each with a scrolling concave crestrail over a conforming slat and caned trapezoidal seat, 33¹/₂in. high.
(Christie's)   (Twelve)
                    $5,500

Two of a set of five early 19th century Provincial mahogany dining chairs, the shield shaped backs in the Hepplewhite manner.
(Phillips)   (Five) $1,440

One of a set of six oak side chairs designed by A.W.N. Pugin, on turned and chamfered legs joined by chamfered stretchers.
(Christie's) (Six) $2,363

DINING CHAIRS

One of a set of three Dutch 19th century floral marquetry side chairs, the arcaded top rails with barley twist central supports.
(Tennants)   (Three) $930

Two of a set of four Japanese bamboo and lacquer sidechairs, late 19th century, each with a rounded-arched top.
(Butterfield & Butterfield)
      (Four) $4,400

One of a set of six Regency mahogany dining-chairs and a pair of later open armchairs, on fern-headed reeded saber legs.
(Christie's)
      (Six) $7,038

An early George III carved mahogany dining chair, after a design in Chippendale's Director, on molded chamfered square legs united by 'H'-stretchers.
(Phillips) $1,602

A pair of 18th century Dutch walnut veneered elm and floral marquetry dining chairs in the Queen Anne style, the balloon shaped backs with mask inlaid top rails.
(Phillips) $2,531

One of a pair of George III mahogany dining chairs each with waved pierced back, the vertical splat carved with arcading headed by honeysuckle.
(Christie's)   (Two)
        $3,678

One of a set of six Regency mahogany dining chairs, each with curved bar top rail, on molded saber legs.
(Christie's)
      (Six) $3,024

A pair of early 19th century Dutch mahogany floral marquetry and brass strung music chairs, with bar top rails and lyre shaped splats.
(Phillips) $1,168

One of a set of six Italian walnut Renaissance Revival dining chairs, with arched upholstered backs and seats on scale carved square tapering legs.
(Bonhams)   (Six) $864

DINING CHAIRS

A pair of mahogany chairs, designed by George Walton, the curved backs with vase-shaped splats pierced with a heart, circa 1900, 48in. high.
(Christie's) $1,772

A Charles X mahogany chaise, circa 1820, with tufted seat above a shaped rail on ring-turned legs, upholstered in claret cut-velvet.
(Christie's) $5,520

Two of a set of four Dutch beechwood, mahogany and marquetry side chairs on saber legs.
(Christie's)
(Four) $1,986

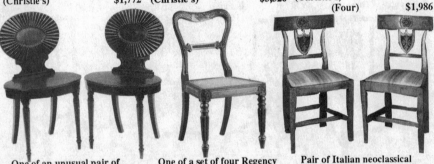

One of an unusual pair of Regency carved mahogany hall chairs, the wide oval panel backs with radiating reeded ornament, having solid seats, on turned tapered legs.
(Phillips) $2,067

One of a set of four Regency Goncalo Alvez dining-chairs by Gillows, each with waisted balloon back, on turned tapering reeded legs and turned tapering feet.
(Christie's) $2,111

Pair of Italian neoclassical carved walnut side chairs, circa 1800, each with a broad bowed crestrail centered by a floral medallion above a pierced urn-form splat.
(Butterfield & Butterfield)
$660

A pair of important oak arm chairs designed by C. F. A. Voysey, each with a slatted back rest with tapering square section supports, carved arms, above rush seats with shaped apron.
(Christie's) $34,452

A classical carved mahogany sidechair, attributed to Duncan Phyfe, New York, 1815-1825, the paneled scrolled tablet crest above a vine-carved lyre support.
(Christie's) $7,475

A pair of paint decorated side chairs with plank seats, Maine, early 19th century, the crest rail painted with two green and brown pears and red and brown oak leaves.
(Sotheby's) $6,900

EASY CHAIRS

Wing chairs have been made since the 17th century, this being one of the few designs to have remained virtually unchanged since its conception, only the legs changing shape according to the dictates of fashion.

The Queen Anne wing chairs had high cabriole legs canted from the corners which demanded extra stretchers for strength. The legs were later straightened and squared off with the inside legs chamfered, before the Georgian influence saw a return of the cabriole legs, but shorter this time and terminating in ball and claw feet.

The armchair by Thomas Chippendale is one of the best chairs ever made. Beautifully constructed to a superbly elegant design, it is strong, graceful and comfortable; a truly classic example of everything a chair should be.

The strong rectangle of the back is softened by the flow of the humped top rail and the arm supports, molded and richly carved with feathers, terminate in cabochon ornament above the graceful acanthus carved cabriole legs with claw and ball feet.

The mid Victorian period abounds with furniture showing the exaggerated curves and floral and leaf carving which clearly reflect the Louis XV rococo influence and beautifully designed chairs of this period simply cry out to be sat in.

Earlier examples had filled-in arms and rather plain frames of mahogany or rosewood but, within a few years, they developed open arms and grandly flamboyant lines.

Pair of Italian baroque giltwood armchairs, early 18th century, each with a domed tapering tall back and molded outswept arms.
(Butterfield & Butterfield)
$13,200

A George III giltwood open armchair with oval padded back, arms and bowed seat covered in light blue silk, the frontrail re-supported, stamped *T M* and with ink inscription.
(Christie's) $2,710

Pair of Louis XV carved polished beech fauteuils à la reine, third quarter 18th century, on molded cabriole supports, brown leather upholsteries.
(Butterfield & Butterfield)
$13,200

One of a pair of early George III mahogany library open armchairs, each with slightly-arched studded rectangular padded back, arms and seat covered in crimson velvet, 28½in. wide. (Two)
(Christie's) $46,265

A pair of mahogany library armchairs of mid-Georgian design, each with a tapestry back and seat, on square molded legs joined by an H-stretcher.
(Christie's) $4,684

Continental rococo walnut armchair, mid-18th century, the cartouche-paneled back, center-pad arms and serpentine seat upholstered in green velvet.
(Butterfield & Butterfield)
$2,750

EASY CHAIRS

One of a pair of George IV
white-painted and parcel-gilt
bergères attributed to George
Seddon, covered in black-
ground 'Adamite' silk.
(Christie's)   (Two)

$12,243

A pair of Victorian mahogany
elbow chairs, the high waisted
backs with 'paper-scroll'
crestings, scroll arms and scroll
front supports.
(Lawrence Fine Art)

$1,386

Italian Empire style parcel-gilt
and green-painted walnut
armchair, the downswept arms
on parcel-gilt and green-painted
swan-form supports.
(Butterfield & Butterfield)

$3,025

One of a set of green and gray
painted seat furniture of
Transitional style comprising
four bergères and a canapé each
with padded curved back, late
19th century.
(Christie's)   (Five)

$6,939

Pair of Restauration carved
mahogany bergères, circa 1830,
each arched and curved
backrest continuing into
armrests and scroll carved arm
supports.
(Butterfield & Butterfield)

$2,875

A George IV mahogany caned
bergère, with deeply curved
back and scrolled toprail, with
scrolled arms and on baluster-
turned legs and brass caps with
pierced wheels.
(Christie's) $2,815

A Neoclassical blue and gilt-
painted open armchair with
striped upholstery, the
rectangular padded back with a
toprail carved with bellflowers,
circa 1800.
(Christie's S. Ken) $1,995

A pair of Empire mahogany
bergères, circa 1810, each
stamped *Jacob. R. Meslee*, on
square tapering legs ending in
paw feet, upholstered in
burgundy striped cotton.
(Christie's) $36,800

Louis XV style painted and
parcel-gilt fauteuil à la reine,
circa 1860–1880, with cartouche
paneled back, centerpad arms
and serpentine feet.
(Butterfield & Butterfield)

$1,980

EASY CHAIRS

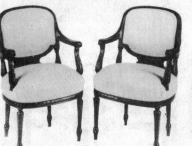

A late Victorian Morris & Co. oak reclining armchair, after a design by Philip Webb, the buttoned back with turned finials above padded arms. (Christie's) **$1,010**

Two of a set of four Continental neoclassical carved walnut armchairs, second quarter 19th century, each with guilloche and acanthus carved frame. (Butterfield & Butterfield) (Four) **$1,725**

A George IV mahogany caned bergère, the rectangular back and sides with squab cushions covered in florally-patterned red silk damask. (Christie's) **$2,521**

A George III mahogany open armchair with arched padded back, with downswept arms carved with acanthus on square legs joined by an H-shaped stretcher. (Christie's) **$7,607**

A pair of giltwood fauteuils of Louis XVI style, each with rectangular padded back, arm rests and bowed seat, on stop-fluted turned tapering legs and on toupie feet, third quarter 19th century. (Christie's) **$5,313**

A good Victorian walnut open armchair, with a cushion molded cresting rail richly carved with stylized dolphin masks, over a buttoned spoon back. (Spencer's) **$1,301**

One of a pair of early Victorian rosewood nursing chairs, with padded back and seat on foliate-headed cabriole legs with scroll feet, late 19th century. (Christie's) (Two) **$2,566**

A pair of mid-Victorian rosewood easy chairs, each with a rounded rectangular button down back, low scrolled arms and serpentine seat on cabriole legs. (Christie's) **$2,208**

Louis XIV carved walnut tapestry upholstered fauteuil, on scroll supports united by flattened wavy X-form stretchers. (Butterfield & Butterfield) **$6,600**

ELBOW CHAIRS

Possibly the greatest problem confronting a designer of chairs has always been that of creating a style robust enough to survive while retaining a degree of elegance

Very few designers achieved this happy blend, most coming down on the side of strong practicality and a few, such Sheraton and Hepplewhite, concentrating on a fashionable delicacy at the expense of strength. Chippendale was the man who came closest to combining the two elements and it is this which has made chairs based on his designs among the most popular ever made.

Beside the elegance of his designs, Hepplewhite is to be remembered for the explicit instructions given in his book regarding the materials to be used for the purpose of covering his chairs: for japanned chairs with cane seats, cushions covered in linen; for dining chairs, horse hair material which may be either plain or striped; for upholstered chairs, red or blue morocco leather tied with silk tassels.

While most surviving Sheraton chairs are made of mahogany, they can also be found in satinwood, painted white or gold or even japanned.

The delicacy of his designs demands that a fine fabric be used to cover the upholstery, green silk or satin being generally considered the most suitable.

More suited to the parlor than the dining room, his chairs must be treated with the utmost delicacy for, not being a manufacturer himself, Sheraton concerned himself more with the aesthetics of design than with the practicalities of use.

Two of six L. & J.G. Stickley chairs, circa 1912, comprised of one armchair, no. 802, and five side chairs, no. 800, 36¹/₂in. high.
(Skinner Inc.) $1,700

A yew wood and elm Windsor arm chair, early 19th century, the low back with pierced splat, solid seat and turned legs united by a crinoline stretcher.
(Tennants) $1,023

Two of a set of six classical mahogany chairs, attributed to Charles-Honore Lannuier, New York, 1810–1819, on paneled klismos legs with carved animal paw feet.
(Christie's)
        (Six) $57,500

One of a pair of George III red-painted simulated bamboo cockpen armchairs, each with arched back and splayed arms filled with pierced Chinese paling.
(Christie's)
        (Two) $4,223

Two of a set of six antique English George II mahogany dining chairs comprising one armchair and five side chairs, circa 1760.
(Selkirk's)   (Six)
                $3,750

A late Victorian painted satinwood bergère, the cane back centered by an oval portrait medallion, the downswept arms continuing into tapering turned legs.
(Bearne's) $1,514

ELBOW CHAIRS

A Charles II oak open armchair with rectangular paneled back carved with scrolls and flowerheads and *THOMAS IEPSON*, on baluster legs.
(Christie's)   **$4,145**

Two of a set of fourteen mahogany dining chairs, each with oval back and pierced uprights, on square tapering legs.
(Christie's)   (Fourteen)
     $4,475

A mid-Georgian elm armchair with waved toprail and solid paneled back, on square tapering legs with paneled sides and back.
(Christie's)   **$669**

One of a set of six Morris & Co. ebonized Sussex open armchairs, each back with four horizontal turned rails and spindles, on turned tapering legs with double stretchers.
(Christie's)
    (Six)   **$2,488**

Two of a set of six North African Moorish ivory-inlaid walnut and parquetry armchairs, late 19th century, each with an incised brown leather back, in a curule-form frame, on down-curved trestle legs.
(Christie's) (Six)   **$10,925**

One of a set of eight Regency mahogany dining chairs, each with an outswept bar toprail and spiral-twist bar above a padded seat, on ring-turned tapering legs.
(Christie's S. Ken)
    (Eight)   **$6,650**

A painted, stenciled and decorated pine and maple Windsor arrowback rocking armchair, New England, circa 1820.
(Sotheby's)   **$1,725**

A rare pair of paint decorated pine open armchairs, New England, early 19th century, painted white with floral decoration on the crest rail, slats, seat and front legs.
(Sotheby's)   **$5,175**

A rare early 19th century Dutch mahogany and floral marquetry metamorphic library step chair after a patent by Morgan and Saunders.
(Phillips)   **$4,620**

ELBOW CHAIRS

One of a pair of Victorian oak armchairs, the spirally turned toprails above rectangular paneled backs carved with foliage and centered by a shield, on X-framed supports.
(Christie's) (Two) $591

Two of a set of ten Regency carved mahogany dining chairs, first quarter 19th century, comprising eight side chairs and two armchairs.
(Butterfield & Butterfield)
(Ten) $6,600

One of a pair of Morris & Co. ebonized beech open armchairs, with spindle top-rails above rush seats on turned legs with stretchers.
(Christie's) (Two) $456

A Robert 'Mouseman' Thompson oak armchair, the horseshoe-shaped arm and back with carved splats bearing carved shield.
(Christie's) $985

A pair of red lacquer chairs with crossed legs (kyokuroku), black leather seats, 19th century, 102.7cm. high.
(Christie's) $10,350

A George III mahogany ladderback open armchair, the gadrooned back with four pierced serpentine crossbars.
(Bearne's) $1,130

One of a set of six mahogany dining chairs, of mid Georgian design, with a drop-in seat, on square chamfered legs joined by stretchers.
(Christie's) (Six)
$3,839

Two of a set of ten Colonial hardwood and brass-mounted dining chairs including two open armchairs, on saber legs, late 19th century.
(Christie's) (Ten)
$4,102

A Spanish walnut X-framed chair, with leather-upholstered seat, the foliate-headed downswept arms with paterae terminals on claw feet, mid 19th century.
(Christie's) $771

CHESTS OF DRAWERS

Throughout the transitional period from coffer to chest of drawers, there were a great many variations on the basic theme but, eventually, a practical and attractive formula emerged about 1670. Not slow to respond to the demand, cabinet makers produced vast quantities of chests of drawers, employing, as a rule, the familiar wood, oak, for the purpose.

Architectural geometric moldings proved popular as decoration and these were glued and bradded in position – a practice which continues to the present day.

As taste developed, there arose a need for more sophisticated chests in more exotic woods such as figured walnut, which was put on to an oak or pine carcass.

The use of veneers made the manufacture of molded drawer fronts impractical and, consequently, more emphasis was placed on the figuring of the veneers as a decorative feature. The oyster design was particularly popular and results from careful cutting of the veneer from a tree bough. This is glued vertically on to the drawer front, the figuring being meticulously matched, and it is crossbanded on the edges, often with an intermediate herringbone inlay.

The drawers are now found to slide on the horizontal partitions which separate them and they are finely dovetailed, where earlier they were more crudely jointed or even nailed together.

Walnut continued as the most favored wood for chests of drawers until the middle of the 18th century, when it gave way to Spanish mahogany.

Antique American Sheraton four-drawer chest in cherry, scrolled splashguard, turned and ribbed legs, brass knobs, 43in. wide.
(Eldred's) $1,210

Federal applewood inlaid chest of drawers, Haddam, Connecticut, early 19th century, with inlaid canted corners, 39¹/₂in. wide.
(Skinner) $4,400

Dutch rococo walnut and marquetry chest of drawers, second half 18th century, the top of rippled outline above a bombé front fitted with four long graduated drawers, 35¹/₂in. wide.
(Butterfield & Butterfield) $11,000

George II walnut chest of drawers, the cross-banded rectangular top with canted corners above two short and three graduated long drawers, 39¹/₂in. wide.
(Butterfield & Butterfield) $3,025

A walnut chest with herringbone bandings, fitted with two short and three long drawers, on ogee bracket feet, 31in. wide, part 18th century.
(Bonhams) $850

A George III mahogany chest, the rectangular molded top, above four graduated long drawers, on bracket feet, 34in. wide.
(Christie's) $3,273

CHESTS OF DRAWERS

A Chippendale applewood serpentine-front chest of drawers, Massachusetts, circa 1785, the oblong top with incised edge, 39in. wide.
(Sotheby's) $4,950

An Empire carved and painted pine chest with drawers, New England, circa 1830, the shaped apron continuing to turned legs ending in ball feet, 41¾in. wide.
(Sotheby's) $9,775

A William and Mary oyster-veneered chest-of-drawers, the molded rectangular top inlaid with concentric circles within boxwood borders, 37in. wide.
(Christie's) $5,630

A William and Mary red-painted chestnut and pine chest-of-drawers, Eastern Connecticut, 1725–1735, the rectangular top with molded edge, on turned feet, 39½in. wide.
(Christie's) $12,100

A Chippendale mahogany block-front chest-of-drawers, Massachusetts, 1760-1780, fitted with four graduated drawers over a molded conforming base with central drop, 33¼in. wide.
(Christie's) $79,500

A Federal inlaid mahogany chest-of-drawers, Mid-Atlantic, 1790–1810, the bowfront top with line inlay surrounding four graduated cockbead and line-inlaid drawers, on French feet, 41in. wide.
(Christie's) $2,640

A Queen Anne walnut chest of two short and three long drawers, with quartered top inlaid with feather bands, on bracket feet, 39½in. wide.
(Lawrence Fine Art)
                    $3,948

A walnut and oak chest, the coffered rectangular top above four long fielded, graduated drawers on bun feet, late 17th century, 42in. wide.
(Christie's) $2,879

An unusual paint decorated pine chest with drawers, attributed to Thomas Matteson, South Shaftsbury, Vermont, circa 1830, 39¼in. wide.
(Sotheby's) $20,700

CHESTS ON CHESTS

In the early 18th century, the tallboy, or chest on a chest, began to replace the chest on a stand and, by about 1725, had virtually superseded it.

Tallboys are made in two parts, the upper chest being slightly narrower than the lower and, although they are inclined to be bulky, this is often minimized visually by means of canted corners.

Early examples were veneered in finely grained burr walnut and often sport a sunburst decoration of boxwood and holly at the base, which usually has the fashionable bracket feet.

As an added bonus, buyers of these superb pieces of furniture often get a secret drawer in the frieze as well as the brushing slide fitted above the oak lined drawers in the lower section.

Despite the obvious difficulty in reaching the top drawers and the competition from wardrobes and clothes presses, tallboys were made in vast quantities throughout the second half of the 18th century. So common were they, in fact, that George Smith, in his *Household Furniture* observed that the tallboy was an article "... of such general use that it does not stand in need of a description".

As a rule, tallboys were made of mahogany and ranged in quality from rather plain, monolithic but functional pieces to magnificent, cathedral-like specimens with elaborate cornices, fluted pillars flanking the upper drawers, low relief carving on the frieze and fine ogee feet.

Their popularity lasted until about 1820 when the linen press, with cupboard doors to the upper section, proved to be more practical.

A George I burr-walnut secretaire-tallboy inlaid overall with feather-banding, 41in. wide.
(Christie's) $50,622

A mid-18th century mahogany chest-on-chest of small proportions, with two short and two long drawers to the upper section, three graduated long drawers below, 27$\frac{1}{2}$in. wide.
(Bearne's) $1,166

The Samuel Morris Chippendale carved mahogany chest-on-chest, Philadelphia, 1760–1780, in three sections, on ogee bracket feet, 95$\frac{1}{2}$in. high, 43$\frac{1}{2}$in. wide.
(Christie's) $74,800

A George I walnut chest on chest, the lower part with three graduated long drawers, on later ogee bracket feet, 3ft. 6in. wide.
(Phillips) $7,250

George III mahogany chest on chest, third quarter 18th century, rectangular dentil molding above three short and three long graduated drawers, 45in. wide.
(Skinner) $2,530

A George III mahogany chest on chest, the molded cornice above two short and three long graduated drawers, on splayed feet, 45$\frac{3}{4}$in. wide.
(Bonhams) $1,751

CHESTS ON STANDS

Towards the end of the 17th century, many chests were raised on stands, often with an extra drawer in the lower section. The reason for this may have been to create a sense of fit proportion between furniture and the high ceilinged rooms of the period, or it may have reflected the stiff backed deportment which was considered proper at that time, raising furniture to a height at which the operative parts could be reached without stooping or bending in an unfashionable manner.

Legs of stands were either turned or barley twist, and were braced with shaped stretchers ending in bun feet.

There were a few pieces made of oak but most, if we are to judge by the survivors, were made of pine with walnut veneer and oak lined drawers. Some sport fine arabesque marquetry decoration, their tops having an oval design in the center and triangular corner pieces. There are half round moldings between drawers which, with the ovolo lip on the top of the stand, are characteristic of pieces of this period.

It is not uncommon to find later bases under these pieces for, although they were generally pretty well made, when full they were inclined to be just that bit too heavy for the rather delicate stands on which they originally stood.

Although of delicate constitution, the chest on stand continued to be made in the early part of the 18th century but, instead of the barley twist legs with shaped stretchers, we find that the later pieces have flowing cabriole legs with ball and claw feet .

A William and Mary walnut chest-on-stand, with molded cornice above a pair of doors enclosing seven variously-sized drawers around a central door, 28¼in. wide.
(Christie's) $7,438

A William and Mary oak high chest-of-drawers, English, late 17th century, on six spiral-turned legs joined by shaped stretchers with compressed ball feet, 38½in. wide.
(Christie's) $3,300

A walnut and feather-banded chest-on-stand, with molded cornice, three short and three long drawers, on stand with three drawers, early 18th century and later, 41in. wide.
(Christie's) $2,104

A Queen Anne tiger maple high chest of drawers, North Shore, Massachusetts, 1740–1760, in two sections, on cabriole legs with pad feet, 38in. wide.
(Christie's) $7,150

A burr-elm and floral marquetry chest-on-stand, the crossbanded top with central inlaid oval depicting birds amongst foliage above two short and two long drawers above two dummy drawers, 32½in. wide.
(Christie's) $2,512

A Queen Anne tiger maple high chest-of-drawers, New Hampshire, Dunlap School, 1740–1770, the upper case with molded cornice above three thumbmolded short drawers 40¼in. wide.
(Christie's) $24,200

CHIFFONIERS

This delightful piece first put in an appearance around 1800 when it achieved instant popularity. The name is from the French chiffonier, defined as 'a piece of furniture with drawers in which women put away their needlework'.

It was designed, possibly as an alternative for the large sideboards of the period, or as a replacement for the commode, whose flowing lines and profuse decoration were not to the taste of the leaders of Regency fashion.

Whatever its parentage, the chiffonier was made, often in pairs, with a glass fronted cabinet in the lower part and, usually, shelves above, which were frequently constructed with lyre or fine scroll shaped supports.

Earlier pieces were made usually of rosewood and, occasionally, of satinwood, while those of later manufacture were of either of those woods and mahogany. In Loudon's *Encyclopaedia of Furniture*, the virtues of the chiffonier are extoled as follows: 'A most useful object for families who cannot afford to go to the expense of a pier or console table.'

A Regency giltmetal-mounted brass-inlaid rosewood and simulated rosewood bonheur-du-jour in the manner of John McLean, 32¾in. wide. (Christie's) $12,370

A Regency brass-inlaid rosewood side cabinet, 45in. wide. (Christie's) $10,276

A Regency lacquered-brass-mounted rosewood breakfront chiffonier attributed to Gillows, the mirrored superstructure with pierced quatrefoil three-quarter galleried shelf on reeded stiff-leaf and part-gadrooned baluster supports, 66in. wide. (Christie's) $11,833

A Regency mahogany chiffonier, with raised superstructure on scroll uprights, above rectangular top and gadrooned frieze above pair of glazed doors, 34in. wide. (Christie's) $2,188

A Regency rosewood and banded chiffonier, the rectangular brass three-quarter galleried mirrored ledged back top with turned supports, 36¾in. wide. (Christie's) $2,303

A William IV mahogany chiffonier, the single shelf superstructure on turned front supports, on a plinth base, 41½in. wide. (Bonhams) $1,780

An early 19th century colonial calamander chiffonier, the scroll-carved back with two graduated shelves, 36¼in. wide. (Bearne's) $2,250

CLOTHES PRESSES

These were the earliest form of wardrobe, with which they became synonymous in the 18th century. They were essentially cupboards for storing clothes, the lower section usually with drawers, and the upper with doors concealing either shelves, sliding trays, or hanging space.

Early examples were generally of oak, and decoration was mainly confined to carving, though occasional examples are found with friezes picked out in color.

Chippendale and his contemporaries produced a number of patterns for clothes presses, some interesting ones with bombé, commode-style lower sections.

The evolution of the clothes press is closely allied to changes in the style of the clothes they had to contain, as, for example, padded trunk hose, doublets and farthingales gave way to thinner materials, which could be folded and laid away.

A George III satinwood clothes press, the cupboard doors enclosing five slides, 49½in. wide. (Christie's) $7,800

A small Regency mahogany clothes press on saber feet with square toes, 36¼in. wide. (Christie's) $7,240

A late 18th century Dutch kingwood side cupboard inlaid with boxwood and ebonized lines, with a cavetto molded cornice above a pair of paneled doors, with splayed legs, 5ft. 5in. wide. (Phillips) $4,602

A mid-Victorian bird's-eye maple and mahogany clothes-press by C. Hindley and Sons, the rectangular eared top above a molded cornice and paneled frieze flanked by flowerheads, 65in. wide. (Christie's) $4,719

A George III mahogany clothes-press, the upper section with rectangular cavetto cornice above a pair of paneled doors enclosing five blue paper-lined slides, 49½in. wide. (Christie's) $4,934

A George III oak press, fitted with a paneled cupboard door, surrounded by a pair of paneled cupboard doors and two crossbanded short drawers, 70in. wide. (Christie's) $3,234

A George III mahogany clothes-press with molded cornice above a pair of oval paneled doors, the base with two short and two graduated drawers, 52½in. wide. (Christie's) $3,178

COMMODE CHESTS

The name commode was first used in France, where it served to describe diverse pieces of furniture. Some took the form of a heavy table with drawers below, while others resembled sarcophagus-shaped coffers with lids, but the most widely accepted use of the term refers to those elaborate and ornate chests of drawers destined for the drawing room.

Most early French commodes had their basic rectangularity softened by subtle curves in the rococo manner – a popular style from the accession of Louis XV in 1715. Good examples are often beautifully inlaid with birds, garlands of flowers and musical instruments besides having superb ormolu mounts and handles made by such masters as Cressent, Gouthière and Caffieris.

By the 1780's, many commodes appeared with fine decoration after the styles of Angelica Kaufmann and Pergolisi – often painted in the form of cupids set in ovals surrounded by painted flowers and scrolls. Another style, particularly favored by Adam, was that of a white ground on which were colored urns set amid wreaths and surrounded by friezes of gilt molding. Toward the end of the century, however, the commode slipped somewhat from its former importance in fashionable drawing rooms and the quality took a predictably downward turn.

Early in the 19th century, commodes lost their flamboyance altogether, returning to a rectangular form and resembling more the chiffonier.

A George III mahogany commode of serpentine form, the eared quarter-veneered top above four graduated long drawers, the top drawer fitted with a ratcheted baize-lined writing-slide, 52¹⁄₂in. wide. (Christie's) $10,435

An Italian walnut and marquetry dwarf commode, inlaid overall with geometric lines and feather-banding, mid 18th century, 21¹⁄₂in. wide. (Christie's) $2,359

A good French Vernis Martin commode, Paris, circa 1885, the molded sage green marble top with a gilt-bronze flower-head guilloche frieze above a wide door, on toupie feet, 110cm. wide. (Sotheby's) $22,550

Louis XV style gilt-bronze-mounted burled fruitwood commode, circa 1900, raised on cabriole legs with gilt-bronze mask-form espagnolettes, ending in animal paw sabots, 4ft. ¹⁄₂in. wide. (Butterfield & Butterfield) $2,750

A George III mahogany commode attributed to Thomas Chippendale, the eared concave-sided rectangular top with molded edge above two cupboard doors, 62¹⁄₄in. wide. (Christie's) $1,654,950

A Louis XV style gilt metal mounted marquetry bombé commode with mottled red marble top on splayed legs, with gilt clasps and sabots, 28in. wide. (Christie's) $2,299

COMMODE CHESTS

Régence inlaid tulipwood and gilt-bronze-mounted bombé commode, circa 1725, the angled projecting stiles applied with gilt-bronze foliate mounts continuing to conforming sabots, 4ft. 3¹/₂in. wide.
(Butterfield & Butterfield)
$20,900

A South German cherrywood, walnut and inlaid reversed breakfront commode, 18th/19th century, 47¹/₂in. wide.
(Lawrence Fine Art)
$4,250

A 19th century French ormolu mounted black lacquer and mother-o'-pearl inlaid bombé commode, in the manner of Dubois, surmounted by a molded gray breccia serpentine top, 5ft. ¹/₂in. wide.
(Phillips)
$9,540

An 18th century Dutch walnut and marquetry commode of bombé form, the serpentine front rectangular top with molded edge and rounded angles, over four shaped long graduated drawers, 112cm. wide.
(Spencer's)
$4,205

A French rosewood-veneered petite commode, circa 1910, in Louis XV/XVI Transitional manner, the pierced heart-shaped gallery with marble top, 79cm. high.
(Sotheby's)
$3,673

A French ormolu-mounted tulipwood and rosewood bombe commode, of Louis XV style, with a serpentine-shaped red marble top, above a pair of quarter-veneered drawers, late 19th century, 53³/₄in. wide.
(Christie's)
$8,567

A French mahogany ormolu-mounted mahogany and marquetry bombé commode with white-veined liver marble serpentine top, late 19th/early 20th century, 52¹/₂in. wide.
(Christie's)
$4,747

A late 18th century Milanese walnut and marquetry commode, the rectangular quarter veneered top with a pastoral scene of a figure and oxen within an oval, on square tapering legs (water damaged), 4ft. 2in. wide.
(Phillips)
$12,816

An Italian painted pine and marblised commode of canted outline, with two drawers on shallow bracket feet, 43¹/₂in. wide.
(Christie's)
$2,284

COMMODES

Commodes made an appearance in Britain as early as the 16th century, when Henry VIII possessed one. It was covered in black velvet, garnished with ribbons and fringes and studded with over 2,000 gilt nails. Seat and arms were covered in white fustian filled with down and it came complete with lock and key, which Henry kept about his person to prevent illicit use.

Britain, however, was for a long time sadly lacking in examples of the plumber's art for, by the late 16th century, it was still generally deemed sufficient to retire a mere 'bowshot away'.

Chippendale walnut commode chair, 1760, with pierced splat, above a deep scrolled skirt.
(Skinner) $1,430

An antique French Provincial carved walnut bidet in the Louis XV taste, with raised padded end with hinged compartment.
(Phillips) $1,570

A Louis XV beechwood commode chair, mid 18th century, with caned back and seat, the apron and sides carved with scrollwork; bearing the stamp *Tilliard JME*.
(Sotheby's) $897

A set of George III mahogany bed-steps with three-quarter galleried columnar top step above tambour shutter slide, the sliding middle step with hinged lid enclosing a fitted interior with later removable lid and white porcelain pot, 18in. wide.
(Christie's) $1,903

An early George III mahogany tray top commode, with a shaped three-quarter gallery and pierced carrying handles above a pair of cupboard doors and fitted pull-out commode drawer, 1ft. 9in. wide.
(Phillips) $2,314

A George III mahogany bedside commode, the sides pierced with carrying-handles, above a pull-out-section with later green leather-lined top and waved apron, 21in. wide.
(Christie's) $1,328

A George III mahogany serpentine-fronted bedside commode, the part-galleried hinged top and paneled sides above a hinged flap enclosing a well, on square legs, 22½ in. wide.
(Christie's) $2,574

A George III mahogany bedside cupboard, with waved gallery and rectangular top above a paneled door and pull-out section, on square legs, 21½in. wide.
(Christie's) $1,935

CORNER CUPBOARDS

Broadly speaking, there are three basic types of corner cupboards and, of these, the earliest was the hanging variety. This was followed, in early Georgian days, by the free standing corner cupboard or cupboard-on-stand and, later and less successfully, by the low-level standing cupboard.

The earliest examples of hanging corner cupboards to be found are usually japanned in the Oriental style.

By the mid 18th century, as architectural styling of furniture became popular, many corner cabinets sported fine pediments whose details reflected the fashionable variations of the period.

Broken-arch pediments were featured on many of the more sophisticated pieces – often in the swan-neck style with a center entablature – but hanging corner cabinets were largely neglected by the major designers at this time.

Most of the antique corner cupboards found today date from the last quarter of the eighteenth century – the period during which the greatest number were produced, and those of the best quality made.

Bow-fronted models were popular, made of mahogany, with double doors about twelve inches across.

Decoration was usually kept to a minimum, most of the good pieces relying on the figuring of the wood, but some were embellished with satinwood stringing or an inlaid conch shell motif on the door.

Broken pediments continued to be used to some extent, together with dentil cornices and pear-drop moldings.

A mid 18th century Continental kingwood and walnut serpentine corner cupboard of arc en arbelette outline enclosed by a pair of parquetry doors, 1ft. 10in., German or Scandinavian. (Phillips) $1,947

A Continental japanned corner cabinet, possibly south German, second quarter 19th century, the tiered superstructure above a double bow-fronted drawer and conforming pair of cupboards, 107cm. wide. (Sotheby's) $6,347

A Louis XV period fruitwood, purpleheart and ormolu mounted encoignure, in the style of Adrian Delorme, on shaped bracket feet, 2ft. 6¹/₂in. wide. (Phillips) $3,540

A Dutch mahogany and floral marquetry corner cupboard, the breakfront top above a pair of doors, 19th century, 24in. wide. (Christie's) $1,543

George III pine corner cupboard, last quarter 18th century, with a stepped and dentilled cornice above an arched aperture disclosing a blue painted interior, 4ft. 2¹/₂in. wide. (Butterfield & Butterfield) $3,300

A Federal red-painted corner-cupboard, Northern New England, early 19th century, the upper section bowed with molded cornice hung with spherules over a frieze , 56¹/₂in. (Christie's) $11,000

COURT CUPBOARDS

The term court cupboard first begins to appear in English inventories in late Elizabethan times and seems to have been derived from the French 'court' or short. Generally made of oak, those of this period usually consist of two or three shelves supported on square columns, and are seldom more than four feet high. They would be used for displaying silver or pewter vessels.

As the 17th century wore on, however, they tended to become much wider than their height, and by the last years of the century, a sideboard type was being introduced, the upper stage consisting of a pediment over a recessed back with doors, the lower with drawers and further cupboards under. Some walnut examples are found, and styles vary from the very plain to elaborately molded and carved.

Court cupboards of the latter type continued to be made into the early 18th century for the country yeomanry, among whom they were often given as wedding presents.

A small oak court cupboard, basically early 17th century, 27½in. wide.
(Christie's) $12,000

A walnut court cupboard, in the manner of A. W. Pugin, 147cm. wide.
(Christie's) $1,800

An early 17th century James I inlaid oak court cupboard, 49in. wide.
(Skinner Inc.) $6,675

Joined, paneled and painted oak court cupboard, probably Massachusetts, 17th century, refinished, 50in. wide.
(Skinner Inc.) $12,100

A Welsh oak tridarn of good patination, the top tier on turned supports tied by stretchers, on square section feet, 33in. wide, 17th century.
(Bonhams) $10,654

An oak court cupboard, with molded cornice above frieze dated *1690 R.H.*, late 17th century, 54in. wide.
(Christie's) $2,992

An antique oak court cupboard in the mid 18th century style, the recessed upper portion having three 'cupid's bow' paneled doors, 4ft.8in. wide.
(Russell Baldwin & Bright) $4,844

CRADLES

The earliest cradles were simply made from hollowed out sections of tree, the natural shape of the wood being ideally suited to rocking. Others were slightly grander, being made in the form of a box suspended between X supports. This method of construction allowed the cradle to be rocked while raising it clear of the damp floor.

At first they were paneled, box-like structures with turned finials at the corners and mounted on rockers. At the end of the 16th century, the end and sides at the head of the cradle were extended to offer protection against draughts.

The basic style of the 17th century cradle lasted throughout the following century, often with a curved hood, and even into the 19th century when it often bore Gothic decoration. By far the most important development, however, was the return of the swinging cot which made a brief appearance early in the 18th century before really coming into its own after Sheraton and Hepplewhite had honored it with their attentions.

A North Swedish carved cradle, the gadrooned sides painted with diamonds, the ends with polychrome fleur de lys and the date *1849*, 87cm. long. (Auktionsverket) $497

A rare heart-decorated chestnut and cherrywood child's cradle on stand, Pennsylvania, 1780–1800, on an arched base joined by a double medial transverse, length 39in. (Sotheby's) $5,750

A Venetian giltwood cradle, the canopy hung with bells, the scrolled headboard carved with foliate trails and strapwork with dished base, first half 18th century, 24in. wide. (Christie's) $6,068

An Arts and Crafts oak crib, the cylindrical barrel type rocking body supported by tall triangular rounded plank ends, 1.27m. high x 1.10m. long. (Phillips) $545

A painted Venetian cradle, in 18th century style, of gondola form, carved with scrolls and masks, 112cm. long. (Sotheby's) $2,132

A late Federal mahogany child's crib with tester, American, first half 19th century, with a serpentine tester, width 48½in. (Sotheby's) $2,990

An 18th century oak cradle with hinged canopy, baluster-turned finials and fielded panels to the sides, 33½in. long. (Bearne's) $1,639

CREDENZAS

Although these items have been classed as anything from sideboards to chiffoniers, most dealers refer to them as credenzas. The word is Italian and applies to a long, low cabinet with up to four doors, a style which first made its appearance in this form during the last quarter of the 18th century.

They are quite large but have the virtue of combining the functions of various pieces of furniture, being suitable for displaying both china and silver while providing a covered storage area for less worthy pieces.

Many are veneered in burr walnut with ormolu mounts on the pilasters and have a small amount of inlay in the center door. Another decorative style used on French credenzas made by various firms is that known as Boulle. This is the inlay of interlocking pieces of brass and tortoiseshell, introduced by Andre Charles Boulle back in the late 17th century. During the later Victorian period many were subjected to the fashion for 'ebonizing' wood, which was popular at that time.

A Victorian gilt metal mounted walnut breakfront side cabinet, the frieze and central door inlaid with fruitwood scrolls, 58in. wide.
(Peter Francis) $2,161

Victorian burl walnut credenza, late 19th century, cabinet doors enclosing three shelves, 60½in. wide.
(Skinner) $1,650

Renaissance Revival rosewood and marquetry credenza, third quarter 19th century, the shaped rectangular top above a central cabinet door enclosing three shelves, 46in. wide.
(Skinner) $2,200

A Louis XVI style ormolu and porcelain-mounted mahogany and parquetry console desserte, late 19th century, with an eared D-shaped violet and white marble top over two paneled conforming doors, flanked by two open marble shelves, on toupie feet, 61¼in. wide.
(Christie's) $25,300

A fine French mahogany side cabinet, Napoléon III, by Grohé of Paris, circa 1860, in Louis XVI manner, with a veined-marble molded top above three frieze drawers and three paneled cupboard doors, 178cm. wide.
(Sotheby's) $13,363

A mid-Victorian walnut credenza, the eared top with bowed ends, the central drawer with a mirrored circular panel, flanked by two glazed paneled doors enclosing open shelves, 72in. wide.
(Christie's) $4,376

A 'Boulle' side cabinet and mirror, probably London, circa 1855, in the French manner, the arched cresting with a mirror plate above a serpentine side-cabinet with a bowed central door, 210cm. wide.
(Sotheby's) $7,016

CUPBOARDS

Cupboards tended to become plainer as their development progressed, with hardly any ornamentation beyond the turned pediments below the frieze which, occasionally, had a wisp of foliated scroll carving.

The cupboard doors in the lower section are usually divided into an arrangement of one horizontal and two vertical panels, which is typical of 17th century furniture, and the doors on the upper section are fielded.

Totally genuine pieces should be open to the floor inside the bottom cupboard.

Early English furniture was usually made of oak, this being the tried and tested native hardwood but, by the end of the 17th century, the more refined tastes of the fashionable town dwellers demanded furniture of more exotic woods such as walnut.

The supply of walnut was met mainly from Europe but, in 1709 an extremely hard winter killed off most of the trees and the French, perturbed by the depleted state of their stocks, placed an embargo on the export of walnut in 1720.

About 1730, as a result of public pressure, the import duty on Spanish mahogany was lifted and designers were able seriously to turn their attention to exploiting the possibilities of this wood.

As trade was developing and the demand for finer detail, such as astragal glazed doors for example, importers turned their eyes towards Jamaica and the West Indies from where the fine grained Cuban mahogany was obtained and so great was the demand that in 1753 alone, over half a million cubic feet were imported.

18th century oak veneered Frankfurt cupboard, paneled doors and sides on a spreading plinth, on bun feet, 200cm. wide. (Arnold) $8,239

A poplar hanging cupboard, Ephrata, Penn., 1743-60, 18½in. wide, 24½in. high. (Christie's) $1,200

A good late 17th century north of England oak press cupboard, the frieze carved with a band of stylized flowerheads, 75in. wide. (Tennants) $9,000

Saxon burr walnut and cedar inlaid hall cupboard, the stepped breakfront pediment above two cupboard doors with drawers under, on bun feet, early 18th century, 197cm. wide. (Kunsthaus am Museum) $6,917

A 16th/17th century Spanish walnut cupboard with two pairs of paneled doors, 37½in. wide. (Christie's) $4,500

A rare Federal grain painted step-back cupboard, Vermont, early 19th century, the entire surface painted olive with brown sponge painted grain decoration, 63½in. wide. (Christie's New York) $44,000

CUPBOARDS

An oak and walnut food
cupboard fitted with a pierced
and carved rectangular paneled
cupboard door, 17th century,
36in. wide.
(Christie's) $3,267

An early 17th century oak
food cupboard on turned
legs and platform stretcher,
50¼in. wide.
(Christie's) $6,000

19th century Chinese apothecary's cupboard, with
numerous drawers, 81cm. wide.
(Auktionshaus Arnold)
                  $1,800

A Charles II walnut, elm and
ash hanging-cupboard, the
rectangular top with later
molded cornice and bolection-
molding frieze above a pierced
door, 33in. wide.
(Christie's) $7,160

One of a pair of Regency plum-
pudding mahogany cupboards,
with gothic arcaded molding,
the interior with arched
molding and single shelf, on
reeded bun feet, 17½in. wide.
(Christie's)(Two) $14,520

An 18th century Chippendale
pine step-back cupboard in
two sections, Penn., 73½in.
wide.
(Christie's) $13,200

An oak aumbry, the front with
two doors pierced with roundels,
flanked by pierced panels,
44¾in. wide, part 16th/17th
century.
(Bearne's) $4,619

South German walnut two-door
cupboard with elaborate
fruitwood inlay, on turnip feet,
early 17th century, 168cm. wide.
(Kunsthaus am Museum)
                $2,767

A 17th century Flemish rosewood,
oak, ebonized and tortoiseshell
cupboard, 64½in. wide.
(Christie's) $4,500

CUPBOARDS

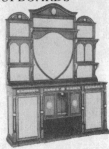

An antique French ebonized fruitwood buffet inlaid with amboyna wood and kingwood, with gilt bronze mounts and Sèvres pattern Paris porcelain plaques, 19th century.
(Selkirk's) $3,600

Louis XV Provincial fruitwood buffet with shaped paneled doors with ebonized outline, raised on simple shaped feet, 4ft. 7in. wide.
(Butterfield & Butterfield)
                               $2,750

An 18th century oak cupboard, with a molded cornice above a pair of fielded arched panel doors, the lower part with fielded panels and two drawers below, 4ft. 2in. wide.
(Phillips) $1,440

German walnut and burr walnut cupboard, the rounded rectangular pediment above two paneled doors over shaped apron, on cabriole legs, 88cm. wide.
(Kunsthaus am Museum)
                               $2,214

Scandinavian Baroque style cupboard with two ornately carved doors flanked by carved columns, two drawers under, on bun feet, Lysberg & Hansen, 228cm. wide.
(Herholdt Jensen) $3,005

Fine Elizabethan Revival oak two-part cupboard, upper section with two carved paneled doors flanked by supporting columns, on bun feet, probably early 20th century, 43in. wide.
(Eldred's) $1,540

Painted cupboard, probably Georgia, mid 19th century, opens to a two-shelved interior, all over original red paint and pulls, 59¹/₂in. wide.
(Skinner Inc.) $4,950

A mid 18th century Cardiganshire oak cupboard with dentil cornice above three drawers, having a pair of doors beneath, 58in. wide.
(Peter Francis) $3,427

Pine slant back cupboard, New England, 18th century, four thumb molded shelves, old stain and varnish, 75in. high.
(Skinner Inc.) $6,000

DAVENPORTS

This is a very delightful little desk which originated during the final years of the 18th century.

Primarily a lady's desk, it is one of those rare pieces in which the virtues of practicality and elegance are beautifully combined to produce a comfortable yet compact piece of functional furniture.

Earlier davenports were usually made of rosewood or satinwood and were boxlike in structure apart from the sloping top, which would either pull forward or swivel to the side in order to make room for the writer's lower limbs.

While most examples are about two feet wide, it is well worth looking for the smaller ones, (about 15 inches to 18 inches wide), for these can fetch twice as much as larger models even though they usually have only a cupboard at the side instead of drawers.

It was during the William IV period that the davenport gained its name and its popularity.

The story goes that one Captain Davenport placed an order for one of these writing desks with Gillows of Lancaster, a well-known firm of cabinet makers at the time. Known during its manufacture as 'the Davenport order', the first desk was completed and the name stuck, being applied to all subsequent orders for a desk of this particular style.

Davenports were, at the middle of the 19th century, at the height of their popularity and at peak quality for, although they remained in vogue to a certain extent for the remainder of the century, the standard of workmanship employed in their construction declined steadily.

A late Victorian ebonized **davenport banded in burr walnut, 22in. wide. (Dreweatt Neate)** **$1,521**

A Regency brass-inlaid mahogany patent davenport printing-desk, inlaid overall with fleurs-de-lys and lozenges, in two sections, 23½in. wide. (Christie's) **$12,938**

An Irish Killarney arbutus davenport inlaid with scenes of ruins, Irish motifs and foliage, on dark stained foliate carved mahogany supports and inverted plinth base, 32¼in. wide. (Christie's) **$4,748**

A George IV rosewood davenport inlaid overall with boxwood lines, with rectangular top above a green leather-lined hinged slope, enclosing a mahogany-lined interior, 18in. wide. (Christie's) **$2,638**

A late Victorian walnut and ebonized davenport, the top with three quarter gallery above a hinged leather lined slope, supported by scrolling corbels, 28½in. wide. (Bonhams) **$1,788**

A Victorian burr walnut-veneered davenport, the rising stationery compartment with fret-carved front and hinged top, the projecting piano front enclosing an adjustable writing slide, 22½in. wide. (Bearne's) **$3,618**

DAVENPORTS

A walnut davenport, Victorian, circa 1860, in well figured wood, the hinged top with pull-out writing drawer, 58.5cm. wide.
(Sotheby's) $3,343

A George IV ormolu-mounted bird's eye maple and amaranth davenport, the sides with candle-slides and a hinged secret drawer, on plinth base, 18$\frac{1}{2}$in. wide.
(Christie's) $5,947

A late Victorian bamboo and black-lacquer davenport decorated with birds amongst foliage, on splayed feet, 23$\frac{1}{2}$in. wide.
(Christie's S. Ken.) $1,089

A late Victorian brass-mounted ebonized and burr-walnut davenport, the three-quarter gallery above a pair of paneled doors, with oval jasper panels depicting classical figures, 22$\frac{1}{2}$in. wide.
(Christie's) $1,507

An Anglo-Indian Vizigatapam ivory, sandalwood and tortoiseshell davenport engraved overall with scrolling foliage, Indian figures, deities and beasts, 18in. wide.
(Christie's) $21,450

A Victorian walnut davenport, the molded rectangular top fitted with a sliding counter-weighted stationery compartment, on foliate-carved cabriole supports and bar feet, 24in. wide.
(Christie's) $3,546

A Regency rosewood davenport, the sliding top with tooled leather inset to the sloping flap and a hinged pen and ink side drawer, 19in. wide.
(Bearne's) $3,384

A William IV carved mahogany davenport of small size, the ratcheted top with inset tooled leather surface and gadrooned edge, 1ft. 8in. wide.
(Phillips) $3,828

A laburnum davenport with leather-lined slope and fitted interior above a pen drawer and four drawers, 19th century, 21in. wide.
(Christie's S. Ken) $1,070

DISPLAY CABINETS

In the early 18th century, Oriental porcelain and Delftware became extremely popular and a need arose for suitably fine cabinets with glazed upper sections in which to display it to its full advantage.

Early styles had straight cornices and doors glazed in half round moldings, the whole supported on turned legs with stretchers. As taste developed, however, heavy architectural styles in the manner of William Kent became popular, often displaying dentil cornices, and broken-arch pediments, with fielded paneled doors below the glazed section.

It was not long before the heavy, architecturally styled cabinets were recognised as being inappropriate for the display of delicate china and porcelain. They were quickly relegated to the libraries of the nation for the storage of books, their places being taken in fashionable drawing rooms by far more graceful display cabinets.

Never slow to turn an imported fashion to their advantage, designers such as Chippendale helped to perpetuate the taste for things Oriental by producing fine Chinese-influenced styles incorporating some incredibly delicate fretwork.

Dutch marquetry was another popular decorative style consisting of naturalistic birds and flowers executed in shaped reserves. Shading of the leaves and flowers was, during the first half of the 18th century, achieved by dipping the veneered shapes part way into hot sand but this later gave way to a method of engraving the shading on to the actual surface.

Oak Art Nouveau design display cabinet with two leaded glazed doors with inlaid decoration on shaped supports, 47½in. wide. (Bigwood) $1,365

A French kingwood vitrine, Paris, circa 1900, in Transitional manner, with three shaped glazed doors and side, 175cm. wide. (Sotheby's) $19,239

A Louis XVI style ormolu-mounted tulipwood vitrine, late 19th century, with a stepped rectangular top with three violet and white marble tops above a rectangular case fitted centrally with a door inset, on toupie feet, 52½in. wide. (Christie's) $12,650

A Dutch rosewood and floral marquetry display cabinet of canted outline, the arched upper section with a molded cornice above a pair of glazed doors flanked by glazed panels, on bun feet, late 18th/early 19th century, 59½in. wide. (Christie's S. Ken) $12,191

A Louis XV style ormolu-mounted tulipwood vitrine, with a serpentine molded brown and white marble top above a conforming case fitted with two glazed paneled doors, on bracket feet, 62½in. wide. (Christie's) $7,475

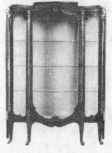

A good French gilt-bronze-mounted vitrine, Paris, circa 1900, of serpentine form, veneered in kingwood with shaped top, central door and six cabriole legs, 148cm. wide. (Sotheby's) $13,642

DISPLAY CABINETS

A good French rosewood and amboyna breakfront secrétaire display cabinet, Napoléon III, by Grohé of Paris, circa 1860, 120cm. wide.
(Sotheby's) $5,247

A Glasgow style mahogany display cabinet, the rectangular top with mirror back above a pair of stained and leaded glass doors, 69in. high.
(Christie's) $1,969

A Dutch walnut and marquetry bombé display cabinet with overall checkered and floral inlay, the arched cresting above a pair of astragal glazed doors, 19th century, 72¹/₂in. wide.
(Christie's) $21,021

A good French mahogany display cabinet, by Lexcellent of Paris, circa 1880, the cresting with a ribbon-tied drape above glazed doors and sides, 114cm. wide.
(Sotheby's) $14,600

A late Victorian gilt-metal-mounted, walnut and floral-marquetry dwarf display cabinet, with overall rosewood banding, the rectangular top above a pair of arched glazed doors, 44¹/₂in. wide.
(Christie's) $1,689

A George IV ormolu-mounted amboyna and marquetry display-cabinet, the pierced foliate-galleried top above a pair of glazed doors, the frieze above a further pair of green pleated silk-lined doors, 36¹/₄in. wide.
(Christie's) $30,429

A large French mahogany vitrine, Paris, circa 1890, the arched cresting flanked by winged acanthus capitals above a pair of shaped bevel-glazed doors.
(Sotheby's) $6,682

A good rosewood and kingwood-veneered side cabinet, circa 1850, the arched mirror back with a glazed door, flanked by open shelves with gilt-bronze mounts throughout, 4ft. 2³/₄in. wide.
(Sotheby's) $4,603

An unusual Continental painted display cabinet, probably German, circa 1880, of architectural form imitating the English Adam manner, 100cm. wide.
(Sotheby's) $4,722

DRESSERS

The name 'dresser' could possibly derive from the fact that its sole original function was to provide a surface on which the food could be dressed before serving, completion of this stage of culinary activity being signaled to ravenous diners by the beating of a drum.

In order to simplify their work and cut costs, cabinet makers of the late 17th century often neglected to produce elaborately turned legs for their products, making do with wavy shapes cut from flat boards instead.

It has been recorded that a few mediaeval cupboard-type dressers had a form of shelving above them but it was not until the beginning of the 18th century that the idea really caught on and became a fully developed, everyday reality.

Another popular innovation in the early 18th century was the inclusion of a row of small spice drawers set in front of the backboard along the top.

Most early dressers with shelves had no backboards to them, these often being added later in the century.

One of the reasons for shelves – apart from the obvious one that people were using more cooking utensils than hitherto – was to display the English Delftware which served most families as a substitute for the expensive Chinese porcelain displayed in the homes of people of wealth.

By the mid 18th century dressers had been ousted from fashionable dining rooms by large side tables or sideboards made of mahogany, the faithful old dressers being relegated to the kitchens.

A George III oak and mahogany inlaid dresser with later plate-rack, the molded cornice above three open shelves, 66¹/₂in. wide.
(Christie's) $3,085

A George III pine dresser, the molded cornice above a two shelf plate rack, the lower section with three frieze drawers above a pair of fielded arched panel cupboard doors, 54in. wide.
(Bonhams) $3,099

An oak dresser, with associated, boarded plate rack, above three frieze drawers and open shelf below, early 19th century, 76in. wide.
(Christie's) $3,198

A George III oak dresser, the associated top and shelves above three drawers, about 5ft. 6in. wide.
(Riddetts) $2,243

Grain painted pine open cupboard, New England, circa 1820, retains original simulated burnt sienna mahogany and mustard graining, 61in. wide.
(Skinner) $3,850

Chippendale walnut step back cupboard, possibly Pennsylvania, late 18th/early 19th century, in two parts, the upper section with molded cornice above two glazed doors, 6ft. 8in. wide.
(Butterfield & Butterfield) $4,675

A mid-Georgian oak dresser banded overall in mahogany, the rounded rectangular top with re-entrant corners, on ogee-bracket feet, 79¹/₂in. wide. (Christie's) $5,276

A rare late Georgian Welsh oak corner dresser, in four sections, the superstructure with molded cornices, length 64in. and 58in., height 78in. (Peter Francis) $5,665

A George II oak dresser with molded rectangular top above three drawers and two paneled doors, on stile feet, on foot repaired, 53¹/₂in. wide. (Christie's) $9,009

An oak dresser designed by Sidney Barnsley, the shaped superstructure with open grid-work back, supporting two open shelves, on shaped bracket feet, 140.8cm. wide. (Christie's) $17,226

An 18th century oak Welsh dresser, the delft rack with shallow swept and stepped molded cornice, over a deep scalloped frieze, 6ft. 8in. wide. (Spencer's) $8,395

A Georgian oak dresser, the plate rack with molded cornice and arcaded frieze above two shelves fitted with iron hooks, 57in. wide. (Christie's) $6,000

A George III oak dresser, the raised plate rack with molded cornice above three open shelves, three frieze drawers and three central dummy drawers flanked by two cupboard doors, 67in. wide. (Christie's) $3,739

A Heal & Son black stained elm dresser, designed by Sir Ambrose Heal, the rectangular superstructure with two cupboard doors enclosing three shelves, circa 1914, 123.3cm. wide. (Christie's) $2,954

A mid-Georgian oak dresser, with molded cornice above two shelves, the lower section with three drawers above two fielded arched paneled doors, 62³/₄in. wide. (Christie's) $3,365

HIGHBOYS

This is a uniquely American design, consisting of a tall chest of drawers mounted on a stand, or lowboy. The chest is often topped by a broken arch pediment with finials. They are often found in Cuban mahogany or walnut, or lacquered or veneered. The lowboy usually has cabriole legs. Tallboys were made in three styles, William & Mary, Queen Anne, and Chippendale.

Queen Anne tiger maple high chest, Stonington, Connecticut area, 1760–1800, 37½in. wide. (Skinner) **$35,200**

Queen Anne maple highboy, New England, mid 18th century, 36in. wide. (Skinner) **$7,700**

Queen Anne tiger maple bonnet top highboy, probably Connecticut, circa 1740–1760, in two parts, the upper section with molded swan's neck cornice flanked by three baluster-turned finials, width 40in. (Butterfield & Butterfield) **$16,100**

Queen Anne walnut and maple flat top highboy, New England, 1740–1760, the upper section with a molded cornice above two short and three long thumb-molded edge drawers, on cabriole legs ending in pad feet, width 38¼in. (Butterfield & Butterfield) **$8,625**

Provincial George I oak and walnut highboy, first half 18th century, the flat rectangular cornice above two short and three full cock beaded and molded drawers, upon a conforming base, 39in. wide. (William Doyle Galleries) **$3,335**

A Queen Anne walnut high chest of drawers, Massachusetts, 1740-1760, on cabriole legs with pad feet, the rear legs of maple, 41½in. wide. (Christie's) **$10,000**

A Queen Anne curly maple bonnet top highboy, New England, circa 1770, 36¾in. wide. (Robt. W. Skinner Inc.) **$3,750**

Queen Anne carved cherrywood flat top highboy, Connecticut, circa 1750, the upper section with dentil molded cornice above three thumb-molded edge short drawers centering a stylized shell, width 40in. (Butterfield & Butterfield) **$5,175**

KNEEHOLE DESKS

Kneehole desks were originally designed for use as dressing tables and are, basically, chests of drawers with recesses cut to accommodate the knees of persons seated before the mirror which stood on top.

It soon became apparent, however, that they made ideal writing tables and they stayed as dual purpose pieces of furniture until the latter half of the 18th century.

A particularly fine example comes from the William and Mary period and is made of walnut with ebony arabesque marquetry panels. These are inlays of floral and geometric scrolls, usually found within a simple, rectangular frame. This desk rests upon small bun feet typical of the period and has a recessed cupboard with a small drawer in the apron above.

Although the kneehole desk with a center cupboard was still popular in the mid 18th century, the style developed somewhat to incorporate two pedestals, each having three or four drawers, surmounted by a flat table top which itself contained two or three drawers.

At first these were made as single units, often double sided to stand in the center of a room, and soon became extremely popular in libraries. They were, however, rather large and cumbersome in this form and later models were made in three sections to facilitate removal and installation.

Pedestal desks date from about 1750 until the end of the 19th century and the difficulty in pricing them stems from the fact that the style changed hardly at all during that time.

A mid-Victorian burr-walnut kidney-shaped desk with inset gilt-tooled tan leather writing-surface above a central kneehole with paneled back flanked by two tiers of four graduated drawers, 48in. wide.
(Christie's) **$10,143**

A gilt-metal-mounted ebonized, brass-inlaid and simulated tortoiseshell bureau mazarin, the rectangular top above three central kneehole drawers flanked by three further drawers, 53in. wide.
(Christie's) **$3,197**

An early Victorian mahogany cylinder bureau, with rectangular top above sliding fall enclosing fitted interior, three frieze drawers above a cupboard door with three dummy drawer fronts, 42in. wide.
(Christie's) **$1,767**

A George I chestnut and walnut kneehole desk inlaid overall with boxwood lines, with frieze drawer and six short graduated drawers around a central kneehole, on ogee shaped bracket feet, 30^1/$_2$in. wide.
(Christie's) **$5,071**

A George I burr-walnut and walnut kneehole desk, the rectangular quarter-veneered top inlaid with feather-banding above a baize-lined slide, on shaped bracket feet, 30in. wide.
(Chrisite's) **$12,851**

A Regency mahogany roll top desk, inlaid stringing, the front with three drawers to the frieze and three drawers to each pedestal, 4ft. 1in.
(Woolley & Wallis) **$7,566**

A walnut-veneered pedestal desk inlaid with panels of seaweed marquetry, the top with tooled leather insert, 51¹/₂in. wide.
(Bearne's) $2,150

A late Victorian Chippendale Revival carved mahogany kidney-shaped knee-hole desk, the leather-lined top above three frieze drawers, on C-scroll carved bracket feet, 51in. wide.
(Christie's) $6,815

An early Victorian walnut pedestal desk with rectangular green leather-lined top and shaped arched kneehole flanked on each side by four drawers, 48in. wide.
(Christie's) $7,607

A Queen Anne figured walnut bureau in two parts, the lower section with central kneehole below two drawers and flanked to each side by three drawers, on later bun feet, 40³/₄in. wide.
(Christie's) $9,424

A Regency style painted and simulated rosewood and gilt-decorated kneehole writing table, the eared rectangular top above a bank of five drawers, 35in. wide.
(Christie's) $1,180

A mid-Victorian brass-mounted burr-walnut kidney-shaped desk with pierced interlaced gothic gallery and green leather-lined writing-surface within a tulipwood, boxwood and ebonized border, 48¹/₂in. wide.
(Christie's) $17,135

A late George II mahogany kneehole desk, the rectangular molded top above a frieze drawer and ogee arched apron drawer, on ogee bracket feet, 3ft. wide.
(Phillips) $5,303

An early Victorian burr walnut writing-desk, the molded rounded rectangular top with leather-lined reading slope with ledge, the frieze with single drawer, 41¹/₂in. wide.
(Christie's) $19,305

A George III mahogany kneehole desk, the rectangular top above a later slide and a frieze drawer, with seven other drawers around a recessed cupboard, 31in. wide.
(Christie's) $2,281

LINEN PRESSES

These are similar in form to clothes presses, except that the doors conceal a further arrangement of drawers, rather than hanging space. These drawers are always low-fronted, so that the contents can readily be seen before they are pulled out.

Its changes in style at various times were largely to accommodate the changing fashions in the clothes it was designed to contain.

A 19th century Dutch marquetry press or cupboard on chest, decorated with scrolling foliage and oval panels centered with birds, urns and floral bouquets, on bracket feet, 4ft. wide. (Phillips) **$6,052**

A George III mahogany linen press, the molded cornice above a pair of oval paneled doors, on bracket feet, the cornice associated, 55in. wide. (Christie's) **$1,683**

A Chippendale figured maple linen-press, Pennsylvania, 1760–1780, the upper section with elaborately molded cornice above two arched paneled cupboard doors fitted with three shelves, on bracket feet, 48in. wide. (Christie's) **$14,300**

A Chippendale mahogany and mahogany veneer linen press, circa 1780, 48in. wide. (Robt. W. Skinner Inc.) **$16,000**

A George III mahogany linen press with molded and dentil cornice, two paneled doors over two short and two long drawers, 50in. wide. (Andrew Hartley) **$2,442**

A North European polychrome-decorated linen-press, decorated overall with foliate arabesques upon an ebonized ground, 18th century, 58¼in. wide. (Christie's) **$8,568**

A Regency mahogany linen press with molded cornice above a pair of oval inlaid doors with two short and two long drawers below, on outswept bracket feet, 51½in. wide. (Christie's) **$2,726**

A Federal mahogany linen press, New York, circa 1820, the removable projecting cornice above a pair of hinged paneled doors, 54in. wide. (Sotheby's) **$4,400**

LOWBOYS

Although many more sophisticated dressing tables were constructed during the 18th century, the lowboy remains extremely popular – probably a sign of its great versatility as a piece of furniture.

The normal construction was an arrangement of three drawers disposed around a kneehole, though some examples have an additional pair of drawers, or one long, single drawer, set immediately below the top.

The most expensive examples are those made of mahogany or walnut, with bold cabriole legs, often enhanced with shells on the knees, but their country cousins of elm or oak are much more reasonably priced. The latter usually have straight, square legs chamfered on their inside edges or rounded legs with pad feet.

The lowboy was often set against the wall below one of the new Vauxhall plate glass mirrors, which were about eighteen inches high and set in plain molded frames.

An early Georgian walnut and oak side table, with two drawers flanking a kneehole drawer, on cabriole legs and pad feet, 32in. wide.
(Christie's) $10,725

A walnut veneered lowboy, the top with herringbone banding and cross banding, on cabriole legs to club feet, 31in.
(Woolley & Wallis) $1,275

English lowboy or dressing table, circa 1740, walnut with crossband and string inlay, one long drawer over two small drawers with flanking chamfered and fluted corners, on cabriole legs, 30in. wide.
(Eldred's) $2,200

A Queen Anne burr walnut and fruitwood lowboy, the rectangular quarter veneered top with cusped corners above a long drawer and two short drawers flanking a false drawer in the shaped apron, 2ft. 6in. wide.
(Phillips) $5,664

A very fine Chippendale carved mahogany lowboy, Philadelphia, circa 1770, the shaped skirt continuing to shell-carved cabriole legs ending in claw-and-ball feet, 36⅞in. wide.
(Sotheby's) $104,500

A walnut and feather-banded lowboy with rectangular molded top and three drawers about an arched pendant apron, on cabriole legs with pad feet, early 18th century, 30in. wide.
(Christie's) $1,752

A fine Chippendale mahogany lowboy, Pennsylvania or New Jersey, circa 1765, the shaped skirt continuing to cabriole legs, 34¼in. wide.
(Sotheby's) $27,500

POT CUPBOARDS

Pot cupboards are exactly what they say they are, bedside cupboards for holding a chamber pot. It was thus that they were known in the 18th century, before the prissier Victorians coined the more decorous term, 'night table'. There is usually a solid or tambour door to the front and sometimes a sliding cabinet below with a close stool. The top is sometimes of marble with a galleried top. By and large, however, they are smaller and plainer than their relative, the commode.

Pair of Venetian rococo painted bedside cabinets, mid 18th century, 18¹/₂in. wide.
(Skinner) $9,900

Mid 19th century mahogany cylinder cabinet of fluted outline with inset marble top on plinth base.
(Lots Road Galleries)
                                    $557

A pair of George III mahogany bedside cupboards, inlaid overall with boxwood and ebonized lines, on square tapering legs, 15in. wide.
(Christie's) $10,557

One of a pair of late Victorian inlaid walnut bedside cupboards, in the style of Christopher Pratt & Sons, each with rectangular top and frieze drawer above a paneled door, 16in. wide.
(Christie's) $2,020

A pair of 19th century walnut veneered Lombard bedside tables, with colored fruitwood inlay of female heads within ornate palm leaf borders, 88cm. wide.
(Finarte) $3,914

One of a pair of mahogany cylindrical bedside step commodes each on a fluted support fitted with a single drawer, 16in., 19th century.
(Christie's) $800

A pair of Regency ebonized and ebony-inlaid oak and brown oak bedside cupboards, attributed to George Bullock, on turned tapering legs headed by roundels, 19¹/₄in. wide.
(Christie's) $14,565

A George III mahogany bedside cupboard attributed to Thomas Chippendale, on tapering legs headed by roundel bosses, 29in. high.
(Christie's) $58,410

SCREENS

Screens have been in widespread use since at least the fifteenth century, for warding off draughts, for protecting sensitive complexions from the fire's heat or for privacy.

Not surprisingly, perhaps, the quality of screens manufacture has varied but little from those early days, and the materials used are still very much the same too; from simple buckram, wickerwork, wood and needlework to extravagant finishes for royalty, including gold lace and silk. During the reign of Charles II, some fine examples, having up to twelve folds, and decorated with superb lacquer work, were imported from the East. Today, of course, one of these would cost many thousands of dollars.

By the William and Mary period, small screens fitted with sliding panels of polished wood or embroidery had become popular and these developed into the cheval screens of the 18th century. Small pole screens also put in an appearance at this time.

A pair of George III mahogany cheval fire-screens, each with a Regency silk-embroidered sliding panel, one depicting Minerva, 46in. high
(Christie's) $5,483

A Japanese carved wood and Shibayama two-fold screen, the gold lacquered panels inlaid in mother-of-pearl and hardstone with peacocks and flowering shrubs, 11¹/₂in. high.
(Bearne's) $2,118

Charles X paper four-panel floorscreen, second quarter 19th century, grisaille decoration, 84in. high.
(Skinner Inc.) $1,320

An Arts and Crafts mahogany-framed four-fold draught-screen, decorated and gilt with pomegranates and meandering foliage, 75in. high.
(Christie's) $1,083

A four-fold transfer printed screen, designed by Piero Fornasetti, one side polychrome decorated with birds in an ornate aviary, 136.6cm. high.
(Christie's) $11,484

A pair of Regency rosewood firescreens, each with circular adjustable banner, above spiral-turned foliate-carved column on trefoil platform base with scroll feet, approximately 52in. high.
(Christie's) $1,599

A four-fold screen, designed by Piero Fornasetti, one side depicting a collector's bookshelves, the other showing guitars, each panel 130cm. high x 35cm. wide.
(Christie's) $5,300

197

SCREENS

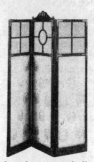

Louis XVI style giltwood four-panel floor screen, panels painted with neoclassical motifs, 68¹/₂in. high.
(Skinner Inc.) **$1,650**

A Louis XVI five leaf screen, of green lacquered wood, painted with musical trophies on a yellow ground, each leaf 49cm. wide.
(Finarte) **$9,252**

A French mahogany and gilt-metal-mounted three-fold screen, each panel with beveled astragal glazed upper section, 19¹/₂in. wide.
(Christie's) **$1,669**

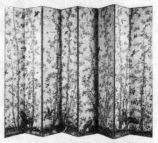

A Chinese coromandel lacquer six-leaf screen, decorated overall with cranes, mandarins, ducks and other birds, late 18th/early 19th century, each leaf 67¹/₄ x 16in.
(Christie's) **$2,760**

A Regency tapestry panel, now set into a giltwood firescreen of Louis XVI style, depicting de la Fontaine's 'Fable of the fox and the stork' in a classical surround, tapestry panel early 18th century, 43¹/₂in. high.
(Christie's) **$3,072**

A painted eight-leaf 18th century screen decorated with Chinese wallpaper panels painted with exotic birds and butterflies among bamboo shoots, flowering shrubs and rockwork, each leaf 105 x 20in.
(Christie's) **$4,948**

A George II mahogany and needlework cheval fire-screen with a petit point needlework scene depicting The Rape of Proserpine in a chariot, 32in. wide.
(Christie's) **$107,085**

A French painted canvas screen in Louis XV style, the four arched leaves painted with chinoiserie scenes in the style of Pillement on a stone-colored ground, 161cm. high.
(Sotheby's) **$4,485**

An early Victorian walnut firescreen, the central glazed section with a display of exotic stuffed birds, 46in. high.
(Bearne's) **$825**

SECRETAIRE BOOKCASES

Not unnaturally, secrétaire bookcases were developed at about the same time as bureau bookcases and were dictated by the same fashionable taste.

A useful, though not absolutely reliable guide to dating a piece is to look closely at the interior fitting of the secretaire drawer; generally speaking, the better the quality the earlier the date. It is often disappointing to find that, among the late 19th century reproductions of earlier furniture, the rule was, 'what the eye doesn't see, the heart doesn't grieve over' – finely finished exterior surfaces concealing a considerable amount of scrimping on the small drawers and pigeon holes in the fitted compartments of secrétaires and bureaux.

Attention should also be centered on the oak lined drawers as a guide to date of manufacture, for it was in about 1770 that a constructional change occurred.

Until this time, the drawer bottoms were made with the grain of the wood running front to back but, from this time onward, the grain will be found to run from side to side, the bottom often being made of two separate pieces of wood supported by a central bearer.

It still has the basic shape of an 18th century piece but the classical pediment with its scroll ends is typical of the Regency period as is the delicate carving on the curved pilasters.

Pieces of this kind are made of mahogany or rosewood, the latter being the most expensive, and they always present an attractive and well finished appearance.

Federal mahogany veneered glazed secretary, New England, 1830's, interior with four open compartments above small drawers, 37½in. wide.
(Skinner Inc.) $2,200

An Edwardian inlaid mahogany breakfront secrétaire library bookcase with overall satinwood bands and boxwood and ebony lines with molded cornice above four astragal glazed doors, 80½in. wide.
(Christie's) $4,868

Late Georgee III satinwood bureau bookcase, first quarter 19th century, upper case with a pair of glazed doors, on bracket feet, (restorations), 66in. high.
(Skinner Inc.) $4,500

An American 'Aesthetic Movement' parcel-ebonized walnut and marquetry secretary bookcase, third quarter 19th century, by Herter Brothers, with a reeded rectangular top above a fall-front door, 57½in. wide.
(Christie's) $18,400

A fine Louis XVI style ormolu-mounted amboyna and mahogany secretaire, twice stamped *Henri Dasson*, with an eared rectangular ocher and violet marble top, bearing the date 1881, 34in. wide.
(Christie's East) $8,800

A Regency mahogany secretaire bookcase, with molded cornice above open shelves flanked by spiral-reeded uprights, 69in. wide. (Christie's S. Ken)
$2,904

SECRETAIRE BOOKCASES

Regency mahogany secretary-bookcase, circa 1825, 46in. wide. (Skinner Inc.) **$3,300**

A Regency mahogany secrétaire bookcase, the arched pediment centered by a figure of a music-making goddess, 42¹/₂in. wide. (Christie's) **$7,038**

Regency mahogany secretary/bookcase, early 18th century, 42in. wide. (Skinner) **$2,200**

A fine and rare Classical secretaire bookcase, New York, 1822-1838, the double glazed cupboard doors with gothic pattern mahogany and gilt-wood muntins, 58in. wide. (Christie's New York) **$42,000**

A mahogany breakfront secrétaire library bookcase, with Greek-key molded cornice and four glazed doors, above central hinged fall enclosing fitted interior, part 18th century, 91in. wide. (Christie's) **$14,603**

A Regency mahogany secrétaire-bookcase with two geometrically-glazed doors, the molded base-section with a central oval-paneled secrétaire drawer enclosing a fitted interior above a pair of further paneled doors, 49¹/₄in. wide. (Christie's) **$16,059**

A late George III mahogany secrétaire bookcase, with molded cornice above a pair of astragal glazed doors above a dummy twinned drawer fall front, 44in. wide. (Christie's) **$2,710**

A George III brass-inlaid mahogany breakfront secretaire-bookcase, with four glazed doors filled with gothic arcading bars and lined with pleated green silk, 100in. wide. (Christie's) **$15,488**

A late George III mahogany secrétaire bookcase, the broken scrolled pediment above a molded and dentiled cornice fitted with a pair of geometrically glazed doors, 106in. high. (Christie's) **$6,730**

SECRETAIRES

The name escritoire (or, scritoire as it was originally) was applied to the piece of furniture produced towards the end of the 17th century in answer to the demand for a cabinet with a falling front; prior to this time, all larger pieces had been equipped with double doors.

Although this design has been used ever since with only minor variations, it has never achieved the overwhelming popularity attained by some of the other writing cabinets and desks. The upper level, revealed by dropping the front, contains a multitude of drawers with pigeon holes above.

A secrétaire chest is, basically, a chest of drawers whose deep fitted top drawer has a fall front which pulls forward to allow a sizeable writing area with room below for the knees.

Having been made from the last quarter of the 18th century until the present day, they are to be found in an extremely wide range of styles, qualities and prices.

When buying such a chest it is wise to bear in mind the similarity between it and a chest of drawers – you might well be buying an old chest of drawers which has undergone a modern conversion.

Look carefully at the sides of the secrétaire and the depth of the top drawer; the sides need to be thicker and stronger for a secrétaire than an ordinary drawer, therefore a conversion will show if the sides appear to be of newer wood than those of the other drawers. The depth of the top drawer should be the largest in the chest and marks will show on the side of the carcass if the supports have been altered to achieve this.

A Beidermeier walnut secrétaire chest, with rectangular molded top and fall front drawer below with galleried sides, central European, 52in. wide.
(Christie's) $1,485

A George III mahogany secrétaire chest, the rectangular top above twin-drawer dummy fall enclosing leather-lined fitted interior above three long graduated drawers on bracket feet, 35in. wide.
(Christie's) $2,889

A Victorian mahogany secretaire campaign chest, the central drawer fitted with four bird's-eye maple-veneered drawers and pull-out writing slide, 39in. wide.
(Bearne's) $2,236

A Biedermeier figured mahogany secretaire chest, circa 1820, the top with molded edge concealing secret compartments above a drop-front drawer, 38¼in. wide.
(Tennants) $1,581

American butler's secretary, circa 1830–1840, walnut, upper drawer with paneled front pulling down to reveal a fitted interior, 39½in. wide.
(Eldred's) $358

A George I walnut secrétaire-chest inlaid overall with fruitwood and ebonized lines, the rectangular quarter-veneered top above a fitted secrétaire-drawer, 31in. wide.
(Christie's) $5,279

SECRETAIRES

An early 18th century burr walnut secrétaire à abattant, the fall quarter veneered and checker banded, 107cm. wide.
(Tennants) $21,750

A Regency rosewood secrétaire breakfront cabinet, the top crossbanded with tulipwood and kingwood, the frieze with a fall front secrétaire drawer, 4ft. 6in. wide.
(Phillips) $4,602

An Empire ormolu-mounted bois satiné secrétaire à abattant, early 19th century, possibly Austrian, 38½in. wide.
(Christie's) $31,050

Biedermeier mahogany and part ebonized fall-front secretary, probably German, second quarter 19th century, on shallow block feet, 46in. wide.
(Butterfield & Butterfield) $3,025

An early 19th century German walnut escritoire à abattant, the rectangular top with a molded frieze drawer above a hinged flap enclosing a carved fitted interior, on shortened carved feet, 3ft. 10in. wide.
(Phillips) $2,700

A George III mahogany secrétaire-chest, the rectangular galleried top above a secrétaire drawer, enclosing a green leather writing-surface, on later bracket feet, 29¼in. wide.
(Christie's) $2,521

George I inlaid walnut oyster-veneered drop-front secretary on stand, circa 1720–1725, the oyster-veneered cabinet enclosed by a drop-front inlaid in fruitwood, the stand fitted with two drawers, width 39in.
(Butterfield & Butterfield) $8,050

A Federal mahogany butler's-desk, New York, early 19th century, fitted with a pair of cockbeaded short drawers above a crossbanded secretary drawer, on turned tapering reeded legs and brass ball feet, 51½in. wide.
(Christie's) $3,850

A Dutch mahogany and marquetry secrétaire à abattant, with eared rectangular top above frieze drawer and hinged fall enclosing fitted interior, on baluster-turned legs, early 19th century, 37in. wide.
(Christie's) $4,478

SETTEES & COUCHES

Settle, settee, sofa, chaise longue or daybed – they are all basically alike yet each has its exclusive character and shape and its exclusive place in the scheme of things. A settle is a wooden bench having both back and arms; a settee is a settle with an upholstered seat, arms and back. A sofa is a more luxuriously upholstered settee; a couch, a luxurious sofa, although more suitable for reclining than sitting on. A chaise longue is a daybed with the addition of an armrest.

There are a number of Regency couches, all of which are influenced by the styles of Egypt, Rome or early Greece.

It was Sheraton in his *Cabinet Dictionary* who first introduced a couch of this style to England and its scroll ends and lion's paw feet made it one of the most elegant fashions to have been seen at that time.

Until the decline of the Regency period, the upholsterer played a very minor role in the production of home furnishings and was really not in the same league as the cabinet maker, his work consisting mainly of hanging curtains and tapestries and lining walls with material.

Around the 1840's, however, there was a small, bloodless revolution within the furniture factories, the upholsterer rising to hitherto unheard of heights in his craft, virtually dictating the shape and style of chairs and settees and leaving the cabinet maker only the responsibility for making relatively simple frames of birch or ash.

Pine settle, probably England, late 18th century, curving hooded back, shaped sides, fixed seat, old refinish, 60³/₄ in. high. (Skinner Inc.) $1,300

Child's painted and decorated settee, America, circa 1840, light green ground with green and yellow pinstriping and pink roses, 24³/₄ in. wide. (Skinner Inc.) $1,300

A fine and rare Imperial zitan rectangular throne, the inner face of the back and two side panels elaborately and crisply carved in relief with five-clawed dragons, the seat plain, Qianlong/Jiaqing, 127cm. wide. (Christie's) $48,944

A painted and turned maple double-back conversation 'Courting' chair, New England, 1780–1810, painted brown with yellow highlights, length 43in. (Sotheby's) $7,475

An oak settle after the design by M. H. Baillie-Scott, rectangular paneled back-inlaid with pewter, ebonized and fruitwood roundels, 136.5cm. wide. (Christie's) $2,488

A red painted ebonized and parcel-gilt boat shaped daybed of antique Egyptian style, the dished seat covered in black horsehair, 76in. wide. (Christie's S. Ken) $3,218

SETTEES & COUCHES

Mahogany and maple inlaid sofa with carved outscrolled arms and drapery carved skirt, Hamburg, circa 1840.
(Kunsthaus am Museum) $3,597

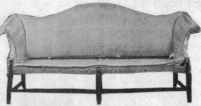

A Chippendale mahogany camel-back sofa, Philadelphia, 1770-1790, the serpentine back with scrolled arms, 89⁵/₈in. wide.
(Christie's) $32,200

A George III style mahogany sofa, the hump back, bowed arms and seat in distressed chinoiserie decorated blue silk, on square tapering legs, late 19th century, 75in. wide.
(Christie's) $2,142

A mid-Victorian mahogany sofa, the back with central oval button upholstered panel with foliate gold cresting, with serpentine padded seat on foliate headed cabriole legs, 77in. wide.
(Christie's) $2,324

A Louis XV walnut and beechwood canapé à oreilles, the molded frame carved with flowerheads, the undulating padded back and seat upholstered in gros and petit point needlework, 6ft. 5in. wide.
(Phillips) $5,303

A mahogany triple chair back sofa, each with a shell carved shaped toprail and pierced vase splat above a drop-in seat, mid 18th century, 66in. wide.
(Christie's) $3,071

A Regency mahogany chaise longue, upholstered in pale blue and gold-watered silk, with scrolled ends and scallop-shell-decorated top-rail, 79in. wide.
(Christie's) $3,029

A Regency brass-inlaid rosewood sofa, the padded back, arms and squab cushions covered in striped green close-cut velvet, on gadrooned and reeded tapering feet, 72¹/₂in. wide.
(Christie's) $8,114

SIDEBOARDS

Most pieces of furniture have clearly traceable roots planted firmly in the distant past. Not so the sideboard. In the form we know it today, this particular item first appeared on the scene in or around 1770.

Prior to that, certainly, there were sideboards, (Chaucer – and who would argue with his evidence? – mentions a 'sytte bord') but these were no more than side tables, sometimes marble topped, which contained neither drawers nor cupboards.

The introduction of a sideboard as a piece of furniture designed for storage came about for one main reason; the hard-drinking habits of 18th century Englishmen established a need for a convenient hidey-hole in which to keep large quantities of drink close by the dining table.

It is Adam, who, along with Shearer, Gillows, Sheraton, Chippendale and Hepplewhite, contends for the title of 'Father of the Modern Sideboard' i.e. of being the first to couple the drawerless side table with a pair of pedestals, one to either end, often placing knife boxes on top. One of the pedestals houses a wine drawer, and the other, a tin-lined cupboard with racks for stacking plates. Some also contained a pot cupboard in one of the pedestals, the door to which is usually quite inconspicuous and opens by means of a catch at the back. The explanation for this quaint variation seems to be that gentlemen, left by the ladies to put the world to rights over port and cigars, would often prefer not to permit calls of nature to interrupt the conversation!

A classical figured maple and mahogany sideboard, New York, 1815-1825, the splashboard with volutes and brass rosettes above a rectangular top, 63in wide. (Christie's) $6,325

A Regency ebony line-inlaid mahogany bowfront sideboard, with central frieze drawer and arched apron flanked by five drawers and one cupboard door, 58in. wide. (Christie's) $1,694

A Victorian carved mahogany sideboard, the crested back above a rectangular re-entrant top with three frieze drawers and three panel doors below, 65in. wide. (Christie's S. Ken) $2,130

A George III inlaid mahogany bowfront sideboard with tulipwood banded top above central frieze drawer and arched fan inlaid apron, 56in. wide. (Christie's) $3,894

An Arts and Crafts inlaid and brass-mounted oak sideboard, the raised back with castellated cornice above bead and copper whip-lash glazed central door, 72in. wide. (Christie's) $1,507

An attractive early Victorian mahogany small sideboard, set with a breakfront shallow shelf, the projecting base with three cushion molded drawers to the frieze over recessed cupboards, 155cm. wide. (Spencer's) $1,450

SIDEBOARDS

Rare Gustav Stickley sideboard, circa 1902, the top shelf galleried on three sides, unsigned, 48in. wide.
(Skinner Inc.) $3,500

A Federal mahogany and satinwood inlaid serpentine-front sideboard, Massachusetts, 1790–1810, the shaped top with alternating line inlays above a conforming case, 66¼in. wide.
(Christie's) $21,850

An inlaid walnut and parcel-gilt sideboard, the crossbanded rectangular top with scrolling foliate marquetry above three frieze drawers, on bun feet, 50½in. wide.
(Christie's) $1,431

An Art Nouveau sideboard by Johnson & Appleyard, the upper section with railed gallery and repoussé copper panels depicting stylized trees and fruit, 6ft. wide.
(Spencer's) $1,567

An early Victorian D-shaped side cabinet, covered overall with paper scrap design, on plinth base. (Lawrence Fine Arts) $3,700

Gustav Stickley sideboard, circa 1907–12, no. 816, plate rack on rectangular top, long drawer over two central drawers, 48in. wide.
(Skinner Inc.) $1,600

A diminutive Federal bird's-eye maple inlaid mahogany sideboard, Salem, Massachusetts or Portsmouth, New Hampshire, 1790-1810, with D-shaped top, the edge with rosewood crossbanding, 60½in. wide.
(Christie's) $23,000

A Victorian Lamb of Manchester pollard oak and ebonized breakfront pedestal sideboard, the superstructure having a pediment with central carved cartouche, 81in. wide.
(Peter Francis) $1,788

A George III line-inlaid mahogany breakfront sideboard, the crossbanded top above two central drawers, flanked by a deep cellaret drawer and a cupboard door on square tapering legs, 49in. wide.
(Christie's) $3,366

STANDS

Such was the ingenuity of past craftsmen and designers that there is a purpose built stand for just about everything from whips to cricket bats.

The 17th century ancestor of the anglepoise lamp was the candlestand. Its purpose was to supplement the general lighting, and the ordinary style was made of walnut or elm and consisted of a plain or spiral turned shaft supported on three or four plain scrolled feet.

At the turn of the 18th century a vase shape was introduced at the top of the pillar. This was often as much as a foot across and decorated with acanthus.

There were a number of delicate little stands made during the second half of the 18th century for the purpose of supporting books or music. The earliest of these resemble the mahogany tables which were popular at the time, having vase-shaped stems and tripod bases but with the addition of ratchets beneath their tops which permitted adjustment of the surface angle.

Ince and Mayhew improved the design by adding candle branches either side of the top and Sheraton (anything you can do …) made his stands adjustable for height by means of a rod through the center column which was clamped or released by the turn of a thumb screw.

The Victorian walnut duet music stand is particularly good with its turned central column and carved cabriole legs. These stands often have intricate fretwork tops, and the lyre design may give way elsewhere to a series of scrolls or leaf patterns.

A pair of Louis XVI ormolu-mounted mahogany jardinières, late 18th century, each with circular fluted vessel fitted with a tin liner, 20in. high.
(Christie's) $5,750

Pair of Régence style gilt-bronze-mounted mahogany pedestals, each black and white-mottled marble top above a coved frieze, the tapered shafts mounted with gilt-bronze rocaille cartouches, width 18in.
(Butterfield & Butterfield)
                    $9,200

Pair of Continental late baroque polychromed and parcel giltwood console pedestals, 18th century and later, each with a green faux marbleised top over an acanthus-carved niche inset with a putto, width 30¼in.
(Butterfield & Butterfield)
                    $7,475

A William IV mahogany library folio-stand with three channeled spreading uprights and a pair of hinged adjustable reading-slopes, 56in. wide.
(Christie's) $6,686

A rare and important Momoyama period Christian folding missal stand (shokendai), decorated in aogai and hiramakie with a central sunburst halo containing the monogram of the Society of Jesus IHS, late 16th/early 17th century, 36cm. high.
(Christie's) $112,948

A famille rose bidet, the interior painted with a flowering tree peony and a butterfly, Qianlong, 22½in. long, now mounted in a late George III mahogany frame.
(Lawrence Fine Art) $6,448

STANDS

A carved pine bucket bench, Pennsylvania, early 19th century, the arched back with scalloped sides centering three shelves, 46¾in. wide.
(Sotheby's) **$1,495**

A George III circular mahogany jardinière with a shallow everted rim and fluted frieze, 18in. diameter.
(Lawrence) **$2,603**

A Federal mahogany basin stand, Boston, Massachusetts, circa 1820, the shaped splashboard above a projecting pierced basin, 20½in. wide.
(Sotheby's) **$2,013**

A Louis-Philippe red and green-painted and gilt-gesso pedestal table of Gothic style with later leather-lined quatrefoil top, 23in. diameter.
(Christie's) **$12,870**

A fine and unusual carved and painted pine planter, New England, circa 1835-40, the sides painted with stylized fruit and flower forms, 12in. high.
(Sotheby's) **$12,650**

American Renaissance inlaid maple and rosewood nightstand by Herter Brothers, New York, circa 1872, the later faux marble top within a molded walnut border, 17in. wide.
(Butterfield & Butterfield)
$990

A George I style walnut urn stand with circular inset marble top and laurel-leaf swag frieze, on acanthus-carved scroll uprights joined by cross stretchers, 29in. high.
(Christie's) **$1,168**

A George II mahogany reading stand, the rectangular ratchet adjustable hinged top with a rising bookcase and two drawers to each side of the frieze, 2ft. 4in. wide.
(Phillips) **$3,186**

A Chinese gilt and polychromed black lacquered table stand, late 18th century, the eight-sided top formed by two interlocked squares, 35¼in. high.
(Christie's) **$6,900**

STOOLS

Stools have not always occupied the humble position they are accorded today, and in the Middle Ages they were an essential part of the social equipment of every household. At court, the sovereign alone sat on a chair, raised on a dais to ensure that no head was higher than his, while stools were provided for the wives of princes, dukes and other important court officials.

A similar hierarchy was observed in most households, which would boast at best only one or two chairs. It was not till Elizabethan times that chairs became more plentiful, by which time too, as a further concession to comfort, stool seats were often padded and upholstered. By the Restoration period stools were being made to match the new chairs which were being imported from the Low Countries.

For the next century and more, stool styles tended to follow those of chairs, though they retained their status, and in the great saloons of houses designed by Robert Adam, an elegant and stately effect was achieved by long stools ranged against the walls, or before windows. Both Hepplewhite and Chippendale feature stools in their Directories, and though Sheraton omits them from his Drawing Book, he does mention them later in his Dictionary. Style thereafter changed little until the anglicized version of the Empire style became popular, but by late Victorian times, the stool had become as often used for resting one's feet upon as any other part of the anatomy.

A late Regency adjustable rosewood piano stool with circular padded seat, cased pedestal and triform base.
(Christie's) $365

A pair of Louis XIV walnut tabourets, late 17th century, on shaped legs joined by an H-stretcher, 19¹/₂in. wide.
(Christie's) $8,625

A pair of Russian neo-classic brass-mounted mahogany tabourets de voyage, late 18th century, on detachable baluster-turned legs, 19³/₄in. wide.
(Christie's) $21,850

An oak and walnut stool, in the Carolean style, with a stuffover seat, on cabriole legs joined by pierced stretchers with cherubs supporting a crown.
(Phillips) $900

A Regency mahogany child's exercise-horse with bellow rectangular seat upholstered in close-nailed red leather, 17in. wide.
(Christie's) $1,470

A pair of caned footstools, Duncan Phyfe, New York, 1810–1833, each on four saber reeded legs with ebonized medallions, 13in. wide.
(Christie's) $4,830

Empire fruitwood curule form banquette, circa 1810, with a salmon pink corded seat above paneled X-frame supports, length 21in.
(Butterfield & Butterfield)
$1,610

A fancy-painted and decorated footstool, New England, first quarter 19th century, the bowed rectangular top centering a rush seat, on turned cylindrical legs joined by ring and block stretchers, 15¼in. long.
(Christie's) $3,520

Empire carved walnut curule form banquette, circa 1810, with ring and baluster-turned ends, the uprights terminating in down-turned swans' heads, length 25¼in.
(Butterfield & Butterfield)
$1,840

Fine Louis XV carved giltwood tabouret, second quarter 18th century, the circular upholstered top above a frieze pierced and carved with palmettes, foliage and scrolls, height 18¼in.
(Butterfield & Butterfield)
$2,588

A pair of Willam IV mahogany stools with rectangular needlework tops on baluster turned legs, 11in. wide x 9in. high.
(Christie's S. Ken) $728

A Charles X ormolu-mounted mahogany piano stool, circa 1820, on lappet-carved legs joined by an incurved triangular undertier, 14in. diameter.
(Christie's) $4,140

An Empire parcel-ebonized walnut tabouret, circa 1810, stamped *J.J.B. Demay*, on saber legs headed by chimerae, 18½in. wide.
(Christie's) $16,100

An early Victorian oak gout stool, the hinged and ratcheted close-studded green leather rest on baluster-turned front legs, 22¼in. wide.
(Christie's S. Ken) $385

A mahogany stool with needlework-covered seat, on cabriole legs joined by stretchers, 22½in. wide.
(Christie's) $4,485

ARCHITECTS TABLES

The architect's table was a
product of the upsurge of
popular interest in
architecture and building
design which occurred in the
18th century, the amateur
enthusiast requiring a surface
on which he could execute
and study his inspirations.
These tables come with many
variations, but all incorporate
leaves and some sort of
adjustable top, under which
there are usually drawers and
partitions for storing pens,
brushes and the like. Some
have pillar bases, while
others are supported on four
legs and resemble a writing
table.

A 19th century architect's
walnut table, the rectangular
top with rosewood crossbanding
and boxwood stringing, on
square tapering supports, 86cm.
wide.
(Spencer's) $955

A George II walnut archi-
tect's table with brass candle
slides, 3ft. wide. $6,000

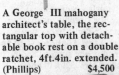

A George III mahogany
architect's table, the rectangular
molded top with easel support
and mechanical book rest,
3ft. wide.
(Russell Baldwin & Bright)
                        $9,114

A late George III mahogany
architect's table, the triple
ratcheted rising rectangular
drawing slope above two frieze
drawers on ring-turned tapering
legs, 36in. wide.
(Christie's) $2,177

A George III mahogany
architect's table, the rectangular top with detach-
able book rest on a double
ratchet, 4ft.4in. extended.
(Phillips) $4,500

An early George III mahogany
architect's table, the frieze
with pull out drawer, on chamfered legs with turned inner legs,
36in. wide.
(Christie's) $1,500

A late George II mahogany
architect's table with fitted
interior and a candlestand,
3ft. wide, circa 1750.
                     $3,500

An early George III mahogany
architect's table with crossbanded hinged and ratcheted
rectangular top above a frieze
drawer, on square chamfered
legs, 34in. wide. (Christie's
London) $8,600

BREAKFAST TABLES

A special form of table for breakfasting seems to have existed at least since Tudor times, when it appears in inventories of the day. During the Stuart period gateleg and flap types were often used for this purpose, but the 18th century habit of rising late and breakfasting upstairs led to the introduction of a small table designed to match the bedroom furniture. These are often of a flap type, with a cupboard or shelf under.

In the Regency period, the breakfast table once again descended the stairs and popularly consisted of a pedestal base with splayed legs.

A George III mahogany and plum-pudding mahogany breakfast-table, the canted rectangular tilt-top crossbanded with satinwood and amaranth and inlaid with boxwood and ebonized lines, 46¼in. wide. (Christie's) $1,690

A good Victorian walnut oval breakfast table, the top with matched burr-walnut quartered veneered panels, on central column composed of four turned, fluted and lobed supports, 52 x 38in. (Canterbury) $2,400

An early Victorian walnut breakfast table, the circular radially-veneered top on faceted tapering column, circular platform base with paw feet, 48in. wide. (Christie's) $2,188

A classical carved mahogany and tropical wood breakfast table, New York, 1810–1820, the rectangular top with double-elliptical drop leaves, 47¾in. wide (open). (Christie's) $48,300

A Victorian walnut breakfast table, the circular molded top above a shaped frieze on a foliate-carved baluster shaft and arched tripod support ending in scrolled toes, 52in. diameter. (Christie's) $2,102

An early Victorian mahogany breakfast table, the circular top on faceted bulbous column and trefoil base with paw feet, 53½in. wide. (Christie's) $2,299

A good Victorian walnut oval breakfast table of shaped outline, with figured quartered veneered top, on four scroll supports, 59in. (Canterbury) $1,575

A Regency brass-inlaid rosewood breakfast-table, the circular tilt-top inlaid with a band of scrolling foliage and with a gadrooned edge, 52in. diameter. (Christie's) $11,965

CARD & TEA TABLES

As the design of card tables progressed, tops tended to become square in shape, but with circular projections on the corners which were dished to hold candlesticks and which also had oval wells for money and chips.

The legs became progressively bolder, the earlier spade and club feet giving way to lions' paws or ball and claw designs. In about 1720, mahogany superseded walnut as the most widely used wood in the construction of gaming boards, though, occasionally, more exotic woods, such as laburnum, were used.

Prior to this time, carving had generally been rather limited – perhaps a shell motif on the knee – but with the introduction of the harder mahogany, more intricate designs, such as lion masks, were added and hairy lions' paw feet employed.

By the 1770's, gambling had reached such a peak that King George III felt it necessary to forbid the playing of cards in any of the Royal Palaces and Horace Walpole, that indefatigable commentator on the fashions of his time, is reported to have remarked that the gaming at Almacks, where young blades were losing as much as £15,000 in a night, was "... worthy of the decline of the Empire".

Although the Prince of Wales, who was later Prince Regent and finally King George IV, extolled the virtues of games of cards, it would appear that the popularity of the pastime had waned somewhat, for 19th century cabinet makers were producing far fewer card tables than their predecessors.

A Victorian walnut card table, the serpentine rectangular top on cabochon tapering shaft and scrolling quadruple supports, 36in. wide. (Christie's S. Ken) $1,800

A Regency brass-inlaid and ormolu-mounted amboyna, calamander and ebonized card-table, on a quadripartite pierced scrolled X-frame base centered by a hexagonal shaft, 36in. wide. (Christie's) $7,776

One of a pair of Regency rosewood card-tables, each with D-shaped red baize-lined top above a well, on tapering octagonal shaft and concave-sided rectangular platform base, 36in. wide. (Christie's) (Two) $4,792

A Dutch mahogany and floral marquetry card table, the rectangular top above frieze drawer and waved apron on square tapering legs, early 19th century, 30¹/₂in. wide. (Christie's) $1,440

A George III mahogany tea-table, the shaped frieze centered by a crisply carved foliate clasp and carved with fruiting vines and flowerheads, on square legs, 35¹/₂in. wide. (Christie's) $25,311

A George I burr walnut and walnut concertina-action card-table crossbanded and inlaid overall with featherbanding, the eared rectangular top enclosing an interior with four square candle-stands, 32¹/₄in. wide. (Christie's) $17,750

CARD & TEA TABLES

A Victorian walnut and floral marquetry inlaid demi lune card table, carved baluster column on four cabriole legs, 41¼in. wide. (Andrew Hartley)
$2,072

A late Victorian rosewood and marquetry envelope card table, with overall foliate-scroll decoration, 21½in. wide. (Christie's)
$1,757

A Regency rosewood D-shaped card table with swiveling top on shaped square shaft and quadripartite platform with splayed legs, 35½in. wide. (Christie's)
$1,609

A late Federal carved mahogany card table, Salem, Massachusetts, 1800–1815, the hinged serpentine top with outset rounded corners over a conforming frieze on rope-turned legs, 37in. wide. (Christie's)
$1,540

A George II Colonial mahogany and mother-o'-pearl inlaid card table, the crossbanded baize lined top with projecting corners with mother-o'-pearl inlaid counter recesses, 3ft. wide. (Phillips)
$4,110

A Chippendale carved mahogany card-table, Philadelphia, 1760–1770, the hinged rectangular top on four cabriole legs with ball-and-claw feet, 34⅛in. wide. (Christie's)
$35,650

A mid 18th century mahogany demi-lune tea table, the double hinged top enclosing an open compartment, on cabriole legs and claw and ball feet, 2ft. 8in. wide. (Phillips)
$1,682

A mahogany and rosewood strung D-shaped card table with a swiveling baize-lined top, on four later fluted column supports and quadripartite platform, first quarter 19th century. (Christie's S. Ken)
$1,884

A classical carved mahogany card-table, attributed to Duncan Phyfe, New York, 1805-1810, the rectangular top over rope-turned columns above a platform base, 35¾in. wide. (Christie's)
$4,600

214

CENTER TABLES

These were tables designed to be free-standing and were often circular. Italian examples dating from the 15th century are often elaborately decorated, and the form became increasingly popular through the 16th century. In the 17th century examples are usually of oak or walnut, but from around 1750 mahogany came to be commonly used in both England and America. During the Directoire and Empire periods, marble-topped center tables were popular.

A William IV rosewood, calamander, amaranth, satinwood, amboyna and bird's-eye maple center table, on paw feet, 62in. diameter. (Christie's) $26,235

A mahogany circular center table with gadrooned edge, on rectangular platform with paw feet, mid 19th century, 45in. diameter. (Christie's) $1,728

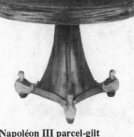

An Edwardian rosewood and marquetry octagonal center table, on square tapering legs headed with bell flower decoration and joined by stretchers united by a raised under tier, 36in. wide. (Christie's) $1,401

Napoléon III parcel-gilt mahogany center table, mid-19th century, the circular top above a plain frieze over a coved spreading triangular pedestal ending in carved giltwood winged birds, diameter 39¹/₂in. (Butterfield & Butterfield) $3,737

English Aesthetic rosewood center table, designed by E.W. Godwin, circa 1870, the octagonal top with moulded edge stamped *Collison & Lock, London* over eight ring-turned legs, width 36¹/₂in. (Butterfield & Butterfield) $10,925

A parcel-gilt and black-painted bronze center table, of Empire style, with a circular black fossil marble top with a molded edge, above three seated winged sphinxes, 38¹/₄in. diameter. (Christie's) $10,281

A Tyrolean inlaid mahogany and burr-veneered center table, the serpentine tip-up top inlaid with an Alpine scene with four roundels depicting wild life, late 19th century, 39¹/₂in. wide. (Christie's) $1,340

A mid-Victorian center table with octagonal inset slate marble top inlaid with various marbles, including Blue John, on scroll carved pedestal support and four splayed legs, 25in. wide. (Christie's) $4,283

CONSOLE TABLES

Console tables are so named for the console, or bracket, which is used to support them against the wall in the absence of back legs.

Perhaps surprisingly, their development came later than that of most other tables for they did not appear until the early 18th century, when house interiors became more sophisticated, with furniture being designed to blend into the entire decorative scheme. It was not, in fact, until about 1730 that eagle console tables achieved real popularity following their appearance in the court of Louis XIV where, as a rule, they were placed beneath a pier glass and sported superbly figured tops of Italian marble.

On the original tables, the marble tops were regarded as being by far the most important features (console tables were described as 'marble slab frames' in early inventories) and they were carefully selected for fine grain and exquisite color gradation and harmony from such notable suppliers as Signor Domenico de Angualis. The Victorians, having rather less flamboyant tastes, tended to go more for plain white tops in preference to the pinks and greens of the earlier examples and were inclined to build up the rococo ornamentation with gesso.

Later still in the Victorian period, the original marble and gilt materials were often abandoned in favor of a much more prosaic style, made either of mahogany or walnut. These are generally about three and a half feet wide, though a smaller example exists with a single cabriole front leg support.

Italian baroque parcel-gilt and painted console, the shaped triangular scagliola top with a molded outline above a parcel-gilt and painted foliate-scroll frieze, 46in. wide.
(Butterfield & Butterfield)
$6,600

A giltwood console table, in the Louis XVI style of semi-lune outline, on circular fluted tapering legs, united by a shaped stretcher and centered by an urn, second half 19th century, 43in. wide.
(Christie's) $3,896

A Louis XV giltwood console table with later serpentine mottled green marble top and pierced frieze carved with flowerheads, 32in. wide.
(Christie's) $7,854

One of a pair of George II style parcel-gilt mahogany eagle-form consoles each with rectangular salmon marble top within a parcel-gilt and floral-carved border, 4ft. wide.
(Butterfield & Butterfield)
$6,600

Italian rococo parcel-gilt and polychromed console table, mid 18th century, the blue marbleised top of shaped outline with inswept sides above a conforming frieze carved with rocaille, 40¹/₂in. wide.
(Butterfield & Butterfield)
$5,500

One of a pair of Milanese ebonized console tables, each supported by a kneeling blackamoor and scrolling back panel, mid 19th century, 40¹/₄in. wide.
(Christie's) $7,294

DINING TABLES

Dining tables, of course, come in many shapes and sizes, several of which, gateleg, dropleaf and large, have their own sections in this book. The circular, tilt top table is another variant, having much in common with the loo table.

No, we are still in the dining room ... Loo tables are named for the three to five handed variety of whist which became a fashionable craze in the mid 19th century. The tables had a circular top and central pillar design, which meant that all players could sit round them in comfort, unhindered by distant corners and constricting table legs.

Usually made of mahogany or rosewood, they have reeded or turned central columns on a platform base with either bun, claw or lion's paw feet. In Victorian times they became more elaborate, with superbly carved bases and often figured walnut tops which have a useful tip up action operated by two screws underneath, enabling them to be stood to one side when not in use. Later too, they often became more ovoid in shape, and the central pillar was enlarged into a cage of four columns. During the Regency period extending, pillar dining tables became popular. These were extremely versatile, and the Victorians were quick to see the advantages in having a table which could stretch or contract to accommodate the number of guests on the night. Their styles however tended to be very much more massive, of the leg-at-each-corner-type, and having center leaves which could be added by turning a handle to open the table.

A Victorian mahogany extending dining table, the two central baluster supports each with two splayed scroll-carved legs, 94in. wide.
(Bearne's) $3,442

A Louis XIV walnut refectory table, the detachable rectangular top pegged and fitting onto a cross frame, on ring-turned columns with bun feet, 1.1m. x 89cm.
(Phillips) $2,301

An early Victorian burr walnut and walnut dining-table by Gillows, the circular top with plain frieze and on part-gadrooned turned spreading fluted legs, 60in. diameter.
(Christie's) $36,465

A George IV loo table, the circular tilt top veneered in figured rosewood, with a band of brass marquetry and a gadroon edge, 4ft. 2in. diameter.
(Woolley & Wallis) $5,995

A large William IV rosewood veneered loo table, the triform base on knurled toes with tulip scrolls, 4ft. 5in. diameter.
(Woolley & Wallis) $1,987

A mahogany dining table with Cumberland action on canti-levered quadripartite baluster-turned supports and splayed legs, early 19th century, 49¹/₂in. wide.
(Christie's) $4,991

DINING TABLES

A Victorian carved walnut 'Capstan' extending dining table, the circular top opening to accomodate two sets of eight leaves of a different radius.
(Phillips) $26,284

A Robert 'Mouseman' Thompson oak dining table, on chamfered column trestle ends joined with single chamfered square section stretcher, 183cm. wide.
(Christie's) $3,347

A mid-Victorian burr-walnut loo table with oval quarter-veneered tip-up top and cabochon carved baluster shaft, 39in. wide.
(Christie's) $1,091

L. & J.G. Stickley dining table, circa 1912, no. 720, circular top, straight apron, supported on five tapering legs, with four extension leaves, 48in. diameter.
(Skinner Inc.) $1,800

A Dutch oak draw-leaf table with rectangular twin-flap top, on baluster legs joined by box stretchers and on block feet, 17th century, 79½in. wide.
(Christie's) $6,783

A Regency mahogany extending dining table, the rounded rectangular top including five extra leaves with a reeded edge and plain frieze, 12ft. long.
(Phillips) $10,605

"Bonnie" dining table, designed by Ferruccio Tritta, produced by Studio Nove, New York, on three columnar supports, 56in. diameter.
(Skinner Inc.) $2,600

A Capstan mahogany extending dining table, the circular revolving top opening to incorporate two sets of leaves, on a reeded quadripartite base terminating with claw-and-ball feet, 67in. diameter.
(Christie's S. Ken) $26,598

A late Victorian mahogany extending dining table with circular molded top on fluted and cabochon-carved turned legs, 114in. extended.
(Christie's) $4,204

DRESSING TABLES

Large dressing tables complete with mirrors were, if we are to judge from the design catalogs, made in profusion throughout the eighteenth century and some, Chippendale's in particular, were very fine indeed.

Designers of the period vied with each other to see who could cram in the greatest number of ingenious little fitments, each designer claiming every innovation as his own and decrying all others for having pinched his ideas. Sheraton, in particular, was fascinated by the challenge and his designs became more and more complex as he progressively widened the scope of his ideas until, toward the end, it would seem that he was attempting to develop the ultimate, all-purpose item of furniture. One of his later creations was a superbly eccentric construction incorporating hinged and swing mirrors, numerous drawers, a washbasin, compartments for jewelery, writing materials and cosmetics, not to mention the commode.

By far the most popular dressing tables to come from the second half of the eighteenth century were described by Shearer as 'dressing stands'. These were usually of quite small size, standing on fine, elegant legs.

During the Victorian period, there were a few small dressing tables but, as a rule, the Victorians preferred them rather more solidly proportioned. The Edwardians, on the other hand, seem to have taken to them with a little more enthusiasm and reproduced a number of styles of the late eighteenth century.

A Queen Anne walnut dressing table, Massachusetts, or Rhode Island, 1740-1760, on cabriole legs with pad feet, 34¹/₈in. wide. (Christie's) $36,800

An early 19th century mahogany tray top dressing table, 38¹/₂in. wide. (Dreweatt Neate) $895

A classical carved mahogany dressing table, New York, 1810-1815, the upper section surmounted by acanthus and rosette-carved serpentine arms centering a rectangular mirror, 40¹/₂in. wide. **(Christie's)** $4,025

A Robert 'Mouseman' Thompson oak dressing table, with rectangular cheval mirror on rectangular, molded and chamfered top, on two pedestals each with three short drawers and eight octagonal feet, 106.7cm. (Christie's) $3,300

A George III mahogany dressing table with molded rectangular top above three frieze drawers above a pair of recessed doors, the sides with carrying-handles, 36in. wide. (Christie's) $6,195

A black and gilt-japanned dressing-table decorated overall with figures, geese and houses in a chinoiserie landscape, on turned tapering legs with brass caps, 42in. wide. (Christie's) $5,148

DROP-LEAF TABLES

From about 1750 until the end of the 18th century, furniture designers strove to break away from traditional styles in the attempt to create something completely different and this period saw a multitude of legs, flaps and movements built into tables which extended, opened, hinged, turned and folded up in order to achieve the maximum possible surface area in the smallest practicable space.

One of the simpler designs to emerge from this orgy of inventiveness was the envelope table – obviously so called from the triangular shape of the flap – which has all the attributes of a good Georgian table, being made of nicely grained mahogany and having cabriole legs.

Another form of drop-leaf table has rectangular flaps which sometimes reach almost to the ground. Though essentially country made and of simple design, with straight, square legs chamfered on the inside edge, units of this kind were often used to form part of the large extending tables so popular throughout the 18th century.

Made from about 1850 and continuing in popularity until the end of the 19th century, Sutherland tables were manufactured in a variety of woods; earlier examples are usually of rosewood and burr walnut, later ones employing walnut or mahogany.

This little table, named after Queen Victoria's Mistress of the Robes is ideal for the small dining room for it will seat six when fully open yet, closed, will stand quite comfortably out of the way.

Queen Anne cherry and maple dining table, New England, circa 1770, 45in. wide open. (Skinner) $1,760

A Federal painted birchwood drop-leaf dining table, New England, circa 1810, on square tapering legs, the base painted red, length 39½in. (Sotheby's) $1,495

A Victorian burr-walnut Sutherland table, on turned tapering column end-standards and foliate carved splayed legs, 35½in. wide. (Christie's S. Ken) $1,007

A Victorian walnut Sutherland table, the molded rectangular top on baluster turned legs with down curved feet. (Bonhams) $976

A George III mahogany hunt-table with oval twin-flap top on square molded legs and four gatelegs joined by molded stretchers, 95in. long. (Christie's) $12,584

A rare George III mahogany drop leaf table, raised on cabriole legs with molded and carved knees, terminating on hoof feet, the top 40½ x 35¾in. (Tennants) $8,556

DRUM TABLES

These rather elegant tables are also known as 'library' or 'rent' tables, and first appeared in the second half of the 18th century. They remained popular throughout the Regency period and well into the Victorian era.

Most earlier examples are of mahogany, while those dating from the Regency period may also be of rosewood. The Victorians used both these woods, but seemed on the whole to prefer burr walnut.

Drum tables were often used in estate offices and commonly had revolving tops.

An early Victorian mahogany drum top library table, the circular leatherette inset top above four frieze drawers on a turned spreading shaft, 3ft. 6in. diameter.
(Phillips) $2,880

A Victorian mahogany drum table, the circular lined top above four frieze drawers and four dummy drawers on turned pillar and tripod, 50in. diameter.
(Christie's) $2,632

A good George IV mahogany drum table, the tooled leather inset top within an ebony inlaid border of scrolling foliage, upon a plain turned lotus capped column and tri-form base with scroll feet, 49³/₄in. diameter.
(Tennants) $3,348

A Regency mahogany drum-top library table, the circular revolving top with four real and four false drawers, 29in. diameter.
(Bearne's) $3,000

A Regency brass-mounted and brass-inlaid rosewood library table, upon a concave-fronted triangular spreading scrolled plinth and further platform base and stiff-leaf-carved scroll feet, 48in. diameter.
(Christie's) $11,833

A late George II mahogany and ebony inlaid drum table, on a ring-turned pedestal with four splayed legs, brass caps and castors, 48in. diameter.
(Christie's) $8,762

A Regency mahogany drum-table, on gadrooned baluster shaft and quadripartite support with fluted leaf-headed scroll legs, 27¹/₄in. diameter.
(Christie's) $26,235

19th century Continental fruitwood library table with segmented inlaid top on vase column and tripod base.
(Lots Road Galleries) $2,494

DUMB WAITERS

Dumb-waiters were extremely fashionable during the final quarter of the 18th century and throughout the Regency period, although there is evidence that they were available as early as 1727, when Lord Bristol purchased one from a cabinet maker named Robert Leigh.

It was Sheraton, with a turn of phrase as elegant as one of his own chairlegs, who described the dumb-waiter as "a useful piece of furniture to serve in some respects the place of a waiter, whence it is so named".

A George III mahogany dumb waiter, of two graduated circular tiers, each with reeded edge and two drop flaps, on a ring turned pillar with brass collar.
(Spencer's) $4,396

George III mahogany dumb waiter of three circular tiers on in-curved tripod with brass castors.
(Lots Road Galleries)

$1,614

A George IV faded mahogany two tier dumb waiter, the circular fixed trays graduated with fluted borders and brass pillar supports, 23¹/₂in. diameter.
(Woolley & Wallis)

$1,584

A William IV mahogany three tier dumb waiter with serpentine acanthus and gadrooned rectangular galleried top, on brass castors, 50¹/₂in. wide.
(Christie's S. Ken) $1,839

A George III mahogany two-tier dumb-waiter, the dished molded rotating upper tier supported by a spirally-gadrooned urn-shaped stem with similar rotating lower tier, 18¹/₄in. diameter.
(Christie's) $5,916

A George III mahogany twin tier dumb waiter with revolving dished tops and reeded edges, on tripod splayed legs, 2ft. diameter top.
(Phillips) $1,363

A mid-Victorian mahogany metamorphic three-tier dumb waiter, with standard ends and dual supports with turned feet joined by a stretcher, 44in. wide.
(Christie's) $1,489

A mahogany three-tier dumb waiter, the graduating circular tiers on turned uprights above three cabriole legs, mid 18th century, 24in. wide.
(Christie's) $1,005

GATELEG TABLES

The gateleg table has remained one of the most popular styles ever since its introduction during the 17th century, even those being made today having the same basic design and movement as the originals.

Usually made of oak, though occasionally of more exotic woods such as yew or walnut, the majority of gateleg tables have tops of round or oval shape and the legs are braced with stretchers which, like the main frame, are cut to take the pivoting 'gate' leg. (Larger tables are constructed with two gatelegs on each side.)

Although these tables have been made since the 17th century, the vast majority date from the late 19th and early 20th centuries.

As a rule, prices reflect top size and, when the length of the closed table is greater than four feet, they really begin to soar into large figures.

The cabriole leg is so called from its likeness in shape to the leg of an animal (it's derived from the French word meaning "goat's leap") and implicit in the meaning is the suggestion of a free, dancing movement which would obviously be destroyed if stretchers were employed.

The change from gateleg to gate tables was a direct result of the switch in fashion towards cabriole legs and, once free of encumbering stretchers, the table's movement could be simplified in that two of the actual legs could now be swung out to support the flaps. This cleaned up the lines of the leg section by allowing the omission of the two extra 'gatelegs'.

William and Mary maple turned tuck-a-way table, New England, 18th century, old refinish, 30in. wide.
(Skinner) **$6,900**

A Charles II oak gateleg table with oval twin-flap top, on turned slightly-spreading supports joined by stretchers, 49½in. wide.
(Christie's) **$3,392**

George III mahogany spider-leg table, last quarter 18th century, the rectangular top with drop leaves, length open 29½in.
(Butterfield & Butterfield) **$3,500**

A 17th century oak credence table, the top turning over to form eight sides, raised upon four columnar turned legs, 37in. wide.
(Boardman) **$2,100**

An oak gateleg table with elliptical leaves and two end drawers, on baluster and bobbin turned supports, 51¼in. wide, basically late 17th century.
(Bonhams) **$2,280**

A mahogany gateleg table, the oval twin-flap top with molded edge, on turned legs and fluted scroll feet, 35¼in. wide.
(Christie's) **$5,483**

LARGE TABLES

Named after the monastic dining rooms in which they were originally used, refectory tables are based upon a very old design.

The name is now given to virtually any long table with legs on the outside edge although it originally applied only to those having six or more legs joined by stretchers at ground level.

Widely used until the end of the Jacobean period (1603–1688), refectory tables dwindled in popularity after that time, though they have been made in small numbers ever since.

The design of tables changed at the beginning of the 19th century from the rectangular and D-ended styles to tables which were either round or sectional.

The latter were extremely practical tables for, besides allowing ample leg room, they could by the simple addition of more units be extended at will from four seaters to a length more suited to a banquet.

Bases had plain or turned columns with three or four splayed legs which were either plain or reeded, terminating in brass castors.

Another large table is the Victorian extending dining table which, being heavy and massive, most people instinctively associate with the Victorian period. This type of table, usually made of mahogany, though sometimes of oak, extended by means of a worm screw operated by a handle in the center and allowed the addition of one or two extra leaves. Occasionally the center leaf was equipped with drop-down legs as a means of providing extra stability when the table was fully extended.

An oak extending dining table designed by Arthur Romney Green, with carved scalloped details, on four hexagonal carved legs supporting platform shelf, on X-shaped stretcher, 187cm. wide (extended). (Christie's) $3,062

Charles and Ray Eames segmented base table, design date 1972, manufactured by Herman Miller, rosewood veneer top, 78in. long. (Skinner Inc.) $600

A Regency mahogany extending dining table, the rounded rectangular top including five extra leaves with a reeded edge and plain frieze, 12ft. long. (Phillips) $10,605

Italian baroque carved walnut draw-leaf table, raised on turned cylindrical legs headed by Ionic columns, 47in. wide. (Butterfield & Butterfield) $825

A Capstan mahogany extending dining table, the circular revolving top opening to incorporate two sets of leaves, on a reeded quadripartite base terminating with claw-and-ball feet, 67in. diameter. (Christie's S. Ken) $26,598

Federal walnut inlaid banquet table, probably Virginia, circa 1800, 92in. wide open. (Skinner) $2,640

A Dutch oak draw-leaf table with rectangular twin-flap top, on baluster legs joined by box stretchers and on block feet, 17th century, 79¹/₂in. wide. (Christie's) $6,783

A Louis XVI mahogany dining-table with two D-shaped end-sections and turned tapering legs with brass caps, 58in. wide. (Christie's) $7,585

LARGE TABLES

Louis XV cherrywood draw-leaf dining table, the later rectangular top over a shaped valance, raised on cabriole legs, width closed 8ft. 9in.
(Butterfield & Butterfield) $5,750

Continental baroque walnut refectory table, rectangular top above molded frieze, raised on turned legs joined by a stretcher, 89in. long.
(Skinner Inc.) $3,100

An early 19th century mahogany twin-pedestal dining table, on ring-turned knopped column and quadruped splayed reeded legs terminating in paw feet and castors, 6ft. 6in. extended.
(Phillips) $8,925

A Regency mahogany extending dining-table, with two D-shaped end sections, with plain frieze and on removable broad-reeded turned baluster legs, 113in. long, overall.
(Christie's) $9,853

A fine Federal mahogany three-part dining table, American, probably Boston, circa 1810, on turned and reeded tapering legs ending in ball feet, length extended 13ft. 3½in.
(Sotheby's) $7,700

A late George III mahogany and banded D-end dining table, with later central section, on square tapering legs with spade feet, 126in. extended.
(Christie's) $2,719

An early 19th century mahogany D-end dining table with reeded edge to the top, on tapering legs with ebonised ring-turned details, 108in. long.
(Bearne's) $5,295

An early Victorian mahogany D-ended extending dining table, the molded top on five massive gadroon and flute molded baluster legs, 170in. long.
(Peter Francis) $2,950

OCCASIONAL TABLES

Tables have come a long way from the mediaeval board and trestle variety, and as social life became more sophisticated so tables of various designs were devised for all relevant activities.

It is perhaps with the Restoration that the age of specialized tables really begins and many distinct varieties were made for the requirements of a luxurious and pleasure loving society. Center tables, similar to consoles, but with decoration on all four sides, became popular, and huge sums were also paid for silver tables which were quite the dernier cri of the time – if you could afford them.

Decoration was a common factor however in all types of occasional tables. They could be intricately carved, decorated with scagliola, particularly towards the end of the 17th century, or painted with gilt gesso or lacquer.

By the later 18th century, many craftsmen were concentrating on the ingenuity of their designs, and patents were taken out for all types of collapsible or extending devices. People, it seemed, loved 'the facility of changing the flaps at pleasure'.

In the Regency period, the new exotic woods such as zebrawood and mahogany became popular for occasional tables, the decoration often being of ormolu. Animal supports with classical and Egyptian motifs were also favored for center and side tables at the time. By the mid 19th century other forms of decoration, such as papier mâché were becoming popular and found application also on occasional tables.

A rare French bronze and onyx low table, probably Paris, circa 1900, the circular top with figured green, purple and brown marble, on four double pierced inswept legs and leaf-cast socle, 109cm. diameter.
(Sotheby's) **$15,367**

A mahogany and plate glass two-tier trolley, by Cesare Lacca, Italy c.1955, 40in. wide.
(Christie's) **$337**

A pair of William IV red and black-painted lamp-tables decorated overall in the Etruscan style, each with canted square tilt-top rising as a pole screen, the decoration possibly late 19th century, 29¹/₂in. high.
(Christie's) **$10,624**

Louis XV Provincial fruitwood tric-trac table, mid-18th century, the leather-inset lift-off rectangular top revealing a later needlepoint playing surface, 36in. wide.
(Butterfield & Butterfield) **$4,950**

An attractive William IV rosewood occasional table, the rounded rectangular top crossbanded, a drawer to each opposing side frieze, raised upon a waisted rectangular pillar, 68cm. wide.
(Spencer's) **$899**

An attractive Edwardian mahogany 'etagère', of two graduated oval tiers divided by curved uprights, the upper tier inset with an oval glass bottomed tray, 88cm. wide.
(Spencer's) **$2,610**

OCCASIONAL TABLES

A mahogany tripod table, the hexagonal top with pierced fretwork gallery on triple S and C-scroll supports, 26½in. high. (Christie's) $4,792

South German oval rosewood table raised on lyre form supports joined by a wavy stretcher, circa 1820, 79cm. wide. (Kunsthaus am Museum) $1,660

A George III mahogany tripod table, the hinged octagonal top with pierced arcaded gallery on a birdcage support and baluster shaft, 29in. high. (Christie's) $21,780

Scandinavian polished birch round table on central column support with three swan neck curved supports, on concave platform base, early 19th century, 80cm. diameter. (Kunsthaus am Museum) $1,827

A late Victorian inlaid mahogany octagonal table, with foliate marquetry border on turned uprights joined by shaped undertier on splayed legs, 30in. wide. (Christie's) $1,711

A specimen marble and hardwood table, the associated circular top centered with a star within a radiating pattern, inlaid with various marbles, mid-19th century, 32in. diameter. (Christie's) $3,652

An Empire brass-mounted and parcel-gilt gueridon, circa 1810, possibly German, with circular black fossilized marble top on tripartite scaly serpent supports, 29in. diameter. (Christie's) $19,550

A carrara marble topped mahogany table, on foliate headed scrolled uprights joined by a foliate-carved stop-fluted ring-turned stretcher, the base early 19th century, 50in. wide. (Christie's) $1,525

A Napoléon III ormolu and malachite occasional table, with a malachite-veneered circular top, the trefoil base with scrolled supports with pineapple finials, 28¼in. diameter. (Christie's) $9,424

PEMBROKE TABLES

This useful table, introduced during the 1760's, was, according to Sheraton, named after the Countess of Pembroke, who was the first to place an order for one.

Essentially, the Pembroke table has a rectangular top with a drawer and small flaps that are either squared or oval in shape. Beyond this, there are any number of different bases, ranging from elegant center columns with tripod splay feet to bulbous, turned pine legs as on the late Victorian examples.

From 1770, Pembroke tables were often made of inlaid satinwood and painting was often also used for their embellishment. They served for meals and, according to Sheraton, "were suitable for a gentleman or lady to breakfast on."

Towards the end of the 18th century, the Harlequin Pembroke was introduced. This ingenious variation comprised a box-like structure fitted with drawers or small receptacles which were concealed in the table body and made to rise by means of weights. Great numbers of small Pembroke-type tables were made in the last decade of the 18th century.

A George III inlaid satinwood and painted Pembroke table, the oval top banded with partridgewood and kingwood, centered by a burr yew panel, 35¼in. wide.
(Bearne's) **$7,413**

A George III mahogany and satinwood serpentine Pembroke table, crossbanded overall in tulipwood and inlaid with boxwood and ebonized lines, 32in. wide.
(Christie's) **$3,871**

A fine George III satinwood and marquetry Pembroke table, attributable to William Moore of Dublin, on square tapering legs inlaid with paterae hung with husk chains united by an undertier with gaitered feet, 2ft. 9in. long.
(Phillips) **$15,350**

A Federal mahogany pembroke table, labeled by Charles Christian, New York, 1810–1815, on reeded tapering legs with baluster and ring turned capitals and feet, 43¾in. wide (open).
(Christie's) **$5,750**

A George III mahogany Pembroke table, the frieze inlaid with ebonized banding and one drawer, on square tapering legs with brass caps, 38½in. wide.
(Christie's) **$1,646**

A George III mahogany Pembroke table, on associated quadripartite base with turned spreading shaft, the downswept reeded legs with brass caps, 48in. wide.
(Christie's) **$3,098**

A satinwood inlaid plum-pudding mahogany Pembroke table, circa 1900, 19in. wide opening to 41in.
(Michael Bowman) **$1,911**

SIDE TABLES

Side tables are the root from which occasional tables grew, dating from the 15th century and resembling, in their earliest form, a kind of chest of drawers under a table top. They were used in large households only, for storage of cutlery, linen and condiments in the dining room and, true to the fashion of the time, were made of oak. Few of these have survived and as such command exceptionally high prices.

From about 1850 fine tapering legs gave way to massive turned ones with heavy brass cup castors.

A fine Federal mahogany two-drawer side table, New York, circa 1810, on reeded tapering legs ending in ebonized vase and ball feet, 20½in. wide. (Sotheby's) **$4,125**

A walnut and oyster-veneered side table, the rectangular molded top inlaid with geometrical lines, on spiral-twist supports joined by flattened wavy stretchers, on bun feet, late 17th century, 37in. wide. (Christie's) **$8,158**

A walnut side table with smaller associated brèche violette rectangular top, the waved frieze carved with acanthus-scrolls centered by a lion-mask, 19th century, 44in. wide. (Christie's) **$7,744**

A mid-Georgian walnut side table, the frieze with one drawer with compartments and a simulated short drawer to the front, on lappeted club legs and pad feet, 27¼in. wide. (Christie's) **$2,073**

A classical brass-inlaid and carved mahogany pier-table, stamped *H. Lannuier, New York*, circa 1815, on four waterleaf and hairy-carved animal legs with paw feet, 33in. wide. (Christie's) **$34,500**

A George II burr-elm side table inlaid overall with feather-banding, the rectangular top with re-entrant corners above three frieze drawers and a waved apron, 33¼in. wide. (Christie's) **$13,196**

A giltwood and gesso side table, the rectangular verde antico marble top with molded edge, the frieze with an arcaded foliate moulding and Vitruvian scroll, early 20th century, 72in. wide. (Christie's) **$3,799**

A Dutch walnut and foliate marquetry side table inlaid with mother of pearl and bone, with single frieze drawer, on square tapered supports joined by a flattened cross stretcher, 18th century and later, 42½in. wide. (Christie's) **$6,230**

SOFA TABLES

The sofa table was originally introduced to the world by Sheraton towards the end of the 18th century. He suggested that the length should be five feet six inches, (with flaps raised) the width two feet and the height 28 inches.

Basically, of course, this is simply the Pembroke table stretched a bit into more elegant proportions and it is interesting to consider how, give the fundamental idea of a table with drawers and flaps, three such successful designs as the Pembroke, sofa and Regency supper tables can be produced.

Earlier sofa tables were made of mahogany or, occasionally, satinwood but later, in the early 19th century, a variety of woods was used including rosewood, amboyna and zebra wood. These are good tables in every sense of the word and, as such, command high prices. Although the 19th century examples are the more flamboyant with their use of exotic woods, inlaid brass and lyre end supports, it is the more austerely elegant late 18th century variety which are the most sought after and, therefore, the most expensive.

The Regency supper table is basically a sofa table with the flaps being hinged from the long sides instead of the short, and having one long drawer in the apron with a dummy front at the opposite end.

Usually made of mahogany or rosewood, the Regency supper table was popular from the beginning of the Regency period through to the start of the Victorian.

A George III mahogany sofa table, on slender trestle supports and outswept legs tied by an inverted 'U'-shaped stretcher. (Bonhams) $1,728

A Regency calamander sofa table, the canted rectangular top crossbanded in satinwood and ebony, with part cedar-lined frieze drawers, 60¼in. wide. (Christie's) $11,995

A Regency mahogany sofa table with rounded rectangular twin-flap top crossbanded in calamander above a frieze drawer and on solid end-supports, 38¾in. wide. (Christie's) $5,997

A late Regency mahogany sofa table with two drawers opposite two dummy drawers, on solid trestle end supports joined by turned stretcher, 41½ x 61in. extended. (Lawrence Fine Art) $4,268

A Regency rosewood sofa table, the two central shaped flat supports on a rectangular platform with four hipped splayed legs, 55½in. wide. (Bearne's) $3,269

A mahogany and rosewood crossbanded sofa table with two true and two false frieze drawers, on solid end supports and outswept legs, 19th century. (Bonhams) $1,469

WORKBOXES & GAMES TABLES

Well before the introduction of playing cards, in the 15th century, proficiency at chess, backgammon and dice was considered to be an essential part of the education of anyone intending to take his place in society. Indeed, all forms of gaming were so popular that *The Complete Gamester* was felt to be almost compulsory reading and, in the edition of 1674, we find the declaration "... he who in company should appear ignorant of the game in vogue would be reckoned low bred and hardly fit for conversation." Since there were, at that time, dozens of games widely played, including glecko, primero, ombre, picquet, basset, quadrille, commerce and loo, to name but a few, there must have been a considerable number of people wandering about with inferiority complexes.

And another thing, people in society rarely messed about with gambling for loose change; in many of the higher gaming establishments, the dice were rarely thrown for less than £100 a throw.

Early games were played on marked boards (as chess and draughts) which were placed either on the floor or on a table. Towards the end of the 17th century, however, the business of losing a fortune was civilised somewhat by the introduction of beautifully made gaming tables specifically designed for players of particular games.

Although a few earlier pieces do exist, it was during the 18th and 19th centuries that gaming tables really came into their own, often being combined with a workbox.

A classical mahogany poudreuse, Duncan Phyfe, New York, 1812-1825, on double-swelled waterleaf-carved feet with brass castors, 30¹/₂in. high. (Christie's) $40,250

Directoire burl walnut sewing table, circa 1800, raised on X-form supports joined by a ring-turned stretcher, 26¹/₂in. wide. (Butterfield & Butterfield) $2,090

A Chinese Export padouk-wood games-table inlaid overall with ebony and satinwood lines, the rounded rectangular twin-flap top banded in satinwood with sliding central section, early 19th century, 48in. wide. (Christie's) $17,336

A George IV maple, grained and ebonized work-table, the rectangular twin-flap top banded in mahogany above three mahogany-lined drawers, on bobbin-turned tapering legs with brass caps, 37³/₄in. wide. (Christie's) $4,187

A Victorian figured walnut games table, with hinged swivel action to reveal an inlaid draughts board and backgammon, 35³/₄in. wide. (Tennants) $2,106

A George III inlaid rosewood work table, the elongated octagonal top and frieze outlined with sharks'-tooth banding, originally with work bag. (Bearne's) $3,384

A mid-19th century mother-of-pearl inlaid ebonized work table, the sarcophagus body decorated throughout with floral sprays and gilt foliage, 23½in. wide.
(Bearne's) $441

A rare and important paint decorated single-drawer work table, South Paris Hill, Maine, early 19th century, 29in. high.
(Sotheby's) $37,950

A mid-Victorian yewwood-veneered octagonal work table with hinged top, on acanthus-carved tripod base, 28¼in. high.
(Bearne's) $1,144

A Victorian burr-walnut work table, the banded hinged top above a well on a turned support on four carved cabriole legs, 20½in. wide.
(Bonhams) $885

A Regency rosewood work table with rounded rectangular hinged top banded in calamander on spirally-reeded column support and quadripartite concave-sided base, 20½in. wide.
(Christie's) $6,195

A Federal brass-mounted and inlaid mahogany two-drawer work table, Philadelphia, circa 1810, with ring-turned three-quarter-round columns at each corner, width 20in.
(Sotheby's) $3,738

A William IV rosewood combined games and work table, on standard end supports joined by a ring turned stretcher with bar bases and bun feet, 1ft. 9in. wide.
(Phillips) $2,070

A rosewood lady's sewing, writing, reading and painting table, circa 1840, inlaid with a star and with Vandyck borders, 31in. high.
(Sotheby's) $2,728

A Federal mahogany two-drawer work table, Boston, Massachusetts, circa 1810, the rectangular top above a case with two drawers, 21in. wide.
(Sotheby's) $3,850

WRITING TABLES & DESKS

Between 1775 and 1825 there were a number of beautifully made desks designed in a delicately feminine manner yet strongly built so that many have survived in good condition to the present day.

There is a fascination in any piece of furniture which has an action like that which is incorporated in some desks, for, when the drawer is opened, the tambour automatically rolls back into the frame to reveal a fitted compartment which may be used for storing paper and envelopes. The drawer also acts as a support for the flap, which can now be lifted from the center of the desk and folded forward to provide an ample, leather covered writing surface.

Tambours were widely used during this period, both vertically and horizontally, to cover everything from desk tops to night commodes.

Made of thin strips of wood glued on to a linen or canvas backing, they run in grooves on the frame and follow any path the cabinet maker wishes them to take.

Another elegant and highly desirable writing table which was made from the end of the 18th century until about 1825 and then again during the Edwardian period when the styles of this era were revived, is described by Sheraton in his Drawing Book as "a Lady's Drawing and Writing Table". It adopted the name Carlton House table from the residence of the Prince of Wales for whom the design was originally prepared.

Basically a D-shaped table on fine square tapering legs, it has a bank of drawers and compartments ranged round the sides and back.

A Louis XV ormolu-mounted kingwood and tulipwood bureau à compartiment, the waved superstructure inlaid with quarter-veneered parquetry panels, above four serpentine-fronted drawers and three compartments, 45¼in. wide. (Christie's) $11,549

An ormolu-mounted tulipwood, kingwood and marquetry table à écrire, the reading-slope flanked by two hinged silk-lined wells, on cabriole legs with foliate sabots, 26in. wide. (Christie's) $46,750

An English ormolu-mounted walnut, burr-walnut, ebonised and marquetry library-table, the bow-ended rectangular top inlaid in ebonized and boxwood lines with a foliate spray to each end, circa 1870, 50¼in. wide. (Christie's) $9,740

A French ormolu-mounted red tortoiseshell and ivory-inlaid kingwood and marquetry table à écrire, by J. Boremans, inlaid overall with tulipwood lines, the shaped rectangular top above a pair of frieze drawers, 19th century, 30in. wide. (Christie's) $9,740

Louis XV style gilt bronze and porcelain mounted bonheur du jour, the upper section with two doors mounted with 'Sèvres' porcelain plaques, 36in. wide. (William Doyle Galleries) $2,990

A Napoléon III ormolu-mounted ebonized, red tortoiseshell and boulle marquetry bureau-plat, of serpentine form, the top inlaid in premier partie, the paneled frieze with one drawer on cabriole legs, 54in. wide. (Christie's) $4,428

A French ormolu-mounted rosewood, mahogany and burr walnut writing table inlaid overall with boxwood and harewood, on toupie feet, mid-19th century, 55in. wide.
(Christie's) **$9,207**

A Régence ormolu-mounted ebonized bureau plat, early 18th century, with rectangular brass-bound leather-lined top, 46in. wide.
(Christie's) **$17,250**

An oak and ebonized library writing table with rounded rectangular leather-lined top, six frieze drawers and turned and reeded tapering legs, mid 19th century, 60in. wide.
(Christie's) **$2,402**

Italian rococo walnut slant-front desk, last quarter 18th century, the rounded rectangular inlaid top continuing into sides over an inlaid slant front, raised on cabriole legs, width 35in.
(Butterfield & Butterfield) **$5,175**

A gilt bronze mounted kingwood writing table, circa 1900, after the model by Riesener, the leather-lined top with rounded corners above a frieze centered by marquetry panels depicting the Arts and Sciences, 109cm. wide.
(Sotheby's) **$6,849**

An Edwardian mahogany and marquetry writing table, the raised superstructure with open compartment with fitted drawer flanked by inlaid panelled doors, on square tapering legs with spade feet, 36in. wide.
(Christie's) **$1,539**

A classical mahogany writing table, New York, 1820-1840, the hinged rectangular top with canted corners and crossbanded edges, 23in wide.
(Christie's) **$1,150**

A Regency mahogany writing table, the rectangular top with hinged compartment above frieze drawer on ring-turned reeded legs, 29in. wide.
(Christie's) **$1,491**

A late Louis XVI mahogany table à ouvrage, late 18th century, stamped *Canabas*, fitted with a hinged writing panel above a long drawer, 29in. wide.
(Christie's) **$13,800**

TALLBOYS

The tallboy is essentially a double chest of drawers, one on top of the other, the lower section being, for obvious practical purposes, rather broader and deeper than the upper.

Tallboys were first introduced around 1700, and were surmounted either by a straight, hollow cornice or by a curved and broken pediment. By 1725 they had virtually superseded the chest-on-stand and they remained popular until the mid-Georgian period.

Additional features of the tallboy often include a secret drawer in the frieze and a brushing slide fitted above the oak-lined drawers in the lower section.

Tallboys look cumbersome, and it is a major operation getting up to the top drawers in the upper section. Many were split in half, and their tops veneered to make two smaller chests. Buyers of early walnut chests of drawers should, therefore, beware of any where the top is of a slightly different color to the rest of the carcase.

A George III mahogany tallboy chest with dentil molded cornice and blind fret frieze, on bracket feet, 44in. wide.
(Christie's) $2,930

A George III mahogany and crossbanded tallboy chest, the upper part with a molded cornice, two short and three long graduated drawers, 3ft. 4in. wide.
(Phillips) $1,800

A George I walnut and crossbanded tallboy chest with a molded cornice and fitted with three short and six long drawers, on later bracket feet, 3ft. 5in. wide.
(Phillips) $3,540

A George III mahogany tallboy, the upper part with a dentil molded cornice, the frieze and canted angles decorated with blind fretwork, 3ft. 7in. wide.
(Phillips) $8,181

A George III mahogany chest on chest, the lower section with a brushing slide above three long drawers, 42in. wide.
(Bonhams) $2,334

A George III Welsh walnut and oak tallboy, the later molded cornice above three short and three long graduated drawers, flanked to each side by fluted angles, 42¼in. wide.
(Christie's) $3,425

A late George III mahogany tallboy with molded and reeded cornice, satinwood-veneered frieze with shell medallions, on shaped bracket feet, 46½in. wide. (Bearne's) $1,354

235

TEAPOYS

The word teapoy comes from the Hindi *tin* and *ter*, three, and the Persian *pai*, a foot. It started life therefore as a small tripod table, and only by erroneous association with tea did it arrive at its final form, a small tea chest or caddy standing on a small three-footed stand.

The teapoy is mentioned in inventories as early as 1808, by which time taking tea was well established as an elegant social habit, tea as a commodity still being sufficiently expensive for the hostess to wish to dispense it herself from a locked box.

A Regency ormolu-mounted rosewood teapoy banded overall in satinwood, lyre-shaped end-supports, 30in. high. (Christie's) **$2,243**

A Regency satinwood teapoy of sarcophagus form, the rectangular lid enclosing two canisters, 16½in. wide. (Christie's) **$871**

A George IV rosewood teapoy, the sarcophagus-shaped body with hinged stepped top enclosing a fitted interior, 32½in. high. (Christie's) **$1,232**

A Regency kingwood and specimen wood parquetry teapoy, with rounded rectangular hinged top with central parquetry panel enclosing a fitted interior with removable and twin removable parquetry caddies, 15¼in. wide. (Christie's) **$8,225**

An early Victorian rosewood teapoy, the rising circular top enclosing two tea canisters and two bowl apertures, on reeded fluted shaft and triform base with scroll toes, 81½in. diameter. (Christie's) **$614**

A Regency mahogany teapoy, circa 1830, opening to fitted compartment over tapering sides, tripartite legs, 32½in. high. (Robt. W. Skinner Inc.) **$1,900**

A William IV mahogany teapoy, with canted rectangular hinged lid and lapeted frieze enclosing fitted interior, on faceted shaft and quadripartite platform with paw feet, 18½in. wide. (Christie's) **$666**

A George III mahogany teapoy with octagonal hinged lid enclosing three lidded boxes, the reeded spreading legs headed by lotus leaves, 16¾in. wide. (Christie's) **$4,752**

TRUNKS & COFFERS

The coffer, or chest, is one of the earliest forms of furniture.

It was used as a convenient, safe receptacle for clothes and valuables, doubling as a seat and even, in the case of the larger ones, as a bed.

It was Henry II, in 1166, who really started the boom in coffers when he decreed that one should be placed in every church to raise money for the crusades. Despite the holy cause, all those coffers were fitted with three locks whose keys were held separately by the parish priest and two trustworthy parishioners, just in case any insular minded local felt that he could put the money to better use.

On most early coffers, the stiles form the legs but others were made without such refinements, being made to be fastened down to the floor. There were still other designs, which were entirely of plank construction, the front and back being lapped over the sides and fastened with dowels or hand wrought nails. The side planks extend down below the bottom of the coffer to raise it off the damp, straw covered floor.

The 16th century saw a notable advance in the method of construction of coffers. A number of wide upright stiles were joined with mortise and tenon joints on top and bottom rails, muntins (vertical framing pieces) being added to make the paneled framework.

Decoration on these coffers was usually confined to the panels and took the form, particularly in the early models, of a linenfold design.

A Momoyama period rectangular wood coffer with domed cover decorated with panels of samegawa-togidashi within shippo-hanabishi border, circa 1600, 45.5cm. long. (Christie's) $26,500

A French walnut cassone with hinged rectangular top edged with gadrooning, the front carved with twin panels with reclining figure of Juno, 16th century and later, 67in. wide. (Christie's) $20,790

A Flemish giltmetal mounted and kingwood strongbox on stand, the rectangular top with pierced hinges and foliate border enclosing a fitted interior, 17th century, 28in. wide. (Christie's London) $5,250

An important large roironuri ground domed seventeenth century export coffer decorated in gold, silver and black hiramakie, takamakie, nashiji, hirame with a central lobed panel depicting stags beside rocks and autumnal flowers, 138cm. wide. (Christie's) $298,375

A German steel armada chest, the lock engraved with mermaids and foliate scrolls and locking at fourteen points around the rim, early 17th century, 49in. wide. (Christie's London) $1,200

An Italian pietra paesina-mounted ebonized box with fielded panelled rectangular hinged lid centred by a rectangular panel, depicting the story of Noah, early 17th century, 16in. wide. (Christie's) $13,860

TRUNKS & COFFERS

A Flemish oak coffer, the panelled front headed by an entrelac molding above flower-filled guilloche, on channelled stile feet, late 17th century, 46in. wide.
(Christie's) $1,036

South German baroque marquetry coffer, early 18th century, the hinged rectangular domed lid inlaid with entwined scrolls, the canted sides inlaid with heraldic crests, above a molded base, width 4ft. 1/2in.
(Butterfield & Butterfield) $1,840

A fine paint decorated two-drawer dower chest, Pennsylvania, circa 1830, the whole grain-painted in orange and yellow, 46in. wide.
(Sotheby's) $12,650

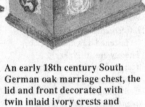

An Afro-American painted and decorated yellow pine slave's trunk, Southern, 19th century, the rectangular hinged lid opening to a divided well, 24in. wide.
(Sotheby's) $1,870

A Chinese coffer-on-stand, the rectangular domed top with a central cartouche with Chinese landscapes of pavilions within a border of inlaid mother-of-pearl, with English carrying handles, the coffer 18th century, 39 1/4 in. wide.
(Christie's) $7,920

An early 18th century South German oak marriage chest, the lid and front decorated with twin inlaid ivory crests and coats-of-arms representing the two families, 53cm. wide.
(Phillips) $1,414

A Chinese black and gilt lacquer chest-on-stand decorated overall with chinoiserie scenes, the domed lid decorated with figures holding nets, the sides with carrying-handles, late 18th century, 34in. wide.
(Christie's) $3,920

A 19th century Kashmir lacquer dower chest, paneled, painted in a floral design, iron clasps and carrying handles, on panel feet, 3ft. 8in.
(Woolley & Wallis) $1,200

A 17th century iron strongbox, of Armada design, the hinged top with nipple studs to release the key cover to a twelve shutter locking device, 58cm. wide, probably German.
(Phillips) $1,591

WARDROBES

Wardrobes are, surprisingly, quite close relations to corner cupboards, for both were born in recesses in walls. Wardrobes were late developers, however, failing to break free from their enclosing walls until the second half of the eighteenth century.

Presses with shelves and drawers were in fairly widespread use by the end of the seventeenth century, before which clothes had been stored in trunks and chests. It had sufficed, for a very long time, to store clothes by packing them flat in horizontal containers but, with the advent of a more sophisticated and clothes-conscious society in which both sexes tended to have increased numbers of garments, it became common sense to hang them vertically.

Although the vogue for wardobes of different kinds seems to have dissipated as abruptly as it arose, a few nice examples have remained with us.

All the fashionable decorative quirks found in other pieces of furniture appear on wardrobes, including dentil cornices, applied moldings and canted front edges. Chippendale favored serpentine fronts, often with bombé fronted drawers below, while Sheraton and Hepplewhite both featured bow-fronted designs. Adam's hallmark on the other hand, was a frieze decorated with low relief carving depicting classical motifs, or panels inlaid with designs of contrasting woods.

Various styles of feet abound, including bracket, ogee and the superbly sweeping French-style foot.

A Victorian bird's eye maple and kingwood crossbanded wardrobe, on a plinth base, 74in. wide.
(Christie's) $1,035

A mahogany wardrobe, the rectangular cornice above a pair of doors, each inset with an oval and a circular panel, 57in. wide.
(Christie's) $528

A Gillow & Co., walnut and oak wardrobe in three sections, with three quarter spindle-turned gallery above molded cornice and two mirrored doors, flanking central cupboard doors with painted panels, 84in. wide.
(Christie's) $1,401

A Robert 'Mouseman' Thompson oak and burr-oak carved paneled wardrobe, with one long cupboard door and one short enclosing two shelves, 119.5cm. wide.
(Christie's) $10,239

An antique English Victorian mahogany wardrobe with a tall pair of serpentine-fronted doors with conformingly shaped molded cornices, circa 1850, 7ft. 4in. high.
(Selkirk's) $3,100

A Tyrolean painted cupboard/ wardrobe, with overall polychrome decoration, the arched molded cornice above a pair of doors between canted angles, early 19th century, 43in. wide.
(Christie's) $1,094

WARDROBES

Classical mahogany carved and mahogany veneer wardrobe, labeled *Manufactured ... at Mathews Cabinet and Chair Factories ... New York*, circa 1820, 55in. wide.
(Skinner) $4,400

A wardrobe, with a broken arched pediment, centered by a seated flute-playing cherub, with a central beveled mirror panel door flanked by a door to each side, 95in. wide.
(Christie's) $11,511

An oak wardrobe designed by Peter Waals, of rectangular form, the two cupboard doors each with four panels and wooden latch, 182.5cm. high.
(Christie's) $4,268

An oak chequered inlaid wardrobe, possibly designed by M.H. Baillie Scott, the molded cornice above a curved recess flanked by a pair of doors inlaid with flowers, 85in. wide.
(Christie's) $3,347

A pine Gothic Revival wardrobe inset with quatrefoils above a pair of pointed arched doors, late 19th century, probably French, 71in. wide.
(Christie's) $1,313

A Regency mahogany wardrobe in four sections, the waved cornice centered by an anthemion and divided by turned finials above two panelled doors enclosing five trays, 98in. wide.
(Christie's) $4,522

A Heal & Son mahogany wardrobe designed by Sir Ambrose Heal, from the 'Five Feathers Suite', London circa 1898, 191.5cm. wide.
(Christie's) $3,150

A Christopher Pratt & Sons late Victorian Arts and Crafts mahogany and ebonized wardrobe, with dog tooth cornices, 66in. wide.
(Christie's) $1,565

A George III oak wardrobe with molded rectangular breakfront cornice and Greek-key moulding, on ogee bracket feet, 78¼in. wide.
(Christie's) $4,522

WASHSTANDS

Wash basins and ewers were introduced as early as the 16th century when Sir John Harrington deemed it essential to "wash all the instruments of the senses with cold water".

Soap balls had been manufactured since the 14th century; toothbrushes had had to wait until the end of the 17th, but it was not until midway through the 18th century that furniture designers thought to design an article specifically for the housing and use of these essential aids to personal hygiene.

A late Regency mahogany washstand with raised back and sides, on turned supports joined by undershelf, 121cm. wide. (Lawrence Fine Arts) $1,800

Federal mahogany and bird's-eye maple veneer corner chamber stand, Massachusetts, early 19th century, 21in. wide. (Skinner Inc.) $2,090

A Liberty & Co. oak washstand, the shaped superstructure with two tiled panels, above rectangular marble top flanked by two shelves, on bracket feet, 104cm. wide. (Christie's) $716

Shaker painted pine washstand, Harvard, Massachusetts, 19th century, the hinged lid opens to a storage compartment above a cupboard, 36in. wide. (Skinner Inc.) $11,000

A Federal carved mahogany wash basin stand, Boston, 1800–1810, with reeded and shaped splash board above a rectangular top with reeded edge fitted for three wash bowls, 30½in. wide. (Christie's) $1,430

A late Federal curly maple single-drawer washstand, Pennsylvania or Middle Atlantic States, circa 1825, 21¼in. wide. (Sotheby's) $2,415

A late Victorian Arts & Crafts oak washstand, attributed to E. & J. Jones of Oswestry, circa 1870, with tiled galleried raised back, 48in. wide. (Christie's) $1,320

A Beidermeier satinbirch and ebonised wash-stand, the circular top with later center above an opening, 29¼in. high. (Christie's) $2,056

WHATNOTS

Formerly of French design, the whatnot made its English debut in about 1790 and was enthusiastically received as the ideal display piece for books and bric a brac.

The earlier examples are generally of rather simple designs and usually of rosewood or mahogany. Subsequent styles, late Regency and Victorian, are often found to be quite elaborate with shaped shelves and fretwork galleries, while some of the Victorian whatnots were made to fit into a corner or enlarged up to four feet in length and designed to be placed against a wall. Some were also fitted with a drawer or drawers.

The whatnot is one of those pieces which could have been called anything at all. The original French name was etagère, but this apparently taxed the memory or linguistic talents of our ancestors to the extent that they fell back on just the kind of name we would be likely to use today; thingamebob, oojah or whatsit.

A pair of gilt-lacquered brass-mounted three-tier mahogany whatnots each with ball finials to the corners, 19th century, 15in. wide.
(Christie's) $12,075

A late Victorian walnut three-tier buffet with pierced fret carved gallery on scroll and spiral twist uprights, 45in. wide.
(Christie's) $1,613

A pair of late Victorian kingwood and satinwood crossbanded etagères, each fitted with three oval graduated shelves, engraved with trailing flowersprays and with pierced brass galleries, 33in. high.
(Christie's) $3,039

An oak Gothic Reform etagère, in the manner of Charles Bevan for Marsh and Jones, circa 1870, with three shelves on trestle supports stencilled with gothic devices, 2ft. 1/2in. wide.
(Sotheby's) $1,364

A Louis XVI ormolu-mounted mahogany étagère d'homme, stamped *Garnier* thrice, late18th century, with ratcheted rectangular galleried top, 47in. high.
(Christie's) $13,800

A pair of mid-Victorian ormolu-mounted burr walnut, amaranth and trellis-pattern parquetry three-tier whatnots by Gillows, 20in. wide.
(Christie's) $27,600

A French gilt-bronze and parquetry etagère, Paris, circa 1885, the removable glass tray-top held by four mer-children, the rectangular table base with caryatid supports, 80cm. wide.
(Sotheby's) $14,699

WINE COOLERS

Records indicate that there were wine coolers in use as early as the 15th century, and examples from the following two centuries are to be seen in many a contemporary tapestry or painting.

They were made for cooling the wine in ice or cold water, and were usually of oval or bowl shape, supported on legs and made in a variety of materials including bronze, copper, silver or even marble and other stones. Some of the silver pieces in particular were very extravagant affairs, and one, in the inventory of the possessions of the Duke of Chandos, is recorded as weighing over two thousand ounces.

Wine coolers made of wood with lead liners were first introduced in about 1730, and these were often supported on cabriole legs with finely carved paw feet.

Some have a nice little brass tap on the side for ease of emptying. Others have brass carrying handles so they could be lifted out of the way with minimal risk of slopping the contents over the guest of honor.

Cellarets were introduced in about 1750 and, at first, were usually of octagonal shape, the earliest often having short feet decorated with carved foliage.

Most are made of mahogany with brass bandings, are lined with lead and partitioned to take nine bottles. At first they were of quite large proportions to take the wide green bottles used at the time but, as these slimmed, cellarets followed suit.

Later in the 18th century, cellarets tended towards an oval shape.

A pair of Regency brass-bound mahogany wine-coolers, each with removable gardrooned and fluted domed top surmounted by a foliate-carved oval handle, 25in. deep.
(Christie's) $108,770

A George II mahogany wine-cooler, the tapering body mounted with pierced carrying-handles, the waved shaped base edged with foliage centred by bunches of grapes, on hairy-paw feet, 27³/₄in. wide.
(Christie's) $292,050

A Regency mahogany wine cooler, the rectangular tapered body with a lead lined interior, canted angles and paneled sides with ebony scroll lines, 3ft. x 1ft. 10in.
(Phillips) $4,242

A George II oval brass-bound mahogany wine-cooler of bombé shape, the sides with giltmetal carrying-handles, on short cabriole legs and hairy paw feet, 28in. wide.
(Christie's) $104,016

A pair of George II brass-bound mahogany oval wine-coolers on George III octagonal stands, each with removable beaten-tin lining and tapering oval body mounted with lion-mask handles, 28in. wide.
(Christie's) $13,464

An early George II walnut cellaret, the moulded hinged top with canted corners and divided interior, the sides with carrying handles, 1ft. 6in. wide.
(Phillips) $3,889

A bronze and rosso marble bird bath, centered by four addorsed dolphins, on a rusticated square base with stepped marble foot, on wooden plinth, 24in. wide. (Christie's)　　　$2,429

A marble and mosaic bench, the rectangular top inlaid with geometric tessuto fragments, on solid lion's claw monopodia base, 39in. wide. (Christie's)　　　$5,855

A Coade stone royal coat of arms, with lion and unicorn supporters, centered by a crown with the heraldic device below, 70$^{1}/_{2}$in. wide. (Christie's)　　　$33,006

A Victorian limestone pulpit, carved with bands of oak leaves and acorns, the foliate branches with pigeons, doves and squirrels, on spreading naturalistic foot, 87in. high. (Christie's)　　　$8,096

A pair of white marble brackets and a matching armorial tablet, the brackets each elaborately carved overall with acanthus, second half 19th century, the brackets: 8$^{1}/_{4}$in. wide. (Christie's)　　　$3,850

Large cast-stone planter on stand, 19th century, on an associated rusticated square pedestal, 35$^{1}/_{2}$in. high. (Butterfield & Butterfield)　　　$1,980

One of a pair of Doulton terracotta figures of eagles with outstretched wings, on square bases stamped *Doulton, London,* 37in. high. (Christie's S. Ken)　Two　　$5,250

An Italian carved pink marble fountain-mask with grotesque face flanked by floral arabesques, now mounted on a rectangular ormolu base, late 17th century, 11in. high. (Chrities)　　　$4,250

A modern patinated copper armillary sphere, supported by four lead cherubs, the sphere with intersecting rings pierced by an arrow, the sphere 31$^{1}/_{2}$in. high. (Christie's)　　　$2,111

A wrought-iron armillary sphere, the interlocking rings pierced by an arrow, on a circular stone foot, 47¼in. high. (Christie's) $548

A white marble bath, of tapering form with rounded ends, the front carved with two rings, 69in. wide. (Christie's) $3,643

A rosso marble well-head, carved in high relief with figures, scrolling foliage and flower-filled vases, on moulded foot, 33in. high. (Christie's) $13,156

An Italian white marble tabernacle surround, in the Florentine late 15th century style, the arched aperture flanked to each side by two angels at prayer, 19th century, 27¼in. wide. (Christie's) $1,643

Pair of large cast-stone fruit baskets on stands, raised on a lobed hemispherical stand above a fluted spreading socle, 45in. high. (Butterfield & Butterfield) $5,225

One of a pair of stone jardinières, each of square tapering form, the paneled sides each with fluted and arcaded decoration and paneled center, 19th century, 18½in. square. (Christie's)
(Two) $4,077

A late 18th century Coade stone keystone, modeled with a mask of an elderly bearded man with cap, stamped Coade, London 1790, 16in. high. (Christie's) $4,000

A carved stone royal coat of arms of Edward VII, with lion and unicorn supporters, within an arched frame, 50in. wide. (Christie's) $1,844

A Venetian Istrian stone well head, with a square molded cornice with rope-twist band, the circular body carved with four acanthus scrolls, probably 14th/15th century, 56in. wide. (Christie's) $38,830

A Coalbrookdale fern and blackberry pattern cast-iron garden seat, scrolled arms with slatted wooden seat, 59¼in. wide.
(Christie's) **$1,660**

A green-painted cast-iron garden chair, the curved back with foliate scrolls and upturned handles, with pierced oval seat, late 19th century.
(Christie's) **$815**

A cast-iron and pine-plank 'Swan' bench, the swan supports centering five rectangular transverses, length 6ft. 1in.
(Sotheby's) **$3,738**

One of a set of four French folding iron garden chairs, the slightly arched backs with down curved scroll arm rests.
(Christie's) **$3,000**

An early 19th century iron garden seat in two half-round sections designed to encircle a tree, on twelve supports with pad feet, maximum diameter 55in.
(David Lay) **$2,664**

A white-painted cast-iron chair, the pierced floral back above a drop-in pierced seat and scrolled cabriole legs.
(Christie's) **$1,323**

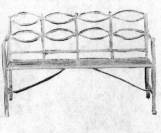

A green-painted cast-iron bench, the pierced back, sides and seat cast with leafy branches, 50½in. wide.
(Christie's) **$1,933**

A Victorian white painted cast iron garden seat, with stiff leaf back and grape vine feet. (Christie's) **$450**

An early 19th century white-painted wrought-iron garden seat, the oval sectioned back above a slatted seat, 61½in. wide.
(Christie's) **$1,300**

A cast-iron double-sided garden bench, the end pieces decorated with eagle-mask hand terminals, on paw feet, 57in. wide. (Christie's) $3,867

One of a set of six white-painted cast-iron chairs, the waisted backs above pierced seats and cabriole legs. (Christie's) (Six) $1,425

An unusual Coalbrookdale pattern cast-iron double-sided bench, with iron slatted seat, the arcaded back pierced with foliage, 56in. wide. (Christie's) $3,441

A white-painted cast-iron gothic armchair, the pierced back and down-curved arm-rests on iron slat seat. (Christie's) $712

A Coalbrookdale laurel pattern cast-iron bench, of semi-circular form with pierced arched back, the arms with griffin head terminals, on winged monopodiae, 46in. wide. (Christie's) $3,036

A cast-iron garden seat, with vine and grape pattern of curved outline with pierced seat, the legs united by stretchers, 36¼in. wide. (Christie's) $810

One of two Coalbrookdale nasturtium pattern cast-iron seats, with wooden slatted seats, the back stamped *C.B. Dale & Co.*, 51¾in. wide. (Christie's) (Two) $2,226

A green-painted cast-iron garden bench, the pierced scrolled back on S-scrolled end supports, 28½in. wide. (Christie's) $509

A white-painted cast-iron seat, with shaped arm supports and triple slat wooden seat, on shaped legs, 57in. wide. (Christie's) $925

FIGURES

A Coadestone figure of a river goddess, from the design by John Bacon, R.A., shown reclining in the form of a triumphal Grecian Naiad, 68¼in. wide.
(Christie's) $47,476

A stone figure of Mercury, wearing a winged cap and holding in his left hand a small bag, 19th century, 68½in. high.
(Christie's) $5,630

Cast iron garden ornament in the form of a Newfoundland dog, America, mid 19th century, 52in. long.
(Skinner) $24,200

A fine Italian white marble figure of a Greek slave girl, by Scipione Tadolini, the maiden shown lightly clad, her hair elaborately dressed in a chignon and head-dress, second half 19th century, 65½in. high the sculpture.
(Christie's) $163,680

Pair of cast stone garden lions on bases, 19th/20th century, each animal recumbent on a stepped and molded rectangular plinth, length 26in.
(Butterfield & Butterfield) $2,875

A 19th century white marble figure of Rebecca at the Well, seated on a rocky outcrop in pensive mood, with water jar at her feet, signed indistinctly, on naturalistic base, 55in. high.
(Christie's) $16,280

A large carved stone figure of Nelson, by Robert Forrest, depicted standing, in military uniform and with his cloak draped over his shoulders, circa 1836, 88in. high.
(Christie's) $29,123

An attractive pair of sandstone garden figures of pixies, each seated cross-legged, eating an apple, 21in. high.
(Spencer's) $1,138

One of a pair of carved red sandstone lions, each sitting back on its haunches and with its paws held before it, 18th/19th century, 34in. high.
(Christie's)
(Two) $5,048

FIGURES

A stone figure of St. George, after Donatello, the saint standing with feet apart, his left hand holding his shield before him, 24½in. high. (Christie's) **$673**

A glazed composition stone group of a lion attacking a kid, after Oscar Waldmann, the lion lying down, snarling, with his right paw clutching the kid, inscribed *O. WALDMANN/ CR(?)ES Emile Muller*, late 19th/ 20th century, 70in. wide. (Christie's) **$6,160**

Zinc garden ornament of a classical figure, A B and W T. Westervelt, New York, late 19th century, 80in. high. (Skinner) **$6,600**

A pair of carved sandstone gate pier finials of heraldic beasts, each sitting on its haunches, its tongue protruding, holding a blank cartouche before it, 19th century, 40in. high. (Christie's) **$2,912**

Monumental cast-stone figure of Diana holding a bow and drapery across her thighs, leaning with her right arm around her deer, 7ft. 1in. high. (Butterfield & Butterfield) **$3,300**

A pair of stoneware gate-pier heraldic lions, each wearing a crown and regarding one another, seated upright on their hind legs and grasping a cartouche-scrolled shield, late 19th century, 46½in. high. (Christie's) **$3,519**

One of a pair of carved Portland stone salamanders, each beast shown seated, wearing a collar and engulfed by 'flames', 18th century, 24in. wide. (Christie's) (Two) **$8,737**

A Victorian stoneware heraldic griffin, seated on his haunches and supporting a shield with his forelegs, on a square stepped base, 42½in. high. (Christie's) **$5,825**

A painted cast-iron dalmatian, American, probably Vermont, 19th century, the freestanding form painted with white and black Dalmatian coloring, 43in. long. (Christie's) **$6,325**

FOUNTAINS

Lead garden birdbath, English, 19th/20th century, in the form of a putto on a shell and raised on triple dolphin supports, 22in. high.
(Butterfield & Butterfield)
$935

An Italian carved Verona marble wall fountain, the rectangular bowl with tapering upright and lion mask fountain head, late 19th/20th century, 69in. high.
(Christie's)
$6,213

A cast-iron fountain, with two circular dishes, the first supported by two cherubs, shown facing each other, on a naturalistic base, 19th century, 57in. high overall.
(Christie's)
$4,453

A Doulton stoneware fountain, probably designed by John Broad, the quatrefoil base of serpentine outline with two putti astride dolphins between two swans, late 19th century, 62in. high overall.
(Christie's)
$13,156

One of a pair of stoneware octagonal fountain bowls and pool surrounds, possibly by John Marriott Bashfield, decorated alternatively with a satyr mask with foliate scrolls between pendant swags, second half 19th century, 51^{1}/4in. high.
(Christie's)
(Two)
$9,677

A cast-iron fountain, the circular dish supported on three seated Egyptian sphinxes, each with ornate headdress and swept back wings, 19th century, 56in. high.
(Christie's)
$3,104

Continental carved marble figural fountain, circa 1900, the figure of Cupid with a drape across his hips, looking down at a butterfly on his right arm, 37in. high.
(Butterfield & Butterfield)
$3,850

Italian baroque Verona marble lion fountain, late 17th century, in three sections, 36^{1}/2in. high.
(Butterfield & Butterfield)
$6,600

A bronze fountain figure of a winged putto carrying a duck, the putto striding forward, on associated circular bronze base with Sabatino de Angelis foundry mark, late 19th century, 21^{5}/8in. high.
(Christie's)
$1,445

SUNDIALS

A glazed stoneware sun-dial plinth, on addorsed swan support, and square sloping base, incorporating a bronze sun-dial inscribed *Thomas Grice, 1705*, 34½in. high.
(Christie's) $1,628

A George III Portland stone and bronze sundial, the bronze dial signed *Simson/Hertford*, with solid gnomon and engraved with chapters and points of the compass, 49in. high.
(Christie's) $2,639

A French limestone wall sundial, surmounted by a square stepped finial, the dial carved with the chapters above a molded arch, 18th century, 20in. wide.
(Christie's) $1,113

A Scottish carved stone sundial pedestal, the circular top with a gadrooned edge and molded support, above an octagonal faceted shoulder with the compass points, late 18th century, 52in. high.
(Christie's) $3,495

Continental carved carrara marble sundial in the Neoclassical taste, probably Italian, second half 19th century, on a concave sided plinth, 41in. high. (Butterfield & Butterfield) $2,200

The Hampton Court Moor by John Van Nost, kneeling and supporting a Portland stone salver with a bronze sundial, wearing a feathered skirt, his hands held above his head, the Moor circa 1701, the dial early 18th century, the figure: 41¾in. high.
(Christie's) $55,770

A Scottish stone sundial, surmounted by a spherical finial, the four sides with arched pediments, each with a carved dial and a bronze gnomon, early 18th century, 66in. high.
(Christie's) $12,620

A stone sundial, with a circular stepped top, supported on four scrolled inverted volutes, with quadruped base, on stepped octagonal foot, the dial: 12in. diameter.
(Christie's) $1,720

A rare terracotta sundial, designed by Archibald Knox, supported on octagonal pedestal cast with leaves and Runic knots, designed and manufactured by Liberty & Co., 3ft. 8in. high.
(Sotheby's) $1,705

URNS

One of a pair of carved white marble urns, each with a molded overhanging rim, the body with drapery suspended between four mask heads, 19th century, 34in. diameter. (Christie's)

(Two) $8,737

A pair of cream marble urns and stands, each with a turned bowl and lip, the body carved with ferns, on tapering turned columns, 37in. high. (Christie's) $704

Carved white marble urn in the neoclassical taste, English, 19th/20th century, carved in low relief with acanthus leaves, 26½in. high. (Butterfield & Butterfield) $770

A Doulton stoneware urn and pedestal, the urn with a waisted body, the lower bowl gadrooned and flanked by twin masks and loop handle to each side, stamped *Doulton Lambeth*, late 19th century, the urn: 33in. high. (Christie's) $1,021

Set of four French polished iron garden urns, signed *Alfred Corneau*, late 19th century, each of compressed circular urn form with tall openwork scroll-handles, height 17in. (Butterfield & Butterfield) $3,163

One of a pair of blue-painted cast-iron urns, the tapering body with gadrooned lower part on circular molded socle with square foot, late 19th century, 29½in. high. (Christie's)   (Two) $822

Large Victorian cast-iron two-handled garden urn, second half 19th century, with coved fluted sides and applied with side handles modeled as grotesque swans, 42in. high. (Butterfield & Butterfield) $2,200

Pair of early Victorian tulip-form cast-iron garden urns, mid 19th century, each with a scalloped lip above a lappet-cast flat-reeded socle, 20½in. high. (Butterfield & Butterfield) $935

One of a pair of monumental George III stone urns, each with an overlaid leaf carved neck, the frieze carved in high relief with ram's mask, foliate festoons and rosettes, 45in. high. (Christie's)

(Two) $8,798

URNS

A rare terracotta garden urn on stand, designed by Archibald Knox, the circular bowl with four outset handles divided by stylized foliage, 3ft. high.
(Sotheby's) $1,023

A pair of parcel-gilt bronze-painted cast-iron urns, after the Warwick vase, each with 'X'-shaped handles in the form of entwined branches, second-half 19th century, 32½in. wide.
(Christie's) $3,871

One of a pair of large composition garden urns of fluted and reeded campana form, 53in. high.
(Bearne's)   (Two) $1,118

One of a pair of monumental white marble urns, after the Warwick Vase, each boldly carved in high relief with masks of Bacchus and Silenus, 20th century, 63in. high.
(Christie's)   (Two)
          $17,204

Pair of Victorian green painted iron garden urns, second half 19th century, of campana form, the inswept sides applied with swags of flowers above a lobed lower section, height 24in.
(Butterfield & Butterfield)
          $1,610

One of a pair of red stoneware urns and pedestals, the waisted body raised with grapes and vine leaves, the lower part gadrooned on a spreading circular socle and stepped square base, the urns, 20½in. high.
(Christie's)   (Two) $1,012

One of a pair of stone urns, in the Neo-Classical style, each with a bead-molded rim and pair of rams-mask handles, with drapery swags above upright water leaves, 20½in. high overall.
(Christie's) (Two) $880

A matching pair of Italian marble urns, after the Medici and Borghese vases, each of campana form, intricately carved overall, first half 19th century, 19½in. high.
(Christie's) $53,900

One of a set of seven stone urns, acanthus-carved upper part, the lower bowl with molded gadrooning, on a circular stepped tapering socle, 18th century, 49½in. high.
(Christie's)
          (Seven) $12,317

A rare circular gas cooker by Hare & Co., with single wrought-iron boiling ring on top and another in oven base, 38in. high.
(Christie's) $1,778

An amber enamel French table gas cooker 'Le Vatel' type 400 by Lilor Paris, with six brass taps to feed oven burner, circa 1915.
(Christie's) $1,333

A New World Junior gas cooker by Davis & Co. under Radiation Patents with front tap rail with four brass lever taps feeding three Rado burners.
(Christie's) $249

A 'Eureka' No 405 gas cooker by John Wright & Co., with front tap rail for two rack-type boiling burners and grill, 21½in. high, circa 1907.
(Christie's) $622

A 'Metropolitan' No 211 double gas range, by the Davis Gas Stove Co., 200/210 Camberwell Road, London SE, with front tap rail, eight taps and cast plate rack.
(Christie's) $338

A 'Davis Wee Cooker' by the Davis Gas Stove Co., Metropolitan Works 200/210, Camberwell Road, London SE, with front tap rail, circa 1898.
(Christie's) $1,067

A rare gas range (Model 140. New pattern) by Richmond & Co., Warrington & London, with original copper hot water urn and gas attachment.
(Christie's) $1,778

A 'Cheerful' gas fire and boiling stove by John Wright & Co., Birmingham, with wrought-iron boiling ring on top.
(Christie's) $160

The 'Great Duck' portable deflector cooker, of sheet steel with four cast iron cabriole feet, thre boiling rings fed from one large ring burner, 32½in. wide, circa 1915.
(Christie's) $249

BASKETS

WMF Alpaca basket, Germany, circa 1905, reticulated form in low relief Art Nouveau decorated style, with clear glass liner, 13¹/₂in. high. (Skinner) $316

A 19th century silverplate 'strawberry' glass centerpiece basket, hand- enameled case blue to white liner, full relief strawberries about the handle. (Du Mouchelles) $200

Tiffany gilt bronze and Favrile basket, pastel yellow glass bowl with vertical leaf pattern and stretched iridescence, 6³/₄in. high. (Skinner) $770

Victorian glass basket, attributed to Stevens & Williams, opaque opal glass cased to raspberry pink, applied with amber leaves and fruits, 11in. high. (Skinner) $660

Escalier de Cristal ormolu basket, attributed to Baccarat, stylized trees and floral enamel decorated on clear bowl mounted with gilt metal double dragon handle, 6³/₄in. high. (Skinner) $660

A Venetian latticinio small bucket in vetro a retorti, the body of compressed baluster form supported on a merese above a spreading conical foot, late 16th century, 12.5cm. high. (Christie's) $1,993

19th century cranberry glass to opalescent white glass bride's basket, set in white metal frame, 6in. wide. (Du Mouchelles) $100

Rare Val St. Lambert cameo glass basket, overlaid in emerald green, cameo cut and wheel cut in Vintage pattern, 11in. high. (Skinner Inc.) $2,000

An amberina bride's basket and holder, set into a silver plated basket with applied leaves and cherries, 9in. high. (Robt. W. Skinner Inc.) $675

One of a group of four green glass Roman beakers, with a thick band of trail around the upper body, 3¹/₂in. high, circa 4th century A.D.
(Bonhams) (Four) $406

A Baccarat cylindrical tumbler with an oval panel set with the Badge of the Legion d'Honneur enameled in colors on a gilt ground, 9.5cm. high.
(Phillips) $884

A German glass beaker, dated *1722*, enameled in colors with a horse seller leading a pack of horses, 5¹/₂in. high.
(Bonhams) $1,500

A North Bohemian 'Lebensalter' cylindrical tumbler engraved with the 'Ages of Man', depicted as an arched bridge, each step supporting a pair of figures, circa 1820, 11.5cm. high.
(Christie's) $5,833

A pair of lithyalin green tinted remembrance beakers from the workshop of Friedrich Egermann, of faceted, waisted form, 11cm.
(Phillips) $2,431

An engraved cylindrical tumbler decorated with a continuous scene of a standing figure of Britannia, with facet-cut footrim, circa 1800, 11.5cm. high.
(Christie's) $807

Bohemian white and cranberry overlay spa glass, mid 19th century, with six vertical panels each with a named engraved and gilt architectural view, 5in. high.
(Butterfield & Butterfield) $357

An armorial cylindrical tumbler, engraved with a coat-of-arms and inscribed above *Prosperity to the House of Downing*, circa 1817, 10.5cm. high.
(Christie's) $1,653

A dated engraved barrel-shaped tumbler, one side with a view of Yarmouth Church, the reverse with the initials *JRP* above the date *1798*, 12.5cm. high.
(Christie's) $1,698

Poison bottle, skull figural poison bottle, cobalt blue, 4³/₈in. high, late 19th century.
(Skinner) $440

An early sealed 'shaft and globe' wine-bottle of green tint, circa 1670, 19.5cm. high.
(Christie's) $7,711

Ruby glass bottle vase, 19th century, the metal of a deep rich purplish-red tone, 10¹/₂in. high.
(Butterfield & Butterfield)
$2,200

Enamelled cordial bottle, colorless with enameled florals and Germanic inscription, metal threads, possibly silver, pontil scar, half-pint, 6³/₄in. high, Bohemia, mid 18th century.
(Skinner Inc.) $176

A pair of green glass bottles, probably Dutch, late 18th/early 19th century, 17¹/₄in. high.
(Sotheby's) $1,000

Early decorated spirits bottle, medium sapphire blue with white loopings, pewter threads, pontil scar, 7⁵/₈in. high, Germany/Northern Europe, circa 1750.
(Skinner Inc.) $1,210

Emile Gallé Islamic style enameled bottle, squared transparent oval-form decorated overall with colorful enameled foliate devices, 6¹/₄in. high.
(Skinner) $7,150

A sealed and dated 'onion' wine-bottle of olive-green tint, applied with a seal inscribed T. Burford 1718, the tapering neck with a string-ring and with kick-in base, 16cm. high.
(Christie's) $1,525

Early decorated bottle, decorated with quilled rigaree and prunts, two swirled rings around neck, 10in. high, probably Spain, late 17th/early 18th century.
(Skinner Inc.) $264

BOWLS

René Lalique, bowl, 'Calypso', after 1930, opalescent glass, 11³/₄in. diameter.
(Sotheby's) $3,920

Murano studio glass bowl, Barovier and Toso, designed by Ercole Barovier in the "Cathedrale" or "Athena" series, 8¹/₄in. diameter. (Skinner Inc.) $4,400

René Lalique, bowl, 'Lys', after 1924, opalescent glass, 9¹/₄in. diameter.
(Sotheby's) $570

An Irish cut circular bowl, the sides with panels of exaggerated step-cutting beneath a fan-cut rim, circa 1830, probably Waterford, 25.5cm. diameter.
(Christie's) $770

A Stuart clear glass bowl designed by Graham Sutherland, flared shallow form on tapering foot, with waved bands of intaglio decoration, 35cm. diameter.
(Christie's) $2,760

Early engraved compôte, bowl engraved with wreaths and tassels, 8¹/₄in. high, New England, 1825–35.
(Skinner) $1,320

A cut deep bowl, the polygonal sides with horizontal prisms beneath a fluted dentil rim, circa 1820, 20.5cm. diameter.
(Christie's) $1,028

An Art Nouveau acid-etched and carved cameo bowl, in gilt metal wirework stand, 17cm. diameter.
(Christie's) $368

Webb gem cameo glass bowl, bright cobalt blue sphere layered in both blue and white, 5in. diameter.
(Skinner Inc.) $6,050

French gilt-bronze-mounted enameled opaline glass box, mid 19th century, with canted corners molded with a diamond pattern, 9in. wide. (Butterfield & Butterfield) $2,475

'Amour Assis', a Lalique satin finished circular box and cover, the top surmounted by a seated cherub, 5³/₄in. high. (Christie's S. Ken) $3,855

A Louis Philippe ormolu-mounted baccarat toilet box with square cut facets and hinged lid, the border with bands of lotus leaves, 5¹/₂in. wide. (Christie's) $1,517

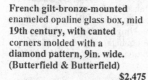

A fine late Victorian tantalus, with three square decanters and four glasses, with games drawer below, 14in. high. (Bearne's) $1,174

'Figurines et Violes', a Lalique circular box and cover, the exterior molded in relief with classical maidens dancing with scarves, stained green, 4in. diameter. (Christie's S. Ken) $2,356

A late Victorian metal mounted oak box pattern tantalus, with three cut glass decanters, 35cm. (Phillips) $660

A Gallé acid-etched and carved circular box and cover, pale gray glass overlaid in purple with trails of wisteria blossom, 6¹/₂in. diameter. (Christie's S. Ken) $1,105

A rare and unusual Venetian glass jewel casket and cover of rectangular shape, the sides formed of rectangular filigree panels of trellis with circular florettes at the junctions, 18.5cm. x 14cm. (Phillips) $2,431

A Gabriel Argy-Rousseau pâte-de-verre circular box and cover, of pale amber glass, the cover molded with yellow and purple stylised petals, 11.2cm. diameter. (Christie's) $6,006

CANDLESTICKS

Pair of dolphin candlesticks, wafer attachments, electric blue sockets, 10¼in., Sandwich Glassworks, 1845–70. (Skinner) **$2,200**

Tiffany gold iridescent Art glass candlestick vase with ribbed twist stem, marked on base, *LCT*, 5¼in. high. (Eldred's) **$440**

Pair of early pattern molded candlesticks, with domed radial molding, colorless lead glass, 6⅛in. high, England, 1715–30. (Skinner) **$550**

'Cariatide', a pair of Lalique frosted glass table decorations, with delicate pinky-brown tint, each modeled as the stylized torso of a young woman, 12in. high. (Christie's S. Ken) **$30,401**

A set of four late 19th century Murano gilt heightened and white enameled glass three light candelabra, each with a central branch flanked by two scrolling arms, 21in. high. (Christie's S. Ken) (Four) **$4,477**

A pair of facet-cut tapersticks with barbed everted lips, flattened collars and central knops between diamond faceting, 15.5cm. high. (Phillips) **$1,020**

Pair of blown and pressed candlesticks, hexagonal base, attached by five tooled wafers to a Pittsburgh-type blown socket, deep blue, 9in., possibly Pittsburgh, 1840–1860. (Skinner) **$4,400**

One of a pair of pressed candlesticks, deep amethyst, 9⅛in. high, New England Glass Co., 1840–50. (Skinner) (Two) **$550**

A rare pair of George III cut-glass candlesticks, each with two tiers of prismatic drops, on 'Bristol' blue glass cylindrical plinths, 12in. high. (Bearne's) **$12,708**

CLARET JUGS

A Victorian silver-mounted cut-glass claret jug, 11in. high, John Grinsell and Sons, London 1897. (Bearne's) $1,103

An English gilt-metal mounted blue glass parrot claret jug, complete with stopper, 11³/₄in. high.
(Christie's) $864

A late Victorian silver-mounted cut-glass flaring claret jug on a star-cut base, J.G. & S., London 1898, 10¹/₄in.
(Christie's S. Ken) $620

An extremely finely engraved Stourbridge claret jug with ovoid body, intaglio engraved with a Grecian charioteer with a helmet and a shield, 26.5cm.
(Phillips) $2,590

A pair of Bohemian gilt and clear glass decagonal claret jugs, each decorated with a band of grapes and vine leaves, 13¹/₂in. high.
(Christie's) $1,132

A good early Victorian claret jug, engraved with an oasis depicting two camels, one recumbent under a palm tree and an Arab kneeling beside his tent, 31cm. high.
(Spencer's) $320

A Victorian mounted glass ovoid claret jug with waisted neck engraved with anthemions and foliage, by J.C. Edington, 1865, 37.5cm. high.
(Phillips) $2,917

A silver mounted claret jug by Heath and Middleton, London, the globular body with wrythen ornament, 1889–90, 22cm. high.
(Finarte) $605

A Victorian claret jug, the ovoid glass body finely engraved with daisies and leafy stems, Sheffield 1900.
(Russell Baldwin & Bright)
$940

Pair of German silver and engraved glass decanters, 19th century, rectangular with rococo scenes, 10in. high.
(Skinner Inc.) $1,760

A very attractive Bohemian cased decanter and stopper, the ruby body cased in white and green opaline glass, 28cm.
(Phillips) $4,183

A pair of green glass mallet decanters, with panel cut decoration and spire stoppers, 13in. high.
(Spencer's) $788

A pair of unusual Venetian or Bohemian millefiore decanters and stoppers of globe and shaft form, 31.5cm.
(Phillips) $1,992

A pair of Continental decanters and silver-gilt stand, French, early 19th century, the central extension of twisted vine motif, with blue glass decanters decorated with twisted vine gold leaf decoration, maker's mark *LB*, 28cm. high.
(Lawrence) $3,323

A pair of amethyst gilt-decorated decanters and stoppers for Hollands and Brandy, of club shape, named in gilt within linked navette, early 19th century, 30.5cm. high.
(Christie's) $2,218

A pair of engraved and cut decanters and stoppers of club shape, decorated with a rounded turf stack flanked by two trees on a sward, early 19th century, 25.5cm. high.
(Christie's) $1,361

A Hukin & Heath electroplated and glass 'crow's feet' decanter, designed by Christopher Dresser, on three metal feet, 24cm. high, October 1878.
(Phillips) $8,200

A pair of magnificent magnum cut decanters and stoppers, printed in colored enamels with figures symbolic of Asia and Africa, 35cm., probably Irish.
(Phillips) $15,200

DISHES

An Irish cut oval turnover center-dish, the bowl with a band of facet ornament, circa 1800, 35cm. wide.
(Christie's)   **$2,742**

A pair of cut oval two-handled deep dishes, the flared sides with horizontal prisms beneath dentil rims, circa 1815, 20.5cm. wide.
(Christie's)   **$942**

Blown three-mold hat whimsey, deep sapphire blue, pontil scar, 2¼in., New England, 1825–40.
(Skinner)   **$825**

A Venetian enameled armorial low tazza, the shallow tray enameled in iron-red, blue and ocher with a coat-of-arms with pendant scrolling tendrils, early 16th century, 23cm. diameter.
(Christie's)   **$18,271**

A J. & L. Lobmeyr large circular dish engraved by Karl Pietsch with 'The Marriage of Neptune and Amphitrite', the center with a running figure of Bacchus holding a goblet beside a leaping panther, 42.5cm. diameter.
(Christie's)   **$73,882**

A J. Couper & Sons Clutha dish, circular with pulled and undulated rim and shallow well, green tinted glass with milky-white and red striations, 22.5cm. wide.
(Christie's)   **$1,244**

Ribbon edge compote, amethyst, 8¾in. wide, wafer attachment, hexagonal base, probably Sandwich Glassworks, 1840–1860.
(Skinner)   **$9,900**

A pair of large cut glass cylindrical two-handled coolers and liners, circa 1820, 26cm. wide.
(Christie's)   **$11,138**

A baluster tazza, the stem with a triple annulated knop above a plain section enclosing an elongated tear and basal knop, circa 1725, 24cm. diameter.
(Christie's)   **$915**

DRINKING GLASSES

A diamond-engraved ale-glass, decorated with two peacocks perched among scattered stylized flowerheads and foliage, circa 1695, 12.5cm. high. (Christie's) $3,322

An airtwist firing-glass with a bell bowl, the stem filled with spiral threads above a thick foot, circa 1750, 10cm. high. (Christie's) $532

A Jacobite dram-glass, the bell bowl engraved with a six-petaled rose, a bud and a half-opened bud, circa 1745, 9.5cm. high. (Christie's) $1,578

A balustroid champagne glass with a double-ogee bowl, the stem with a beaded knop between two plain sections above a domed foot, circa 1730, 12cm. high. (Christie's) $432

A Venetian drinking-glass, the shallow bowl supported on a wrythen-molded slender tapering stem, late 16th/early 17th century, 14.5cm. diameter. (Christie's) $2,990

A balustroid molded champagne-glass, the double-ogee bowl with everted rim molded with allover honeycomb ornament, circa 1735, 15.5cm. high. (Christie's) $598

A color-twist firing-glass, the stem with an opaque gauze core entwined by a pair of translucent green and a pair of opaque spiral threads, circa 1770, 11cm. high. (Christie's) $2,824

A Venetian drinking-glass, the radially ribbed small bowl with a wide everted rim supported on a merese, early 17th century, 12cm. high. (Christie's) $2,824

An engraved rummer attributed to William Absolon, the pointed funnel bowl decorated with a wheat-sheaf within a circular cartouche, early 19th century, 14.5cm. high. (Christie's) $747

EWERS

A cut and stained-amber ewer of tapering oviform with a scroll handle, cut with three rows of sunburst medallions, circa 1830, 24.5cm. high.
(Christie's) $1,113

A cut glass ruby-stained claret ewer, circa 1865, the ovoid body cut overall with large diamonds, the shoulder and slender neck with printies, 11³/₄in. high.
(Sotheby's) $1,620

A Venetian small ewer lightly molded with vertical flutes, the scroll handle applied with pincered ornament, late 17th century, 14cm. high.
(Christie's) $622

A Stourbridge green flash slender oviform ewer with hinged silver cover, engraved with lilies issuing from stylized foliage, early 20th century, 12⁵/₈in. high.
(Christie's) $875

A 'Façon de Venise' diamond-engraved ewer of slightly straw-tinted metal, decorated with panels of flower-sprays, scroll and dot ornament, Spain or Italy, early 17th century, 17cm. high.
(Christie's) $3,397

A fine silver-mounted cameo claret ewer, probably Thomas Webb and Sons, circa 1884, the deep amber-tinted glass overlaid in opaque-white and carved with dahlias, a raspberry and insects, 10³/₈in. high.
(Sotheby's) $5,115

A Schneider 'Le Verre Français' cameo glass jug of oviform, the mottled pink body overlaid with red glass shading to brown, 50cm. high.
(Phillips) $695

A fine engraved armorial claret ewer, possibly John Baird Glassworks, Glasgow, circa 1860, finely engraved possibly by Henry Keller, with a Grecian warrior and chariot, 9⁵/₈in. high.
(Sotheby's) $2,131

A Bohemian enameled green-ground slender oviform ewer and stopper, decorated in the Persian taste in bright colors with stylized foliage, circa 1890, 46cm. high.
(Christie's) $1,661

FIGURES

'Danseuse Drapée', a Sabino opalescent figure, molded as a nude female, walking arms outstretched with a long cloak flowing behind, 23.6cm. high.
(Christie's) $1,140

Pair of Steuben cut crystal pigeons, 6824 Carder birds, inscribed *Steuben*, 6in. high.
(Skinner) $1,725

'Gros Poisson, Vagues', a Lalique sculpture, the clear glass molded as a large-finned fish, 39cm. high with base.
(Christie's) $4,867

'Espagnole', a Sabino opalescent figure, molded as a Spanish dancer, poised holding a tambourine, with engraved signature *Sabino Paris*, 27.4cm. high.
(Christie's) $1,300

Pair of René Lalique auto mascot Longchamp bookends, of solid grayish crystal molded as thoroughbred racehorses, mounted to black glass platform bases, 6¹/₂in. high.
(Skinner) $7,475

Gino Cenedese & Cie Studio glass figure, attributed to Alfredo Barbini, iridized opal mauve colored glass sculpture of bearded oriental fish vendor, 18in. high.
(Skinner Inc.) $1,485

'Suzanne au Bain', a Lalique opalescent glass figure, molded as a nude girl poised on one leg, her arms outstretched supporting a drape, 22.5cm. high,
(Christie's) $1,762

A pair of glass horse heads, designed by Archimede Seguso, the dark blue glass covered with white fragments, Murano, Made in Italy, 16.5cm. high.
(Christie's) $1,566

'Jeune fille aux colombes', a Sabino opalescent statuette, molded as a nude woman kneeling with three doves, with molded signature *Sabino Paris*, 15.8cm. high.
(Christie's) $815

Pitkin-type flask, broken swirl, deep golden amber, sheared lip-pontil scar, half-pint, 6⅝in. high, Midwest America, 1790–1830.
(Skinner) $495

A Netherlands turquoise globular flask, the lower part molded with 'nipt diamond waies', late 17th century, 24.5cm. high.
(Christie's) $7,475

Eagle masonic historical flask, aqua, sheared lip-pontil scar, pint, Kensington Glassworks, Philadelphia, 1822–25.
(Skinner) $143

A Central European dated tailor's spirit-flask, enameled in colours with accoutrements of the tailor's trade, the reverse with an inscription and the date *1771*, 14cm. high.
(Christie's) $1,663

A German engraved flask and screw-cap cover, the flattened oviform body with a dragon-fly alighting on the hump of a camel, perhaps Nuremburg, circa 1700, 28.5cm. high.
(Christie's) $7,431

A Bohemian dated enameled rectangular flask amusingly painted with a farmer, with a hoe in one hand and holding a goblet in the other, 1792, 21cm. high.
(Christie's) $6,664

Grotesque head men arguing pictorial flask, aqua, sheared lip-pontil scar, possibly Continental Europe, early 19th century.
(Skinner) $385

A Spanish latticinio cruet-flask with opposing slender curved spouts, Barcelona or Catalonia, late 17th/18th century, 17cm. high.
(Christie's) $832

A Central European amber-tinted spirit-flask of rectangular section with allover honeycomb molding, second half of the 18th century, 15cm. high.
(Christie's) $2,772

GLASS

GOBLETS

A heavy baluster goblet, set on
an inverted baluster stem
enclosing a large tear above a
folded conical foot, circa 1700,
19cm. high.
(Christie's) $747

A pair of glass goblets, each bowl
engraved with national emblems,
hops and barley, dated 1829,
13.4cm.
(Bearne's) $627

A baluster goblet with a bell
bowl, the stem with a beaded
knop above an inverted baluster
section and basal knop, circa
1730, 21cm. high.
(Christie's) $583

A 'Façon de Venise' latticinio
goblet, the compressed oval
bowl with a band of vetro a
retorti between white threads,
South Netherlands, second half
of the 16th century, 13cm. high.
(Christie's) $11,666

Six René Lalique wine goblets,
colorless crystal bowl stemmed
by plump frosted amethyst
birds, 4⅝in. high.
(Skinner) $2,750

An interesting 'Façon de Venise'
vetro a retorti goblet with
entwined corkscrew spirals,
above five knops and a tall
conical foot, 16.5cm. high.
(Phillips) $3,720

A lithyalin goblet of marbled
blue/gray color, the ovoid
hexagonal bowl with raised cut
bosses, perhaps Johann Zich,
Waldviertel, circa 1832, 15.5cm.
high.
(Christie's) $2,033

Two Orrefors goblets designed
by Gunnar Cyrén, each with
deep bowl on thick cylindrical
colored stem and circular foot,
8¼in. high.
(Christie's S. Ken) $1,474

Bohemian white and cranberry
overlay glass goblet, mid 19th
century, enameled with floral
bouquets or cut with blocks of
diamonds, 6¾in. high.
(Butterfield & Butterfield)
                            $605

JARS

Bohemian Art Glass covered jar, colorless bowl cased to caramel and internally decorated in red random squiggles, 5¹/₂in. high. (Skinner) $172

Pair of yellow Peking glass ginger jars and covers, circa 1900, the ovoid sides of each carved in deep relief, 6³/₈in. high. (Butterfield & Butterfield)
$1,980

An early 19th century glass jar, cover and stand, each piece cut with a diamond design within a serrated rim, 23.4cm. high. (Bearne's) $448

Jeweled Crown Milano biscuit jar, with pale yellow and orange mottled floral background, 5in. high. (Skinner Inc.) $425

A collection of eleven 19th century deep bottle-green and brown specie jars, with numbered, gilt oval labels, 14¹/₂in. high. (Christie's S. Ken)
(Eleven) $2,317

Gallé spider web dresser jar, 'fire polished' amber glass with interior frost and sapphire blue over-layer, 4¹/₂in. high. (Skinner) $1,725

A pair of pedestal sweetmeat jars and covers set on square stepped bases, the body and cover cut with scrolls and vertical flutes, 32.5cm. (Bearne's) $546

A 19th century glass specie-jar, with painted and gilded royal coat of arms and gilded lid, 35in. high. (Christie's S. Ken) $685

A pair of cut jars and covers with mushroom finials, with spiral fluted decoration on square star cut bases, 11¹/₂in. high. (Christie's S. Ken) $805

A baluster jug with a ribbed lower section on a spreading foot and a ribbed strap handle, 1799, 20.5cm.
(Phillips) $785

'Griffith Hyatt & Co/Baltimore' handled jug, deep golden amber, 7¼in., America, 1840–60.
(Skinner) $412

A blue overlay oviform jug, decorated with panels painted in colors and gilt with flowers, 12in. high.
(Christie's S. Ken) $4,026

A Spanish 'Façon de Venise' latticinio baluster jug decorated with vertical marvered opaque-white threads, late 17th/18th century, 9in. high.
(Christie's) $585

A Spanish 'ice-glass' small jug of straw tint, the 'ice-glass' globular body beneath a plain rim applied with turquoise trailed thread, late 17th century, Barcelona or Castile, 5½in. wide.
(Christie's) $2,750

A W.M.F. lemonade jug, the tapering cylindrical glass body cut with diamonds and swags, 13½in. high.
(Christie's) $428

A jug designed by E. Léveillé, with cylindrical neck and curved handles, internally decorated with mottled undulating stripes of white and maroon, 9¾in. high. (Christie's) $1,460

Pillar molded syrup jug, with pewter spout and lid, colorless, hollow blown handle, pontil scar, 9½in., Pittsburgh area glass house, 1820–1850.
(Skinner) $440

An engraved topographical jug, possibly J. B. Millar, John Ford and Co., Edinburgh, circa 1865, engraved with titled views of Holyrood Palace, Calton Hill and Edinburgh Castle, 9in. high.
(Sotheby's) $2,216

MISCELLANEOUS

An unusual Varnish & Co. ring stand with ruby glass over the silver, and tall pointed spire, 13cm. high.
(Phillips) $672

A very unusual glass teapot and cover, of globular shape with a trailed loop handle, wide spout and stylized bird finial, 15.5cm.
(Phillips) $1,793

English cameo mirrored épergne, four bulbed flower bowls of lustrous red overlaid in white, 10½in. high.
(Skinner Inc.) $3,400

Pair of Louis XVI style gilt-bronze-mounted cut glass urns, with upstanding foliate handles issuing from female masks at the shoulder, 16¾in. high.
(Butterfield & Butterfield) $1,980

An oval pâte sur pâte plaque by Frederick Rhead, signed, decorated with a young maiden holding a basket of fruit and dressed in a diaphanous costume, 27cm.
(Phillips) $3,248

A pair of Victorian mushroom opaque glass lusters, the cylindrical bowls printed in colors with eight oval panels enclosing female heads, on a gilt decorated ground, 33cm. high.
(Spencer's) $354

A St. Louis macedoine wafer-stand, the rim to the ogee bowl applied with a cobalt-blue twisted ribbon entwined with white latticinio thread, mid-19th century, 7.5cm. diameter.
(Christie's) $997

A George III two-handled oil and vinegar frame, with ram's mask and scroll handles and beaded border, by Andrew Fogelberg, 1775, 8¾in. long, 17oz.
(Christie's) $4,117

A Stourbridge glass millefiori inkwell with stopper, the canes arranged in concentric rows including four showing the date *1848*, 4½in. diameter.
(Russell Baldwin & Bright) $526

PAPERWEIGHTS

A St. Louis pink dahlia weight, the flower with three rows of deep-pink lightly ribbed petals about a yellow-dotted red center, mid-19th century, 7.2cm. diameter.
(Christie's) $1,284

An Almaric Walter pate-de-verre paperweight designed by H. Berge, 8cm. high.
(Christie's) $15,500

A Clichy flower weight, the daisy-like flower with radiating white petals tipped in pale-yellow about a red, white and pale-yellow center, mid-19th century, 7.5cm. diameter.
(Christie's) $9,424

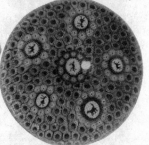

A Baccarat flat bouquet weight, the central pink 'thousand-petaled' rose surrounded by a cobalt-blue and white primrose, a pansy of conventional type, a yellow wheatflower and dark-blue and red buds, mid-19th century, 7.8cm. diameter.
(Christie's) $9,970

A Clichy double-overlay close concentric millefiori mushroom weight, the tuft with five circles of canes in shades of moss-green, white, dark-blue and including five pink roses, mid-19th century, 7cm. diameter.
(Christie's) $6,976

A St. Louis green carpet-ground concentric millefiori weight, the central silhouette of a devil within a circle of white and dark-blue canes surrounded by five silhouettes, mid-19th century, 6.8cm. diameter.
(Christie's) $6,976

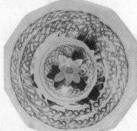

A St. Louis faceted upright bouquet weight, edged with green leaves and including a large white flower with yellow 'match head' center, mid-19th century, 7.5cm. diameter.
(Christie's) $4,983

A Clichy sulphide garlanded swirl weight, the sulphide portrait of the young Queen Victoria in profile to the left, mid-19th century, 7.8cm. diameter.
(Christie's) $1,113

A Clichy flower weight, the daisy-like flower with radiating purple petals tipped in pale-yellow about a blue and pale-yellow center, mid-19th century, 7.4cm. diameter.
(Christie's) $6,976

PITCHERS

Free blown pitcher, with applied and crimped handle, deep cobalt, folded rim-pontil scar, 6in.
(Skinner) $303

Victorian Art Glass pitcher and tumbler, attributed to Thomas Webb & Sons, of opaline with internal red striping and gold enamel floral decoration, 8³/₄in. high.
(Skinner) $345

Antique amberina water pitcher with applied ribbed amber handle, New England, circa 1860, 8¹/₈in. high.
(Eldred's) $193

Rare pillar molded pitcher, cranberry body with clear cased cranberry blown handle, 9½in., possibly Pittsburgh area, 1850-1870. (Robt. W. Skinner Inc.) $9,000

A Richardson's water-set, comprising a baluster water-jug with loop handle and two goblets, circa 1848, the jug 20.5cm. high.
(Christie's) $1,885

Moser enamel decorated glass pitcher, trefoil rim on sapphire blue coin spot pitcher with multicolored scrolls and stylized foliate designs, 7¹/₂in. high.
(Skinner) $747

Mt. Washington Royal Flemish pitcher, bulbous-form with molded raised fishnet design handpainted with seashells, marine plants and two realistic fish, 8in. high.
(Skinner) $1,100

'A. A. Adams – Pittsburgh PA' engraved water set, pitcher and five tumblers, colorless upper bodies with ring pattern, 1870–1880's.
(Skinner) $330

Fleur de lys pitcher, circa 1895, etched glass, heightened with gilding, with gilt mark *Daum Nancy*, 7¹/₂in. high.
(Sotheby's) $927

273

English intaglio cut glass vase, attributed to Stevens & Williams, sapphire blue cased to opal white squat bowl with ruffled crimped rim, 7¹/₂in. diameter.
(Skinner) $440

A pair of Palme Konig iridescent green glass vases of baluster shape, with twisted body having applied lines in spider web effect, 27cm.
(Phillips) $323

An iridescent glass shell vase, attributed to Loetz, frilled rim conch shell on a frilled foot, 16.4cm. high.
(Bonhams) $1,130

A Loetz iridescent glass vase, of squat baluster form with an irregular flared mouth, in clear glass covered with a golden iridescence, 13.5cm. high.
(Phillips) $550

Pair of green Peking glass vases each of slender baluster form flaring towards the base and surmounted by a tall waisted neck, 11¹/₂in. high.
(Butterfield & Butterfield) $1,760

A Loetz vase, with everted rim and applied lattice decoration, the yellow ground with areas of rainbow iridescence, 18.5cm. high.
(Christie's) $1,416

An Argy-Rousseau smoky gray glass vase, centered in enamel with a huddled group of white chicks flanked by similar solitary birds, 17.80cm. high.
(Phillips) $1,556

A pair of fine bronze mounted intaglio-carved glass vases, with carved decoration of a song bird perched on a blossom branch watching a flying insect, 31cm. high.
(Christie's) $1,958

An impressive Art Deco Daum acid-etched green glass vase, the heavily moulded vessel deeply etched with a frieze of circular volutes against a textured ground, 35.50cm. high.
(Phillips) $19,061

VASES

A Lalique bucket-shaped vase molded with six birds perched among berry-laden branches, incised *R. Lalique*, 5³/₄in. high. (Christie's) $1,505

Fine pair of cranberry vases, tapering ovoid form, Mary Gregory style decoration of girl with bird and boy with hat in landscape, 12in., circa 1900. (G. A. Key) $453

'Orléans', a Lalique blue vase, molded with a band of flowers of leafy stems, with engraved signature *R. Lalique*, 20cm. high. (Christie's) $5,742

Loetz Art Glass handled vase, brilliant emerald green jardinière-form with three gold iridescent oil spot handles, 5¹/₂in. high. (Skinner) $550

Good pair of green overlay Peking glass vases, 19th century, each of slender baluster form with a recessed circular foot and surmounted by a wide trumpet mouth, 8³/₈in. high. (Butterfield & Butterfield)
                                  $1,320

A Loetz iridescent glass vase, with three applied scrolling handles, the blue glass decorated with a silver/blue oil splash pattern, 17cm. high. (Christie's) $1,096

A Loetz octopus vase, cased amber glass over white decorated between the layers with an air trap scrolling motif, covered with a gilt painted scrolling design, 15.1cm. high. (Christie's) $1,369

A very fine pair of blown and engraved ruby glass vases: The President's House, Washington, and Battle Monument, Baltimore, Bohemian, circa 1860, 14in. high. (Sotheby's) $29,700

'Bacchantes', a Lalique opalescent glass vase of flared form, heavily molded in relief with a frieze of naked female figures, 24.50cm. high. (Phillips) $14,004

WINE GLASSES

A very unusual facet-cut wine glass, the heavy bowl deeply cut with diamond facets, on an opaque twist stem, 11.8cm. (Phillips)   **$478**

A Jacobite wine-glass, the bell-shaped bowl engraved with a portrait medallion of Prince Charles Edward Stuart, 4¼in. high. (Christie's)   **$2,541**

A baluster wine glass with bell bowl, the stem with a teared swelling knop between shoulder a basal knops, 16.5cm. (Phillips)   **$637**

A dark-amber goblet, the slender funnel bowl and short waist-knopped stem with opaque herring-bone decoration, late 17th/early 18th century, perhaps Tyrol, 15.5cm. high. (Christie's)   **$2,105**

A Beilby masonic opaque-twist firing-glass, the ogee bowl inscribed *Antient Operative Lodge DUNDEE.*, the short stem with a laminated corkscrew core, on a terraced foot, circa 1770, 9.5cm. high. (Christie's)   **$11,666**

An Anglo-Venetian wine-glass, with spiked gadroons to the lower part, supported on a merese above a four-bladed propeller-knopped stem terminating in a basal knop, 1685–90, 14cm. high. (Christie's)   **$4,277**

A Jacobite portrait firing-glass of drawn-trumpet shape, engraved with a portrait of Prince Charles Edward within a circular double-line cartouche, mid-18th century, 10cm. high. (Christie's)   **$9,332**

A façon de Venise wine glass, the funnel bowl 'nipt diamond waies', set in two rings above a hollow-blown quatrelobed knop, 13.3cm., end 17th century. (Phillips)   **$2,244**

A small color-twist wine-glass, the short stem with a yellow multi-ply spiral core enclosed within an opaque laminated corkscrew edged in translucent pink, circa 1775, 9cm. high. (Christie's)   **$2,000**

WINE GLASSES

A light baluster wine glass with pan-topped bowl engraved with a border of vines, the stem with a teared central knop, 15cm.
(Phillips) $518

A deceptive baluster wine-glass, the thick funnel bowl supported on an inverted baluster stem above a folded conical foot, circa 1715, 11cm. high.
(Christie's) $2,236

A Jacobite plain-stemmed wine-glass, the funnel bowl engraved with a rose and bud, on a conical foot, circa 1750, 16cm. high.
(Christie's) $1,885

A small color-twist wine-glass, the stem with a central translucent green core enclosed within an opaque laminated corkscrew edged in translucent cobalt-blue, circa 1775, 10.5cm. high.
(Christie's) $3,650

'Fountains', a Baccarat crystal drinking glass, designed by Georges Chevalier, the bell-shaped bowl with engraved decoration on long, swollen stem and circular foot, 15.4cm. high.
(Christie's) $557

An interesting and amusing Schwarzlot decorated glass, the small cup-shaped bowl decorated with an amusing scene of an irate woman belaboring a man with a stick, 9.3cm., probably Silesian.
(Phillips) $411

A North Bohemian (Kronstadt) 'Schwarzlot' wine-glass painted by Ignatz Preissler, with three horses in various stances on a continuous grassy band, circa 1715, 12cm. high.
(Christie's) $11,666

A composite-stemmed wine-glass of drawn shape with a tulip bowl, the stem filled with airtwist spirals, circa 1750, 15cm. high.
(Christie's) $465

An emerald-green incised-twist wine-glass with a generous round-funnel bowl, the stem with a swelling waist knop and incised with spiral twists, circa 1765, 14cm. high.
(Christie's) $1,361

An early 19th century 2 inch terrestrial globe, inscribed *Model of the Earth by J. Manning*, 13¾in. high. (Christie's S. Ken)

$1,834

A pair of globes of Louis XIV style with brass indicator rings, the terrestrial with dedicatory panel, on Italian ebonized and parcel-gilt stands, the stands and globes 33in. high. (Christie's)

$13,860

A Dutch de Elsevier globe, by Dr. G. J. Dozy, Rotterdam, manufactured on a similar principle to the Betts portable globe, 30in. long. (Christie's)

$588

A Newton 12in. celestial globe on stand, English, published 1830, with printed label *Newtons New & Improved Celestial Globe*, composed of twelve printed and hand-colored gores with brass hour circle and meridian, 45.5cm. high overall. (Bonhams)

$1,301

A miniature terrestrial globe inscribed within a circle *CARY'S/Pocket/GLOBE;/ agreeable/to the latest/ DISCOVERIES/LONDON*, 3½in. diameter. (Bearne's)

$1,730

C. Smith & Son, *Smith's Terrestrial Globe Shewing the latest discoveries to the present time*, mid-19th century, a 6 inch terrestrial globe, with hand-colored and engraved paper gores. (Christie's)

$1,279

A Regency turned mahogany and engraved brass terrestrial globe, English, dated *1833*, on ring-turned legs joined by turned stretchers, height 15in. (Sotheby's)

$1,610

A fine pair of George III mahogany Cary's terrestrial and celestial globes, the basket stands on reeded tapered legs and united by stretchers below, 3ft. 9in. high. (Phillips)

$55,650

An instructional globe, unsigned, dated *1910*, the horizon ring with zodiac, time and calendar scales on plinth base, 10½in. diameter. (Christie's)

$798

Vintage classroom globe, 'The Excelsior Globe by G. W. Bacon & Co. Ltd., 127 The Strand, London', on an ornate ebonized base, 9in. high.
(G. A. Key) $210

Pair of terrestrial and celestial table globes, J. & W. Newton, 88 Chancery Lane, London, early 19th century, total height 26½in.
(Skinner) $4,675

A Louis XV giltwood globe, now with terrestrial globe published by James Wyld, Leicester Square and dated *1855* and English chapter ring, 23in. high.
(Christie's) $10,400

A Cary 18 inch terrestrial library globe, English, 1816 corrected to 1839, titled *Carys New Terrestrial Globe ... made and sold by J&W Cary, Strand March 1st 1816, with corrections and additions to 1839*, overall 120cm. high.
(Bonhams) $21,114

A rare 18th century 2¾ inch terrestrial globe, with label inscribed *A Terrestrial GLOBE G: Adams No. 60 Fleet Street LONDON*, the colored paper gores showing Anson's Voyage.
(Christie's S. Ken)
                              $6,945

An early 19th century 16in. terrestrial globe, inscribed *J. & W. Cary, Strand, March 1st 1816 with corrections and additions to 1839*, 3ft. 8½in. high.
(Phillips) $11,100

C. Smith, Smiths terrestrial globe, a rare 12 inch diameter terrestrial table globe, with twelve colored paper gores, showing the voyages of Capt. Gore and Capt. Cook.
(Christie's) $2,426

Good pair of William IV library globes on stands by Newton, Son & Barry, London, 1830 and 1832, each revolving in a mahogany stand with ebonized line decoration, 43in. high.
(Butterfield & Butterfield)
                             $24,750

An early 19th century 3¾ inch celestial globe, with makers label inscribed *SMITHS CELESTIAL GLOBE*, the constellations named and lightly colored, 6¾in. high.
(Christie's S. Ken)
                              $2,703

A fine French octagonal vari-colored gold and piqué tortoiseshell snuff-box, the cover piqué with a windmill on a hill, by Adrien-Jean-Maximilien Vachette, Paris, 1789–90, 2⁵/₈in. long.
(Christie's) $39,600

A rare gold zodiac figure, standing barefoot on a tripod base, wearing an armor-like studded suit with a long tunic and shoulder pads, 12th/13th century, 13cm.
(Christie's) $20,273

A Swiss rectangular gold snuff-box, the hinged cover chased and engraved with Naval Trophies, the engine-turned walls and base with laurel and bead border, maker's mark *C C S*, 19th century, 3³/₈in. long.
(Christie's) $6,171

A George III rectangular gold snuff-box, the cover chased with Venus attempting to hold Adonis back from leaving her to go hunting with his dogs, by Alexander James Strachan, 1807, 2³/₄in. wide.
(Christie's) $9,346

A gold-mounted enamel and gemset rock-crystal parasol-handle, engraved with sunflowers around the stem and set with red stones, late 19th century, 2³/₈in. long.
(Christie's) $1,950

An important Frederick Augustus III oval gold and hardstone snuff-box, set on all sides with a Zellenmosaik of rural landscapes, by Johann Christian Neuber, Dresden, circa 1770, 3³/₈in. long.
(Christie's) $82,280

A 'Scottish' barrel-shaped gold-mounted agate vinaigrette, formed of hardstone staves and engraved gold hoops, 19th century, 2¹/₂in. high.
(Christie's) $5,634

A very rare pair of inscribed beaten gold lotus cups, each with straight tapering sides thinly beaten and chased with two tiers of lotus petals, Tang Dynasty, 9.8cm. diameter.
(Christie's) $42,680

A George II gold scent-bottle case set with two panels of moss agate, circa 1755, with velvet lining, 1¹/₂in. high.
(Christie's) $2,017

A rare gold foliate box and cover, the cover chased with two lions amidst flower-sprays within a band of raised dots and flower-heads, Liao Dynasty, 6cm. wide.
(Christie's) $34,144

An archaic gold and silver-inlaid bronze axe-head, cast at the angle with openwork dragons biting the blade and gripping the shaft socket, Warring States, 13cm. wide.
(Christie's) $14,938

A fine engraved gold singing bird box by Georges Reymond, Geneva, the movement providing song and motions to head, beak and wings of feathered bird, circa 1805–1815, 71mm. long.
(Christie's New York)
$35,200

A French circular gold-mounted tortoiseshell bonbonnière, the cover set with an enamel plaque of a young couple seated in a landscape, circa 1780, 3¹/₄in. diameter.
(Christie's) $1,408

A Louis XVI gold-mounted glass scent-flask, the front applied with an oval vari-color gold medallion chased and engraved with flowers and foliage, Paris, 1777–78, 4in. long.
(Christie's) $2,600

A Swiss oval enameled gold snuff-box, the cover painted with a couple in a garden with a fountain and statue in the background, Geneva, circa 1800, maker's mark MC, 2⁵/₈in. long.
(Christie's) $5,544

A Louis XV shaped gold and agate snuff-box, the convex cover hinged at one end and set with two panels of agate in borders chased and engraved with foliage, by Nicholas Bouillerot, Paris, 1728–29, 2³/₈in. long.
(Christie's) $6,501

A Swiss rectangular vari-colored gold snuff-box, the cover chased and engraved with a female winged demi-figure between eagles, Geneva, circa 1815, maker's mark M M, possibly for M. Marchinville, 3¹/₈in. long.
(Christie's) $5,544

A fine George II cartouche-shaped gold snuff-box, the interior of the lid set with an enamel portrait of Mary, Countess of Bute by Christian Friedrich Zincke, circa 1750, 2³/₄in. wide.
(Christie's) $71,280

Thorens Excelda cameraphone, ultra portable gramophone in the form of a folding camera with Excelda No 17 sound pick up, crank and arm, circa 1932.
(Auction Team Köln) $512

A 'Trade Mark' gramophone by the Gramophone Company, No. 5219, with March '98 Patent date, Clark-Johnson soundbox, lacquered brass horn, and cam-and-spring brake.
(Christie's) $4,280

A Peter Pan Clock gramophone with Peter Pan soundbox on gooseneck tone-arm and reflector in lid.
(Christie's) $542

A small Klingsor gramophone in oak case with pierced door to upper compartment containing horn aperture and strings, 27in. high.
(Christie's) $1,450

A Primaphone (Bombay) compact portable gramophone in polished wood case, Thorens Imperial soundbox, 9¼in. wide, circa 1929.
(Christie's) $407

An HMV Model 1 automatic gramophone, with Florentine bronze fittings including No. 16 soundbox, 42in. wide, circa 1929.
(Christie's) $1,954

Oak cased Victor Model V table gramophone with unusual mahogany horn by the Victor Talking Machine Co., Camden, NJ.
(Auction Team Köln)
                         $2,812

Pathéphone model 50 table gramophone by Pathé Brothers, with original sound box and integral loudspeaker.
(Auction Team Köln)
                          $359

A Gramophone Company coin-operated gramophone with Clark-Johnson soundbox, wood traveling arm and rectangular oak case with coin mechanism, 1898–9.
(Christie's) $7,326

Cast iron Melodograph child's gramophone with integral horn and manual handle for spring drive, circa 1925.
(Auction Team Köln)
$249

A Colombia Type BN Improved Royal Disc gramophone in oak case, with needle clip soundbox and double spring motor.
(Phillips) $931

A Gramophone Co. Pigmy Grand hornless gramophone with Exhibition soundbox on detachable gooseneck tone-arm, mahogany case with internal horn, 1909 HMV transfer.
(Christie's) $430

A rare HMV Model 10 automatic gramophone with 5A soundbox, re-entrant tone chamber and electric motor driving turntable, 40³/₄ in. high, 1930.
(Christie's S. Ken)
$3,287

A Gramophone & Typewriter Ltd Melba gramophone with G & T Exhibition soundbox on gooseneck tone-arm ebonized case with embossed brass lunettes of a female head in scrolling Art Nouveau surround.
(Christie's) $8,172

An HMV Model 193 re-entrant tone chamber gramophone with 5A soundbox, the oak case of Jacobean design, 44¹/₂ in. high, 1930.
(Christie's S. Ken)
$8,327

A tin toy Electric Phonograph Mod. 777 gramophone by the Lindstrom Corp., Bridgeport, CT, 110v, red and green with bright children's decoration, circa 1955.
(Auction Team Köln)
$254

An Edison Bell Picturegram portable gramophone with Edison Bell 'Era' soundbox and drawer containing panoramic picture apparatus, circa 1925.
(Christie's S. Ken)
$2,112

A German Mammut coin operated gramophone, lacking horn and needing restoration, in richly carved and decorated wooden housing, circa 1910.
(Auction Team Köln)
$772

An E.M.G. Mark IX hand made gramophone with double-spring Paillard motor.
(Christie's) $2,605

The Wonder Portable Chiftophone, portable gramophone, with flat pick up and turntable, circa 1920.
(Auction Team Köln)

$170

A Gramophone Company Senior Monarch gramophone with oak horn and case, triple spring motor, circa 1910.
(Christie's) $2,372

American mahogany cased Columbia Grafonola table gramophone by the American Gramophone Co., Bridgeport, CT., circa 1924.
(Auction Team Köln)

$588

An HMV Model 202 gramophone cabinet with quadruple-spring motor, 'antique silver' 5a soundbox and tone-arm, 49½in. high.
(Christie's) $4,250

Victor Model IV mahogany gramophone by the Victor Talking Machine Co., Camden, NJ.
(Auction Team Köln)

$1,961

The Trade Mark Gramophone, with label of the Gramophone & Typewriter Ltd., London, the first gramophone to carry the world renowned HMV logo with Nipper the dog, 1898.
(Auction Team Köln)

$3,473

An EMG Mark XB 'Tropical' hand made gramophone with four-spring soundbox, Paillard GGR double-spring motor, 29½in. diameter.
(Christie's) $4,880

A Carette cylinder gramophone by Georg Carette, Nürnberg, with red base decorated in relief with flower and bird motifs and a 7-section blue and gold horn, circa 1910.
(Auction Team Köln)

$926

GRAMOPHONES

An HMV Model II (Intermediate Monarch) horn gramophone with single spring motor in mahogany case, 17½in. diameter, dated on base *Nov. 1913*.
(Christie's)   **$2,000**

A Nirona '888' child's gramophone on square tinplate base with nursery scenes and typical Nirona bell resonator.
(Christie's)   **$644**

An HMV Model VIIA mahogany horn gramophone (HFM) with triple-spring motor, rocking turntable, 21¾in. diameter horn, circa 1913.
(Christie's)   **$1,791**

A good H.M.V. Model 460 table grand gramophone with Lumiere pleated diaphragm, gilt fittings in quarter-veneered oak case.
(Phillips)   **$2,134**

A rare Gramophone Company de luxe gramophone with triple-spring motor, yielding turntable, Exhibition Junior soundbox and mahogany horn, 64in. high overall, circa 1920–22.
(Christie's)   **$7,150**

A rare E.M.G. tropical portable gramophone with E.M.G. two-spring soundbox, gooseneck tone-arm and internal horn, circa 1928, and eight albums of records.
(Christie's S. Ken)   **$1,125**

Glass fronted gramophone, with dealer's label, *Chas. Knishott, Cardiff*, with tin for needles, in working order, horn with fine floral decoration, circa 1905.
(Auction Team Köln)   **$709**

An E.M.G. Mark IX hand-made gramophone with electric motor, E.M.G. two-spring soundbox on swan-neck tone arm, in oak case with 23in. papier mâché horn.
(Phillips)   **$3,104**

An HMV Junior Monarch gramophone with Exhibition soundbox, single 1¼-inch spring motor, fluted oak horn and oak case dated *December 1911*.
(Christie's)   **$3,011**

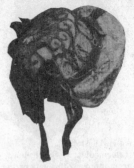

A child's or young lady's hat of ivory silk quilted with a scale design and trimmed with a rosette of ivory ribbons, circa 1820. (Christie's) $900

A top hat of brown felt, with black ribbon, by A. Giessen, Delft, circa 1870. (Christie's) $750

A black satin bonnet trimmed with pleating, circa 1880. (Christie's) $45

A straw bonnet with deep brim, trimmed later with satin with chine silk ribbon and artificial flowers, circa 1830. (Christie's) $450

A top hat of grey beaver, possibly 1829, labelled M. Strieken, 8in. high. (Christie's) $1,200

A bonnet of brown striped plaited straw trimmed with brown figured ribbons, edged with a fringe, circa 1850. (Christie's) $120

A mourning bonnet of black crepe, circa 1830. (Christie's) $210

Winston S. Churchill (1874–1965), a gray Homburg by *Lincoln Bennett & Co., by appointment to her Majesty the Queen*, initialed in gold *W.S.C.*, the up-turned brim with ribbon trim.
(Christie's) $13,213

A gentleman's nightcap of linen worked in cutwork with vines, the cuff also edged with lace, English, circa 1610. (Christie's) $6,625

Harrison Ford's hat from 'Indiana Jones and the Raiders of the Lost Ark', 1980, together with a Continuity Script, issued 28th May, 1980.
(Sotheby's) $1,416

A 16th century man's embroidered cap embellished with sequins and gold lace trim, England, 8in. high.
(Robt. W. Skinner Inc.) $11,000

A rare hand-painted ceremonial parade fire hat: Vigilant, initialled *J.W.W.*, probably Pennsylvania, mid-19th century, 7in. high.
(Sotheby's) $14,850

A gentleman's linen nightcap, embroidered in colored silks, gilt and silver gilt threads, with a repeating pattern of Tudor roses and pansies, English, circa 1600.
(Christie's S. Ken) $27,599

A wide brimmed straw hat with shallow crown, lined with red silk brocaded with flowers, with original green silk ribbons, 1765–70.
(Christie's) $3,366

A bonnet of black satin trimmed with a large bow and rouleaux, circa 1830.
(Christie's) $450

A fine hand-painted leatherboard ceremonial parade firehat: The Independence Hose Company, initaled *A.R.R.*, probably Pennsylvania, mid 19th century, height 7in.
(Sotheby's) $5,750

Late 17th/early 18th century gentleman's green velvet undress hat embroidered in silver and gold thread, 8½in.
     $1,500

Painted and decorated parade fire hat, Philadelphia, circa 1854, decorated with a central medallion depicting William Rush's figure "Water Nymph and Bittern".
(Skinner Inc.) $8,500

A Chinese rhinoceros horn libation cup carved in relief with officials and sages wearing tabbed hats, the handle formed as pine boughs, 16/17th century, 3½in. high. (Christie's S. Ken) $6,000

An Anglo-Indian horn tea caddy of sarcophagus shape, the ivory and ebony interior fitted with two hinged zinc lined caddies, 15in. long. (Christie's London) $750

A late Victorian oak desk stand, incorporating a timepiece supported on silvered metal mounted horns, 17¾in. wide. (Christie's) $700

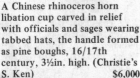

A rhinoceros horn libation cup of tapered square shape, carved on the body with two pairs of confronted kui dragons, 17th century, 14.6cm. wide, carved fitted wood base. (Christie's) $6,000

Scottish staghorn and ivory inkstand, 19th century, mounted with an antler pen holder, a sander, inkwell and small dished tray, the whole raised on three carved ivory claw feet, 9in. wide. (Butterfield & Butterfield) $935

Fine rhinoceros horn libation cup, 17th/18th century, the honey-colored matrix well carved and pierced with a continuous scene, 5¼in. high. (Butterfield & Butterfield) $14,300

A Chinese rhinoceros horn libation cup carved in relief with a figure teaching children, the handle formed as pine boughs coming over the rim of the cup, 17/18th century, 5in. high. (Christie's S. Ken) $10,500

An engraved powder horn, the body decorated with a map of Fort Saint Mark, showing various buildings. (Phillips) $2,310

An engraved Masonic horn cup, American, early 19th century, three circular reserves with Masonic iconography, colored red and black, 3¾in. high. (Christie's New York) $375

A horn hair comb by Fred T. Partridge set with baroque pearls in white metal, formed as an umbellifer.
(Christie's) $1,340

Two erotic horn figures, circa 1800, both semi-naked, their hair coiled at the back of their heads, 4¼ in. high.
(Christie's) $4,500

Hammered copper presentation cup with three horn handles, Thomas G. Brown & Sons, New York, circa 1903, 6¼ in. high. (Robt. W. Skinner Inc.) $270

A rhinoceros horn libation cup carved with two male figures seated under a willow-type tree beside a stream watching two horses at play, 17cm. wide.
(Christie's London)
                    $7,722

A pair of horn hair ornaments by Fred T. Partridge, set with moonstones and detailed with white metal.
(Christie's) $1,914

Rhinoceros horn libation cup, 18th/19th century, the honey brown horn delicately carved as an open peach issuing from a gnarled leafy branch, 3³/₄ in. high.
(Butterfield & Butterfield)
                    $1,100

A rhinoceros horn libation cup carved around the sides with flowering magnolia branches, 17th century, 16.6cm. wide.
(Christie's) $3,875

Pair of armchairs made from steer horns, late 19th/early 20th century, with rust-red leather seat and headrest.
(Eldred's) $1,870

A 19th century Scottish ram's horn snuff mull, with silvered mount and agate set hinged cover, 6.7cm. high. (Geering & Colyer) $175

A 19th century icon of the Mother of God Kazanskaya, the parcel gilt oklad with river and seed pearls, 12½ x 10¼in.
(Christie's) $5,136

An 18th century icon of the Hodigitria Mother of God, the Christ Child with His fingers raised in Benediction, 20 x 16¾in.
(Christie's) $5,583

A 19th century Greek icon of St. Nicholas, the Miracle Worker, 14in. x 10½in.
(Christie's S. Ken) $420

A late 19th century Russian icon of The Old Testament Trinity, realistically painted, with Abraham and Sarah in attendance, 14in. x 12¼in.
(Christie's S. Ken)
                                  $1,933

An 18th century Italo-Cretan icon of the Hodigitria Mother of God, 19in. x 15in., in a carved wood and gesso frame.
(Christie's S. Ken)
                                  $7,983

A 19th century Russian icon of the Mother of God of the Sign, traditionally painted on gilt ground, Christ with an applied halo, 7¼in. x 6¼in.
(Christie's S. Ken) $1,680

A 19th century Russian icon of St. John the Forerunner, with the Christ Child, 17½in. x 14½in.
(Christie's S. Ken) $1,050

A late 19th century Finift icon of the Appearance of the Mother of God to St. Serafim of Sarov, in a silver engraved frame, St. Petersburg 1886, 7½in. x 6in.
(Christie's S. Ken) $1,156

A 19th century Russian icon of Six Chosen Saints, including Catherine, Barbara, Mitrophan and Harlampy, 12¼in. x 10½in.
(Christie's S. Ken) $882

A late 19th century Moscow School icon of the Pokrov, overlaid with a repoussé silver oklad, 15in. x 12in.
(Christie's S. Ken) **$1,050**

A 19th century Russian icon of the Hodigitria Mother of God Iverskaya, 17³/₄ x 15in.
(Christie's) **$1,301**

An 18th century Russian icon of the Virgin of Joy to Those who Grieve, overlaid with a silver gilt oklad, 11¹/₂in. x 9¹/₂in.
(Christie's S. Ken) **$840**

A 19th century Russian icon of the Decollation of St. John the Forerunner, overlaid with a silver oklad with hallmark stamp for 1870, 9 x 7in.
(Christie's) **$1,001**

A 19th century Russian icon of the Transfiguration, the Saviour brightly robed, with standing and kneeling saints before Him, 14in. x 12in.
(Christie's S. Ken) **$798**

A late 19th century Russian icon of The Mother of God Kazanskaya, in a silver repoussé and engraved oklad, 7in. x 5³/₄in.
(Christie's S. Ken) **$1,366**

A 19th century Russian icon of the Vladimirskaya Mother of God, overlaid with a silver oklad, 10¹/₂in. x 8³/₄in.
(Christie's S. Ken) **$945**

A 17th/18th century Cypriot icon of the Mother of God of the Sign, 30in x 25in.
(Christie's S. Ken) **$2,941**

A 19th century Russian icon of the Baptism of Christ, with the Forerunner and angels, the Lord Sabaoth above, 8³/₄in. x 6³/₄in.
(Christie's S. Ken) **$882**

A four-case fundame inro decorated in hiramakie and heidatsu with chrysanthemum flower-heads, signed *Tsunekawa* (or Josen) *saku*, with red tsubo seal, 19th century, 7.8cm. high.
(Christie's)   **$2,167**

A three case Shibayama inro in the form of a tied bag, decorated with a ho-o bird among flowers and foliage, late 19th century, 10cm.
(Christie's)   **$13,475**

A four-case inro richly decorated in hiramakie, aogai and kirikane on a hirame ground with a cicada on a gourdvine, signed *Kajikawa*, 18th century, 8.9cm. high.
(Christie's)   **$7,744**

A large four-case inro decorated in hiramakie, okibirame, kimpun and togidashi with a dragon arising from the sea in clouds of vapor, signed *Koma Kyoryu saku*, late 18th century, 12cm. high, with a walrus ivory ryusa style manju netsuke attached.
(Christie's)   **$8,131**

Four case inro, 19th century, sealed Shiomi Masanari, decorated in gold hiramaki-e with stylized floral and zoomorphic mon on a pale brown lacquer ground.
(Butterfield & Butterfield)
                                  $863

A four-case kinji inro decorated in gold and silver hiramakie, takamakie, kirikane, nashiji and inlaid in Shibayama style, one side with a tea-house girl watching a samurai falling from a bench, signed *Teimin*, late 19th century, 10cm. long.
(Christie's)   **$11,616**

A four-case inro decorated in hiramakie, togidashi and makibokashi with Nitta no Yoshisada casting a sword into the sea as an offering to the gods, signed *Inagawa*, with red tsubo seal, 19th century, 8.2cm. high.
(Christie's)   **$4,259**

A four case somada style inro decorated in mother-of-pearl inlaid on a roironuri ground with a long tailed bird in a pine tree, 18th century, 8.9cm.
(Christie's)   **$4,620**

A three-case roironuri inro decorated in raden, red and gold hiramakie with a flower arrangement in a wicker basket, signed *Shutoho*, 19th century, 7.3cm.
(Christie's)   **$3,034**

A three-case hirame inro decorated in silver, gold and gray hiramakie with three red-capped cranes on the reverse cypress saplings, signed *Koma Yasutada saku*, 19th century, 7.3cm. high.
(Christie's) $8,131

A three-case nashiji ground inro decorated on one side with a gold ground inro with peacocks on a tree, signed *Kajikawa saku*, 19th century, 8.3cm. long.
(Christie's) $13,475

A four-case hirame inro decorated in hiramakie and okibirame with yamabushi-no-oi, the robe container of a warrior monk, standing in an ivy-clad landscape beneath a maple, unsigned, 19th century, 8.2cm.
(Christie's) $6,068

A five-case inro decorated in takamakie, hirame and okibirame with a long-tailed pheasant perched on a rock among peonies, signed Toshosai Hozan, 19th century, 9.2cm.
(Christie's) $4,767

A three case inro decorated in gold hiramakie, hirame nashiji and inlaid in Shibayama style with insects beside two floral displays of irises, chrysanthemums and blossom, 19th century, 7.8cm.
(Christie's) $9,240

A four-case kinji inro decorated in gold and silver hiramakie and kirikane with a blossoming plum tree, with young shoots springing from a gnarled trunk, signed *Gyokujunsai*, 19th century, 9cm. high.
(Christie's) $4,259

An unusual single-case cherry-wood inro containing four cases and a cover, formed as an oi or backplate of a yamabushi, signed *Haritsuo*, probably 18th century, with a silver filigree ojime, 9.9cm. high.
(Christie's) $4,259

A four case kinji ground inro decorated in Shibayama style with a cockerel on a mortar beside a pestle, the reverse with a hen and a chick, late 19th century, 9.8cm.
(Christie's) $10,588

A four-case gold hirame ground inro decorated in gold hiramakie, takamakie, kirikane and foil, decorated with tree peony, signed, 19th century, 8.2cm. long.
(Christie's) $5,420

A brass tulip framed sextant, the index arm with 9 inch radius, with framed vernier, magnifier, tangent screw and clamp, 10¹/₂in. wide.
(Christie's) $684

An 18th-century 'Augsburg'-pattern gilt-brass universal equinoctial compass dial, signed on the base of the compass box *And. Vogler*, 2³/₈in. wide.
(Christie's) $1,261

A late 19th century French noon cannon dial, signed *Darreny Londres a Paris 969*, the cannon molded and modeled with fluted decoration.
(Christie's) $6,820

A fine engraved gilt metal horse pedometer and watch by Ralph Gout, London, the verge watch movement with pierced balance cock chased with trophy of arms, circa 1800, 55.5mm. diameter of pedometer.
(Christie's New York)
                              $9,350

An 18th-century lodestone, with brass mounts and suspension ring, in fishskin case, 2in. high.
(Christie's) $2,311

A fine early 19th century lacquered and silvered brass equinoctial dial, signed on the hour-ring *Watkins & Hill Charing Cross* with inner hour scale, spring loaded gnomon, 3³/₄in. long.
(Christie's S. Ken)
                              $2,124

An early 19th century brass portable sundial, mounted on a walnut quadrant, the turned stem to a molded circular base.
(Woolley & Wallis)
                              $5,910

A late 18th century lacquered and silvered brass universal equinoctial compass dial, signed on the hour ring *Jᶜ Ramsden London*, 7in. wide.
(Christie's) $2,270

A late 17th/early 18th century silvered brass and ivory azimuth diptych dial, signed on the calendar volvelle *Jacques Senecal ADieppe fecit*, 3in. long.
(Christie's) $3,406

A rare equinoctial sundial signed *PHILIPS' SUN-DIAL*, with paper card dial, in paper card carrying box, 8³/₄in. high.
(Christie's) $729

An early 17th century gunner's quadrant, the brass base frame stamped *C.T.D.E.M* and dated *1612* engraved with flower and foliate decoration, 5¹/₄in. wide.
(Christie's) $2,838

A 19th-century mining tacheometer, by E T Newton & Son, Camborne, Cornwall, with trough compass and staff mounting, overall height 12³/₄in.
(Christie's) $546

An 18th-century brass pair of gunner's calipers, signed on one arm *G. Adams London*, with scales for Brafs Guns, Iron Guns, and other scales, 12in. long.
(Christie's) $1,576

A rare pair of William and Mary shield wool-weights, molded with 'simple' royal coat of arms, various touch marks, with suspension loop, 7in. long.
(Christie's) $4,433

A fine and rare 19th century lacquered brass goniometer, signed on the vertical circle *Aug. Oertling, Berlin No. 2840*, with silvered scale and magnifier, 10¹/₂in. high.
(Christie's S. Ken)

    $10,039

A late 17th-century brass perpetual calendar, unsigned, inscribed *Allgemeiner und Imer Werender Calender*, 2in. diameter.
(Christie's) $882

A lacquered brass universal equinoctial compass dial, engraved on the hour ring *Troughton & Simms*, in fitted mahogany case, 19th century, 6in. wide.
(Christie's) $833

A black enameled and lacquered brass airflow meter, by Short & Mason, with eight-bladed aluminium fan, 4³/₄in. wide.
(Christie's) $273

An 18th-century brass 'Butterfield'-type octagonal compass dial, signed *N. BION A-PARIS*, engraved on the underside with the latitudes of twenty-four continental cities and towns, 3¹/₄in. long.
(Christie's) $1,366

A gimballed azimuth compass, the 7 inch compass with silvered quadrantly divided reversed engraved outer ring signed *J. SPEYER AMSTERDAM*, 12in. square.
(Christie's) $1,261

A brass cannon-dial signed *F BARKER & Sons* with calendar dial, engraved quadrant on three pad feet, 9³/₄in. diameter in plush lined carrying case.
(Christie's S. Ken) $1,255

A fine brass universal equinoctial ring dial, the pivoted horizon ring engraved with 24-hour Roman chapters graduated at five-minute intervals, probably English, late 17th century, 15cm. diameter.
(Christie's New York)
                      $3,520

A rare early 17th century brass horological Compendium, unsigned; dated *1605*; comprising a nocturnal, magnetic compass, horizontal sundial and moon dial, 2in. diameter.
(Christie's) $18,920

A George III pocket chronometer by John Arnold, circa 1785, with 1³/₄in. diameter enameled dial, now in later mahogany case as a boudoir clock, 7in. high.
(Bearne's) $8,460

Swiss precision watchmaker's milling machine on mahogany plinth with drawer, brass with almost complete set of equipment, circa 1880.
(Auction Team Köln) $531

A Negretti & Zambra barograph, English, early 20th century, No. 3690 with clockwork recording drum, silvered thermometer and recording apparatus on a brass platform in a glazed oak case with drawer in the base.
(Bonhams) $734

An English Hearson's Patent Biological Incubator, for the culture of micro-organisms, with gas heating regulator.
(Auction Team Köln)
                       $293

A rare mid 17th century horizontal sundial and nocturnal, unsigned, dated *1650*, and engraved with initials: *F/I C B DRID*, 4in. long.
(Christie's) $5,676

A fine 'Solnhofer' stone horizontal dial, unsigned, with finely engraved hour scale numbered 7–12–5, with latitude scale engraved *Elevatio Poli*, 11in. wide.
(Christie's) $1,449

A rare Hygrophant early hygrometer for measuring relative air humidity with turning drum measurement, circa 1929.
(Auction Team Köln) $96

A silver Butterfield dial signed *Butterfield a Paris, Premier Cadran*, inset with glazed compass, engraved with hour scales for 43–46–49–52 degrees, bird gnomon, mid 18th century, 78mm. long.
(Christie's) $2,420

An unusual late 14th (?), 15th (?), or early 16th (?) century brass astrolabe, from France or the Low Countries, with quatrefoil ornamentation on the rete and a dedication dated 1522, unique amongst known astronomical instruments in featuring "Chaldean" or "Astrologers'" numerals, 4⅝in. diameter.
(Christie's) $85,140

A 19th century lacquered brass universal equinoctial inclining dial, signed on the silvered hour-ring *W. Hanks Grice Bond St. London*, in plush-lined leather case, 3in. wide.
(Christie's) $1,364

A late 17th century silvered brass compass, the octagonal plate signed I*eremius Kögler Dantzig Fecit 1680* with well engraved compass rose, iron needle with brass cap, 2⅞in. wide.
(Christie's S. Ken) $1,544

A Gerrard lattice frame sextant, English, second half 19th century, signed *W Gerrard, Maker to the Royal Navy, Wapping, Liverpool*, in fitted mahogany case, with accessories.
(Bonham's) $643

A fine and rare mid 19th century heliostat, signed on the drum *J.T. Silbermann invteur, Soleil Fecit à Paris, No. 7*, on tripod stand with lock and three adjustable feet, 15in. high.
(Christie's S. Ken) $11,583

Cast iron doorstop in the form of a terrier, good early paint, 10in. long.
(Eldred's) $94

A cast-iron royal coat of arms, the arms surmounted by a crown and flanked by a rampant lion and unicorn, banners with *DIEU ET MON DROIT* below, 27in. wide.
(Christie's) $4,660

Inlaid iron and mixed metal teapot, compressed globular form with panels of blossoms in gold and inlay, brass cover, signed, 3½in. high.
(Skinner Inc.) $1,760

Pair of Victorian black-painted cast-iron urns, each fluted flaring form on a circular fluted socle, 34½ in. high.
(Butterfield & Butterfield) $2,200

An early Victorian red-painted and gilt coal scuttle, the sides with lion-mask handles and decorated with eagles, lions and horses, 14in. wide.
(Christie's) $1,287

A pair of Thornton & Downer iron chamber sticks, with circular sconces and drip pans, engraved and stamped decoration, on scrolled feet, 23.2cm. high.
(Christie's) $383

A George III cast iron royal coat of arms, with flanking figures of the lion and unicorn, 50cm. wide approximately.
(Phillips) $1,300

Hagenauer figure of a piano player, nickel-finish, flat stylized representation, impressed with Wiener Werkstatte mark, 8½in. high.
(Skinner Inc.) $1,100

An iron koro and cover on tripod feet, the squat body with three elaborately pierced silver cloisonné lappet panels depicting a dragon, ho-o bird and karashishi among flowers, 19th century, 12.8cm. high.
(Christie's) $6,068

A large russet-iron model of a carp, its body, tail, dorsal and ventral fins fully articulated, signed *Munekazu*, 19th century, 47cm. long.
(Christie's) $14,200

An iron tetsubin of cylindrical form, the sides with a dragon in low relief rising amongst clouds two small handles, 19th century, 14cm. high.
(Christie's) $786

A wrought iron trivet, American, late 18th century, with strapwork and scrolled iron filigree within a pointed arch, on tripod legs, 12$\frac{1}{2}$in. long.
(Christie's) $770

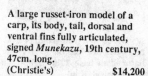

A pair of cast-iron Hessian andirons, American, late 19th century, of typical form with striding figures.
(Sotheby's) $1,760

Two of a set of four mauve-painted cast-iron urns and covers, after the antique, each with anthemion decorated lid, 31$\frac{1}{2}$in. high.
(Christie's)
(Four) $9,240

A pair of French cast iron torchères, each modeled as putto holding a torch with glass shade above his head, one inscribed *Pelees*, late 19th century, 56in. high.
(Christie's) $5,643

A pair of Artificers' Guild wrought iron candelabra designed by Edward Spencer, supporting circular drip pans, numbered 3009, 28.5cm. high.
(Christie's) $2,363

An unusual and rare painted pine and wrought iron 'bone shaker' bicycle, American, late 19th century, 65in. long.
(Sotheby's) $3,575

Coalbrookdale cast iron umbrella stand to hold twelve umbrellas, with pierced sides and carrying handles, approx. 24in. wide.
(G.A. Key) $468

A pair of painted cast-iron dogs, American, 19th century, each full standing and life-size, with tails, raised on a plinth base, 49¾in. long.
(Sotheby's) $4,950

A Gritzner sewing table set, cast iron with colored glass containers, inscriptions on lids, circa 1920.
(Auction Team Köln) $254

A silvered cast iron group of a mare and her foal, on a naturalistic base, 12in. high.
(Christie's S. Ken) $665

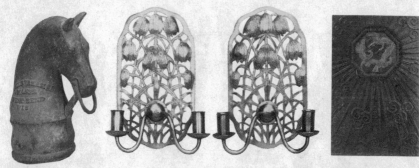

A cast iron hitching post by O. Silberzahn Manufactory, Westbend, Wisconsin, 19th century, the cast horse's-head with wavy mane and molded features, retains traces of yellow polychrome, 14in. high.
(Christie's) $880

A pair of Alfred Bucknell polished steel wall sconces designed by Ernest Gimson, with pierced decoration of fritillaries, the two curved branches with circular drip pans, circa 1940, 32cm. high.
(Christie's) $3,544

'Le Cigognes d'Alsace', an Edgar Brandt wrought iron and bronze decorative panel, embellished in gilt bronze with three storks amid wirework clouds, 194 x 126cm.
(Phillips) $8,185

A demonstration model Holland stove, 23cm. high, circa 1910.
(Auction Team Köln) $54

A decorative cast-iron fireback, cast in relief with an armorial cartouche flanked by supporting lions, surmounted by a visored helmet and a third lion, 44in. wide.
(Christie's) $1,425

A green-painted cast-iron fountain, with two circular tiers, the first supported by two cherubs, 19th century, 57in. high overall.
(Christie's) $2,600

A green painted cast iron umbrella stand, attributed to Dr Christopher Dresser, with rectangular rail, 79cm. high.
(Christie's) $502

'Alberto's Kettle', an aluminium, steel and blue painted kettle, by Ron Arad, the cut and angled form with curved spout and arched strap handle, 21cm. high.
(Christie's) $1,024

A punishment mask or scold's bridle, entirely of steel, composed of flat steel bars riveted together.
(Christie's) $1,361

A pair of molded cast-iron owl andirons, American, 20th century, in the half-round, with cut-out round eyes, height 14in.
(Sotheby's) $4,888

A cast-iron fireback, with the Tudor rose on a shield flanked by a supporting lion and winged grayhound, and surmounted by a crown, inscribed *1571*, 27½in. wide.
(Christie's) $866

A pair of cast-iron horse's head hitching posts, American, 19th century, mounted on ovoid shaped ribbed columnar standards, height 15¼in.
(Sotheby's) $1,840

A cast-iron umbrella stand, possibly Coalbrookdale, circa 1855, in the form of a dog begging with a whip in its mouth, 2ft. wide.
(Sotheby's) $3,751

Painted cast iron lawn ornament of a dog, America, 19th century, 28½in. high.
(Skinner) $3,025

A Victorian green-painted, cast iron umbrella and stick stand, the back cast with a central figure of a footballer holding a ball, 34in. high.
(Christie's) $777

A cast-iron figure of a dog, probably American, late 19th century, with molded fur and curled tail, 24in. high. (Sotheby's) $5,750

North African brass-mounted iron storage chest, 18th century, with arched top and embossed designs, 58in. wide. (Skinner Inc.) $1,500

A cast-iron stag, shown alert and looking forward, with five-point antlers, on a rectangular base, 19th century, 48in. wide. (Christie's) $2,834

A cast-iron dog hitching post, American, late 19th century, the head of a dog in the full-round cast in two parts, 16½in. high. (Sotheby's) $1,495

A pair of white painted iron figures of eagles, the birds staring straight ahead, their wings folded, on square bases pierced for mounting, 34in. high. (Christie's) $3,300

A fine and rare painted cast-iron Washington stove figure, Corona Stove Company, American, late 19th century, overall height 69in. (Sotheby's) $14,950

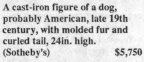

A large decorative cast-iron fireback, the arched top surmounted by a seashell and supporting angels, the main panel decorated with a biblical scene in relief, 38in. wide. (Christie's) $1,925

A white-painted cast-iron jardinière, cast with stylized foliate brackets, on scrolled trefoil supports with black-painted octagonal foot, 19th century, 40½in. high. (Christie's) $2,400

A decorative cast-iron fireback, decorated with two anchors interspersed with rosettes and fleur-de-lis, with rope-twist borders, 21in. wide. (Christie's) $770

A pair of book ends in the style of Hagenauer, each in the form of a lacquered steel stylized figure of a horse, 16cm. high. (Christie's) $334

A painted cast-iron retriever dog garden figure, probably J. W. Fiske & Co., New York, third quarter 19th century, length 52in. (Sotheby's) $9,200

A wrought-iron rack with set of four hanging utensils, possibly Pennsylvania, late 18th/19th century, overall height 27¹/₂in. (Sotheby's) $1,840

A black and white painted cast-iron fountain, by Walter Macfarlane & Co. Glasgow, the circular pediment headed with acanthus and scrolls, 66in. high. (Christie's) $3,325

Pair of Continental black-painted cast-iron urns, second half 19th century, the side handles formed as lion masks each supporting a winged seated putto, 24¹/₂in. high. (Butterfield & Butterfield) $2,750

A Regency red-painted cast-iron lamp base, with a fluted circular shaft cast with outswept foliate scrolls, on shaped, square tapering base, 29in. wide. (Christie's) $2,136

A decorative cast-iron fireback, with an arched top, decorated in relief with a mythological scene, surrounded by putti and fruiting foliage, 30¹/₂in. wide. (Christie's) $1,251

A Japanese iron globular tripod koro and cover with bronze terrapin finial, silver inner liner and cover, 6in. high, signed *Chishinsai Katsunobu (Shoshin)*. (Christie's) $35,000

An Aesthetic Movement cast iron stick stand by Thomas Jeckyll, painted white, cast in relief with sun, moon and cloud motifs, 82cm. high. (Christie's) $635

A Beefall early English cast iron gas iron with front flue turned sideways, 1896.
(Auction Team Köln)

$339

A 19th century Egyptian foot iron, 75cm. long.
(Auction Team Köln)

$617

An English patented Salter's gas iron with air regulator, circa 1910.
(Auction Team Köln)

$117

East Frisian charcoal iron, an early brass iron with cold tip for ironing ruches and bands, 19.5cm. long, circa 1800.
(Auction Team Köln)

$254

An early cast tailor's iron, with handle support and original brass mounted wooden handle, 19cm. long.
(Auction Team Köln)

$232

Charcoal eye iron with 2 segment apertures on each side, with lock, handle possibly renewed, circa 1900.
(Auction Team Köln)

$86

An Omega spirit iron, a pointed nickeled iron with transverse barrel-like tank, 20cm. long, circa 1905.
(Auction Team Köln)

$139

A brass box iron with horn handle and hinged closure, imprinted *Heinrich Thomsen, Boholzau* and dated *1876*.
(Auction Team Köln)

$77

An American Steam-o-Matic Model B-300 early electric steam iron made by Waverly Prod. Inc in cast aluminium housing, 1944.
(Auction Team Köln)

$27

The American Fluter pleating iron by the American Machine Co., Philadelphia, the heated plate hinged for inserting the heating iron, 1895.
(Auction Team Köln) $123

Ox tongue iron, cast brass with pusher and nailed on handle, circa 1860.
(Auction Team Köln) $55

An English The Rhythm No. 375 U Radiation gas iron, enameled in black and green, complete with enameled stand.
(Auction Team Köln) $69

An early Diamond Self Heating Iron gas iron with 45° calibrated nickeled tank, wooden handle and inscribed *Patented 27 Oct, 1914*.
(Auction Team Köln)
                        $170

A brass charcoal iron, lacking wooden handle, with cold tip and spring-hinged lid, circa 1900.
(Auction Team Köln) $66

A charcoal iron, richly decorated with dragon closure and American handle, circa 1870.
(Auction Team Köln) $69

Geneva Hand Fluter, a small American pleating iron, 14cm. long.
(Auction Team Köln)
                        $186

American Hand Fluter, a hinged heatable pleating machine by North Bros. Mfg. Co., Philadelphia, 17cm. long, circa 1880.
(Auction Team Köln)
                        $186

Westphalian Oxtongue iron, with asbestos heating mantel in the interior and porcelain handle, 19cm. long, circa 1870.
(Auction Team Köln)
                        $254

An ivory basket and cover, of lobed circular shape, with a domed lid and twin high loop handles, 9¹/₂in. high. (Lawrence Fine Art) $422

An ivory peach-shaped carving with a scholar and three young attendants beside a pavilion next to trees on a rocky river bank, 18th/19th century, 15cm. wide. (Christie's) $1,707

A Dieppe silver-mounted ivory ewer and dish, the ewer carved in relief, the central panel showing the Triumph of Bacchus and Ariadne, 19th century, 19¹/₂in. high. (Christie's) $36,520

Fine pair of American 19th century scrimshaw vases, made from whale's teeth with notch-carved edges inset with two turned wood bands. (Eldred's) $1,980

Fine Anglo-Indian etched ivory table bureau cabinet, Vizagapatam, first quarter 19th century, with an interrupted triangular pediment centering a turned finial above four drawers, 23³/₈in. wide. (Butterfield & Butterfield) $23,100

A pair of fine ivory tusk vases, boldly carved with birds among flowers and foliage on wood bases, late 19th century, 46cm. high. (Christie's) $10,346

A Vizigapatan ivory workbox in the form of a house, engraved with penwork, the hinged lid enclosing a fitted interior, late 18th century, 6³/₄in. wide. (Christie's) $11,616

Portuguese colonial carved ivory birdcage, early 20th century, of typical cylindrical form with dragon-carved hanging hook, enclosing carved and painted ivory birds, 12¹/₄in. high. (Butterfield & Butterfield) $1,500

A late 19th century ivory Japanese model of the takarabune, the seven gods on the canopied two tiered deck, each with their respective attributes, 11in. tall. (Spencer's) $1,790

An Italian ivory relief of Diana the Huntress, the goddess shown in a central panel striding forward armed with bow and spear, 19th century, 8 x 5in. (Christie's) $1,405

A finely detailed ivory okimono style netsuke depicting five Sika stags in a compact maple grove, signed *Masatoshi* (Shinkesai), 19th century, 4.2cm. (Christie's) $846

An unusual Anglo-Indian carved ivory miniature chiffonier, the upper section with mirror back and scroll supports, 19th century, 7in. high. (Bearne's) $919

An impressive pair of ivory temple ornaments with double pagoda roofs above carved hexagonal bodies, 25in. high. (G.E. Sworder) $4,650

An ivory tonkotsu carved in high relief with the seven sages of the bamboo grove, assisted by karako carrying scrolls and musical instruments, signed *Kihodo Masakazu horu*, late 19th century, 9.6cm high. (Christie's) $5,279

A pair of Chinese carved ivory vases, of hexagonal section intricately carved with figures in landscapes, the necks with floral scroll handles, 19th century, 9in. high. (Woolley & Wallis) $648

French ivory inlaid marquetry wall plaque, third quarter 19th century, depicting a garden detail with an exotic bird with long plumage closely observing a grasshopper, 15³/₄in. diameter. (Butterfield & Butterfield) $4,400

A German ivory lidded tankard, the sides finely carved in relief with an animated hunting scene, with riders, hounds and bears, 19th century, 9in. high. (Christie's) $8,593

One of two carved and painted ivory plaques, Meiji period, with stained and incised details, each within carved hardwood frames, 8in. x 6⁵/₈in. (Butterfield & Butterfield) (Two) $3,025

ANIMALS

Ivory study of frogs, early 19th century, comprised of a baby riding in its mother's back as she rests upon a bed of leaves, 1½in. long.
(Butterfield & Butterfield)
$575

Good ivory animal study, 19th century, depicting a badger with black-inlaid eyes peeping out of a folded lotus leaf, 1¼in. long.
(Butterfield & Butterfield)
$1,265

Good ivory study of a rat climbing on clam shells, late 18th/early 19th century, the base with large himotoshi, 2in. wide.
(Butterfield & Butterfield)
$863

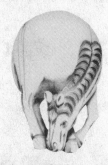

An ivory okimono of Bashiko the Chinese doctor healing a dragon, the physician bending forward to examine the mouth of his patient, signed *Mansanari*, late 19th century, 10.8cm. high.
(Christie's) $3,484

Late 19th century boxwood, rootwood and ivory group of doves attending their young, signed Mitsuhiro, 49cm. high. (Christie's)
$19,000

Fine ivory study of a grazing horse, late 18th century, the steed with black-inlaid eyes shown lowering its head to the level of its four closely spaced legs, 2½in. high.
(Butterfield & Butterfield)
$1,840

Ivory study of a Shishi, late 19th century, the playfully ferocious beast with inlaid eyes shown grasping a moving ball in his open mouth, 2⅝in. high.
(Butterfield & Butterfield)
$34,500

A well carved ivory group of a cockerel, hen and three chicks on wood stand, late 19th century, overall 18cm. wide.
(Christie's) $2,000

Ivory animal study of an eagle and Namazu, 19th century, signed *Deme*, with black-inlaid eyes shown pulling with its beak the forehead skin of the 'earthquake fish', 1½in. high.
(Butterfield & Butterfield)
$690

Good ivory study of two puppies, late 18th/early 19th century, the two little dogs with black-inlaid eyes shown exploring a length of plaited rope, 2⅝in. long.
(Butterfield & Butterfield)
$1,035

A wood and ivory carving of an oni on a turtle in two sections to constitute a box, the ivory oni crouching and scowling in a wicked fashion, signed *Sekkosai Masayoshi*, late 19th century, 15.3cm. long.
(Christie's) $2,129

An ivory okimono of a recumbent horse, its head turned to the rear, its mane and tail engraved and stained, unsigned, style of Rantei, 19th century, 4.8cm. long.
(Christie's) $1,517

A finely patinated ivory netsuke of a magic fox dancing on its hind legs, the cord attachment formed by the tail, unsigned, 18th century, 11cm.
(Christie's) $11,165

Fine pair of large ivory carvings of horses, Rajasthani style, 19th century, each depicting a majestic steed with flaring nostrils and large eyes accentuated by alert ears and long mane, 13¾in. high.
(Butterfield & Butterfield)
$30,250

Unusual Asakusa School ivory study of a kirin, 19th century, the mythical unicorn shown poised with reticulated legs upon an oval plinth, 1⅞in. high.
(Butterfield & Butterfield)
$2,070

Ivory study of a spotted puppy playing with a ball, 19th century, signed *Gyokko*, the charming creature with its forepaws upon the ball and head turned away as though enticed by some new distraction, 1⅛in. high.
(Butterfield & Butterfield)
$316

Fine carved ivory study of a boar, signed *Kaigyokusai/Masatsugu* (1813-1892), the recumbent animal resting on a bed of leaves arranged with one hind hoof forming the himotoshi, 1¾in. long.
(Butterfield & Butterfield)
$107,000

Fine carved ivory study of a seated Shishi, late 19th century, from the atelier of Kaigyokusai Masatsugu (1813-1892), boldly rendered with hind paw scratching an irritated chin, 5.5cm long.
(Butterfield & Butterfield)
$123,500

IVORY

Good ivory study of a man seated on a clamshell, late 18th century, the man shown dressed in plaited rain skirt as he prepares to pry open a giant clam shell, 2¹/₈ inch wide.
(Butterfield & Butterfield) $1,725

Japanese ivory okimono, 19th century, Samurai doing battle with tengu, a boy at his side, 8¹/₂in. high.
(Skinner) $1,760

Good pieced ivory study of an old man and a sleeping child, Meiji Period, signed *Homin*, the elderly man shown seated at a milling stone, his right arm cradling the young child asleep on his lap, 9¹/₂in. long.
(Butterfield & Butterfield) $6,325

Ivory figural study of Jurojin, 19th century, signed Kinryusai (Tomotane), shown standing with his staff and holding a scroll as a kneeling karako plays with the minogame at his feet, 2¹/₈in. high.
(Butterfield & Butterfield) $1,150

Ivory figural study of Matsuri revelers, Meiji Period, signed *Norinobu/Hosho*, comprising two masked dancers moving to the music of three seated musicians, 2in. high.
(Butterfield & Butterfield) $575

Ivory study of a skeleton holding a skull, 19th century, the kneeling skeleton wiping off the skull he holds in front of him, 1³/₈in. high.
(Butterfield & Butterfield) $546

An ivory carving of a seated man, a tortoise emerging from a cut down wooden barrel filled with water in front of him, 3³/₄in. long, signed Meiji period.
(Bonhams) $392

A wood and ivory carving of Ebisu kneeling beside a large floundering sea bream, signed on a rectangular reserve Ryumei, Meiji period, 17cm. high.
(Christie's) $3,750

Good ivory study of two Karako, 19th century, signed *Tadachika*, the two closely seated young boys playfully taunting each other, 1⁹/₁₆in. high.
(Butterfield & Butterfield) $460

FIGURES

Ivory study of Ono No Komachi, late 19th century, signed *Chikusai*, the gaunt figure dressed in ragged clothing resting on an overturned grave post with walking stick in hand, 1³/₈in. high.
(Butterfield & Butterfield) $1,035

An ivory group of The Three Sake Tasters and a sake bowl, their faces most expressively carved, the tasters wearing robes and tasseled girdles, the figures signed *Mitsuaki*, 19th century, 21.5cm. high.
(Christie's) $32,912

Ivory figural study, late 19th/early 20th century, signed *Ono Ryomin*, the jolly mythical priest shown seated on his sack of presents and teasing a kneeling karako, 2in. high.
(Butterfield & Butterfield) $690

An ivory carving of two dignitaries, one standing pouring from a vessel, the other seated, 4in. high, Meiji period.
(Bonhams) $1,026

A 19th century German or Austrian ivory group of an aristocratic couple accosted on their travels by two fortune tellers, 29cm. high.
(Christie's) $20,450

Ivory figure study of Shoki and Oni, late 19th century, signed *Komin*, the writhing limbs of the demons and the flowing robes of their adversary all deeply undercut, 2¹/₄in. high.
(Butterfield & Butterfield) $1,035

A fine ivory carving of a child on a wheeled hobby-horse, the details inlaid in mother-of-pearl, an uchiwa in his hand, signed *Kozan*, late 19th century, 13cm. high.
(Christie's) $3,292

A Japanese carved ivory group of a woodcutter, the smiling man cutting a half-sawn tree trunk, Meiji period, signed, 7¹/₂in. high.
(Bearne's) $884

A large okimono group of a fruit seller surrounded by children including one holding a tortoise and tobacco pouch, 19th century, 27cm high.
(Christie's) $3,343

JADE

A white jade baluster vase and cover carved in high relief on one side with a phoenix perched on rockwork among flowers, 18th century, 19.5cm. high. (Christie's) $5,600

A white and brown jade quail, carved with a plump body resting on two thin legs tucked under and small head tilted upward, the long feathers well defined, 17th century, 7.2cm. long. (Christie's) $2,600

A pale celadon jade vase, carved as an upright hollowed curling lotus leaf issuing from ribboned leafy and flowering stems, 18th century, 21.5cm. high. (Christie's) $12,799

A very fine white jade table screen, Qianlong, carved according to the theme of Lanting Tsu by Wong Xizhi, to the front with scholars gathered along the bank of the winding stream, 9⁵/₈in. high. (Christie's) $170,680

A white jade mythical-beast vase, 18th century, well carved from a stone of lightly mottled pale celadon tone with a winged beast with dragon-like head, 4¹/₈in. high. (Christie's) $4,267

Fine carved nephrite brushpot, late 18th/early 19th century, carved in the form of a hollow tree trunk to simulate the natural pitting and knotting of wood, 7¹/₂in. high. (Butterfield & Butterfield) $59,400

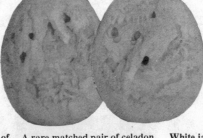

A yellow jade vase and cover, of flattened baluster shape with elephant-mask handles and animal finial, the base carved with three goats amongst rockwork, early 18th century, 18.5cm. high. (Christie's) $22,000

A rare matched pair of celadon jade boulders carved from a single stone, one with Shoulao and a deer standing on a cliff, the other with a recumbent doe beneath a pine tree, 18th century, Qianlong, 19.5cm. high. (Christie's) $7,000

White jade cricket cage, 19th century, carved in shallow relief to depict a continuous landscape scene of flowering lily, prunus and chrysanthemum branches, 4¹/₂in. high. (Butterfield & Butterfield) $1,760

A celadon jade carving of double gourds carved and pierced with a large central double gourd and leafy tendrils with two smaller double gourds, 18th century, 10.5cm. high. (Christie's) $3,544

A pair of linked jade bangles, Ming dynasty, each carved as two confronted archaistic crouching dragons, the stone of even light brownish tone, 2in. diameter. (Christie's) $5,184

A fine jadeite globular bowl and cover, the spherical body raised on three cabriole legs and crisply carved with two mask handles suspending loose rings, 13.5cm. wide. (Christie's) $11,420

A celadon jade carving of Shoulao and a boy, standing among rockwork and a fruiting peach tree, Shoulao with a staff and ruyi sceptre, the boy holding up a small peach, mid Qing Dynasty, 10cm. high. (Christie's) $4,268

A pale celadon jade figure of a camel naturalistically carved and detailed with a thick mane, bushy tail and thick hair on the top of the humps and legs, Qing Dynasty, 19cm. wide. (Christie's) $5,762

A longquan celadon figure of Budai, Ming Dynasty, the seated figure in a casual attitude, resting one arm on a large peach, holding a tablet in the opposite hand, 6¹/₄in. high. (Christie's) $4,978

Small white jade square form vase, Ming Dynasty, the sides carved in shallow relief to depict a band of stylized taotie masks bracketed by a leafy tendril and keyscroll band, 4¹/₂in. high. (Butterfield & Butterfield) $4,950

A pale celadon jade censer and cover carved around the lower section with taotie masks on a leiwen ground divided by two fixed-ring dragon-head handles, Qianlong, 15cm. wide. (Christie's) $3,400

A very fine jade monkey, late Ming Dynasty, ingeniously carved using the natural skin and inclusions of an irregular nephrite pebble as a crouching monkey, the posture naturalistic, 4¹/₈in. high. (Christie's) $64,000

BROOCHES

A gold brooch in the form of the bust of an Oriental, his hat set with bands of diamonds, 1ct.
(Finarte)   **$711**

A platinum, pearl and diamond circular brooch of open cagework design with central single pearl.
(Bearne's)   **$1,788**

A clip brooch in the form of an amethyst basket holding flowers in gold with colored enamel petals.
(Finarte)   **$1,505**

'Medusa', a yellow metal, ivory and enamel brooch by George Hunt of the head of Medusa, set with opals and pendent pearls.
(Christie's)   **$3,828**

A half-pearl and ruby brooch, designed as a graduated half-pearl crescent supporting a gold owl with ruby eyes.
(Lawrence Fine Art)
$1,143

An 18ct. gold, ruby and diamond brooch in the form of a chick with fluffed up feathers and ruby and diamond cluster eye, signed *Kutchinsky*.
(Bearne's)   **$894**

A Victorian pendant/brooch, open back collet set with a large faceted oval citrine, the scroll surround set with faceted garnets.
(Spencer's)   **$741**

Hardstone cameo brooch, depicting a classical bust of a woman within a half-pearl and 14ct. gold frame.
(Skinner)   **$748**

A late 19th century gold and diamond flower brooch with six petals pavé-set with old-mine brilliant-cut stones.
(Bearne's)   **$17,710**

BROOCHES

A 1960s Cartier cluster brooch, with rose coral and pavé cut diamond spheres, diamonds 5.5ct.
(Finarte) $5,267

A mid-19th century black enameled gold oval mourning brooch with central 'forget-me-not' design in half-pearls and rose-diamonds.
(Bearne's)   **$515**

A 1940s stylized and pierced shield shaped brooch, in bicolored gold set with cabochon and square cut rubies and diamonds.
(Finarte) $1,501

An early 19th century gold, seed-pearl and hair plait memorial brooch with central hair miniature, dated 1831.
(Bearne's)   **$385**

A Victorian diamond brooch, for Queen Victoria's Jubilee, 1837–1887, designed as a coronet within a border of sunburst rays, pavé-set throughout with rose-cut diamonds.
(Lawrence) $665

An enamel, diamond and half pearl brooch/pendant, circa 1875, of marquise shape, painted with three cherubs seated on a cloud.
(Lawrence Fine Art)
                             $4,826

A 1950s gold bow brooch with a central emerald surrounded by small diamonds, diamonds 0.6ct.
(Finarte) $2,106

A 1950s French Boucheron gold clip brooch as a feather, studded with sapphires, rubies, emeralds and diamonds, in original box.
(Finarte) $6,783

Green bakelite horse-head pin with metal pegged mane, 2¹/₂in. long.
(Eldred's) $61

BROOCHES

Early 20th century gold and green enamel brooch in the form of a four leaved clover, with central diamond.
(Finarte) $1,632

A German Art Nouveau brooch in the form of a woman with long flowing tresses, wearing cloche hat, 2¼in. long.
(Christie's) $6,230

Sterling silver brooch, designed as an open heart centered by a pair of dolphins in marine life surround, signed *Georg Jensen*.
(Skinner) $374

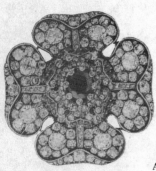

A mid-19th century gold, ruby and diamond flower brooch, with four petals, pavé-set with old-mine brilliants, centering in a larger oval ruby.
(Bearne's) $13,090

A Guild of Handicraft silver brooch designed by C. R. Ashbee in the form of a peacock, detailed and set with enamel, abalone and a ruby, with London hallmarks for 1907.
(Christie's) $2,871

A Victorian gold and shell cameo brooch, last quarter of the 19th century, the oval plaque carved as two female profiles, an owl and a dove, within a gold beaded border.
(Lawrence Fine Art)
                              $2,413

A 14ct. gold and white gold brooch as a seated cat, the body set with pavé cut turquoises, the face with rubies and small diamonds.
(Finarte) $2,056

A platinum and diamond regimental brooch designed as the standard of The Royal Irish Fusiliers, pavé-set with rose diamonds.
(Bearne's) $1,620

18ct. yellow gold, emerald and diamond frog pin, pavé-set emeralds and diamonds with cabochon-cut ruby eyes, signed *Fridel Virgilio*.
(Skinner Inc.) $5,500

EARRINGS

A pair of Swiss gold-mounted pendant earrings with porcelain portraits.
(Christie's) $2,904

Grape cluster gold earrings, the grapes of ruby and onyx spheres, the stems of onyx and pavé cut diamonds.
(Finarte) $2,257

A pair of jadeite pendant earrings, each with a circular wheel of carved jadeite suspended from a square chain.
(Christie's) $423

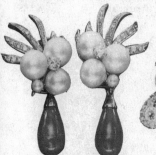

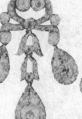

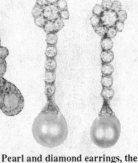

A pair of lavender jadeite, pearl and diamond earrings, the jadeite of pear-drop form, the lavender bright with some inclusions, suspended from pearl and diamond cluster mounts, 4.7cm. long overall.
(Christie's) $13,512

A pair of early Victorian chandelier-drop earrings with three pear-shaped diamond pendant clusters, mounted in silver and gold, circa 1840.
(Christie's) $22,022

Pearl and diamond earrings, the two cultured pearl drops suspended from a diamond rosette by five further diamonds.
(Kunsthaus am Museum)
                    $1,937

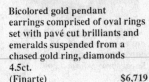

Bicolored gold pendant earrings comprised of oval rings set with pavé cut brilliants and emeralds suspended from a chased gold ring, diamonds 4.5ct.
(Finarte) $6,719

Coral and diamond earrings set in white gold, the coral pendants hung from a floral motif diamond setting.
(Kunsthaus am Museum)
                    $1,661

A pair of pendant earrings, comprised of two heart shapes set with pavé cut diamonds, onyx and two cabochon sapphires, 5.60ct.
(Finarte) $4,890

PENDANTS

A late 19th century miniature portrait of F.W. Young as a boy, painted on ivory, mounted within a glazed frame of moonstones in gold settings as a pendant.
(Bearne's) $750

A fine emerald-green jadeite pendant, carved as a group of gourds with foliage and tendrils, the stone of even semi-translucent tone, 4.6cm. long.
(Christie's) $42,670

A mid-19th century gold, ruby, diamond and half-pearl-set circular crystal pendant.
(Bearne's) $2,880

A white and yellow metal mounted cloisonné enamel pendant by Harold Stabler, designed by Phoebe Stabler, of a cherub with a rose, signed with initials and dated *1914*.
(Christie's) $861

An enamel pendant designed by Sir Frank Brangwyn for La Maison de l'Art Nouveau, Paris, circular with three knots, set with green and mottled white enamel.
(Christie's) $3,828

A fine jadeite and diamond pendant, the stone of very large size and of very even emerald-green tone with good translucency carved to the front with four felines among a lingzhi branch.
(Christie's) $227,573

A mid-19th century gold, emerald, diamond and gem-set crystal circular pendant, the wings pavé-set with emeralds and rose diamonds.
(Bearne's) $3,780

By and after Francesco Bianchi, an oval shell carved cameo depicting Pope Leo XIII, contained in a silver gilt filigree pendant mount.
(Spencer's) $576

A 19th century gold and pietra dura oval pendant, the hardstone panel depicting a floral spray within a gold frame.
(Bearne's) $459

A George III mahogany and boxwood strung knife urn, the lid rising to reveal a stepped cutlery matrix, 2ft. 7in. high. (Phillips) $3,115

A pair of George III mahogany, kingwood banded and herringbone strung knife boxes, with sloping lid, the front of projecting broken outline. (Phillips) $4,872

A George III cutlery box of serpentine form, veneered in mahogany, with parquetry stringing and silver handles and lock plate, 14½in. high, 26oz. (Bearne's) $2,538

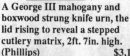

A pair of Regency ebonised and mahogany cutlery-boxes of sarcophagus shape, each with pine-cone finial above a gadrooned domed lid, 28½in. high. (Christie's) $29,130

A George III mahogany and ebony strung cutlery urn, the domed cover with urn finial, the tapering body with triple boxwood strung supports, 61cm. high. (Phillips) $1,511

A pair of walnut and parcel-gilt cutlery-urns of George II style, each with telescopic gadrooned top with pierced strapwork and urn-finials, 24in. high. (Christie's) $4,927

A George III mahogany, kingwood banded and herringbone strung knife box, with sloping lid and arc en arbalette front. (Phillips) $572

A pair of Regency carved mahogany crossbanded and marquetry knife boxes, the domed tops with turned finials concealing fitted graduated interiors for cutlery, 2ft. high. (Phillips) $6,619

One of a pair of George III black shagreen cutlery boxes, one with gilt fittings, the other with silvered fittings, 13½in. high. (Christie's) $750

A roironuri ground koro and cover of lobed form, the body and the base decorated in gold, silver and iroe hiramakie and hirame, unsigned, 17th century, 11cm wide.
(Christie's) $21,114

A silver kodansu chased overall with a dense profusion of flowers and foliage, each side inset with a rectangular ivory panel decorated in Shibayama style, signed on a mother-of-pearl tablet Masamoto, 19th century, 14.5cmx11.4cmx15.3cm.
(Christie's) $7,038

A lacquered palanquin with gold hiramakie on a roironuri ground and gilt metal fittings incised with foliage, the exterior of the rectangular carrying case divided by horizontal bands, 19th century, 105cm. long.
(Christie's) $50,787

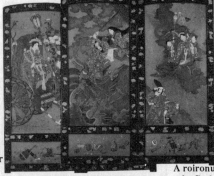

A fine lacquer vase and cover decorated in gold and silver hiramakie, takamakie, hirame, gyobu-nashiji and fundame with two panels elaborately decorated in Shibayama style, signed *Sadatoshi*, late 19th century, 26cm. high.
(Christie's) $34,650

A pair of important two-leaf gold lacquer screens decorated with figurative scenes, the panels bordered by a finely carved wood frame inlaid in mother-of-pearl and ivory, Meiji Period (1863–1912), each panel 225cm. high x 104.5cm. wide.
(Christie's) $376,200

A roironuri ground cylindrical sake flask, food container and cover decorated in gold hiramakie, kimpun and hirame with hydrangea, roundels and geometric pattern, 17th century, 29cm. high.
(Christie's) $11,286

A Japanese lacquer tea caddy, 19th century, decorated in Rimpa style with inlaid mother of pearl hydrangea with gold lacquer and pewter leaves, 5⅝ in. diam.
(Christie's) $2,875

A gold fundame and nashiji ground suzuribako in the shape of takarabune, a treasure boat, unsigned, 18th century, 22cm. long.(Christie's) $36,575

A composite lacquer sage-jubako comprising a carrying frame, a four-tiered jubako, two boxes and a sake bottle modeled as Jurojin with his stag, 18th century, 30.7cm. high.
(Christie's) $8,465

A Momoyama period domed coffer decorated in gold hiramakie and inlaid in mother-of-pearl with panels of birds among tachibana, late 16th century, 79cm. wide.
(Christie's) $53,152

A fine early Edo period Export coffer with coved cover and a samegawa-togidashi ground bordered with bands of scrolling foliage and stylized tessen, early 17th century, 132cm. long with gilt stand.
(Christie's) $116,270

A fine lacquer box and cover decorated in gold, black and silver iroe hiramakie, takamakie, hirame, heidatsu on a nashiji ground, late 18th/early 19th century, 37.5 x 26.5 x 27.4cm.
(Christie's) $22,425

  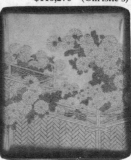

A lacquer koro formed as a cockerel and hen on an alarm drum on a four-legged stand, decorated in hiramakie, togidashi and gyobu, late 19th century, 24.1cm. high.
(Christie's) $9,101

A kinji ground suzuribako with silver rims decorated in gold hiramakie with a profusion of chrysanthemums issuing from behind a brushwood fence, 19th century, 26cm. long.
(Christie's) $17,250

A gold lacquer skull attended by three ivory oni, the three demons with stained detail and decorated with accoutrements in Shibayama style, unsigned, 19th century, overall height 20cm.
(Christie's) $14,520

A lacquer box and cover, decorated in silver and gold hiramakie, on a nashiji ground with aoi mon interspersed among a geometric design, late 18th/early 19th century, 21.3cm. wide.
(Christie's) $6,000

Japanese lacquer kimono boxes, 18in. high, black lacquer ground with hand painted gold motif of leaves and mon.
(Du Mouchelles) $1,500

A fine kojubako, the two tiers and cover decorated on a gyobu ground with raised panels representing framed paintings, 19th century, 12.4cm. wide.
(Christie's) $8,305

A composite lacquer sage-jubako comprising a carrying frame, a small tray, a box, two sake bottles in a tray, a four-tiered jubako, late 17th/early 18th century, 24.5cm. high. (Christie's) $5,643

A Momoyama Period small rectangular wood coffer and domed cover decorated with shippo hanabishi in gold lacquer, late 16th century, 23cm. long. (Christie's) $5,643

A large fine Shibayama style kodansu, the silver ground carved in relief with massed chrysanthemum flowerheads, signed on the nashiji ground base *Masayoshi*, late 19th century, 30.5cm. high. (Christie's) $37,620

A hexagonal gold ground lacquer box and cover on short shaped feet, the sides with panels decorated in Shibayama style with flowers and hanging flower baskets, late 19th century, 15.5cm. wide. (Christie's) $11,130

A pair of cylindrical gold lacquered wood vases decorated in gold and silver takamakie, hiramakie and kirigane and inlaid with wood and ivory with Fikurokuju and Daikoku standing under blossoming boughs, late 19th century, 52cm. high. (Christie's) $16,253

An important seventeenth century ewer and basin decorated in gold hiramakie, 17th century, the ewer 25.5cm. high. (Christie's) $182,875

A rare and fine double lozenge shaped sage-jubako connected by another lozenge-shaped piece, 17th century, 29.7cm. high. (Christie's) $13,167

Good gilt lacquer decorated kodansu, Meiji period, ornamented with a flock of cranes amid pine and above a small hinged double-door compartment, 22½ x 24 x 14³/₈in. (Butterfield & Butterfield) $9,900

A six-case kimpun-scattered roironuri ground inro decorated with stylized ju characters against massed chrysanthemum flowerheads, signed *Shiomi Masanari*, early 19th century, 7.6cm. long. (Christie's) $7,524

LACQUER

A rare 17th century oval barber's shaving bowl, the black lacquer ground decorated in gold hiramakie, kinpun and a little kirigane with lakeside buildings among trees, 31.6cm. wide.
(Christie's) $16,190

A red lacquer zushi containing a Shinto deity Dakini-ten mounted on a fox, late 18th/early 19th century, 22.5cm. high.
(Christie's) $3,010

A wood panel decorated with two fans, the open fan depicting the oil thief beside a temple lantern, the other birds among plum blossom, signed *Kongyokusai*, late 19th century, 70cm. wide.
(Christie's) $1,693

A large export lacquer medallion, the oval plaque decorated in gold hiramakie on a roironuri ground with a bust portrait of Pieter Breughel the Elder, 18th century, 22.5cm. high.
(Christie's) $3,467

A maroon lacquer suzuribako decorated in gold hiramakie, takamakie, kirikane, hirame and kimpun with Chinese scholars and children on a rocky path, unsigned, 19th century, 23.2 x 21.2cm.
(Christie's) $6,738

A finely modeled gold lacquered okimono of a macaque monkey wearing a sleeveless haori and sitting holding a peach, the back of his haori decorated in gold hiramakie with the other eleven zodiacal animals, late 18th/early 19th century, 19cm. high.
(Christie's) $44,480

A gold lacquer ground box and cover shaped as a persimmon decorated in hiramakie and kirikane, 19th century, 7.5cm. wide.
(Christie's) $1,693

A black roironuri ground suzuribako, the cover decorated in gold and silver hiramakie and kirikane with a pair of karashishi, 19th century, 22.7cm. long.
(Christie's) $5,800

A lacquer tobacco set decorated with panels depicting various landscapes, copper fittings and a kizerizutsu, late 19th century, 19.5cm. high.
(Christie's) $3,104

Chrysanthemum lamp, circa 1900, cameo glass, bronze, the shade and base with cameo mark *Gallé*, 11¼in. high.
(Sotheby's) $19,602

A pair of French red marble lamps, Napoléon III, Paris, circa 1870, each in the form of a classical urn, 97cm. high overall.
(Sotheby's) $4,198

Emile Gallé, cherry blossom and humming bird lamp, circa 1900, cameo glass, bronze, 10¼in. high.
(Sotheby's) $27,384

Tiffany bronze and favrile glass oil lamp, broad gourd-form opal glass shade with gold iridescent combed surface, shade diameter 9½in.
(Skinner) $2,860

René Lalique, pair of lamps, 'Grand Depot', after 1928, frosted glass and nickel plated metal, 19¾in. high.
(Sotheby's) $11,097

Tiffany counterbalance desk lamp, brilliant iridescence on cased gold and amber wave design damascene shade signed *L.C.T.*, shade diameter 7in.
(Skinner) $3,190

Bradley & Hubbard paneled table lamp, dome shade composed of six bent panels of closely ribbed glass decorated with painted urns and floral arrangements, 24in. high.
(Skinner) $825

A pair of gilt-bronze mounted Chinese porcelain lamps, mounted in Paris, circa 1880, 80cm. high.
(Sotheby's) $4,373

Tiffany bronze and favrile glass double student lamp, green and iridescent gold damascene ribbed glass shades lined in opal white, total height 30in.
(Skinner) $11,000

Emile Gallé, peony lamp, circa 1900, carved cameo glass, fire polished, bronze, 11³/₄in. high. (Sotheby's) $6,937

Two pewter chamber lamps, *S. Rusts Patent New York*, 19th century, 8⁵/₈in. high. (Skinner) $522

Emile Gallé, dragonfly veilleuse, circa 1900, cameo glass, patinated metal, 6³/₄in. high. (Sotheby's) $10,223

A Regency bronze and giltmetal colza oil-lamp attributed to William Bullock, the circular molded top with removable burner, 11in. high. (Christie's) $2,973

A pair of French gilt-bronze lamps, Paris, circa 1895, in the Art Nouveau influenced Louis XV manner, 66cm. high overall. (Sotheby's) $2,099

Dirk Van Erp copper and mica table lamp, circa 1911, vented cap on conical shade of four mica panels, separated by riveted hammered columns, 16¹/₂in. high. (Skinner) $22,000

A Lalique frosted glass illuminated table ornament, cataloged 'Oiseau de Feu', total weight 47cm. (Bearne's) $27,000

A pair of French porcelain-mounted oil lamps, Napoléon III, Paris, circa 1870, fitted for electricity, 57cm. high overall. (Sotheby's) $4,198

Arts and Crafts oak table lamp, hexagonal base with open lattice work, oil lamp insert under hexagonal lamp shade, unsigned, 23in. high. (Skinner) $385

René Lalique, lamp, 'Suzanne', after 1925, 11in. high overall. (Sotheby's) $12,474

A painted bronze, spelter and blue glass table lamp by Limousin, in the form of four elephants facing outward from a central square column, 15³/₄in. high. (Christie's) $1,066

A ship's external lantern of copper and brass with red glass for the stern, fitted for electricity, 'Red Light', Japan. (Auction Team Köln) $117

A cameo giltmetal-mounted oil-lamp base, overlaid in opaque-white and carved with a branch of trailing prunus pendant from a band of stiff leaves, circa 1885, 24cm. high. (Christie's) $1,264

Pair of French mantel lamps with Muller shades, silvered metal reticulated stick-shaft torchère forms with amethyst, pink, green and white mottled glass shades, 15¹/₂in. high. (Skinner) $1,320

A Clarice Cliff lamp base, of ovoid form molded in relief with a young girl in swimming costume riding a water buffalo, 21cm. high. (Christie's) $217

Pairpoint etched glass dragon lamp, cased red to white closed top shade with etched and gold enameled dragon decoration, 18in. high. (Skinner) $770

A Loetz and Osiris table lamp, the cylindrical shade with pinched quatrefoil rim, the yellow ground decorated with iridescent silver splashes and green and blue trailing. (Christie's) $1,168

Muller Frères and Chapelle Stork lamp, composed of wrought iron reticulated cage in form of a stork, 15in. high. (Skinner Inc.) $8,250

An early Victorian brass two light oil lamp, the reservoirs with vine chased holders, supported by a figure of Hercules, 33in. high.
(Christie's S. Ken)
$1,933

A William IV bronze colza oil lamp, in the form of a campana shaped urn with fruiting cone finial, on a circular plinth, 39cm. high.
(Phillips)
$1,408

Tiffany lotus leaf lamp, flared Oriental parasol shade of green and white favrile glass segments arranged with raised leaded ribbing, 22in. high.
(Skinner)
$40,700

German bronzed and metal glass figural lamp, designed as a tile-roofed outbuilding with three children gazing into a tub of water, 14in. high.
(Skinner Inc.)
$880

A pair of Empire ormolu and bronze lamps in the form of Atheniennes, each with later vertical shaft and white pleated silk shades, possibly Austrian, 34in. high.
(Christie's)
$35,530

One of a pair of mahogany wall-lanterns, each with broken pediment centered by an ivory acorn finial above a mirror-backed body with three glazed panels, 12in. wide.
(Christie's)
$4,202

Dirk Van Erp copper and mica table lamp, circa 1909, raised cap over conical shade of four mica panels separated by riveted hammered columns, 19½in. high.
(Skinner)
$4,400

A William IV bronze colza-oil lamp, in the manner of Thomas Messenger, in the form of a rhyton horn with lotus leaf top and fruiting finial, 9½in. wide.
(Christie's)
$2,178

Victorian bent panel table lamp, elaborate floral decorated metal shade and base frames for green-amber slag glass curved panels, 19in. diameter.
(Skinner)
$715

A George III lead cistern, of rectangular form, the paneled front centered with the initial *P*, with two cherub mask heads, dated *1781*, 40in. wide.
(Christie's) $4,660

A lead caricature figure of an obese drunkard, standing on circular base, 15in. high.
(Christie's) $450

George III lead cistern, dated *1765*, the front cast with a raised molded geometric design framing a central standing figure of a bacchic reveler, 39in. wide.
(Butterfield & Butterfield) $3,300

A large lead figure of a nymph, attributed to John Cheere, emblematic of Spring, depicted bare-breasted, flowers in her hair and a basket of flowers in her right hand, 18th century, 59in. high.
(Christie's) $29,123

A pair of lead sphinxes, possibly depicting Madame du Barry and Madame de Pompadour, each seated on their haunches, with their front legs crossed, early 20th century, 36in. wide.
(Christie's) $9,319

Lead figural fountain head, first half 19th century, in the form of a standing naked infant strangling a cockerel, 33in. high.
(Butterfield & Butterfield) $1,870

A pair of English lead figures, attributed to John Cheere, emblematic of Summer and Autumn, Ceres representing Summer, Bacchus representing Autumn, mid 18th century, 53³/₄in. high.
(Christie's) $50,479

One of a set of four lead urns, each with a foliate-cast molded rim, the body cast with a seam to each side, and with two scrolled dragon head handles, mid-18th century, 23¹/₄in. wide.
(Christie's)
(Four) $6,795

A pair of patinated lead maquettes cast from models by George J. Frampton, for Queen Mary's Dolls House, of two young maidens in mediaeval costume, 26.2cm. high.
(Christie's) $1,378

A lead corner trough, the faceted front cast with vintage scenes, 41in. high. (Christie's) $4,500

A pair of lead urns, the upper part of the body decorated with vine, above a frieze of classical figures, late 19th/early 20th century, 30in. high. (Christie's) $6,795

One of a pair of lead jardinieres of cylindrical form, the sides cast with lion masks, 10½in. high. (Christie's) $525

One of a set of four large lead urns, the waisted body with a satyr mask to each side and hung with a garland of fruit, 31½in. high. (Christie's) (Four) $5,113

A pair of modern lead grayhounds, each shown standing and looking forward, on rectangular stone bases, 36in. wide. (Christie's) $4,271

One of a pair of lead urns, each with a waisted body flanked by stylized handles, raised in relief with cherubs, on a waisted socle and square canted foot, late 19th/20th century, the urns, 17¾in. high. (Christie's) (Two) $688

Two lead cherubs, each with one arm raised, on square stone bases, first half 18th century, 33in. high. (Christie's) $4,854

Fine pair of neoclassical lead urn-form gatepost or balustrade finials, probably English, late 18th century, 26½in. high. (Butterfield & Butterfield) $3,575

One of a pair of lead urns, each of circular tapering form with two ram's masks, the lower part with overlapping petals and acanthus, 30½in. diameter. (Christie's) (Two) $3,036

One of a pair of 19th century lead urns, the wide scrolled rims above squat bulbus bodies, cast with roseheads, 15in. high. (Christie's) $3,250

Charming lead garden figure of a little girl and her rabbit, circa 1930, standing on a rockwork base, 31½in. high. (Butterfield & Butterfield)

$825

One of a pair of lead troughs in the 18th century style, the sides applied with lion masks, 16in. high. (Christie's)
Two $1,000

One of a set of four carved stone gothic finials, each of square tapering form and decorated with crockets, 18th/19th century, 48in. high. (Christie's)   (Four)
                    $2,429

Pair of Regency lead jardinières, first quarter 19th century, with a ram's head projecting from each corner above festoons of berried foliage and flowers, 12½in. high. (Butterfield & Butterfield)
                    $2,200

A fine English lead figure of Acis, attributed to the workshops of John Cheere, the young faun clad in a tightly-fitting bacchic goat-skin with curling hair and pointed ears, circa 1770, 52in. high. (Christie's) $37,000

A George III lead figure of a grayhound, probably by John Cheere, seated on his haunches and wearing a collar, late 18th century, 21in. high. (Christie's) $1,760

A pair of lead jardinières, each of circular form with three lion masks and ogee molded paneled sides, 20th century, 19½in. diameter. (Christie's) $387

A lead fountain figure of a putto, holding aloft a dish with his left hand, the right supporting a festoon of flowers, late 19th/early 20th century, 35in. high. (Christie's) $1,113

One of a set of three modern lead jardinières, the paneled sides cast in high relief with ogee molding, a ship, dolphins and foliate festoons, 31in. square. (Christie's)

(Three) $5,825

A modern lead fountain group of a swan and putto, the swan with outstretched wings and head held high, the boy at his side looking up, 49¼in. high. (Christie's)

$8,154

A rectangular lead cistern, the front with the date *1709*, above a panel centered with the initials *R.D.*, early 18th century, 65¾in. wide. (Christie's)

$6,989

One of a pair of lead vases, each of hexagonal form, the waisted body cast in high relief and with a drilled background, the six sides each with an oval cartouche above a stylized twin-handled flower-filled vase, first half 18th century, 23in. wide. (Christie's)

(Two) $27,181

Pair of Neoclassical style lead circular jardinières, each decorated in relief with sunbursts, height 15in.; diameter 22in. (Butterfield & Butterfield)

$2,300

One of a set of four lead urns, each with bulbous upper section decorated with alternating gadrooning and acanthus leaves, the body with four masks above drapery swags, 18th century, 20in. high. (Christie's)

(Four) $8,154

A lead figure of a shepherdess, after John Cheere, shown holding a staff in her left hand, a lamb supported by her right hand, late 19th/20th century, 48in. high. (Christie's) $9,319

A pair of English lead urns, each with the handles, rim, lower body and foot elaborately cast with acanthus leaf decoration, 18th century, 29in. high. (Christie's) $25,240

A lead cherub sundial pedestal, shown holding a cornucopia in his right hand and supporting a circular stone platform, 41¾in. high. (Christie's) $1,942

An Avanti Laterna Magica/
Liesegang slide projector, with
original components in portable
case, circa 1910.
(Auction Team Köln)
$247

A metal-body Lapierre magic
lantern with lens, lens cap and
chimney.
(Christie's) $68

Georg Bing, Nürnberg, a
metal-body magic lantern with
spirit burner, lens and twelve
transfer strip slides, in maker's
box.
(Christie's) $212

A metal-body Cinematographe
Lumiere projector marked *J.
Carpentier, Paris* with hand-
crank, brass bound lens with
rack and pinion focusing, a
spare lens and flange.
(Christie's) $5,405

The 'Improved Phantasmagoria
Lantern', by Carpenter & Westley,
with patent argand solar lamp
with a quantity of lantern slides.
$515

F. Cox, London, a metal-body
child's phantasmagoria lantern
with chimney, lens, spirit burner,
and applied metal plate *F. Cox,
Optician, 100 Newgate St.,
London.*
(Christie's) $326

Ernst Planck, Germany, a
metal-body projecting
praxinoscope lantern with
integral spirit burner, chimney,
hand-crank, shutter
mechanisms.
(Christie's) $978

A mahogany and brass-fitted
biunial lantern with chimney,
condensing lenses, shutter, a
pair of brass bound lenses.
(Christie's) $2,495

An Ernst Plank Laterna Magica
projector for 90mm. slides,
lacking burner, with original
case and four slides, circa 1890,
35cm. high.
(Auction Team Köln)
$170

A mahogany and brass-fitted Merito Optical lantern with red-leather bellows, brass bound lens, metal chimney, electric illuminant and plate *Thornton-Pickard Merito Optical Lantern*. (Christie's) **$212**

An upright cylinder lantern with red and gilt decoration on barrel with chimney by Ernst Planck, Nuremberg. **$1,432**

G. Carette & Co., Germany, a metal-body child's lantern with chimney, lens, illuminant and twelve transfer strip slides, in maker's fitted box. (Christie's) **$178**

A pair of metal-body Improved Phantasmagoria magic lanterns each with 3½ inch condensing lenses, Carpenter & Westley, 24 Regent St, London. (Christie's) **$2,233**

A Jean Schoenner, Nurnberg, toy spherical magic lantern with polished metal body and black painted support. **$385**

Ernst Planck, Germany, a blue-painted metal-body child's magic lantern with gilt decoration, polished metal chimney. (Christie's) **$196**

A mahogany and brass biunial magic lantern with brass bound lens section, a pair of three-draw rack and pinion focusing lenses. (Christie's) **$5,583**

Ernst Planck, Germany, a metal-body child's lantern with lens, chimney and slides, in maker's box. (Christie's) **$131**

A mahogany body biunial magic lantern with lacquered brass fittings, in fitted wood box. (Christie's) **$1,605**

A Napoleon III ormolu-mounted griotte marble urn with everted egg-and-dart rim flanked by beaded foliate scroll-handles, 20³/₄in. high.
(Christie's) $3,287

A St. Annes marble oval cistern, the waisted body on conforming spreading foot, 18th century, 27¹/₂in. wide.
(Christie's) $5,436

A circular marble table top, including numerous marble types, in a radiating geometric pattern, 19th century, 27in. diameter.
(Christie's) $3,850

A pair of 19th century French pentallic marble and ormolu mounted vases and covers, on square marble feet with applied foliate spandrels, 54cm. high.
(Phillips) $5,653

An Italian white marble jardinière, after the Antique Albani cinerary urn, of octagonal form, each side carved in relief with a winged dancing putto, 19th century, 18¹/₈ x 17⁷/₈in.
(Christie's) $3,388

A pair of black marble and pietra dura urns with pinched necks and baluster-shaped bodies decorated with scrolling floral ivy, 17in. high.
(Christie's) $3,287

Italian specimen marble and agate table top, late 18th century, centered by a gameboard, surrounded by various stones, 47³/₄ x 27¹/₂in.
(Skinner Inc.) $6,050

A pair of Austrian ormolu and bardiglio marble profile medallions depicting Emperor Francis II, Francis I of Austria, and Empress Maria Theresa in court dress, 14 and 17cm. high.
(Christie's) $15,991

A large Italian black marble vase, mid 20th century, flecked with white marble, 75cm. high.
(Sotheby's) $2,624

A 19th century Italian marble panel, carved in low relief with the Virgin and Child, 26¹/₂ x 16³/₄in.
(Christie's S. Ken) $1,552

A carved white marble relief, depicting Christ kneeling within a pointed arch, His arms outstretched, inscribed *HOMO DEUS CHRISTUS PONTIFEX*, circa 1942, 17³/₄in. wide.
(Christie's) $1,320

An English white marble oval portrait plaque of Queen Victoria, in profile, by Frank Theed, carved in high relief, the Queen wearing a lace veil, signed, 24in. high.
(Christie's) $1,452

A pair of marble and gilt bronze urns, the mottled white and green marble forming the baluster body, with gilt bronze feet decorated with stylized foliage, 19th century, 6¹/₄in. high.
(Christie's) $2,396

A modern carved white marble horsehead, with open mouth, signed *D. Lott*, 31in. high.
(Christie's) $2,287

A pair of ormolu, bronze and red marble urns, of campana shape, flanked by loop-and-mask handles, on fluted socle with laurel-cast foot, late 19th century, 7¹/₂in. diameter.
(Christie's) $6,198

A Regency white marble occasional table, on a tapering gadrooned central column, the trefoil foot carved with acanthus scrolls, on claw feet, early 19th century, 26³/₄in. high.
(Christie's) $2,374

Pair of monumental gray marble footed urns in the Neoclassical taste with foliate swags and swan neck handles, 45in. high.
(Butterfield & Butterfield) $4,400

Fine Italian micro-mosaic and specimen marble table top on later base, circa 1900, centred by a circular scene depicting the Roman Forum, 29¹/₂in. high.
(Butterfield & Butterfield) $9,900

Italian marble bust of a satyr,
19th century, 16½in. high.
(Skinner Inc.) $3,080

A white marble portrait bust of
a girl, by Larkin Goldsmith
Mead, American, late 19th
century, 19³/₈in. high.
(Christie's) $1,495

A 19th century white marble
bust of Michelangelo, 55cm.
high.
(Finarte) $2,491

A fine English white marble bust
of a maiden, by Holme Cardwell,
with delicate classical features,
her hair swept into a graceful
chignon, signed and dated
*HOLME CARDWELL SCULPt
ROMA 1868*, mid-19th century,
23½in. high.
(Christie's) $4,501

Monumental Italian carved
Carrara marble bust of a
seventeenth century nobleman
in the style of Roubilliac, Prof.
Aetrilli, 19th century, the
nobleman with moustache and
projecting underlip with
arrogant expression, 30½in.
high.
(Butterfield & Butterfield) $8,250

A French white marble bust of
Napoléon after Canova,
inscribed on the plinth, *Donne
par son Altesse Imperiale
Madame la Grand Duchesse de
Toscane a Madame Benoist,
1809*, first quarter 19th century,
24in. high.
(Christie's) $18,595

An Italian white and brown
marble bust of a woman, looking
slightly to her right, wearing a
headscarf tied at the nape of her
neck, early 20th century, 16in.
high.
(Christie's) $4,283

A marble bust of Spring by
Salvatore Albano, Italian, 19th
century, the maiden truncated at
the waist, 26³/₄in. high.
(Christie's East) $5,280

A large white marble bust
depicting The Lord of the Isles,
the bearded figure with long
flowing hair and draped
shoulders, signed on back *J.
Hutchison Sc, Edinr*, 32in. high.
(Christie's) $2,239

BUSTS

An English white marble bust of a young boy, his head turned to the right, his short hair with curls, first half 19th century, 15in. high.
(Christie's) $3,267

A 19th century carved white marble bust of Napoleon, after Canova, the Emperor dressed al'antica, 1.23m. high.
(Phillips) $5,355

An English white marble bust of a Vestal Virgin, looking slightly downwards, her veil drawn forwards over her shoulders, first half 19th century, 15½in. high.
(Christie's) $6,098

An English white marble bust of William Overend Q.C., by Sir Joseph Edgar Boehm, the judge shown bewigged and in robes of office, second half 19th century, 30½in. high.
(Christie's) $3,769

An early 19th century sculpted white marble bust of Pericles, his helmet with raised figures of Hercules, Centaurs and animals, 27in. high.
(Christie's S. Ken) $7,758

An English white marble portrait bust of a young boy, by Edward Hodges Baily, the youth looking slightly to his right, on a spreading circular socle, mid-19th century, 19½in. high.
(Christie's) $6,511

An Italian white marble bust of a lady, by C. Scheggi, in elaborate Renaissance costume, her hair adorned with pearls and tied behind, 28in. high.
(Christie's) $10,623

A marble bust of a girl by A. Piazza, Italian, 19th century, truncated at the shoulders, 18in. high.
(Christie's East) $1,100

A white marble bust of a lady, French School, 19th century, in 18th century manner, her long hair curling over her shoulders, 66cm. high.
(Sotheby's) $2,171

FIGURES

An English white marble group of Diana the Huntress, after the Antique, the goddess striding forward, a leaping stag beside her, 19th century, 30¹/₂in. high.
(Christie's) $1,925

A white marble group of Cupid and Psyche on a spiral column, Italian, circa 1880, after Canova, Psyche leaning back to reach up and kiss the naked Cupid, the marble group 52cm high.
(Sotheby's) $6,013

A 19th century Japanese marble okimono of a young woman spinning silk, signed on base *Rysukeda*, circa 1850.
(Duran) $2,106

An Austrian white marble figure of Venus, by Victor Oskar Tilgner, the goddess shown seated, her light robe falling off her shoulder and revealing her thighs, circa 1896, 50¹/₂in. high.
(Christie's) $91,300

A mid-19th century Italian white marble figure of the crouching Venus, after the Antique, signed *G. Andreoni, Pisa*, a vase at her feet, 34in. high.
(Christie's) $8,140

An Italian white marble group of a girl feeding doves, by I. Possenti, the barefoot girl shown kneeling, offering up her right hand to a dove perched on her left arm, signed, late 19th century, the group 23¹/₂in. high.
(Christie's) $19,481

An alabaster group of Apollo and Daphne after Gianlorenzo Bernini, Apollo chasing a nymph as she metamorphoses into a laurel tree, 26¹/₄in. high.
(Christie's East) $1,320

A French white marble group of a shepherd and shepherdess, by L. Charles Fremont, the couple shown seated on a tree trunk, second half 19th century, 36¹/₄in. high.
(Christie's) $9,936

Italian carved carrara marble group of two putti, circa 1900, both naked but for scanty draperies, 29in. high.
(Butterfield & Butterfield) $3,025

FIGURES

An Italian white marble group, depicting a woman fetching water, with her admirer seated and holding her hand, late 19th century, 25in. high.
(Christie's) $791

An Italian white marble figure of the Sleeping Nymph, after the antique, shown reclining, her drapery falling about her in soft folds, her legs crossed, her head supported on her left arm with asp bracelet, 31in. wide.
(Christie's) $1,186

A white marble group of cherubs, after Thomire, both shown standing and struggling to reach a heart, late 19th/20th century, 17³/₄in. high.
(Christie's) $2,302

An Italian white marble figure of a kneeling cherub, by Pietro Costa, leaning his head against his right hand and holding a wreath, late 19th century, 20in. high.
(Christie's) $3,769

An Italian white marble group of the Wrestlers, after the Antique, the two naked athletes locked in combat, 19th century, 18¹/₄in. high.
(Christie's) $4,138

A fine English white marble figure of Eve, by John Warrington Wood, the graceful Eve shown naked and seated with her legs folded beside her on a grassy mound, signed *J. Warrington Wood Roma*, second half 19th century, 41in high.
(Christie's) $58,432

An Italian white marble figure of the crouching Venus, by V. Livi, on an integrally-carved square base, two fingers repaired and two replaced, circa 1841, 28¹/₂in. high.
(Christie's) $3,646

A white marble group of a boy holding a fish, Italian, by Nicola Cantalamessa-Papotti, 1881, the chubby boy seated in a scallop shell with waves beneath, signed and dated, 66cm. high.
(Sotheby's) $7,350

An Italian white marble figure of the crouching Venus, her hair tied up in a headdress, her right hand sponging herself, 19th century, 37¹/₂in. high.
(Christie's) $4,565

A Gem roller organ with twenty-note mechanism in gilt stenciled ebonized case and six 'cobs'.
(Christie's) $753

A Regina Sublima piano, with 73-note roll-operated mechanism, electric motor drive, coin mechanism with mercury switch, and oak case.
(Christie's) $4,250

A Triola mechanical zither with 25-note roll mechanism and twenty-four hand-played strings, on ebonized base.
(Christie's S. Ken)
                    $4,092

Coinola Mod. CJX electric piano with xylophone, coin operated, with decorative Jugendstil glass front, with folding seat and three rolls, 1916.
(Auction Team Köln)
                    $8,489

A rosewood musical tea caddy, English/Swiss, circa 1840, the hinged lid containing musical movement and opening to reveal two tea compartments, 12in. wide.
(Sotheby's) $781

A forty-four key trumpet barrel organ, playing eight airs, with thirty-five wooden pipes and thirteen exposed brass trumpets, 46in. wide.
(Phillips) $7,760

A Margot piano orchestrion with 44-key action, in oak case with stained glass door, 98in. high.
(Christie's) $5,421

A musical Christmas tree stand, perhaps by Eckardt, Stuttgart, with rotating cast iron, decorated tree holder, playing four melodies on two cylinders, in working order, circa 1890.
(Auction Team Köln)
                    $578

A twenty-three key portable barrel piano, playing eight airs, in mahogany case with pierced fretwork grille, 36$\frac{1}{2}$in. high.
(Phillips) $1,455

Trombino, a rare plated tin 18 tone mechanical trumpet by M. Winkler & Co., Munich, with four paper rolls, circa 1900. (Auction Team Köln) **$1,775**

A cabinet roller organ, twenty-note organette in gilt stenciled oak case, with seventeen combs. (Phillips) **$1,746**

A musical clock base, Swiss, circa 1830, the 8in. cylinder playing four operatic airs on sectional comb in rosewood veneered oval base. (Sotheby's) **$1,996**

A Berlin double flute player organ with wooden cylinders, in walnut case with palisander inlay, playing eight Berlin melodies, circa 1950. (Auction Team Köln) **$7,716**

An Othello Orchestrion by Popper & Co., Leipzig, the cabinet with Art Nouveau decoration and equipped with mechanical piano, mandoline, xylophone, drums, triangle and cymbals, in working order, 1912. **$10,285**

An unusual 19th century Swiss musical box, in the form of an organ of vertical rectangular form, the top, sides and fascia inset with ten enamel plaques painted in colors, 23cm. high. **$2,988**

A Cabinetto 25-note organette in gilt stenciled walnut case with instructions and National Musical Cabinetto importers' label, 17½in. wide. (Christie's S. Ken) **$1,330**

A rare musical necessaire, the sur-plateau movement with two-sets of seventeen separate teeth, four-wing governor and male winding key, 5¼in. wide, circa 1810. (Christie's) **$6,186**

'Symphonia' roll organ, early 20th century, by Wilcox & White Organ Co. of Meriden, oak case with simulated inlay, 18in. wide. (Eldred's) **$358**

A very rare gilt-brass and blued steel mechanical trephine, signed *Evans, London*, with ivory handles, the center pin in the crown, circa 1850–55, 7in. long.
(Christie's) **$11,858**

A lacquered brass enema signed *MAYER & MELTZER*, with double nozzle and release mechanism, in fitted velvet lined case, 11⁹/₁₀in. wide.
(Christie's) **$416**

A rare pair of 'Smellie's' curved forceps, the iron frame with shaped wood handles and handle notches, with leather covers, incorporating the 'English lock', circa 1752, 11³/₄in. wide.
(Christie's) **$3,049**

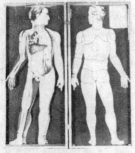

Anatomical teaching device, 'Smiths's New Outline Map of the Human System, Anatomical Regions, No. 2', manufactured by American Manikan Co., Peoria, Illinois, 1888, 44in. high. **$1,065**

A rare early 19th century Laennec-type fruitwood monaural stethoscope, arranged in three sections, overall length, 12³/₄in.
(Christie's) **$7,115**

A fine quality wax model of the human head, in glazed ebonized case, 9³/₄in. high. **$620**

A J. R. Delius sterilizing chamber, with copper boiler on iron legs, with Bunsen burner, circa 1910.
(Auction Team Köln) **$346**

A World War I field surgeon's instruments case, signed *Meyer & Meltzer London*, in velvet lined brass bound mahogany case, with protective metal casing, 17¹/₂in. wide.
(Christie's) **$1,215**

A 19th century mahogany domestic medicine chest, the lid rising to reveal compartments for fourteen bottles, 8¹/₄in. high. (Christie's S. Ken) **$964**

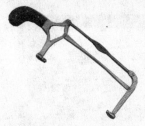

A 'Dr Butcher's' bone saw signed *Perry Greenwich*, with cross hatched ebony pistol grip handle, the wrought iron frame with central adjustment screw, 12³/₄in. wide.
(Christie's) $121

A mahogany medicine chest, English, circa 1801-13, the case with brass carrying handle, double doors opening to a fitted interior containing twenty-one glass bottles, 33cm high.
(Bonham's) $1,301

A rare field surgeon's amputation saw with folding horn handle and blade guard, circa 1780, 17¹/₄in.
(Christie's) $521

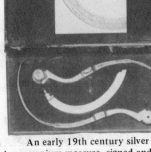

A rare plaster demonstration model of a womb with internal foetus, indistinctly signed and dated *ANZ – Doctr Fecit anno 1875*, probably French, 6¹/₂ x 5in.
(Christie's) $1,128

An early 19th century silver cranium measure, signed and engraved in the quadrant arm *To W. A. F. Brown Esqr. Surgeon,* Edinburgh, 1833, 26.4cm. wide. (Christie's S. Ken) $2,479

A fine set of dental scalers, with interchangeable bone handle, six steel scalers in red velvet lined fishskin case, late 18th century, 2¹/₂in. wide.
(Christie's) $474

A Maw pattern enema pump with ivory plunger handle and articulated nozzle, the reservoir of oval form decorated with gilt banding, in leather case, 10¹/₂in. long.
(Christie's S. Ken) $463

An early 19th century? Persian steel saw; with a decorative cartouche, damascened in gold on the blade which reads: *Its owner is Aqa Muhammad, year 1245,* (H. = A.D. 1829–30); with mother-of-pearl handle, 10³/₄in. long.
(Christie's) $473

A silver plated 'London dome' ear trumpet signed *F.C. Rein & Son Patenteed,* with decorative engraving, and bone earpiece, circa 1865, 6¹/₂in. high.
(Christie's) $781

A mahogany medicine chest, English, early 19th century, with hinged lid and drawer containing bottles, scales and measuring vessels, 22cm wide.
(Bonhams) $532

A Ritter SA dental X-Ray machine, electrics in wooden case under bakelite X-Ray protector, circa 1922.
(Auction Team Koln) $742

A surgical instrument case, containing three saws, three Liston knives, forceps, tourniquet and other items in a fitted mahogany case, 17in. wide. (Christie's S. Ken) $750

A late 19th century brass enema syringe by S. Maw Son & Thompson, complete with accessories in mahogany case 12in. wide.
(Christie's S. Ken) $385

McConnell dental folding chair with curved headrest and foot-rest, American, circa 1900.
(Auction Team Koln) $268

A 19th century French pewter enema douche with accessories in fitted oval japanned case, 8in. wide. (Christie's) $450

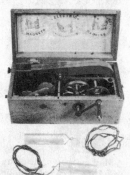

Cupping set with brass cupper and three glass cups, in original velvet-lined mahogany case, circa 1880.
(Auction Team Koln) $106

An 18th century medical saw, the blade secured by rivet and wing nut, and with tapering walnut handle, 9¾in. long.
(Christie's S. Ken) $300

Electric Magneto Machine for treating nervous and other ailments, in mahogany case, circa 1880.
(Auction Team Koln) $90

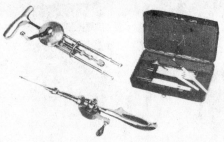

A small skull-shaped poison container probably French, 19th century unmarked, with red stone eyes, hinged face mask, hinged jaw and suspension loop, 2cm.
(Bonhams) $152

Two surgeon's drills and dissecting sets.
(Auction Team Koln) $68

A silver plated resonator ear trumpet, signed *F C Rein & Son*, with decorative engraving, fretwork funnel cover, and bone earpiece, circa 1865, 7½in. high.
(Christie's) $1,128

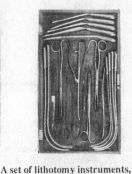

Traveling medicine set, cupping set, glass cupper and brass enema set, circa 1880.
(Auction Team Koln) $106

A case of Smith surgical instruments, English, 1850's signed 'Smith surgical inst. maker 21 S. Augustines parade Bristol' in a plush lined case, 24cm wide.
(Bonhams) $608

A set of lithotomy instruments, some signed *STODART*, in velvet lined mahogany case, 16¾in. wide, mid-19th century.
(Christie's) $1,187

A late 19th-century mahogany slide cabinet of 24 drawers, containing a large collection of professional and amateur slide preparations by various preparers, 24in. high.
(Christie's) $1,891

A 19th century amputation saw by Weiss, with anti-clog teeth and ebony handle, 15½in. long.
(Christie's) $150

A 19th century mahogany domestic medicine chest, the lid rising to reveal compartments for sixteen bottles, 8¾in. high.
(Christie's S. Ken) $1,606

A rare and important French compound microscope to the design of the Duc de Chaulnes, unsigned, sundry accessories, overall height 16½in.
(Christie's) $20,460

An early 19th century 'Jones Most Improved' monocular microscope, on a turned pillar with folding tripod stand signed *Dollond London*, 1ft. 5¾in. high.
(Phillips) $2,035

A good 19th century lacquered brass compound monocular and binocular 'Van Huerck' microscope, the tripod support signed, *W. Watson & Sons*.
(Phillips) $6,290

A fine lacquered brass binocular microscope signed *C. BAKER*, the body tubes with rack and pinion eyepiece focusing, in fitted mahogany case, with a substantial collection of accessories.
(Christie's) $6,247

A mid 19th-century lacquered brass compound monocular microscope, sgned on the Y-shaped base *A. ROSS, LONDON*, in a mahogany case with six graduated drawers, 20⅝in. high.
(Christie's) $4,202

A rare Culpeper-type compound microscope, possibly by Matthew Loft, with brass eyepiece, lignum vitae carrier, green vellum body tube, in shaped pyramid case with brass handle, circa 1740, 18¾in. high.
(Christie's) $15,345

A late 19th-century lacquered brass compound monocular universal microscope, signed on the body tube *A Microscope Achromatique Universal de Charles Chevalier, Imperieur Opticien, Palais Royal, Paris.*
(Christie's) $2,311

An early 19th-century lacquered brass 'Cary'-type pocket botanical microscope, unsigned, the rectangular pillar with rack and pinion focusing, 5½in. wide.
(Christie's) $672

A fine lacquered brass monocular microscope, signed *Smith & Beck*, with rack and pinion focusing, triple nosepiece, square mechanical stage, and plano-concave mirror.
(Christie's) $1,041

A microscope by Zeiss, with lacquered brass body on black 'jug-handle' stand, coarse and fine focusing, 12in. high. (Christie's S. Ken) $593

A 19th-century lacquered brass inverted microscope, signed *NACHET a Paris*, with circular stage, in case, 10in. high. (Christie's) $3,572

A late 18th century brass Cuff-type compound microscope, unsigned, in shaped pyramid mahogany case, 16¼in. high. (Christie's) $4,433

A Henry Crouch brass binocular microscope, English, last quarter 19th century, signed, with rack and pinion adjustment to the eyepieces, rack and long lever focus, together with two boxes of microscope slides. (Bonhams) $887

A 19th century brass binocular telescope by Broadhurst Clarkson & Co London, in fitted mahogany carrying case. (Andrew Hartley Fine Arts) $1237

A lacquered brass monocular microscope signed *Chatelain 51 rue Bisson Paris*, with rack-and pinion and fine focusing screw, with accessories in fitted mahogany case, 12½in. wide. (Christie's) $599

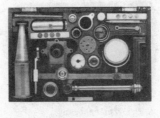

A rare mid-19th century simple and monocular microscope, signed *Charles Chevaliers Ingeniers Opticien Brevete Palais Royal 165 Paris*, 12in. wide. (Christie's) $2,217

A 19th century lacquered brass 'Jones's Most Improved'-type compound monocular microscope, signed on the folding tripod stand *Cary LONDON*, 11¼in. wide. (Christie's) $2,270

A black enameled "Bactil Binocular" microscope by W. Watson & Sons Ltd., in fitted mahogany case, 17in. high, with accessories. (Christie's S. Ken) $381

A miniature Georgian mahogany drop-flap oval dining table with gateleg action, raised on tapering turned supports and pad feet, 40cm. extended. (Phillips) $3,382

A George II mahogany miniature tripod table, the circular snap top on an urn-shaped shaft on tripod legs, 9in. wide. (Phillips) $863

A miniature painted pine document-box, the rectangular top lifting above a conforming case over a shaped apron, on bracket feet. (Christie's) $462

A mahogany miniature bureau inlaid with boxwood lines, the sloping fall with oval fan inlay and conforming spandrels enclosing an interior of four drawers and pigeonholes, 11in. wide. (Phillips) $1,339

A miniature Chinese-Export ivory open armchair in the George III Chippendale style, the pierced rectangular back with waved toprail above a pierced vase-shaped splat, on canted square legs, 18th century, 5¹/₂in. high. (Christie's) $9,805

A miniature William and Mary dower-chest, New England, 1710–1725, on four ball and baluster-turned feet, 12¹/₄in. wide. (Christie's) $4,620

A mid-Victorian oak miniature cabinet in the form of a six-panelled door-case flanked by half-columns and surmounted by a pediment, 16in. high. (Christie's) $2,479

A Victorian mahogany miniature sample dining-table, the molded extending rectangular top above four bulbous baluster legs with a patent-brass mechanical extending action, fully extended: 13¹/₄in. wide. (Christie's) $4,832

A miniature slat-back chair, American, 19th century, the two arched slats painted with flowers, centered by leaves, 10in. wide. (Christie's) $437

A fine paint decorated miniature pine foot stool, Landis Valley, Pennsylvania, early 19th century, 8in. long.
(Sotheby's) $2,300

A George III mahogany miniature tripod table with circular tip-up top on turned stem and cabriole base, 12½in. high.
(Christie's) $7,399

A George III mahogany miniature chest, the rectangular top banded with ebonized and boxwood lines, above four short and two graduated long drawers, 16¾in. wide.
(Christie's) $1,224

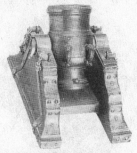

A Regency rosewood and satinwood miniature chest, inlaid overall with boxwood and ebonized lines, the rectangular top above a pair of brass-grilled doors with carrying-handles to the sides, 19in. wide.
(Christie's) $6,752

A miniature Dutch bronze mortar in three stages, turned and molded at the muzzle, reinforced and rounded base, vent with shell-shaped pan behind the signature, *AD 1752*, 6in. barrel, 2¼in. bore.
(Christie's) $2,374

A mid-Georgian walnut miniature chest crossbanded overall in yewwood, the rectangular top above four graduated long drawers and on later bun feet, 15¼in. wide.
(Christie's) $2,986

A 19th century Dutch walnut and checker strung miniature cabinet with a pair of doors enclosing two short and one long drawer with three drawers below, 1ft. 11in. wide.
(Phillips) $1,593

A Regency mahogany miniature chest, with ebonized stringing, on later ogee bracket feet, 1ft. 1in. wide.
(Phillips) $625

A late Regency mahogany miniature linen press, the plain rectangular top above a pair of paneled doors enclosing four slides, on bracket feet, 1ft. 1in. wide.
(Phillips) $864

A classical carved and gilt looking glass, English 1815–1820, the frame surmounted with an eagle clasping a ball-and-chain, 25¹/₂in. wide.
(Christie's) $27,600

A Regency giltwood convex mirror, with ebonized reeded slip within a fluted and acanthus molded surround with a shell carved foliate cresting and apron, 52¹/₄in. diameter.
(Christie's) $11,901

A giltwood convex mirror, with eagle cresting flanked by scrolling foliage, early 19th century.
(Christie's) $2,549

A Regency giltwood, composition and ebonized mirror with circular convex plate, with reeded slip, the cushion frame decorated with lotus leaves and lozenges, 37 x 23in.
(Christie's) $1,786

A Regency giltwood mirror with circular convex plate and ebonized slip, the molded frame applied with balls and stars, 30in. diameter.
(Christie's) $3,960

A classical giltwood convex mirror, American, early 19th century, the black-painted and carved spreadwing eagle perched on a plinth above a circular reeded frame, 45in. high.
(Christie's) $7,150

A good classical giltwood four-light convex wall mirror, first quarter 19th century, surmounted by a wingspread eagle on a rock work support, 44in. high.
(Sotheby's) $8,800

A Regency giltwood mirror with convex circular plate, ebonized slip and molded frame applied with balls, the plate possibly resilvered, 42in. x 22in.
(Christie's) $3,366

A Regency ebonized and parcel-gilt wood and composition convex mirror, the circular plate within a stiff-leaf and floral patera molded frame surmounted by a scrolling lotus-leaf, 44³/₄ x 42in.
(Christie's) $37,191

GIRANDOLE

A Federal gilt and carved girandole looking glass, American or English, 1810-1815, the concave frame surmounted by a carved eagle, 53in. high.
(Christie's) **$16,100**

One of a set of four Italian girandoles, circa 1920, each cartouche-shaped mirrored plate with five candle arms below a crown, 88cm. high.
(Sotheby's)

(Four) **$5,011**

A Regency style gilt convex girandole, the plate within an ebonized slip and molded frame, surmounted by a displaying eagle, 44 x 33¹/₂ in., late 19th century.
(Bonhams) **$1,433**

A late 19th century French ormolu table girandole, the cartouche shaped frame with chased rocaille ornament, the base with twin candle arms, 24in. high.
(Christie's) **$1,655**

A pair of giltwood girandoles of George III style, with oval plates and beaded fluted frames, with triple branches and conforming pierced scrolling aprons, 50 x 23¹/₂in.
(Christie's) **$2,509**

A Queen Anne silvered-wood and walnut girandole in narrow walnut and molded silvered-wood frame, the plate with a small crack at the base, 34 x 23¹/₄in.
(Christie's) **$33,099**

A gilt girandole mirror, American, 1820–1830, surmounted by an ebonized eagle on a rocky plinth flanked by acanthus leaves, the coved mirror frame hung with spherules, 30¹/₄in. high.
(Christie's) **$15,400**

A good Regency gilt and parcel ebonized girandole, the octagonal plate within an ebonized slip and sphere applied frame, 32 x 16¹/₂in.
(Bonhams) **$3,650**

A George III giltwood girandole, with oval plate in a pierced scrolling foliate frame, the pierced cresting with stylized acanthus-enriched confronting C-scrolls, 26¹/₂ x 15in.
(Christie's) **$4,377**

OVAL

A George III giltwood mirror with oval plate and frame carved with unspringing foliage and flowerheads entwined with ribbons, 45 x 26¹/₂in.
(Christie's) $23,364

An early Victorian giltwood oval mirror frame of George III style, carved as two ribbon-tied acanthus fronds, 45 x 45¹/₂in.
(Christie's) $1,682

A Swedish giltwood mirror, with oval plate, molded frame carved with acanthus and laurel-leaf, mid 18th century, 41in. high.
(Christie's) $1,940

A George III giltwood mirror with later oval plate, the frame carved with ribbon-and-rosette entwined with acanthus, with acanthus-scroll cresting, 32 x 23in.
(Christie's) $2,904

An ebonized and tortoiseshell toilet mirror, the cartouche-shaped frame inset with a Charles II stumpwork panel sewn with a man and woman, 30in. high.
(Christie's) $7,970

An early 19th century Irish ebonized and parcel gilt mirror, the oval plate within a molded and glass studded frame, 2ft. 5in. high.
(Phillips) $936

A George III giltwood mirror with oval plate in a Vitruvian scroll and rockwork surround and florally-entwined scroll frame, 52 x 33in.
(Christie's) $8,291

One of a pair of giltwood oval mirrors, each with later oval plate within a husk molded pierced rockwork frame, crested by a confronting C-scroll and acanthus carved cresting, 50¹/₂ x 51¹/₂in.
(Christie's)
          (Two) $7,574

A George II giltwood mirror with oval plate within a gadrooned frame carved with scrolling oak leaves and acanthus, 50¹/₂ x 30in.
(Christie's) $6,996

OVER MANTEL

An Italian carved giltwood rococo frame mirror, the shaped plate with a scroll spray border, floral open spray surmount, 3ft. x 3ft. 2in.
(Woolley & Wallis) **$666**

A Flemish parcel-gilt carved-wood overmantel mirror, circa 1880, in Renaissance manner, with a rectangular beveled plate, 148cm. wide.
(Sotheby's) **$2,624**

Over-mantel mirror, 19th century, painted green, three panels with griffin and acanthus leaf design, possibly Italian, 59¼in. wide.
(Eldred's) **$660**

A George II giltwood overmantel, with triple-divided plate within a reed and rockwork C-scroll carved frame incorporating a cartouche-shaped panel depicting the gardens at Chiswick House, 50½in. wide.
(Christie's) **$28,739**

Flemish School, early 18th century, a Bacchanalian scene, oil on shaped canvas, approx. 30 x 52½in., incorporated in a carved gilt wood overmantel mirror with three beveled plates, 56in. wide.
(Tennants) **$9,300**

An early Victorian giltwood overmantel mirror by William Thrale Wright, the central rectangular plate flanked by shaped plates and divided by entwined foliate bars, 78½ x 66in.
(Christie's) **$2,099**

Charles X carved pine overmantel mirror, second quarter 19th century, in a broad paneled frame carved in high relief with sprays of chestnuts and foliage, 45in. wide.
(Butterfield & Butterfield) **$3,300**

A Chippendale style mahogany and parcel gilt triple plate overmantel, surmounted by a shaped crest with gilt ho-ho bird finial, 55 x 50½in.
(Bonhams) **$1,186**

A French carved giltwood overmantel mirror, Napoléon III, Paris, circa 1870, the arched cresting pierced with profusely carved ribbon-tied summer flowers, 220cm. by 140cm.
(Sotheby's) **$6,374**

RECTANGULAR

Florentine rococo style carved and painted mirror in a deeply carved and pierced border of scrolling acanthus, 5ft. high. (Butterfield & Butterfield) $3,025

A William and Mary oyster-veneered ebonized and marquetry cushion frame mirror with rectangular plate and foliate scroll surround, 41¹/₂in. high. (Christie's) $5,577

A Franco-Flemish baroque gilt-metal and walnut mirror, late 17th century, with rectangular plate within a cushion-molded frame, 36x26in. (Christie's) $9,775

A William and Mary walnut and floral marquetry cushion frame mirror, the surround with ebonized reserved panels inlaid with vases of flowers and foliate sprays, 3ft. 8¹/₂in. x 3ft. 1¹/₂in. (Phillips) $9,570

A Wiener Werkstätte giltwood mirror, designed by Dagobert Peche, decorated with overlapping stylized leaf design, 48 x 46.6cm. (Christie's) $18,183

A rare parcel-gilt and carved walnut mirror, designed by Alfred Stevens, the divided plates etched with foliage within an egg and dart molding, 5ft. 9¹/₄in. high. (Sotheby's) $8,525

A George III giltwood mirror with shaped rectangular plate, the pierced frame carved with C-scrolls, rockwork, acanthus and flowerheads, 38in. x 22in. (Christie's) $12,276

Rare Charles II metallic thread embroidered silk petit point traveling mirror, circa 1660–1685, 15³/₄ x 15¹/₄in. (Butterfield & Butterfield) $3,025

Florentine giltwood mirror, late 19th century, surround with inset portrait miniatures and hardstone roundels, 37¹/₂in. high. (Skinner Inc.) $2,970

A 19th century Dutch
marquetry toilet mirror,
decorated with scrolling foliage
and floral sprays, on block feet,
1ft. 9¹/₂in. wide.
(Phillips) $623

A mahogany toilet-mirror, the
replaced rectangular beveled
plate in an ebonized slip and
molded hinged frame between
turned fluted supports, 28in.
wide.
(Christie's) $929

A George III mahogany toilet-
mirror with later shield-shaped
plate in a plain surround and on
scroll supports, back feet
replaced, 17in. wide.
(Christie's) $1,237

A Federal carved ebonized
mahogany dressing glass with
drawers, Boston, Massachusetts,
circa 1820, the mirror plate
pivoting between reeded and
scrolled uprights, 20³/₄in. wide.
(Sotheby's) $1,100

A Regency ivory-mounted and
inlaid mahogany dressing
mirror with drawers, first
quarter 19th century, on turned
ivory feet, width 20¹/₄in.
(Sotheby's) $1,035

A George III mahogany toilet-
mirror with oval plate in a plain
surround and eared supports,
the serpentine base with a single
mahogany-lined frieze drawer,
on shaped bracket feet, 17³/₄in.
wide.
(Christie's) $1,522

An early Georgian walnut and
parcel-gilt toilet-mirror, the
later rectangular plate in a
molded foliate surround
between channeled supports,
18in. wide.
(Christie's) $1,609

An Edwardian mahogany toilet
mirror with shield-shaped plate
and scrolling frame inlaid with
paterae, on arched feet, 22in.
wide.
(Christie's) $753

A George II mahogany toilet-
mirror in a narrow frame
carved with scrolling foliage and
rocaille between fluted and
rusticated supports, 29¹/₄in.
high.
(Christie's) $29,205

A 2in. scale model of a Shand Manson Horse Drawn Fire Appliance of circa 1894 built by B. Hatswell, 13³/₄ x 22¹/₂in. (Christie's) $3,476

A well engineered model of a single cylinder pear crank water pumping engine built by H. Beech, 12 x 6⁵/₈in. (Christie's) $826

A well engineered 2in. scale single cylinder, single speed, three shaft general purpose traction engine 'Claire', 20¹/₂ x 30in. (Christie's) $2,824

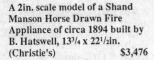

A late 19th century small full size single cylinder vertical reversing stationary engine, 25¹/₂ x 13¹/₂in., with brass bound wood lagged cylinder. (Christie's) $2,081

A well engineered 2in. scale model of the Burrell Special Scenic Showman's Road Locomotive 'Thetford Town', Reg. No. E.L. 1988, built by E. Lofthouse, 23¼ x 47½in. (Christie's) $8,514

A finely engineered model 3in.:1ft. scale model Rider–Ericsson 8 inch hot air driven pumping engine built by J.P. Nazareth, 21¹/₂ x 16¹/₂in. (Christie's) $3,027

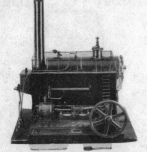

A fine early 20th century live steam stationary steam set with brass labels inscribed *T R Barker Alpha Bristol and Babcock and Wilcox Boilermakers*, 22 x 21in. (Christie's) $2,607

A fine and unusual late 19th century brass model condensing twin cylinder vertical blowing engine, one frame engraved *M Noton, maker, Salford, 1874*, 16¹/₂ x 12³/₄in. (Christie's) $5,214

A Bing 'Phoenix' spirit fired model traction engine, German, circa 1906, with 3 inch cast flywheel and four road wheels hand painted in red and cream, 8¹/₂in. long. (Sotheby's) $607

A 19th century Roman
rectangular mosaic panel,
decorated with a view of
the Piazza del Popolo in
Rome, 2¾in. long.
(Christie's) $1,875

Early 19th century circu-
lar Roman micro-mosaic
decorated with a duck and
duckling, the box 3in.
diam. (Christie's)
                              $1,875

A Roman rectangular
micro-mosaic panel deco-
rated with a bull-baiting
scene, circa 1800, 3in.
long. (Christie's)
                              $4,875

Early 19th century circu-
lar Roman micro-mosaic
decorated in the style of
Rafaelli with a finch, the
box 3in. diam.
(Christie's) $2,250

A 19th century Roman
micro-mosaic panel deco-
rated in bright colors with
a bunch of flowers, approx.
8in. long. (Christie's)
                              $6,000

A circular tortoiseshell snuff
box with detachable cover,
the mosaic circa 1820, 2¾in.
diam.
(Christie's) $1,500

A Roman rectangular micro-
mosaic plaque, depicting a view
of St. Peter's Square, in gilt-
metal frame with suspension
ring, 19th century, 3⅝in. wide.
(Christie's) $3,960

A circular Roman micro-
mosaic of a pannier brim-
ming with flowers, circa
1830, the box 2¾in. diam.
(Christie's) $3,000

A Swiss rectangular gold snuff-
box set with a Roman micro-
mosaic, showing Rinaldo and
Armida, in a wooded landscape
setting, by S. Chaligny, Geneva,
circa 1820, 3¾in. long.
(Christie's) $41,173

A Jawa 350 Junior motorcycle, chassis no. 317, with 4 cylinder V 350 cc engine, 1968. (Finarte) $6,669

A Bimota-Harley-Davidson 250 motorcycle, engine no. 373, with 55 hp engine, circa 1977. (Finarte) $8,004

A Magnat-Debon 2$\frac{1}{2}$ hp motorcycle, engine no. 264 monocylinder, 2.5 hp. engine, circa 1909. (Finarte) $10,227

An AJS 7R 350 motorcycle, engine no. 497R608, with 31 hp engine, 1949. (Finarte) $26,679

A Zündapp K800 motorcycle, chassis no. 140046, 22 hp engine, circa 1936, all parts original. (Finarte) $8,892

A Suzuki 750 Vallelunga motorcycle, chassis no. 31191, with 81 hp engine, top speed 220 km/H, 1972. (Finarte) $3,558

An AJS 350 16MS motorcycle, chassis no. 53/16MS/19548, with 4 speed transmission, professionally restored, 1953. (Finarte) $2,313

A James Twin 600 motorcycle, chassis no. 768, twin cylinder, 600 cc engine, three speed manual gearbox and 26" wheels, circa 1915. (Finarte) $16,008

A Yamaha 350 TR2 motorcycle, chassis no. 900.141, with 350 cc 54 bhp engine, 1968. (Finarte) $7,113

A very rare Motobi 250 Corsa motorcycle, with 250 cc, 90 bhp engine, circa 1967. (Finarte) $16,896

A Benelli 175 Monza motorcycle, chassis no 281, with 175 cc single shaft engine, three speed gearbox, 1927. (Finarte) $15,117

An MV Agusta 125 single shaft motorcycle, chassis no. 150085, with 16 hp engine, circa 1952. (Finarte) $16,896

A Seeley-Norton 920 Special motorcycle, chassis no. CS 335K with Norton 920 cc engine, circa 1969. (Finarte) $11,115

A very rare MV Agusta 600 motorcycle, chassis no. 1990135, with 50 hp engine, odometer reading 18,000 km, 1969. (Finarte) $26,679

A Suzuki 653XR 23B motorcycle, chassis no. 1010, with 138 hp engine, sold with a complete engine and numerous other spare parts, 1979. (Finarte) $48,021

A Yamaha OW 31 750 motorcycle, chassis no. 409.200147 with four cylinder 130 hp engine, circa 1976. (Finarte) $21,342

A twelve-air cylinder musical box, Swiss, last quarter 19th century, in a rosewood grained and inlaid case, 58cm wide. (Bonham's) **$490**

A mandolin musical box by P.V.F., playing six airs (teeth grouped in fours), in feather-banded bird's eye maple case, 19¹/₂in. wide. (Christie's) **$1,465**

Frères Rochat, a fine and rare early 19th century gold and enamel musical singing-bird box, the oval cover to the bird with enamel wreath decoration, 87 x 57mm. (Christie's) **$54,683**

A 19th century walnut cased musical box and table base, the musical box with comb and cylinder movement with white metal lyre cast soft/loud pedal, 41in. wide overall. (Spencer's) **$6,585**

An Orchestral musical box, by S. Troll Fils, Genève, playing eight airs accompanied by drum, castanets, 20-note organ and six engraved bells with bird finials, 29in. wide. (Christie's S. Ken) **$7,670**

A Lochmann's original 48D 11 inch disk musical box, German, circa 1905, the double comb periphery drive movement contained in walnut case, together with thirteen disks, 17in. wide. (Sotheby's) **$1,475**

A 19th century Swiss figured walnut, amboyna and ebonized cased 'Sublime Harmony' musical box, the 13in. interchangeable brass cylinder and two comb movement playing six airs. (Spencer's) **$3,590**

A twenty-air forte-piccolo 'Bells in Sight' cylinder musical box, Swiss, late 19th century, with lever-wound movement, 60 cm wide. (Bonham's) **$1,148**

An early 'Flutina' orchestral musical box by Bremond, No. 6329 playing ten popular and operatic airs accompanied by sixteen-key organ, 30¹/₂in. wide, circa 1862. (Christie's) **$6,776**

A key-wind forte-piano musical box by Nicole Freres, playing eight hymn tunes, with figured ash case with ebony stringing, 19¼in. wide.
(Christie's) $5,000

A white metal singing bird box, Swiss, second half 19th century, the bird with moving perch, wings and bone beak in an engraved case, 10cm. wide.
(Bonhams) $1,301

A twenty-four-air musical box by P.V.F., No. 67805, with large (two-per-turn) cylinder, in case with inlaid lid, 21in. wide.
(Christie's) $1,694

An 'Ideal Sublime Harmonie' inter-changeable cylinder musical box by Mermod Freres, playing six tunes on each cylinder, with tune selector and indicator, 41in. wide overall.
(Christie's) $8,500

A 'Grand Format' musical box by Nicole Frères, playing four overtures, with lever-wind, engraved silver tune sheet in rosewood veneered case, 27½in. wide. Accompanying this musical box is a letter (written in French) from Nicole Freres to their London agents, dated April 1860.(Christie's) $54,780

Stella disk music box, Switzerland, circa 1900, playing 17¼-inch disks on a single comb, handle wound, mahogany case with oak leaf carving, 28½in. wide.
(Skinner Inc.) $2,600

A Swiss rosewood musical box, the 33cm. brass barrel and single steel comb movement playing twelve airs, 66cm. wide.
(Spencer's) $1,249

Gilt sterling and enamel automaton music box, unmarked, circa 1900, the top with hinged lid painted en plein air with a vase of flowers opening to reveal a chirping bird with red feathers, height 2⅝in.
(Butterfield & Butterfield) $1,955

A fruitwood music box, Pennsylvania, 1780–1810, of rectangular form with hinged lid opening to a printed paper-lined interior fitted with works, length 15½in.
(Sotheby's) $2,415

Painted and decorated parade drum, J. & G. Dennison, Freeport, Maine, late 19th century, the green ground decorated in polychrome, 16½in. diam. (Skinner Inc.) $900

An E-flat Helichon, by Boosey and Co., and engraved Solborn class A, and numbered 9908. (Christie's S. Ken) $300

A double action pedal harp by Sebastian Erard, the body, arm and soundboard with gilt lines, forty-three strings, eight pedals, 68⅛in. high. (Christie's) $4,651

The Anaconda, the only known example of a contra-bass C serpent, by Joseph Richard Wood in Upper Heaton, Yorks, circa 1840, overall length 475cm. (Phillips) $8,700

A portable three-octave harmonium by Debain, with burr-walnut case, ormolu mounts and gilt tripod base, 23in. wide. (Christie's) $977

A thirty eight button Anglo-German system concertina by Jeffries, stamped *C. Jeffries, Maker*, with hexagonal nickel plated fretted endplates, in a hexagonal leather case. (Christie's) $2,080

A fifty six button English system Aeola concertina by Wheatstone, with nickel mounted endplates, in the original square leather box. (Christie's) $1,200

A set of Scottish Highland bagpipes, the green covered bag with bass drone and two tenor drones, the rosewood chanter marked *R. G. Lawrie Scone*. (Phillips) $850

Large painted and decorated parade bass drum, inscribed *William Bridget Maker & Painter, Belfast*, late 19th century, 37in. diam. (Skinner Inc.) $4,500

A late Victorian rosewood lute-harp with gilt decoration to the front, on oval foot. (Christie's) $825

A set of bagpipes of Hutcheon of Edinburgh, circa 1920, with later Kintail pipe chanter and bag. (Christie's) $696

Painted poplar chime cabinet, eastern United States, circa 1840, 15in. wide. (Skinner) $660

A Tyrolean Concert zither, circa 1880, in fitted velvet lined case the body of rosewood. (Phillips) $825

A set of Regency period musical glasses, in the original mahogany veneered rectangular case with divided interior, 3ft.9in. (Woolley & Wallis) $3,500

A fifty six button English system accordion by Lachenal, branded *The Edeophone*, with pierced ebonized endplates, 16¹⁵/₁₆in. diameter. (Christie's) $672

A rope-tension side drum of the 4th (Carms.) Bn., The Welch Regiment emblazoned with regimental devices. (Christie's) $525

Chappell Pianino, circa 1815, having twenty blue glass rods (of thirty seven) in a line inlaid mahogany case on turned pedestal. (Christie's) $2,658

Painted and decorated tambourine, America, early 20th century, painted in polychrome, pressed brass bells, 9½in. diam. (Skinner Inc.) $1,500

An ivory netsuke of a man kneeling to polish the character Shin, signed *Ogura* (*Tomoyuki*), late 19th century, 5cm. long.
(Christie's) $1,192

Ivory netsuke of two skeletons wrestling, 19th century, signed *Gyokosai*, 2¼in. high.
(Skinner Inc.) $880

A stained wood netsuke carved as a snail and an aubergine on a pumpkin, signed *Shigemasa to*, early 19th century, 4.5cm. wide.
(Christie's) $2,384

A finely detailed small ivory netsuke of a wild boar asleep on a bed of leaves beside a fallen oak branch, unsigned, late 18th century, 3.3cm.
(Christie's) $5,300

An ivory okimono-style netsuke Raijin the God of Thunder setting out as a traveler with his drum on his back and a young oni carrying a persimmon at his side, signed *Tomomasa to*, late 19th century, 5cm. high.
(Christie's) $14,204

An ivory netsuke of a snake, its body coiled into many loops, its mouth open and eye pupils inlaid, unsigned, 19th century, 3.5cm.
(Christie's) $1,750

An ivory netsuke of a macaque monkey sitting holding a persimmon between its feet and a shishimai headdress on its head, signed *Masatami*, late 19th century, 4cm. high.
(Christie's) $2,600

Ivory netsuke of lion dancer and child, late 19th century, signed *Matatoshi*, the shishimai dancer beating a drum and ringing bells as an excited child reaches for the drumstick, 1⁷⁄₁₆in. high.
(Butterfield & Butterfield) $489

A wood netsuke depicting a human skull entwined by a snake, its body passing through the left orbit, its head with black inlaid eyes, unsigned, 19th century, 3.5cm. high.
(Christie's) $2,600

A finely carved ivory netsuke of a group of three rats clustered together, signed in a rectangular reserve *Masaka*, late 19th century, 3.5cm. wide. (Christie's) $5,634

Wood mask netsuke, early 19th century, grimacing male face, signed *Tadatoshi*, 1¹/₂in. long. (Skinner Inc.) $523

A well-detailed ivory netsuke of a monkey with two young ones, signed in an oval reserve *Naomitsu*, 19th century, 4.5cm. wide. (Christie's) $1,950

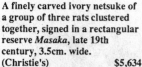

A very fine boxwood and ivory netsuke depicting Choryo kneeling to put on Kosekiko's shoe, with lacquer and metal detail, late 19th century, 4cm. high. (Christie's) $14,150

A well-detailed ivory netsuke of a rat sitting holding a candle with its forepaws, its eyes inlaid in black horn, signed *Tomokazu*, 19th century, 3cm. high. (Christie's) $1,400

An ivory netsuke depicting Kanyu sitting leaning against a low table stroking his beard while reading a military treatise, signed *Kinryusai*, late 19th century, 4.2cm. wide. (Christie's) $1,084

An unusual stained boxwood netsuke depicting Santa Claus holding a small Christmas tree, surrounded by three boys, signed *Gyokuzan*, circa 1900, 6.2cm. high. (Christie's) $1,950

An ivory netsuke depicting Kanyu standing stroking his beard, his retainer Chow Tsang beside him, signed *Shounsai* (*Shounsai Joryu of Edo*), late 18th century, 5cm. high. (Christie's) $2,059

A well-detailed stained boxwood netsuke of the toad and decayed well-bucket model, signed *Masakatsu* (of Ise-Yamada, son of Masanao I), 19th century, 4cm. high. (Christie's) $1,625

A Pilot desk punch, metal on wooden base, circa 1910. (Auction Team Koeln) $30

Early German Courant letter opener, circa 1910. (Auction Team Koeln) $120

Early German DRGM 114.189 stapler, with unusual reverse stapling facility, 1900. (Auction Team Koeln) $130

An Art Nouveau nickel plated cast iron stapler, circa 1890. (Aution Team Koeln) $60

A Sensator Model VIII flat copier in attractive wooden roll top case, circa 1920. (Auction Team Koeln) $225

A Boston Pencil Pointer pencil sharpener. (Auction Team Koeln) $45

An Ergo Extra pencil sharpener, (Auction Team Koeln) $135

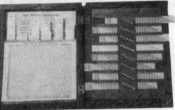

The Jeffers Calculator, calculating aid with interchangeable cardboard strips, in folding wooden case, 1907. (Auction Team Koeln) $1,050

A two tier gold-bronze painted stamp holder, circa 1900. (Auction Team Koeln) $25

A very rare J. N. Williams US cheque writer for Automatic Bank Punch Co., New York City, 1885. (Auction Team Koeln) $300

A calculating ape: Consul the Educated Monkey, a very rare tin calculating toy, in original cover, 1918. (Auction Team Koeln) $750

Automatique Dubuit platen machine, desk top model for printing small items like business cards, circa 1920. (Auction Team Köln) $157

A Karl Krause board cutter for coarser book binding board with manual drive and a rare corner cutter, cut width 70cm. (Auction Team Köln) **$695**

The Rapid adhesive label dampener of decorative Art Nouveau style, German, circa 1900. (Auction Team Koeln) **$185**

A Jupiter pencil sharpener by Guhe & Harbeck, Hamburg, with case, circa 1920. (Auction Team Koeln) **$120**

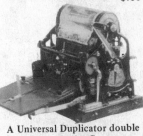

A brass pen brush for quill pens, circa 1900. (Auction Team Koeln) **$45**

A very early American Webb's Adder, double plate, with carry ten facility, 1868. (Auction Team Koeln) **$750**

Parlograph dictating machine with taping and erasing modules and 11 new wax rolls, by Carl Lindstrom AG Berlin, circa 1920. (Auction Team Koeln) **$750**

A late 19th-century Wheatstone-pattern telegraph receiver, the lacquered brass mechanism mounted on a mahogany base, 12¹/₂in. wide. (Christie's) **$945**

A good extensive set of drawing instruments by Elliott Brothers, The Strand, London, including a rolling rule, foot rules, pair of compasses, and curve patterns, 35cm. wide. (Spencer's) **$3,321**

A Universal Duplicator double cylinder copier by Gestetner, complete with cardboard roll with original wax stencils and metal cassette with unused stencils, circa 1925. (Auction Team Koeln) **$128**

An Olympic pencil sharpener. (Auction Team Koeln) **$120**

A decorative block stamp having floral decoration to the sides complete with plug and mat. (Auction Team Koeln) **$120**

English line dial, an early ebony desk telephone with separate earpiece, connection rosette and 10 stage switch, by Walker Bros. Birmingham, circa 1900. (Auction Team Köln) **$275**

An early 18th century monocular, with stamped maker's name on the green vellum body tube *J. Gilbert London*, with lacquered brass segments.
(Christie's) $222

French mother of pearl and brass deluxe opera glasses, circa 1870.
(Auction Team Köln) $131

A rare leather magnifying glass, hand stitched frame with tapered handle (glass cracked), 17th century, 3³/₈in. long.
(Christie's) $1,511

W. Butcher & Sons, Blackheath, a wood-body Reflectoscope lantern viewer with 3¹/₄ inch diameter viewing lens.
(Christie's) $388

Ernst Planck, Germany, hot-air powered child's praxinoscope with spirit burner, condensing piston, connecting pulleys and six-inch diameter mirrored drum.
(Christie's) $6,657

A mahogany-body zograscope with 5 inch diameter magnifying lens and a 10 x 8in. mirror.
(Christie's S. Ken) $1,025

E. Reynauld, Paris, a 5-inch diameter miniature Le Praxinoscope with black drum, turned wood base and four picture strips.
(Christie's) $620

A wood-body hand-cranked projection shutter with applied paper labels *Cinématographe. Fabrication Française Déposé E.V.L. Déposé.*
(Christie's) $701

E. Reynauld, Paris, a hand-cranked pulley-operated 8 inch-diameter Le Praxinoscope on a turned wood base, six picture strips.
(Christie's) $1,060

London Stereoscopic Co, 12-inch diameter Wheel of Life zoetrope on a turned wood stand and with twelve picture strips.
(Christie's) **$631**

Galileo aluminum opera glasses with enameled decoration of dogs playing, circa 1875, marked *Iris, Paris*.
(Auction Team Köln) **$131**

A 7½ x 5¼ inch five-part peep view, the front section printed in German, French and English.
(Christie's) **$1,675**

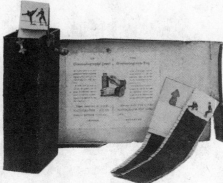

A 9 inch diameter Le Praxinoscope with candle holder, later shade and six picture strips, on a wood base.
(Christie's) **$971**

A cardboard-body The Cinématograph-Toy with five picture strips, metal hand-crank and marble weight, in original box.
(Christie's) **$457**

A cardboard-body New Jewel kaleidoscope with turned wood eyepiece, rotating brass section, on a decorative metal stand.
(Christie's) **$1,051**

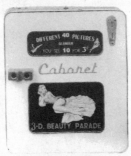

An international Mutoscope reel Co, 'Mutoscope', American, circa 1900–20, with red painted finish, viewing hood, coin slot and stand joined by X-stretchers, 135cm high.
(Bonham's) **$1,070**

A wood-body, electrically-powered, coin-operated Cabaret stereoscopic viewer, the front panel with legend *40 Different Pictures Glamour, You see 10 for 3d.*
(Christie's) **$2,424**

A phenakistiscope part-set comprising five 7 inch diameter double-sided slotted disc, in maker's marbled folder.
(Christie's) **$790**

369

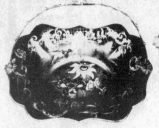

A fine 19th century papier mâché cake basket, the central panel painted with a passion flower, roses and a mythical bird, 11½in. wide.
(Bonham's) $600

A Victorian inlaid and painted small papier mâché writing slope with glass inkwells.
(Greenslades) $410

A Regency papier mäché rectangular tray with monochrome flowers and leaves on a crimson ground within an oak leaf and anthemia border, 32¼ x 24½in.
(Christie's) $3,049

A mid Victorian black, gilt and mother-of-pearl japanned papier-mache table-bureau, 14¾in. wide. (Christie's)
$1,500

A pair of mid Victorian black, gold japanned papier-mache spill vases, 8in. wide.
$895

Black lacquered papier mâché rectangular box, the lid painted with a picture of a woman as 'Autumn', Brunswick, Stobwasser, early 19th century, 6cm. long.
(Kunsthaus Lempertz)

$2,003

An early Victorian papier-mâché tray, decorated in gilt and mother-of-pearl with a cockatoo in an exotic garden, 2ft. 6¾in. wide.
(Phillips) $1,266

Victorian papier mâché snap top table, painted with flowers and inlaid with mother of pearl detail, 24in. wide.
(G.A. Key) $441

A 19th century papier-mâché tray, decorated overall with gilt heightened leaves and flowers, circa 1840, 2ft. 7¾in. wide.
(Phillips) $1,947

A good 19th century shaped rectangular black papier mâché tray, the center painted with lilies, the border dripping foliated scrolls, 31½in. wide. (Anderson & Garland) $2,529

A Victorian mother-of-pearl inlaid black lacquer papier mâché tilt-top table, mid 19th century, attributed to Bettridge and Jennins, 43¼in. high. (Christie's) $3,000

Victorian black papier mâché tray with gilt detail to edges and painted floral center, having mother of pearl inlays, 23 x 19in. (G.A. Key) $435

One of a pair of lacquered papier-mâché hand held screens, of ornate mirror shape, painted with landscape scenes after Constable, 10¾in. wide. (Bonhams) $821

Pair of Chinese lacquered papier mâché vases, 18th/19th century, with incised polychrome landscape and floral reserves on black ground, 13in. high. (Skinner Inc.) $1,540

One of a pair of lacquered papier-mâché hand held face screens, of ornate mirror shape, each inlaid with a central mother of pearl floral bouquet, 11in. wide. (Bonhams) $256

A lacquered papier-mâché blotter, the front painted with a bouquet of garden flowers, heightened with tinted inlaid mother of pearl leaves and petals, 12in. x 9in., circa 1835. (Bonhams) $164

A Victorian papier mâché work table decorated with painted flowers and gilt scrolls, 18½ x 31in. high. (Anderson & Garland) $2,079

A Regency papier-mâché tray decorated with chinoiseries, the two central figures of elders seated at a table taking tea, 2ft. 6¼in. wide. (Phillips) $1,168

A Swedish Art Deco pewter bowl, attributed to Gullsmeds Aktie Bolaggt, supported on four ribbed feet and stepped circular foot, 22cm. diameter. (Christie's) $268

Pewter candlestick, England, circa 1675, octagonal bobeche over conforming ringed standard, medial drip pan and base, 8¹/₂in. high. (Skinner Inc.) $7,700

Orivit Art Nouveau pewter centerpiece, Germany, circa 1900, tall cut-glass liner in a round handled pewter bowl, 8¹/₄in. diameter. (Skinner) $495

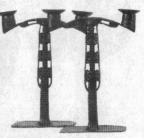

A pair of Liberty & Co. 'Tudric' pewter candlesticks, the design attributed to Archibald Knox, the bullet shaped sconce with flanged rim, 23.5cm. high. (Phillips) $740

An 18th century English pewter charger, 20¹/₂in. diameter, with reeded border, the center later engraved with the Duke of Marlborough, initial *M* and date, *1704*. (Bonhams) $1,575

A pair of Liberty & Co. Tudric pewter twin-branched candelabra designed by Archibald Knox, with pierced decoration of leaves and berries on tendrils, on rectangular flat foot, 27.8cm. high. (Christie's) $3,272

Pewter gallon double volute measure, England, 18th century, unmarked, inspector's excise stamp on rim of lip *CM* and *CC*, 13in. high. (Skinner) $2,070

Possibly Archibald Knox for Liberty & Co., biscuit box and cover, designed 1903, pewter and enamel, 4¹/₂in. square. (Sotheby's) $499

Pewter beaker, John Will, New York, 1750–74, scarce form with earliest known touch of John Will, 4³/₄in. high. (Skinner) $16,100

A Kayzerzinn pewter chalice, with three stag skulls each with full antlers curving up and around the tapering cylindrical bowl, 36cm. high.
(Christie's) $284

Kayserzinn Art Nouveau pewter dish, Germany, circa 1897, designed by Hugo Leven, covered dish raised on tapered feet with sculpted foliate design, 9¹/₂in. long.
(Skinner) $413

A 'Tudric' pewter tankard with hinged cover, the design attributed to Archibald Knox, 21cm. high.
(Christie's) $334

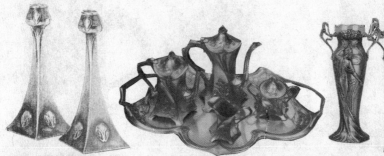

A pair of W.M.F. pewter candlesticks, the tulip-shaped sconces raised on tall squared columns flaring to the bases, 22cm. high.
(Phillips) $775

A W.M.F. pewter tea service, of waisted hexagonal form cast in relief with whiplash foliage and sprays of berried foliage.
(Christie's) $2,531

A pair of W.M.F. silvered pewter twin-handled vases, cast in relief each side with an Art Nouveau maiden, 36.5cm. high.
(Christie's) $2,508

A rare pewter tankard, touchmark of Samuel Hamlin, Providence, Rhode Island, first quarter 19th century, 6in. high.
(Sotheby's) $2,300

A Liberty & Co. hammered pewter rose bowl, the design attributed to Oliver Baker, cast and applied decoration, set with five green glass studs, 15.8cm. high.
(Christie's) $730

A late 18th century japanned metal coffee pot, the stepped domed cover with urn finial, the urn shaped body with gilt decoration.
(Phillips) $3,828

PEWTER

A Liberty & Co. 'Tudric' pewter easel timepiece of irregular circular outline having a raised decoration of leaves and berries, 12cm. diameter.
(Phillips) $550

Pair of Chinese Export polychrome pewter figural pricket candlesticks, early 19th century, each a kneeling gentleman, 12½in. high.
(Skinner Inc.) $7,150

A mid-18th century French pewter lavabo cistern with flat back, serpentine front and twin cherub cast handles, 10¼in. high.
(David Lay) $300

A Loetz pewter mounted vase, the yellow glass decorated with iridescent purple wavy lines and pink ovals, with two-handled pewter mounts, 17cm. high.
(Christie's) $1,818

A W.M.F. electroplated pewter ewer and basin, with repoussé decoration of two profiles of young maidens and stylized flowers, the basin with everted rim, 45cm. high.
(Christie's) $1,340

An American pewter flat-top tankard, Henry Will, New York, circa 1775, the body with shaped handle with bud terminal, on a stepped molded foot, height 7in.
(Sotheby's) $3,450

Pewter lighthouse coffee pot, attributed to the Trasks, Beverly, Massachusetts, second quarter 19th century, 12½in. high.
(Skinner) $517

A pair of W.M.F. pewter candlesticks, the openwork rectangular columns flaring to the base, 15cm. high.
(Phillips) $260

A French Art Deco white metal vase, the body stamped in relief with dense geometric patterns, French poinçon, 5½in. high.
(Christie's S. Ken) $240

A spouted pewter ale jug with domed top and shell thumbpiece, with reeded baluster body, early 19th century, 10in. high.
(Christie's) $748

A pair of Art Deco white metal twin branch candlesticks, each on stepped circular base surmounted by asymmetric curved stems, 6in. high.
(Christie's) $443

A German pewter Guild flagon of conical form, with scroll thumbpiece, the cover with an heraldic lion supporting a shield with owner's initials, 25½in. high, Weismar, circa 1670.
(Christie's S. Ken)
    $5,320

A 'Tudric' twin-handled cylindrical pewter vase, cast in relief with sprays of honesty and bearing the inscription *For Old Times Sake*, 7¾in. high.
(Christie's) $325

Two Liberty & Co. pewter vases designed by Archibald Knox, each bullet-shaped form chased with stylized floral decoration, on tripod bases, 18.8cm. high.
(Christie's) $770

A Charles I pewter flagon with straight sided body incised with lines, and engraved *Kingstone* 1633, 13in. high.
(Lawrence Fine Art)
    $2,280

A Loetz vase with white-metal mount, designed by Koloman Moser, slender flared stem with swollen bowl and everted rim, 23cm. high.
(Christie's) $6,230

Pair of Chinese pewter deer, 17th/18th century, stylized standing animals with glass eyes and articulated tails, 11½in. high.
(Skinner Inc.) $1,500

A late 17th century pewter half gallon measure by Richard Dunne, of baluster form with fluted eared thumbpiece, 27.75cm. high overall.
(Spencer's) $1,853

An Edison red Gem phonograph, Model D, with K reproducer, maroon Fireside horn, crane and thirty-four wax amberols.
(Christie's) $1,547

A small Mikiphone Pocket Phonograph, pocket gramophone with original pick up.
(Auction Team Köln) $1,350

A German phonograph with Puck Type mechanism, cast iron base of Art Nouveau design and horn modeled as a lily flower.
(Christie's S. Ken) $920

An Edison Fireside phonograph, Model A, with K reproducer and No. 10 black Cygnet horn, and approximately forty cylinders, mainly two-minute.
(Christie's) $1,384

A rare mahogany cased Edison Gem phonograph, now with combination gearing and K reproducer, the mahogany case with *Edison Gem Phonograph* banner transfer.
(Christie's S. Ken) $1,936

An Edison disk phonograph, official laboratory model with Diamond reproducer, lateral cut adapter and William and Mary style case, 50¹/₂in. high.
(Christie's S. Ken) $876

An Edison Fireside phonograph, Model A No. 25426, the K reproducer, crane and 36 two-minute and four-minute wax cylinders in cartons.
(Christie's) $750

An Edison Gem phonograph, with patent combination gear attachment, Walshaw-type turnover stylus in C reproducer and black 18-inch octagonal horn with crane, circa 1908.
(Christie's) $7,300

An Edison Triumph phonograph, Model A No. 45259, in 'New Style' green oak case, with 14in. witch's hat horn.
(Christie's) $825

Rare Pathe Le Gaulois French phonograph with decorative red varnish and red aluminium horn, only produced for a short time up to 1903.
(Auction Team Köln)

$1,732

A hand-turned Tinfoil phonograph with brass mandrel on steel threaded arbor with hand wheels at each end, with brass bearings on turned supports with screw release, 15in. wide. (Christie's S. Ken)

$6,545

Edison Home Phonograph Model A, the first Edison cylinder player with decorative banner emblem, with 12 cylinders, 1898.
(Auction Team Köln)

$1,576

German C G Phonograph cylinder player with finely decorated cast socle and horn in the form of a convolvulus head with French 4 minute adapter and 2 each 2 min and 4 min cylinders, only one other example known, 1903.
(Auction Team Köln)

$1,732

A large cabinet phonograph incorporating a Model A Edison Triumph mechanism 45035 with two-speed pulley and Diamond B reproducer, 49in. high.
(Christie's S. Ken)

$3,887

A Baillard's Echophone phonograph with model C reproducer shaped brass horn and transfer printed beech case, 13^1/$_2$in. wide.
(Andrew Hartley Fine Arts)

$600

An Edison GEM phonograph with original horn serial no. 3146330.
(Bonham's)

$361

An Edison Spring Motor phonograph, now with Bettini type 'C' reproducer and recorder, japanned 'funnel' horn with fixed elbow, and light oak case with lid.
(Christie's)

$3,871

Edison Standard Phonograph with large swan neck horn on gallows, oak case, circa 1905.
(Auction Team Köln)

$2,756

A Louis XIV carved and gilded frame, the anthemia corners and flowerspray centers flanked by opposed C-scrolls, 18½ x 21¾in.
(Christie's) $3,579

An Italian eighteenth century carved and gilded leaf frame, the border with cherubs and pierced scrolling acanthus leaves, 50¼ x 43in.
(Christie's) $8,854

An Italian seventeenth century carved and gilded frame, with ribbon-and-stick outer edge, 38¼ x 32⅞in.
(Christie's) $3,768

A Spanish eighteenth century carved, gilded and painted frame, with punched scrolling foliage and flowers running to similar corner panels, 29⅞ x 23⅞in.
(Christie's) $7,912

An Italian seventeenth century carved, gilded and painted cassetta frame, with imbricated leaf outer edge, the central plate with cauliculi centers, 15¾ x 14¼in.
(Christie's) $2,826

A Spanish eighteenth century carved, gilded and painted frame, with marbled central plate, foliate inner edge and bar-and-quadruple-bead sight edge, 30⅝ x 26½in.
(Christie's) $2,261

A Louis XVI carved and gilded frame, with gadrooned raised outer edge and cartouche cresting flanked by foliage and flowers, 24¼ x 18⅝in.
(Christie's) $3,960

A Lombard early sixteenth century carved and gilded tabernacle frame, the entablature supported by pilasters flanked by volutes, overall size 18½ x 14¾in.
(Christie's) $7,524

An Italian seventeenth century carved and gilded frame, with scrolling acanthus outer edge and raking gadrooned knull raised inner edge, 20½ x 34in.
(Christie's) $7,920

An Italian early seventeenth century carved, gilded and marbled frame, the centers and corners with panels of scrolling acanthus leaves, 53¼ x 42½in. (Christie's S. Ken)

$13,552

A Spanish seventeenth century carved and gilded frame, with acanthus and c-scroll corners and centers in high relief, 36 x 31in. (Christie's S. Ken)

$16,456

A Dutch seventeenth century tortoiseshell frame, 13½ x 17¼in. (Christie's S. Ken)

$9,293

A Spanish seventeenth century carved, gilded and painted frame, with scrolling acanthus outer edge, 45⅛ x 39in. (Christie's S. Ken)

$3,160

A Dutch nineteenth century carved ebonized frame, decorated with ivory inlay figures and cherubs' heads, tortoiseshell geometric panels and mother-of-pearl dots, 30½ x 27in. (Christie's S. Ken)

$4,213

A South German seventeenth century carved, gilded and ebonized frame, with various ripple and wave moldings, 25⅜ x 23¼in. (Christie's S. Ken)

$1,510

An Italian late sixteenth century carved, gilded and painted cassetta frame, with raised outer edge, 41¼ x 33in. (Christie's S. Ken)

$15,799

Italian baroque giltwood picture frame, circa 1700, carved with acanthus scrolls and putti, the inner frame carved with laurel leaf clusters, 78½in. high. (Skinner Inc.)

$6,000

A Flemish nineteenth century carved ebonized frame, with various color marble inlays under glass, 27¼ x 24¾in. (Christie's S. Ken)

$1,881

Gnome cheroot holder, with sun and trees, amber stem, fitted case, 4¼ in. long.
(Skinner Inc.) **$150**

Female jockey cheroot holder, ebonized accents, amber stem, fitted case.
(Skinner Inc.) **$225**

A meerschaum pipe, the bowl modeled as an open flowerhead and carved with a running deer, 2¾ in. high.
(Christie's S. Ken) **$321**

Cheroot holder of a fairy, amber stem, adaptor missing, fitted case, 5in. long.
(Skinner Inc.) **$375**

Pipe of a North African man, wearing a fez, amber ferule and stem, fitted case, 6½ in. long.
(Skinner Inc.) **$250**

Pipe of soldiers drinking, silver fittings, no stem or case, 4½ in. long.
(Skinner Inc.) **$550**

Wolf's head pipe, metal ferule, amber stem, fitted case, 7in. long.
(Skinner Inc.) **$200**

Romeo and Juliet pipe, inscribed silver ferule, amber stem, fitted case, 9½ in. long.
(Skinner Inc.) **$1,100**

Pipe of a bearded and hooded man, silver ferule hallmarked Birmingham, amber stem, no case, 7½ in. long.
(Skinner Inc.) **$400**

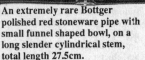

Cavalier cheroot holder, held by the neck, amber stone, fitted case, 5½ in. long.
(Skinner Inc.) **$375**

An extremely rare Bottger polished red stoneware pipe with small funnel shaped bowl, on a long slender cylindrical stem, total length 27.5cm.
(Phillips) **$19,920**

Set of three "Naughty" cheroot holders of a young woman, torso and pair of legs, amber stem, fitted case, 1½–3½ in. long.
(Skinner Inc.) **$650**

Cheroot holder of a gnome stroking his beard, amber stem, fitted case, 5in. long. (Skinner Inc.) $150

Woman's leg cheroot holder, silver ferule, amber stem, no case, 4½in. long. (Skinner Inc.) $150

Gondolier cheroot holder, amber stem, missing adaptor, fitted case, 4½in. long. (Skinner Inc.) $125

Cupid with frog cheroot holder, silver ferule, amber stem, fitted case, 6in. long. (Skinner Inc.) $150

Cheroot holder of a pair of running horses, amber stems, fitted cases, 7in. long. (Skinner Inc.) $225

A massive meerschaum pipe bowl, carved with figures and hounds hunting bears, 7½in. long. (Christie's S. Ken) $381

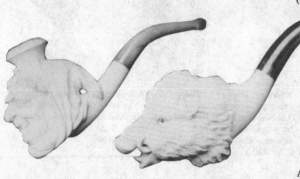

Monk's head cheroot holder, amber stem, fitted case, 6¾in. long. (Skinner Inc.) $950

Boar's head pipe, amber stem, fitted case, 9in. long. (Skinner Inc.) $1,100

A hexagonal pipe-head painted with figures in regional Eastern costumes above molded gilt ribs and green foliage, circa 1840, 9cm. long. (Christie's) $338

Cheroot holder of champagne drinkers, amber stem, fitted case, 5½in. long. (Skinner Inc.) $325

Arab hunter cheroot holder, silver ferule, amber stem, fitted case, 6in. long. (Skinner Inc.) $500

A meerschaum pipe, the bowl carved with the figures of a fox and a bird, fitted with an amber stem, 3¾in. high. (Christie's S. Ken) $261

A pair of South German 18th century baroque sculptures, lacking arms, on wooden plinths, total height 191cm. (Arnold) $5,669

A Richard Garbe plaster figure of a naked kneeling maiden with streaming hair and flowing drapery, 102cm. high. (Christie's) $1,500

A pair of English painted plaster figures, London, circa 1900, each boy with bare feet, one wearing a fez, 1ft. 9½in. high. (Sotheby's) $1,748

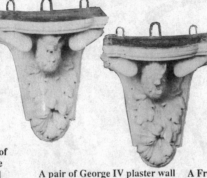

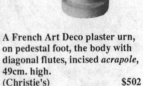

A patinated plaster bust of William Shakespeare, the playwright's head turned slightly to sinister, his cloak draped about his shoulders, on integrally cast circular socle, 27¾in. high. (Christie's) $732

A pair of George IV plaster wall brackets in the manner of Thomas Hopper, each supported by winged chimera with acanthus-cast tails, 17in. high. (Christie's) $1,903

A French Art Deco plaster urn, on pedestal foot, the body with diagonal flutes, incised *acrapole*, 49cm. high. (Christie's) $502

Two Continental painted plaster boys, possibly Austrian, circa 1900, one smiling holding a basket, the other playing a banjo, 2ft. 2in. high. (Sotheby's) $3,845

A composition and plaster overlaid on linen male torso, 51in. high, on a block plinth. (Christie's) $2,250

A pair of 19th century French terracotta colored plaster busts of Bacchantes, with indistinct signature on one (marbled wood socles), 16cm. high. (Christie's) $975

A plaster bust of George II, his hair dressed with laurels. (Christie's) $750

Pair of patinated plaster busts, after Jean-Antoine Houdon, depicting a young boy and girl, 16in. high. (Robt. W. Skinner Inc.) $525

A plaster bust by Phoebe Stabler, of the head of a maiden, on an oval section cut-sided base, 1942, 31.5cm. high. (Christie's) $788

A painted plaster-of-Paris bust of Thomas Edison, head and shoulders, signed *G. Tinworth 1888 and Doulton & Co., Lambeth*, the front inscribed *EDISON with Colonel Gouraud's compliments*, 22½in. high. (Christie's) $2,000

An English patinated plaster bas-relief of 'Cathal and the Woodfolk', cast from a model by Charles Sargeant Jagger, satyrs, centaurs and nymphs in Bacchic abandon, circa 1912–14, 19⁷/₈ x 31¹/₈in. (Christie's) $4,216

A late 19th century French plaster bust of 'L'Espiegle', signed on the shoulder *J.B. Carpeaux*, 51cm. high. (Christie's) $2,850

A late 19th century French original plaster half length portrait of Mme. La Baronne Cecile Demarcay, signed J. B. Carpeaux, 80cm. high. (Christie's) $29,500

A pair of polychrome-painted plaster figures of Chinamen in court dress with nodding heads, both holding ceremonial staffs, early 19th century, 15³/₄in. high. (Christie's) $8,910

One of a pair of oval cream-painted plaster and wood plaques, the moulded frames with foliate cresting, 34 x 27in. (Christie's) Two $2,800

An upright 19⁵/₈-inch Polyphon in walnut case with double comb, coin mechanism and plinth drawer, 36¹/₂in. high, with twenty-eight disks.
(Christie's) $3,388

A Kalliope table model with central spring lift on central spindle, with fifteen 23.5cm. disks, good loud tone.
(Auction Team Köln)
                          $1,889

A Nicol Frères walnut cased 'Penny in slot' polyphon, playing 20in. diameter disks, on baluster turned feet, 27in. wide.
(Spencer's) $3,465

A Regina Corona 27 inch self-changing disk musical box, with double-spring motor, coin mechanism, double combs on horizontal bedplate and magazine below containing twelve disks, 66in. high
(Christie's S. Ken)
                    $24,640

A Kalliope No. 42 musical box for 25cm. disks, with 42-tone comb with four disks, with original hand crank and dealer's label *A. Brandenburger, Berlin*, circa 1900.
(Auction Team Köln)
                          $578

A 15⁵/₈in. upright Polyphon with double comb, dual coin mechanism, in walnut case with glazed door, 35in. high, with one disk.
(Phillips) $6,014

An 11¹/₈-inch Polyphon disk musical box, German, circa 1910, with single comb and top-wind motor in walnut veneered case with print applied to lid interior, 13¹/₂in. wide.
(Sotheby's) $694

A 15⁵/₈in. table Polyphon disk musical box with single comb movement, in walnut case with inlaid panel and monochrome print to lid, with fifty disks.
(Phillips) $3,492

A 15¹/₂-inch Polyphon disk musical box, German, circa 1900, with twin comb movement in walnut case with carved and molded decorations, together with approximately twenty five disks.
(Sotheby's) $3,210

Regina disk music box, circa 1880, table model, 10 x 21 x 18in., mahogany serpentine case, banjo attachment, duplex comb, having thirty 15½in. disks.
(Du Mouchelles) $2,200

An 11¼in. Regina disk musical box, with twin combs, in carved walnut case of Gothic style, with seventeen disks.
(Phillips) $3,104

A Style 45 Polyphon 15⅝-inch disk musical box with Duplex comb in walnut case with inlaid lid, 22¾in. wide, with forty-four disks.
(Christie's) $4,066

A 19.58in. upright Polyphon with coin mechanism and drawer in typical walnut case with pediment, 51½in. high, with thirty-nine disks.
(Christie's S. Ken) $9,203

A Regina musical disk player, playing 15½in. discs, A. Wolff, New York, contained in a blond oak case, together with fifteen disks contained in a breech case.
(Spencer's) $1,402

A walnut cased penny-in-slot wall mounted Polyphon musical disk player, with cast iron money slot to both sides inscribed *Drop a Penny in the Slot*, with sixteen metal disks, 80cm. high.
(Spencer's) $3,822

A Symphonion 'Lyra' 11⅞-inch wall-hanging disk musical box with diametric combs on vertical bedplate, coin-slot mechanism and walnut-veneered case, 20in. high.
(Christie's) $1,850

A 15¾-inch Polyphon disk musical box, German, circa 1900, with double-comb movement, contained in a walnut veneered case, 58cm. wide, together with twenty-eight metal disks.
(Bonhams) $3,060

A 15½-inch Polyphon disk musical box, German, circa 1900, the periphery driven disk playing on two combs, with approximately eight metal disks, 36in. high.
(Sotheby's) $1,735

CHILDREN

Follower of Herman van der Mijn (1684–1741), a young girl, in white chemise and beige-lined blue cloak, oil on copper, oval, 2³/₄in. high.
(Christie's) $676

A portrait miniature of Helen L. and Arthur V. Cunningham by Mrs. Moses B. Russell, 1852, on a shaded orange and brown field, in gold frame, 1¹/₂in. high.
(Christie's) $3,850

Joseph Einsle (1794–died post 1850), a young boy, seated beside his wooden cart, full length on a grassy bank, signed and dated *1821*, 2¹/₂in. diameter.
(Christie's) $1,760

Vittorio Amidio, a fine portrait of Ducci Di Milorja, in navy blue cloak, light blue dress with frilled white border, oil on copper, indistinctly inscribed on reverse, 2⁵/₈in. high.
(Bonhams) $1,764

Miniature of three children and a cat, American School, 19th century, watercolor on ivory 4³/₄ x 3³/₄in.
(Skinner Inc.) $16,000

James Nixon, A.R.A. (1741–1812), Master William Henry West Betty, standing full length before a red curtain and pillar, in yellow jacket and pantaloons, oval, 8in. high.
(Christie's) $9,557

Bernard Lens (1682–1740), Anna Maria Whitmore, holding a fan, in gray dress sprigged in crimson and edged with lace, with gauze bodice and apron, signed with monogram and dated *1791*, oval, 3³/₄in. high.
(Christie's) $10,560

John Barry, a charming double portrait of Eliza and Sarah Bird, wearing white tunics, gilt-metal frame, with plaited hair reverse, 3¹/₄in. high.
(Bonhams) $3,724

Thomas Hargreaves (1774–1847), a girl, in low-cut white dress tied with blue ribbon, landscape background, signed in full on reverse and dated 1816/7, oval, 3¹/₂in. high.
(Christie's) $1,478

CHILDREN

Ozias Humphry, a young boy, wearing green coat and waistcoat, his right hand tucked into his waistcoat, oval, 1¹/₂in. high.
(Bonhams) $785

Abraham Daniel (died 1806), Masters Charles and Samuel Black, the younger boy held in his brother's arms, in brown jackets and white shirts with lace collars, oval, 4¹/₂in. high.
(Christie's) $5,280

Richard Gibson (1615–1690), Elizabeth Capell, Countess of Carnarvon, in low-cut blue dress with scalloped edge over white underslip, diamond and pearl clasps at shoulder and corsage, oval, 3¹/₄in. high.
(Christie's) $29,568

Richard Schwager (1822–1880), a young girl, seated on a cushion, in low-cut white dress edged in lace, red sash and bows at shoulders, a straw hat and child's doll beside her, signed and dated *1868*, oval, 3⁷/₈in. high.
(Christie's) $6,160

Charles Jenour, Henry Christopher Metcalfe (1822–1881), aged 8, wearing a blue tunic trimmed with black ribbon over white pantaloons, rectangular, about 9in. high.
(Bonhams) $1,256

Attributed to Cornelius Durham (fl. circa 1850), a little boy, in light blue coat and waistcoat, an open white shirt with large frilled collar, silver frame, oval, 2⁷/₈in. high.
(Christie's) $299

J. R. Galland, a delightful portrait of a young boy holding a stick and pug dog kneeling in a landscape setting, signed on the obverse and dated *1804*, 4³/₄in. high.
(Bonhams) $2,940

English School, circa 1805, Elizabeth and Marianne Austen as children, three-quarter length, in white dresses, the latter wearing a sprigged bonnet and holding a basket of cherries, oval, 3¹/₄in. high.
(Christie's) $1,848

Richard Crosse (1742–1810), a young man, possibly Edward Crosse, in profile, leaning against a table beside a globe, reading a book, in purple coat and white shirt, oval, 2³/₄in. high. (Christie's) $1,496

FEMALE

William Egley, a lady, wearing a lilac colored dress and long gold chain, a tortoiseshell comb in her brown hair, 2⁵/₈in. high. (Bonhams) $882

French School, circa 1805, a lady, wearing décolleté green dress with lace inset and necklace with gold bordered black jewel, oval, 2¹/₂in. high. (Bonhams) $628

Andrew Plimer, a fine portrait of a lady, in white dress, scarf and bandeau, sky background, oval, 3¹/₈in. high. (Bonhams) $1,495

Edward Nash (1778–1821), a portrait miniature of a lady, nearly full face in white dress and cap (unfinished), in gilt-metal frame with guilloche border, oval, 2³/₄in. high. (Christie's) $983

Circle of Gerard Terborch, circa 1650, a fine portrait miniature of a lady, facing right in black dress with double lawn collar, pearl necklace, oil on copper, in silver frame, oval, 2¹/₂in. high. (Christie's) $5,007

John Smart (1742–1811), a lady, facing right, in white dress with ruffled collar, short dark hair, signed with initials and dated *1800*, gold frame with glass reverse, oval, 3in. high. (Christie's) $19,360

John Hoskins (fl. circa 1645), Lady Mary Glamham, in low-cut black dress trimmed with white lace and brooch at corsage, wearing pearl necklace and earrings, signed with initials and dated 1648, oval, 2⁷/₈in. high. (Christie's) $35,838

Louis-Marie Sicardi (1746–1825), a lady, in décolleté light blue dress gathered with gold brooch at her corsage, her hair dressed with blue ribbons, signed and dated 1797, circular, 2⁷/₈in. diameter. (Christie's) $7,566

Peter Oliver (circa 1594–1647), the Countess of Pembroke, in orange and black striped dress with jeweled border, white fichu and high ruff, wearing earrings and a jewel in her hair, oval, 2¹/₈in. high. (Christie's) $37,829

FEMALE

Christian Friedrich Zincke, a young lady, wearing a pink cloak, and white dress trimmed with matching pink ribbon at her corsage, enamel, 1⁷/₈in. high. (Bonhams) **$2,352**

Attributed to Alexander Gallaway, a lady, half length, facing left, in mourning dress, signed with initials *A.R.G.* and dated *1800*, oval, 2¹/₂in. high. (Bonhams) **$502**

Fanny Charrin (fl. circa 1820), a lady, in low-cut black dress with white underslip, twisted gold colored ropes round her waist, signed in full on obverse, oval, 3in. high. (Christie's) **$796**

Christian Friedrich Zincke (circa 1683–1767), a lady, in décolleté blue dress with a bouquet of pink and white flowers at her corsage, enamel, gilt-metal mount, oval, 2in. high. (Christie's) **$2,957**

Moritz Michael Daffinger (1790–1849), Princess Clementine Melterwich, full face, in white dress secured by a triple strand of pearls, signed on the obverse, oval, 3in. high. (Christie's) **$7,040**

Christian Friedrich Zinche (circa 1683–1767), a lady, in décolleté blue dress with white underslip, her hair falling over her right shoulder, enamel, gold frame, oval, 2in. high. (Christie's) **$1,692**

Sampson Towgood Roch (1759–1847), a lady, facing left, in low-cut pale blue dress with lace neckline adorned with a single strand of pearls, her brown hair up-swept and curls falling to her shoulders, signed and dated *1788*, oval, 2⁵/₈in. high. (Christie's) **$968**

Nicholas Hilliard (1547–1619), a fine portrait miniature of a lady, perhaps Elizabeth of Bohemia, facing left in black dress elaborately slashed in pink, with gold inscription *Ano Dm. 1--0*, on vellum, oval, 2¹/₈in. high. (Christie's) **$62,200**

Nicholas Hilliard (1547–1619), a very fine portrait miniature of a noblewoman, facing left in black dress slashed in white, a thistle and a fly alighting upon a daffodil pinned to the high lace ruff, on vellum, turned ivory frame, oval, 2in. high. (Christie's) **$130,620**

MALE

Walter Stephens Lethbridge, a gentleman, wearing blue coat, yellow waistcoat and white tied cravat, oval, 2¹/₂in. high. (Bonhams) $478

William Thicke, a gentleman, wearing a mole colored coat, gold frame, the reverse with plaited hair, oval, 2³/₄in. high. (Bonhams) $1,884

George Engleheart, an officer, wearing scarlet uniform with buff colored facings and silver epaulettes, oval, 2in. high. (Bonhams) $4,082

Christian Richter (1678–1732), a gentleman, in amber-colored cloak with blue lining and white cravat, full-bottomed wig, on vellum backed with card, possibly by James Seamer, oval, 3in. high. (Christie's) $11,616

John Smart (1742–1811), an officer, facing right, in the uniform of the 2nd Battalion of the Madras Presidency Foot Artillery, white waistcoat and frilled cravat, signed with initials and dated 1791, oval, 2¹/₂in. high. (Christie's) $17,600

Samuel Cooper (1609–1672), a young gentleman, in black doublet, slashed sleeves to reveal white, large lawn collar trimmed with lace, his long curly hair falling over his shoulders, oval, 3¹/₈in. high. (Christie's) $35,838

Flemish School, circa 1600/05, a fine portrait of Emperor Matthias (1557–1619), wearing a gold embroidered black doublet, and lace ruff, on vellum, oval, 2¹/₈in. high. (Bonhams) $53,380

English School, 18th century, Oliver Cromwell, on card, turned gilt-wood frame, the reverse with the hand inscription *This belongs to my son Tom*, 3in. high. (Bonhams) $1,176

Thomas Forster (fl. circa 1700), Sir Thomas Pope Blount, in flowing robes and cravat, full-bottomed wig, plumbago, signed and dated 1700, oval, 4¹/₄in. high. (Christie's) $2,534

MALE

English School, circa 1745, Prince James Francis Edward Stuart, facing left in armor and a sash of the Order of the Garter, oval, 1³/₈in. high. (Christie's) $2,541

Joseph Daniel, a fine portrait of a gentleman, wearing blue coat, gilt-metal mount, the reverse with plaited hair, oval, 2⁷/₈in. high. (Bonhams) $1,884

A portrait miniature of Mr. Thomas Chase by Robert Field, 1804, with brown wavy hair, black coat, on a shaded brown field, 3in. long. (Christie's) $5,500

Peter Paillou (died after 1820), a gentleman, facing left, in brown coat, white shirt and lace cravat, signed and dated 1790 on the obverse, oval, 2¹/₄in. high. (Christie's) $15,840

Flemish School, circa 1550, a rare early portrait miniature of a gentleman, facing left in black doublet with buttons down the front, narrow ruff and flat black hat, on vellum, gold frame with spiral cresting, 1¹/₂in. diameter. (Christie's) $37,553

Attributed to Henry Bone, a gentleman, wearing a lilac-colored coat, yellow waistcoat and lace cravat, oval, 2¹/₄in. high. (Bonhams) $471

James Warren Childe, an officer of the Lancers Regiment, wearing blue uniform with gold epaulettes and gold collar, signed on the obverse, oval, 4³/₄in. high. (Bonhams) $1,334

Nicholas Hilliard (1547–1619), a superb miniature of a man clasping a hand from a cloud, possibly Lord Thomas Howard, on vellum, gilt-metal frame, oval, 2³/₈in. high. (Christie's) $266,250

Christian Friedrich Zincke (circa 1683–1767), Lord William Beauclerk, in white-lined crimson coat, white shirt and black stock, enamel, gold frame, oval, 1⁵/₈in. high. (Christie's) $2,389

A very fine pieced calico and chintz Star of Bethlehem quilt, probably Pennsylvania, mid-19th century, approximately 116 x 114in. (Sotheby's)   **$7,130**

A fine and rare pieced, appliqued and reverse applique cotton and velvet flower basket quilt, probably Pennsylvania, mid-19th century, approximately 104 x 112in. (Sotheby's)   **$6,613**

A fine pieced, applique and reverse applique cotton quilt, probably Baltimore, mid 19th century, composed of brilliantly colored red, yellow, green and blue cotton patches, approximately 72 x 72in. (Sotheby's)   **$4,400**

A pieced cotton quilted coverlet, American, circa 1880, worked in the Thousand Triangles pattern with blue, red, brown, yellow and green calicos decorated with chevron-stitching, with blue calico binding, 73 x 77in. (Christie's)   **$990**

A very unusual pieced cotton and broderie perse Star of Bethlehem quilt, Southern, probably Alabama, early 19th century, arranged in the Star of Bethlehem pattern, 112 x 107in. (Sotheby's)   **$7,150**

A pieced cotton quilted coverlet, American, circa 1880, worked in the Baby Blocks pattern in brown, red, and blue calico, with a blue binding, 76 x 96in. (Christie's)   **$462**

A pieced cotton quilted coverlet, American, circa 1880, worked in green, red and gold diamond-quilted cotton in the Joseph's Coat pattern, with a red binding, 72 x 74in.
(Christie's) $880

A pieced cotton presentation album quilt, Massachusetts, dated 1859, worked in brown, red and green calico blocks with ink inscriptions of children's names and ages, 82 x 84in.
(Christie's) $990

A pieced cotton quilted coverlet, Pennsylvania, circa 1880, worked in the Log Cabin Barn Raising pattern with white, red, green, blue, brown, and yellow calicos, surrounded by a blue calico border, 80 x 84in.
(Christie's) $550

An Amish pieced cotton and wool quilted and embroidered coverlet, Indiana, circa 1930, worked in brown, blue, gray, pink, black, petal, green, and tan wool and cotton with numerous blocks of pieced stripes, 85 x 86in.
(Christie's) $1,540

An unusual pieced and appliqued American flag quilt, probably Virginia, circa 1920, composed of red, white and blue stars and stripes, approximately 84 x 72in.
(Sotheby's) $4,400

A pieced and appliqued cotton quilted coverlet, American, signed *Louise Bryan*, dated *1933*, worked in blue, green, orange and purple calico, 86 x 68in.
(Christie's) $495

A Talisman 308V radio with U-21 valve facing and designer bakelite casing by Tesla, circa 1948.
(Auction Team Köln)
$263

A Philips 'Local Station Receiver' Model 930A 3-valve receiver in 'Arbolite' cabinet, 18in. high, 1931.
(Christie's)
$443

1930's period bakelite cased rocking ship clock, (electrically operated) in the form of a radio case.
(G.A. Key)
$397

A Telefunken 127 WLK single screen receiver with short wave, some parts replaced, 1933.
(Auction Team Köln)
$101

A Crosley Model 124 eight-tube straight receiver in wooden cathedral case, circa 1932.
(Auction Team Köln)
$176

A Telefunken superhet receiver with wooden housing, export model, lacks backplate, circa 1935.
(Auction Team Köln)
$85

A Nora VE 301 W receiver with bakelite housing and original cloth grille, circa 1933.
(Auction Team Köln)
$262

A Telefunken 31W radio with horn speaker, alternating current receiver, lacks key, 1929–30.
(Auction Team Köln)
$849

A Bush Model AC3 mains receiver with molded wood fret in 'Cathedral' style walnut-veneered cabinet, 18in. high, circa 1932.
(Christie's)
$876

A Fada Model 252 receiver in bright yellow bakelite case with bright red bakelite tuning scale surround and turning knobs, 10½in. long, 1946.
(Christie's) $454

A Philco 'People's Set' Model A527 5-valve mains receiver in brown bakelite case, 15½in. high, circa 1937.
(Christie's) $623

A 3-valve receiver with Haynes radio tuning dial in oak case with removeable lid and copper-lined glass fronted doors, 16¼in. wide.
(Christie's) $146

A Kleinempfanger 'People's Set' receiver in upright black bakelite case, 15¼in. high, circa 1933.
(Christie's) $301

A Marconiphone Multivalve Type RB7 receiver in smoker's cabinet style mahogany case with BBC transfer, 20½in. high, circa 1923.
(Christie's) $6,500

A Philco Model 38–60 3-valve upright receiver in walnut veneered plywood cabinet, 17in. high.
(Christie's) $323

An English transparent plastic radio for Zarach 1971, of cube form, 15cm. high.
(Bonhams) $220

A Gecophone 'Victor 3' three-valve receiver in crinkle finish metal case with hinged lid, and an Orphean horn speaker.
(Christie's S. Ken) $348

An early mains Kolsterbrandes Pup radio, with free oscillator loudspeaker, circa 1931.
(Auction Team Köln) $123

An Isaria Type RL in original condition, lacking valves, with RTV stamp for 1924.
(Auction Team Köln)
$3,396

A detector receiver with distributor box and headset, original Daki crystal, circa 1925.
(Auction Team Köln)
$309

A Siemens Riesenskala single screen straight receiver with special coil-variable capacitor arrangement, lacking tuning band, circa 1931.
(Auction Team Köln)
$501

A radiogram television incorporating Baird Televisor with disk and valve in upper two tiers, the base containing speaker, electric turntable and pick-up in drawer, 54in. high.
(Christie's) $3,500

A Schaub Supraphon 52 music center with ultra short wave function, record player, magnetic tape recorder and two tapes, in working order, 1951.
(Auction Team Köln)
$695

An Ideal Blaupunkt Type 2 GD music cabinet with built in Schaub radio, direct current receiver and converter, in mainly original condition, circa 1933.
(Auction Team Köln)
$386

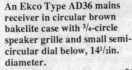

A Gecophone Type BC 2001 3-valve receiver in walnut case with door enclosing control panel and battery compartment below.
(Christie's S. Ken) $920

An Ekco Type AD36 mains receiver in circular brown bakelite case with $3/4$-circle speaker grille and small semi-circular dial below, $14^{1}/_{2}$in. diameter.
(Christie's) $682

A Howe Radio Receiver detector/receiver, circa 1925, rare as patent only applied for and never granted.
(Auction Team Köln)
$232

A Fada 'Streamliner' Model 115 receiver in bright yellow bakelite case with bright red bakelite handle, 10¹/₂in. long, 1941.
(Christie's) $454

A lacquered iron table speaker, signed *Sterling*, London 1920s, 29cm. high.
(Auktionsverket) $265

A Sparton Model 517 receiver in Art-Deco style wooden cabinet with blue mirror-glass panels, 15in. long, 1936.
(Christie's) $1,108

An Awa Radiolette 'Fisk' Model 32 receiver in upright brown bakelite case of Art Deco design, circa 1930.
(Christie's) $454

An S.O.E. agent's suitcase wireless receiver/transmitter (Transceiver no. 3 Mark II, known also as B2) with earphones and tap key, 16¹/₂ x 12¹/₂in.
(Christie's) $2,167

A Gecophone two-valve receiver, type BC 2001, in mahogany 'smokers cabinet' case with instruction card, 16¹/₂in. high, circa 1923
(Christie's) $1,271

An Ekco Type AD75 AC mains receiver in circular brown bakelite case with ³/₄-circle speaker and small semi-circular dial below, 14¹/₂in. diameter.
(Christie's) $488

A G.E.C. mottled brown bakelite electric radio, of rectangular form with white rectangular dial flanked by louvre speakers, 7¹/₂in. high.
(Christie's) $275

A Philips 'Superinductance' Model 830A 4-valve receiver with illuminated dial, in 'Arbolite' case with simulated walnut finish, 19¹/₄in. high, 1932.
(Christie's) $516

A Masudaya battery-operated lithographed tinplate 'Target Robot', circa 1960, 15in. high. (Christie's) **$1,045**

An unusual silver Horikawa Attacking Martian robot, in original box. (Christie's S. Ken) **$689**

A Yonezawa for Cragstan battery-operated tinplate 'Mr Robot', same body pressing as 'Talking Robot', 1960's. (Christie's S. Ken) **$568**

A Nomura painted tinplate 'Battery Operated Mechanised Robot' ("Robbie the Robot"), with black body, red arms and feet, circa 1956, 13in. high. (Christie's S. Ken) **$2,729**

A Yonezawa friction drive tinplate 'Talking Robot' with battery operated speech mechanism, retailed by Cragstan, in original box, circa 1960's (Christie's S. Ken) **$823**

A Yoshia Mighty Robot, Japanese, 1960's, with plastic head with rotating colored cogs, lithographed breast plate, 31cm. (Sotheby's) **$1,225**

A Horikawa battery operated tinplate 'Fighting Robot', with transparent plastic chest cover, 1960's. (Christie's S. Ken) **$400**

A Yonezawa 'Space Explorer' No. 802, finished in brown, transforming from a TV set into a battery operated walking robot, in original box, early 1960's. (Christie's S. Ken) **$975**

Robot ST 1, tinplate German robot by Streng & Co., silver painted, circa 1955. (Auction Team Köln) **$445**

ROBOTS

A Nomura battery-operated lithographed tinplate Mobile Space TV unit and trailer, with mystery action, in original box, 11in. long.
(Christie's) **$1,742**

A Kosuge battery-operated (by remote control) High Wheel Robot, finished in metallic blue, 10½in. long, 1960's.
(Christie's) **$255**

A Yonezawa 'Cragstan's talking robot', Japanese, early 1960's, finished in red with silver face and arms, in maker's box, 10¾in. high.
(Sotheby's) **$347**

A Yoshiya battery-operated painted tinplate 'Chief Robot Man', finished in metallic blue, in original box, 1960's, 12in. high.
(Christie's) **$927**

A Nomura 'Robby' mechanized robot, Japanese, 1950's, the black body with perspex dome to head covering mechanism, in original box, 12½in. high.
(Sotheby's) **$1,735**

A Masudaya battery-operated lithographed tinplate Target robot, red target on chest causing evasive action, 1950's, 15in. high.
(Christie's) **$1,549**

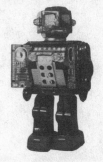

An Asakusa Thunder robot, Japanese, 1960's, finished in brown, with plastic sleeves and hands, 11¼in. high.
(Sotheby's) **$1,215**

A rare Nomura tinplate battery operated 'Robby Space Patrol', with mystery action, clear plastic dome and light dishes, 1950's, 12½in. long.
(Christie's) **$2,323**

Horikawa Toys, 'Attacking Martian', a printed and painted tinplate robot, battery operated with moveable legs, boxed, circa 1960, 11¼in. high.
(Bonhams) **$434**

Malayer rug, West Persia, late 19th century, in shades of blue, rose, gold and light teal, 6ft. 8in. x 4ft. 6in.
(Skinner Inc.) $1,600

An antique Bergama rug, West Anatolia, the copper red field with a characteristic central rectangular panel, 6ft. 1in. x 4ft. 11in.
(Phillips) $5,950

Yomud Ensi rug, West Turkestan, late 19th/early 20th century, the chestnut brown field quartered into rectangles, 5ft. 11in. x 4ft.
(Skinner Inc.) $475

Karabagh prayer rug, South Caucasus, late 19th century, the diamond lattice of red, sky blue, gold and green flowering plants covers the midnight blue field, 4ft. 5in. x 2ft. 8in.
(Skinner Inc.) $1,500

Karapinar rug, Central Anatolia, late 19th/early 20th century, the large ivory and green hexagonal medallion nearly covers the light red-brown field, 5ft. 4in. x 3ft. 10in.
(Skinner Inc.) $1,300

Kazak rug, Southwest Caucasus, late 19th century, the red field contains the Lori Pambak design of a large elongated octagonal ivory medallion, 10ft. 2in. x 5ft. 10in.
(Skinner Inc.) $7,000

Shirvan rug, East Caucasus, late 19th/early 20th century, the abrashed brick red field lavishly decorated with human figures and animals, 5ft. 6in. x 3ft. 9in.
(Skinner Inc.) $4,250

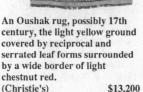

An Oushak rug, possibly 17th century, the light yellow ground covered by reciprocal and serrated leaf forms surrounded by a wide border of light chestnut red.
(Christie's) $13,200

Karagashli rug, East Caucasus, late 19th century, two stepped diamond medallions flanked by two bright red flowerheads decorate the navy blue field, 6ft. 6in. x 3ft. 10in.
(Skinner Inc.) $2,700

Konya area prayer rug, Central Anatolia, mid 19th century, (small areas of restoration), 5ft. 2in. x 3ft. 8in. (Skinner Inc.) $14,000

Yomud Salatshak, West Turkestan, early 20th century, columns of midnight blue, red, apricot and ivory geometric figures, 4ft. 6in. x 3ft. 10in. (Skinner Inc.) $800

Avar rug, Northeast Caucasus, late 19th century, the bold red "many-necked house" design decorates the medium blue field, 4ft. 10in. x 3ft. (Skinner Inc.) $450

Kazak rug, Southwest Caucasus, late 19th century, the central ivory octagonal medallion flanked by two navy blue stepped medallions, 8ft. x 6ft. 5in. (Skinner Inc.) $2,750

Fachralo Kazak rug, Southwest Caucasus, late 19th century, the red field with two blue and one green joined horizontal medallions, 4ft. x 3ft. 4in. (Skinner Inc.) $3,250

Konagend rug, Northwest Caucasus, early 20th century, the sky blue and rose central medallion flanked by four abrashed red octagons, 5ft. 6in. x 3ft. 9in. (Skinner Inc.) $1,800

Shirvan rug, East Caucasus, late 19th century, the abrashed mustard-gold field with octagonal lattice of palmettes, 5ft. 6in. x 3ft. 10in. (Skinner Inc.) $1,600

Shirvan rug, East Caucasus, late 19th century, the dark brown field with six columns of confronting animals, 5ft. x 4ft. 3in. (Skinner Inc.) $3,000

Shirvan rug, East Caucasus, late 19th century, the ivory field with overall Chi-Chi design in shades of dark red, blue, rose and beige, 5ft. 6in. x 3ft. 8in. (Skinner Inc.) $1,100

SAMPLERS

Needlework sampler, *Abigail E. Read*, New England, circa 1820, worked with silk threads in shades of blue, green, pink, yellow, coral, cream and black on linen ground, framed, 17³/₄ x 17¹/₂in.
(Skinner) $5,500

Needlework sampler, *Louisa Perkins at Miss Williams School, Boston, June 18th, 1817*, bands of alphabet and verse over inscription, 14 x 12¹/₂in.
(Skinner) $440

Needlework sampler, *Elizabeth A. Goshen's work*, Chester County, Pennsylvania, circa 1825, worked with silk threads in shades of blue, green, yellow, cream, peach on a natural linen, 23¹/₂ x 27¹/₂in.
(Skinner) $8,800

A fine needlework sampler: signed *Harriet Weiser*, probably Reading, Pennsylvania, dated *1830*, executed in a variety of blue, green, yellow, pink, and brown stitches, 26¹/₄ x 17³/₄in.
(Sotheby's) $11,000

A fine and rare needlework sampler, by Alice Mather, Norwich, Connecticut, 1774, 13³/₄ x 11¹/₂in. (Christie's New York) $49,500

A needlework silk-on-linen sampler by Desire E. Demmen, Scituate, Massachusetts, 1804, worked in polychrome silk threads on a linen ground, the upper register depicting an alphabetic sequence, 19¹/₄in. high, 15¹/₂in. wide.
(Christie's) $6,600

Needlework sampler, *Wrought by Charlotte Chapin in the 12th year of her age 1842*, Massachusetts, worked in silk threads, 18¹/₄ x 15¹/₄in.
(Skinner) $1,540

Needlework sampler, *Lydia Ashleys sampler, aged eleven years, worked September 1798*, Massachusetts, worked in silk threads in shades of pink, green, yellow and burnt umber, framed, 10 x 7in.
(Skinner) $1,045

Needlework sampler, *Margaret A. Cassady's work Washington Oct. 3, 1826*, vivid polychrome silk threads on linen ground, 17¹/₂in. x 16³/₄in.
(Skinner) $54,050

A sampler, by Christian Mackenzie, 1830, with a verse *Why should we start*, also with trailing floral patterns and spot motifs of trees and plants above a large house, 17 x 13in.
(Christie's) $1,456

Rare needlework sampler, worked by Sally Johnson Age 12, Newburyport, Massachusetts, 1799, one of a small and important group of samplers worked in Newburyport from 1799–1806, 19 x 27in.
(Skinner Inc.) $33,000

A fine and rare needlework sampler, Elizabeth Beale, probably Pennsylvania, dated *1832*, worked in a variety of pale pink, yellow, green and blue silk stitches, 21½ x 23½in.
(Sotheby's) $15,525

A fine needlework sampler: Mary Clothilda Dare, Chester County, Pennsylvania, dated *1837*, executed in a variety of pink, blue, yellow, green, white and red silk stitches, 25⅝ x 23½in.
(Sotheby's) $22,000

A long sampler worked in colored silks, with spot motifs, with borders of Tudor roses and sprays of flowers, 34 x 8½in.
(Christie's) $2,722

A fine needlework sampler, signed Hannah McCriller, Canterbury, New Hampshire, dated 1795, worked in a variety of green, blue, pink, white and black silk stitches, 17¾ x 17in.
(Sotheby's) $2,760

A needlework sampler, signed *Elisabeth Landis*, Pennsylvania, dated *1831*, worked in a variety of red, lavender, yellow and green, 15¾ x 15¾in.
(Sotheby's) $1,150

A good early Victorian child's needlework sampler worked with a verse, buildings, sportsmen, birds, butterflies and trees by Martha Bitterson, aged 9, and dated *1845*, 16½ x 17½in.
(Bearne's) $1,412

Needlework sampler, *Polly Wilde Sampler Wrought in Salem, June 1796* and further inscribed *Maffachufetts State Salem*, 13¾ x 12½in.
(Skinner) $8,800

SCALES

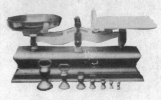

Plated cast-iron Enterprise Colonial ware shop scales, with four weights, circa 1920. (Auction Team Köln) $69

A set of counter-top scales signed on the porcelain slab *J. White & Sons Auchtermuchty Est 1715*, with brass central carrying handle and weights pan, 19½in. wide. (Christie's S. Ken) $318

Classic brass column scales by W. & T. Avery Ltd., Birmingham, on mahogany base, circa 1910, 49cm. high. (Auction Team Köln) $226

A set of early Victorian mahogany jockey scales with ivory plaque De Grave & Co., Makers, London, 39in. wide. (Christie's) $4,500

A lacquered brass precision balance, the beam stamped To Weigh/To Grain, No. 5962, with electrical attachments in a glazed mahogany case, 14¾in. wide. (Christie's) $300

A set of Victorian blond oak jockey scales, the seat with square paneled back, downward outward scroll open arms on a rectangular base, 3ft. 2in. wide. (Spencer's) $726

A late 18th century 'Ladder Scale', the 1oz. and 2oz. beams stamped De Grave & Co. London, 16⅛in. wide. (Christie's) $900

An unusual 56lb beam scale, the beam inscribed *De Grave, Short & Co Ltd Makers London Borough of Scarborough*, with two pans, raised on a stepped mahogany plinth, 56¼in. high overall. (Christie's) $648

A pair of W. & T. Avery snuff scales, to weigh 1lb., class B. No. A189 with brass pans, together with a set of 5 weights. $225

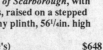

A three-color cameo scent flask, probably Thomas Webb and Sons, circa 1890, the light blue glass overlaid in white and lilac and carved with flowers and leaves, 2½in. high. (Sotheby's) $818

Pair of French porcelain scent decanters, decorated in the Imari style, each with an umbrella shaped stopper, 9in. overall. (G. A. Key) $489

Extremely fine French glass dressing table scent decanter and stopper, signed *E Galle Nancy*, 6½in. overall. (G. A. Key) $667

Abraham, Colomby, a late 18th century French gold, enamel and glass scent bottle containing a verge watch, the chased and engraved gold cap with blue, pink and white enamel decoration, 63 x 47mm. (Christie's) $5,422

'Voltigy', a Baccarat clear bottle for A. Gravier, modeled as a butterfly with outstretched wings, the body stained in pink and black, 3⅝in. (Bonhams) $31,500

A Chelsea gold-mounted scent-bottle and stopper modeled as a cat with brown fur-markings, seated erect with a mouse in its mouth, circa 1755, 6.5cm. high. (Christie's) $3,938

An attractive silver mounted clear glass scent bottle, of globular form with diamond and slice cut decoration, by Levy & Saloman, 12.5cm. high. (Spencer's) $318

'Hantise', a Baccarat black enameled pink opaque bottle for A. Gravier, of multi-faceted ovoid form, with gilt metal bullet-shaped stopper and circular foot, 4⅝in. (Bonhams) $5,950

'Le Jade', a Lalique pale green scent bottle, in the style of a Chinese snuff bottle, molded with an exotic bird amid tangled branches, 8.3cm. high. (Christie's) $2,922

A façon de Venise scent bottle of flattened pear shape and in clear glass trailed with bands of white festooning, 9.5cm.
(Phillips) $223

A Chelsea gold-mounted peach scent-bottle and stopper naturally modeled and colored, stamped gold mounts, circa 1755, 7cm. high.
(Christie's) $8,269

French porcelain set of three scent bottles and stoppers, decorated with floral swags, gilt brass holder, 6in. high.
(G. A. Key) $255

'Malice', a Baccarat enameled clear bottle for A. Gravier, of squared baluster form, the grooved edges enameled in blue, the front enameled in black, 4³/₈in.
(Bonhams) $3,150

A French gilt-metal mounted kingwood and crossbanded scent casket, by Tahan, Paris, the base with a quarter veneered hinged top and parquetry sides, late 19th century.
(Christie's) $553

'La Joie D'Aimer', a Baccarat enameled clear bottle for A. Gravier, of octagonal form, with swollen neck, enameled in black and orange with an abstract pattern, 5¹/₈in.
(Bonhams) $2,450

A cameo globular scent-flask with silver mount and hinged cover, the red ground overlaid in opaque-white and carved with a trailing prunus branch, probably Stevens & Williams, circa 1885.
(Christie's) $444

'Pluie D'Or', a Baccarat enamelled clear bottle for A. Gravier, of triangular section, enameled in black, orange, green and yellow with flower sprays, with triangular domed stopper, 5³/₄in.
(Bonhams) $7,350

A silver mounted glass perfume flask by the Goldsmiths and Silversmiths Co., 1918/9, the silver top incised with stylized garlands, 12.5cm. high.
(Finarte) $428

A cut and enameled scent bottle and stopper, the front with a panel set with a crown enameled in colors on gilt foil, 10.3cm. high.
(Phillips) $1,530

'Dans la Nuit', a Lalique display scent bottle and stopper, of spherical form molded in relief with stars, the reserve stained blue, 10in. high.
(Christie's) $1,363

A cristallo ceramic scent bottle with a head and shoulders profile portrait of a Roman with wavy hair, 8cm.
(Phillips) $609

'Emeraude', a scent bottle and stopper made for Coty, in original fitted box, 4in. high.
(Christie's S. Ken) $300

'Me Voici', a Baccarat enameled clear bottle for A. Gravier, of shoe form, with faceted stopper, the bottle enameled in green, blue, orange and yellow with Egyptianesque floral patterns, 4in. wide.
(Bonhams) $10,850

'Parfum A', a black enameled frosted bottle for Lucien Lelong, of square section, each side molded with black enameled swags, 4¹/₈in. high.
(Bonhams) $8,000

A ceramic scent bottle, Chelsea Pottery, designed as a kneeling young woman and a peacock, silver colored metal mount, 7cm.
(Lawrence) $262

A Dubarry scent bottle and stopper, of rectangular form molded in relief with sunburst motif, 4¹/₄in. high.
(Christie's) $40

A gold-mounted scent-bottle and stopper of 'Girl in a Swing' type modeled as a Chinese family with a Chinaman embracing a Chinese lady holding an infant, 9cm. high.
(Christie's) $5,513

The Original Lincoln shuttle sewing machine by Grimme, Natalis & Co., Brunswick, Germany, circa 1870.
(Auction Team Köln)

$915

An American Willcox and Gibbs chain stitch machine with unusual manual drive, circa 1872.
(Auction Team Köln) $117

An American Grover & Baker double chain stitch grip machine, on turned wooden stand, 1872.
(Auction Team Köln)

$2,470

A Cookson's lockstitch sewing machine with part-plated mechanism on cast iron base and wood cover.
(Christie's) $1,750

Clemens Müller chain stitch sewing machine without gripper on attractive 3 footed stand by E Pruchner, formerly E Boissier, Berlin, circa 1875.
(Auction Team Köln)
          $2,027

A rare hand-operated Wheeler & Wilson No. 1 sewing machine, No. 274943, in D-ended walnut case with angled crank, spare bobbins and a price list, $17\frac{1}{2}$in. wide, circa 1867.
(Christie's) $2,737

German Casige No. 205 collapsible child's sewing machine, circa 1953, very rare.
(Auction Team Köln)
          $232

A Whight & Mann Prima Donna sewing machine, with good gilt decorations and instructions.
(Phillips) $1,745

Union Special industrial sewing machine by the Union Special Machine Co Chicago USA, circa 1910.
(Auction Team Köln) $141

A Hurtu Mod. A, French frame machine with gilt decoration, on a wooden plinth, circa 1890. (Auction Team Köln)

$216

An American Shaw & Clark chain stitch machine, with closed tower, circa 1864. (Auction Team Köln)

$2,315

Weir chain stitch machine described as 'The Globe', 1885, in original metal case, without shuttle. (Auction Team Köln) $390

A rare Nuremburg Clown sewing machine, No. 4024, the seated cast iron figure with nodding head and working arms operated by a porcelain handled crank, on iron base with lions paw feet, 8¾in. high. (repainted) (Christie's S. Ken) $4,500

A rare Kimball & Morton Lion treadle sewing machine, the machine head formed as a standing lion, 26½in. wide, with Registration mark of 1868. (Christie's S. Ken) $7,762

A rare McQuinn lockstitch sewing machine, with scalloped base, partial gilt transfers, Britannia trade-marks, dated *October 20 1878*. (Christie's) $7,750

US patent model John W. Lufkin buttonhole sewing machine, for the US patent no. 242. 462 of 7 June 1881, with all relevant documentation. (Auction Team Köln)

$1,698

The Grover & Baker Family Box Machine, the first boxed traveling sewing machine, with instruction booklet dated *1859*, circa 1860. (Auction Team Köln)

$3,007

A Shakespear lockstitch sewing machine by Royal Sewing Machine Compy. Limited, Birmingham with gilt transfer decoration, nickel-plated stitch plate. (Christie's) $342

A fine lacquer and Shibayama kodansu, the exterior decorated on three sides with wheeling cranes and on the top with a bird of prey, Meiji period, 12.75cm. high.
(Hy. Duke & Son)

$14,000

A spherical tripod koro and cover, decorated in Shibayama style on a gold lacquer ground, the body with birds on a blossoming branch and two oni at kubi-hiki represented in shippo, signed *Gyokukendo*, late 19th century, 19cm. high.
(Christie's)

$13,552

A silver filigree mounted Shibayama inlaid ivory tray, the center with a peacock standing majestically on a rocky outcrop and a peahen below, signed *Naoyuki*, Meiji period (1868–1912), 30.1cm. long.
(Christie's)

$6,068

Red lacquer corner cabinet with gilt lacquer and mother-of-pearl overlay panels, Meiji period, the upper section with a curved curio shelf above two sliding doors overlaid in Shibayama style, 32in. wide.
(Butterfield & Butterfield)

$7,150

A Shibayama tusk vase decorated with geese, butterflies, bees, dragonflies, flowering grasses and chrysanthemums, Meiji period, 14.5cm. wide.
(Hy. Duke & Son)

$700

A fine lozenge-shaped gold lacquer vase, the sides decorated in gold hiramakie, takamakie, okibirame, kirikane, kimpun, hirame and Shibayama style with Shoki searching for oni in the stream, unsigned, 19th century, 18.5cm. high, with European fitted box.
(Christie's)

$19,360

A pair of silver vases decorated in Shibayama style on a gold lacquer ground, the panels depicting birds perched on flowering boughs and panniers, signed *Teiko*, Meiji period (1868–1912), 17cm. high.
(Christie's)

$8,235

A late 19th century Japanese Shibayama ivory tusk section vase, applied with carved and stained ivory reliefs of a young lady wearing fine robes, 1ft. 3in. high.
(Spencer's)

$3,401

A Shibayama box and cover, carved in low relief with branches inhabited with doves, the lid with a finial of a hen and chicks, 3¹/₄in. high.
(Lawrence Fine Art)

$759

A Komai style cabinet, the various doors and drawers inset with ivory panels inlaid in Shibayama style with various bird and floral scenes, late 19th century, 47cm. high.
(Christie's) $10,120

An ivory elephant inlaid in Shibayama style with an elegant caparison, decorated with a profusion of flowers and foliage, unsigned, Meiji period, 14cm. long. (Christie's London)
          $9,000

A silver vase and domed cover, the lobed body suporting five convex panels decorated in Shibayama-style with birds in flight, signed *Kanemitsu*, late 19th century, 24cm. high.
(Christie's) $6,200

A silver and lacquer vase and cover decorated in Shibayama style with two shaped panels, one with egrets by wisteria and chrysanthemums, the other with Daikoku and Bishamonten, signed *Yoshiaki saku*, late 19th century, 25.5cm. high.
(Christie's) $10,600

A pair of small Shibayama style vases with massed flowerheads ground, each with the gold lacquer ground shoulder decorated in gold hiramakie with chrysanthemum flower and foliage, late 19th century, 16.2cm. high.
(Christie's) $8,450

A Japanese silver colored metal and Shibayama two handled vase, cover and liner, the melon fluted body inlaid in mother of pearl and polished hardstones, 26cm. high.
(Spencer's) $4,020

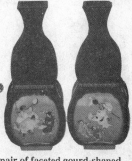

Pair of Shibayama School inlaid ivory tusks, signed *Masayuki*, late 19th century, with roosters and hens among flowers, 12in. high.
(Skinner Inc.) $6,600

A Komai style garniture, each of the vases inset with ivory panels inlaid in Shibayama style depicting various birds and floral designs, 36cm. high.
(Christie's) $16,200

A pair of faceted gourd-shaped tsuishu vases, decorated in Shibayama style with birds and flowers, brushes and books, signed *Ozeki sei*, late 19th century, 23.3cm. high.
(Christie's) $17,305

A rare pair of lady's mules of pale blue satin embroidered in white thread partly wrapped in silver with sunbursts trimmed with sequins, with square toes, circa 1665.
(Christie's S. Ken)
$23,353

A lady's mule of yellow and brown silk brocade woven with abstract designs and cartouches, 2.5in. high, 10in. long, circa 1660. (Christie's)
$25,025

A pair of ladies' shoes of pale blue moiré grosgrain silk with ivory satin covered 2¼in. heels and straps, 1782.
(Christie's)
$911

A pair of ladies shoes of ivory silk applied with ivory silk braid, the tongue lined with blue silk damask, English, early 18th century.
(Christie's)
$6,102

A pair of ladies' button boots, the front of gilt leather with a stitched scalloped edge, with a gilt painted Louis 4in. heel, 1880's. (Christie's)
$6,545

A rare pair lady's shoes of white kid painted in pink and gray with sprigs of flowers, and trimmed with silk rosettes, circa 1700.
(Christie's S. Ken)
$18,046

A pair of 1900's wedding shoes, the ivory silk uppers and cross bar embroidered with diamante and glass beads.
(Phillips)
$142

A fine pair of lady's shoes of purple and white spotted kid, one shoe labeled *Edwd. Hogg Ladies Cheap Shoe Warehouse*, circa 1795.
(Christie's S. Ken)
$4,876

A pair of pink silk shoes, the toes embroidered with metal sequins and coiled metal braid with a floral spray design, circa 1760. (Christie's)
$6,545

A pair of clogs of black kid bound with morocco braid, with wide blue linen band across the toe cap, probably late 18th century. (Christie's) $311

A pair of shoes of mustard colored ribbed silk with 3in. heels, English, circa 1770, inscribed Miss Alsorne. (Christie's) $2,117

A pair of lady's shoes of dark blue morocco, with low wedge heels, circa 1790. (Christie's) $1,800

A pair of ladies' high heeled shoes of ivory silk, circa 1730. (Christie's) $3,118

A pair of ladies' lace-up boots, the fronts of scarlet glace leather with red covered Louis heel 3½in. high, circa 1889. (Christie's) $1,028

A pair of early 18th century lady's shoes of duck-egg-blue silk worked with gold thread embroidery and sequin decoration. (Phillips) $2,670

A pair of ladies' high heeled shoes of crimson damask, trimmed with gold lace with 2in. heels, 9in. long, early 18th century. (Christie's) $1,455

A fine pair of Woodlands tanned skin moccasins, the brown velvet cuffs sewn with flowers and leaves in colored and transparent beads. (Christie's) $3,993

A pair of mid 18th century shoes with fitted clogs of yellow damask silk, bound in yellow silk. (Phillips West Two) $6,120

Miers and Field, circa 1820, Captain W.C. Lemprière, in uniform of the Royal Artillery, silhouette on plaster, oval, 3¹/₄in. high. (Christie's) $498

Augustin Edouart (1789-1861) – Silhouette of Three Children with Toys, Cat and Dog, cut paper applied to a watercolor, 17.8 x 34.6cm. (Skinner Inc.) $2,100

A bronzed silhouette of a gentleman, painted on plaster, by John Field, oval 83mm., in papier mache frame. (Phillips London) $326

Double watercolor and paper portrait silhouette, The Surrender at Yorktown, early 19th century, 6¹/₂ x 8¹/₂in. (Butterfield & Butterfield) $2,500

A full-length profile of a family group, by Augustin Edouart, signed and dated 1825, cut-outs on card, 13in. high. (Christie's) $1,573

A rectangular silhouette on paper by John Buncombe, of Catherine Reynolds of Newport, circa 1785, 90 x 70mm. (Phillips) $226

A. Charles (fl. circa 1780-1807), Mr. Fitzgerald, in profile to the right, in coat, waistcoat stock and hat, his hair tied in a pigtail, silhouette, painted on glass, 3in. high. (Christie's) $2,500

Edouart, a paper cut silhouette, mounted on a colored wash drawing room interior in Gothic style, depicting male and female in costume, signed and dated 1837, 12in. x 9in. (Black Horse Agencies) $511

Mrs. Isabella Beetham (circa 1753-1825), Mrs. Sharland, seated half length in profile to the left, in lace trimmed dress and hat decorated with rosette, silhouette, painted on convex glass, 3⁷/₈in. high. (Christie's) $3,500

Augustin Edouart, dated *1840*, silhouette portrait of Stephen Matlack and his dog, 'Rush', free cut black paper mounted on a wash ground, 9³/₄ x 7³/₄in. (Sotheby's) $2,990

William James Hubard (1807–1862), free cut black paper silhouette with bronzing mounted on white paper with wash, 12 x 19in. (Sotheby's) $3,220

A gentleman standing full-length profile, by Augustin Edouart, cut-out on card, signed and dated 1836, 10³/₄in. high. (Christie's) $495

A bronzed silhouette on plaster of Reverend J. Babington, by J. Miers, oval 80mm., in papier mache frame. (Phillips London) $391

A rectangular conversation piece by Wm. Welling, of a husband and wife taking tea, signed and dated 1874, 280 x 380mm. (Phillips) $4,832

John Field, one of a pair of silhouettes of John Stonor (1771–1846) and his wife Helen (née Chadwick) (1773–1852), bronzed silhouettes, painted on plaster, 3¹/₈in. high. (Bonhams)(Two) $1,078

Augustin Edouart (1789–1861), a full-length group; Monsieur Iaac, Monsieur Edmond Jagot, holding a whip and his grandmother Madame Catherine Hyn, rectangular, 9³/₄in. high. (Christie's) $1,262

H.A. Frith, two children standing full-length in a landscape, the eldest handing the other a rose, dated 1846, rectangular, 8in. high. (Christie's S. Ken) $1,931

Augustin Edouart, Colonel Robert Samuel Hustler, silhouette cut-out on card, signed on obverse and dated *1833*, sepia and pencil background, 11in. high. (Bonhams) $1,019

BASKETS

A sugar basket, pierced and chased with a cartouche, scrolls and paterae amongst pales and flutes, by Burrage Davenport, London 1772, 7³/₄oz., 5¹/₂in. high. (Tennants) $930

A silver cake basket, maker's mark of R&W Wilson, Philadelphia, circa 1830, with die-rolled Greek-key borders, 12in. diameter, 38 oz. (Christie's) $1,100

A large George II circular bread basket, the spreading foot chased with a band of acanthus leaves, by Louis Laroche, 1733, 12¹/₄in. diameter, 79oz. (Christie's) $65,626

A George III circular bread basket, with openwork basket-work sides, basket-weave border and twisted and foliage swing handle, by John Wakelin and Robert Garrard, 1795, 11¹/₄in. diameter, 42 oz. (Christie's) $8,448

German hallmarked silver fruit basket, 19th century, 800 fine, reticulated and chased figural and floral decoration, approximately 46 troy oz. (Skinner Inc.) $2,200

A fine George II shaped-oval bread basket, the everted border cast and pierced with wheat ears, flowers, scrolls and ribbons, by Paul de Lamerie, 1747, 13³/₄in. long, 72oz. (Christie's) $207,273

George II style silver cake basket, clover piercing and engraved crest, side bearing marks of Wm. Plummer, 1759–60, 13in. wide. (Skinner Inc.) $1,760

A sugar basket of hemispherical shape chased and pierced with flowers, scrolls, and a cartouche, by Richard Meach, London 1770, blue glass liner, 4¹/₂oz., 4¹/₂in. diameter. (Tennants) $651

A George II shaped oval bread basket, the sides pierced and chased with quatrefoils, scrolls and beading, by Edward Aldridge, 1759, with blue glass liner, 17¹/₄in. wide, 52oz. (Christie's) $12,813

A silver beaker, maker's mark of Nicholas Geoffroy, Newport, Rhode Island, 1795–1817, 2⅞in. high, 3oz.
(Christie's) $550

A Continental late 19th century tapering circular beaker on spherical feet and with a molded rim, London 1885, 3½in., 5.75oz.
(Christie's) $246

A small beaker, the sides engraved with opposed leaves and initials and date 1756, 18th century, Scandinavian, 5.5cm.
(Lawrence Fine Art) $734

A German silver gilt tapering cylindrical beaker, the body with a broad band of tear drop ornament on a punched ground, by Christoph Zorer, Augsburg, 1570–1575, 4¾in. high, 208grs.
(Christie's) $14,861

A Swiss tapering cylindrical beaker, punched with a broad band of matting and with molded rim, Sion, circa 1700, maker's mark possibly that of Francois-Joseph Ryss, 3¼in. high, 111grs.
(Christie's) $6,068

A Hungarian parcel-gilt beaker, engraved with initials and dated 1670, the base inset with a medallic 1½-Thaler, 1541, struck at Kremnitz, 4in. high, 207grs.
(Christie's) $3,115

A silver beaker of historical interest, maker's mark of Churchill & Treadwell, Boston, 1805–1813, 3½in. high, 4oz. 10dwt.
(Christie's) $4,400

An Art Nouveau beaker, the body stamped with flowers, foliage and scrollwork decoration, Mappin and Webb, Sheffield 1901, 6in., 13.5oz.
(Christie's S. Ken) $619

A late 18th century Channel Isles beaker, with an everting rim and a molded circular foot, 9.5cm. tall, by George Mauger, Jersey, circa 1780–1800, 3oz.
(Phillips) $777

BOWLS

A Queen Anne circular punch bowl, chased with a broad band of flutes and with two applied grotesque male mask and drop-ring handles, by William Fordham, 1706, 11½in. diameter, 65oz.
(Christie's) $22,612

A George II circular sugar bowl and cover, engraved with a band of palm leaves and below the shaped rim with a band of strapwork, latticework and female masks, by John Le Sage, 1730, 4in. high, 17oz.
(Christie's) $14,698

Japanese silver repoussé punch bowl, Meiji period, with lush flowering kakitsubaki (iris) plants executed in high relief on a graduated ground, the base impressed STERLING K & CO., 54oz. 6dwts.
(Butterfield & Butterfield) $6,050

A George III two-handled circular bowl with monteith rim, the body chased in high relief with oriental figures, flowers, scrolls and foliage, 11in. diameter, maker's mark W.B., London 1817, 100.8oz.
(Bearne's) $8,640

Danish silver circular bowl by Georg Jensen, Copenhagen, circa 1940, with lobed sides rising to everted horizontal border, 14in. diameter, 35oz. 4dwts.
(Butterfield & Butterfield) $2,200

George II silver gilt bowl and cover, Phillips Garden, London, 1751, the upper body chased with flowers and a rococo scrollwork band incorporating two blank cartouches, 4¼in. diameter, 9oz. 2dwts.
(Butterfield & Butterfield) $1,540

A Georg Jensen footed bowl, with openwork leaf and berry stem, on flared circular foot, with stamped maker's mark for 1925–32, 11cm. high, 305 grams.
(Christie's) $4,211

A silver footed bowl, maker's mark of Samuel Williamson, Philadelphia, 1795–1810, on a flaring pedestal base over a square foot, 6⅝in. diameter, 15 oz. 10 dwt.
(Christie's) $2,200

An Edwardian silver-gilt and cut-glass rose bowl, the circular lobed cut-glass body with foliate decoration, by William Comyns, 1904, 15cm.
(Lawrence) $1,959

CANDELABRA

One of a pair of six branch candelabra with spiral foliate decoration, on fluted circular bases, 59cm. high, 5000gr.
(Finarte) (Two) $4,070

A pair of Sheffield plate three-light candelabra, each on circular base with tapering stem, vase-shaped sconces, circa 1820, 22in. high.
(Christie's) $2,813

One of a pair of plated five-light candelabra, maker's mark of Tiffany & Co., New York, circa 1885, with foliate decoration, 15¼in. high.
(Christie's) $4,180

One of a pair of Victorian massive seven-light candelabra, the scroll stem entwined with vine tendrils and with frolicking putti, shamrocks and a harp, by John S. Hunt, 1844, 31½in. high, 741 oz.
(Christie's) $61,600

Pair German silver five light candelabra, Friedlander, early 20th century, 800 standard modified reproduction of George III style, 19in. high, 111oz. 14dwts.
(Butterfield & Butterfield) $1,980

A Harold Stabler silver twin-branch candelabrum, tall ovoid fluted and faceted stem with similarly faceted curved branches, stamped facsimile signature *Harold Stabler*, 1935, 29cm. high, 569 grams.
(Christie's) $1,531

A Victorian three-light candelabra, on three foliate and scroll feet and with floral border, by John S. Hunt, 1844, 18in. high, gross 99 oz.
(Christie's) $3,520

Pair of Art Nouveau candelabra, silvered metal with stylised arms supporting candle nozzles, impressed marks, 12¼in. high.
(Skinner) $605

An Edwardian four branch five light table candelabrum, with detachable square sconces, Sheffield 1906, by Martin Hall and Co., 56cm. high overall.
(Spencer's) $2,016

CANDLESTICKS

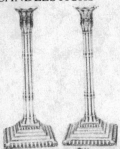

A fine and attractive pair of early George III cluster column candlesticks by Ebenezer Coker, London 1768, 31.5cm. high. (Spencer's) $2,103

Pair of Russian silver gilt and enamel candlesticks, Moscow, late 19th century, approximately 25 troy oz. (Skinner) $1,870

A pair of reproduction cast candlesticks in the William III manner, by Carrington & Co., weight 24oz., 6¼in. high. (Christie's) $1,180

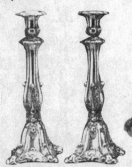

Pair of Continental silver candlesticks, apparently unmarked, 19th century, fitted with detachable nozzles, 12in. high, 18oz. 16 dwts. (Butterfield & Butterfield) $1,100

A set of four Sheffield plate candlesticks by Waterhouse, Hatfield & Co., Sheffield, circa 1840, 9¼in. high. (Butterfield & Butterfield) $1,210

A pair of Queen Anne candlesticks, each on spreading decagonal base and with baluster stem and circular vase-shaped socket, by Ambrose Stevenson, 1711, 7in. high, 35oz. (Christie's) $12,488

A pair of late 18th century candlesticks, the lightly channeled stems with slight spiral swirl, stamped with two crowns, Milan, 19cm. high, 700gr. (Finarte) $4,410

Pair of Danish silver single candlesticks by Georg Jensen, Copenhagen, circa 1940, designer Harald Nielsen, both with circular stepped base, 2¾in. high, 10oz. 14dwts. (Butterfield & Butterfield) $2,200

A pair of George V silver mounted oak barley twist candlesticks by Albert Edward Jones, with planished silver cylindrical sockets, Birmingham 1920, 21.5cm. high. (Spencer's) $371

CANNS

A silver covered cann, maker's mark of Simeon Soumaine, New York, circa 1710, 4³/₄in. high, 10oz. 10dwt.
(Christie's) $6,325

A silver cann, maker's mark of William Taylor, Philadelphia, circa 1775, 5¹/₄in. high, 11oz.
(Christie's) $2,200

A rare silver cann, maker's mark of Charles Oliver Bruff, New York, circa 1770, 4³/₈in. high, 9oz.
(Christie's) $8,250

A silver cann, maker's mark of William Homes, Sr., Boston, circa 1750, the S-scroll handle with molded drop and bud terminal, 5¹/₄in. high, 10 oz. 10 dwt.
(Christie's) $1,320

An American silver small cann, Edmund Milne, Philadelphia, circa 1770, with leaf-capped double-scroll handle, 9oz., height 4¹/₂in.
(Sotheby's) $2,990

A rare silver cann, maker's mark of John Bayley, Philadelphia, 1760–1770, the double scroll handle with acanthus-leaf grip, on molded circular foot, 5in. high, 13 oz. 10 dwt. (Christie's) $3,080

An early 18th century silver cann, probably Boston, possibly by Samuel Edwards, 4in. high, 6 troy oz.
                               $1,256

Mid 18th century footed silver cann, maker's mark on base 'I. Edwards', 5¼in. high, 10 troy oz.
                               $2,352

A silver child's cann, maker's mark of Ebenezer Moulton, Boston, circa 1790, 3in. high, 2oz. 10dwt.
(Christie's) $2,860

CASTERS

A silver caster, maker's mark of Eleazer Baker, Ashford, Connecticut, circa 1785, 5¼in. high, 3oz. 10dwt. (Christie's) $3,850

A pair of George II plain octagonal sugar casters, with pierced domed cover and baluster finial, by Samuel Wood, 1737, 6in. high, 10 oz. (Christie's) $1,760

A Charles II caster, the cap pierced with a variety of scattered motifs below gadrooning and baluster finial, London 1679, 7¹/₂oz., 7¹/₈in. (Tennants) $2,418

A fine octagonal silver pepper box, maker's mark of Andrew Oliver, Boston, circa 1740, of octagonal form on molded base, 4¼in. high, 3oz. 10dwt. (Christie's) $9,200

A set of three Queen Anne octagonal casters, the pierced domed covers with bayonet fittings and baluster finials, unmarked, circa 1710, 5¼in. and 4½in. high, 14 oz. (Christie's) $1,232

A rare and important silver sugar caster, maker's mark of Jacobus van der Spiegel, New York, 1690–1708, the domed cover pierced with fleurs-de-lys 8¼in. high, 16oz. (Christie's) $121,000

A caster with molded girdle and foot, the cap pierced with scrolls, maker probably S. Wood, London, 1728, 6¹/₂oz., 6³/₈in. high. (Tennants) $744

A pair of 18th century Belgian casters of paneled baluster form with knop finials, probably by Ferdinandus Cornelius Carolus Millé, Brussels, 1747/9, 18.7cm. high, 19oz. (Phillips) $16,416

A baluster caster, the pierced domed cover applied with a band of flower buds and with stylized flower finial, by Omar Ramsden, 1936, 6¹/₂in. high, 11oz. (Christie's) $2,972

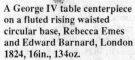

A late Victorian centerpiece
formed as a horse beneath an
oak tree, on rockwork base with
presentation shield plaque dated
1899, 12in. high.
(Christie's) $1,361

A George IV table centerpiece
on a fluted rising waisted
circular base, Rebecca Emes
and Edward Barnard, London
1824, 16in., 134oz.
(Christie's) $7,043

A George V dessert stand
centerpiece, supported on a
panelled tapering stem, 13in.
high, Walker and Hall, Sheffield
1920, 43.7oz.
(Bearne's) $1,585

An antique German
Renaissance Revival solid silver
centerpiece in the form of a
family tree, hallmarked *Posen*
for Lazarus Posen, Frankfurt,
circa 1880, 33^1/$_2$in. high, 339 troy
oz.
(Selkirk's) $8,500

A large French parcel-gilt
centerpiece, the central
hardstone plinth supporting a
detachable loosely draped female
figure, the ground signed *H.
Wadere*, circa 1897, 34^1/$_2$in. high,
gross 25,860grs.
(Christie's) $29,700

A Victorian vase-shaped
centerpiece and cover, the stem
formed as three female figures,
the bowl cast and chased with a
horserace and numerous figures
on horseback, by John S. Hunt,
1861, 20in. high, 266oz.
(Christie's) $13,790

A good late Victorian table
centerpiece by Messrs. Hancock,
supported on the outstretched
arms and head of a nude,
London 1886, 1950 grams,
33cm. high.
(Spencer's) $3,115

'English Sterling' centerpiece,
New York, circa 1870, the boat
form bowl on a narrow waisted
stem over a multi stepped
expanding base, 8^3/$_4$in. high,
42oz.
(Butterfield & Butterfield)
                                $770

An early George V centerpiece,
the central trumpet vase flanked
by three smaller trumpet vases,
the whole with cast reel and
bobbin borders, Sheffield 1913,
906 grams.
(Spencer's) $970

CHAMBERSTICKS

A George III chamber candlestick, with gadroon border and flying scroll handle, 1772 (no maker's mark but nozzle by Ebenezer Coker), 9.5cm., 7.5oz. (Lawrence Fine Art) $347

A rare George IV silver-gilt chamber candlestick, with flower petal socket, cylindrical nozzle and tendril handle, by Philip Rundell, 1821, 4¹/₄in. diameter, 6oz. (Christie's) $3,684

A George III chamberstick, 4in. high, with reeded borders, and vase-shaped socket with detachable nozzle, London, 1807, by William Barrett II, 11 oz. (Bonhams) $620

A William IV shaped circular chamber candlestick with reeded edging, 5³/₄in. diameter, Henry Wilkinson and Co., Sheffield 1835, 11.2oz. (Bearne's) $684

A George III miniature chamber candlestick, the circular base, nozzle and conical extinguisher engraved with crest, 3in. diameter, Peter, Anne and William Bateman, London, 1802, 96 gms, 3.0 oz. (Bearne's) $520

A George III chamberstick, with reed rim, vase shape sconce, detachable nozzle and conical extinguisher, by Peter and Anne Bateman, 1797, 14cm. (Lawrence) $630

A George III chamber candlestick, with flying scroll handle and extinguisher, marked on base and extinguisher by Ebenezer Coker, 1766, 10cm., 10.5oz. (Lawrence Fine Art) $888

Matthew Boulton & Co, an early 19th century circular 'storm' chamber lamp with a matted, globular glass shade, a conical snuffer and gadrooned borders, 15cm. diameter, circa 1815. (Phillips) $415

A George III chamberstick, 4¹/₄in. high, with gadrooned border, vase-form socket with detachable nozzle and scroll handle, Sheffield, 1803, by John Watson, 8 oz. (Bonhams) $736

CHRISTENING MUGS

A mid Victorian christening mug by George Unite, of quatrefoil form, Birmingham 1863, 187 grams, 10.5cm. high. (Spencer's) $314

A Chinese christening mug of tapering cylindrical form, embossed with chrysanthemums, stamped on the base with Chinese characters only, circa 1900, 7.9cm. high, 6oz. (Phillips London) $350

A Victorian silver-gilt campana-shaped christening mug on a domed circular base applied with classical musicians, George Adams, London 1858, 5in. (Christie's S. Ken) $792

An Indian Colonial 19th century gilt-lined campana-shaped christening mug, the fluted body chased and applied with flowers and foliage and with a molded rim, Hamilton & Co., Calcutta circa 1860, 4$^{1/2}$in., 9oz. (Christie's S. Ken) $453

An attractive Victorian silver-gilt christening mug, the baluster body with an overlapping rim embossed on either side with an oval 'disk' cartouche, 12cm. high, E. & J. Barnard, 1862, 7oz. (Phillips) $864

An early Victorian christening mug of paneled waisted cylindrical form, engraved with a presentation inscription, and panels of diapering and foliage, London 1853, maker's mark *RD*, 127 grams. (Spencer's) $277

A Victorian christening mug in the gothic manner engraved with panels of entwined strapwork and foliage and with presentation inscription, Glasgow, 1861. (Christie's) $715

A attractive Victorian christening mug, the cylindrical body paneled and engraved with floral sprays against a shaped background, 13cm. high, by Atherly & Sillwell, 1858, 6oz. (Phillips) $484

A Victorian christening mug of waisted cylindrical form on shell and scroll base, chased and embossed with children playing, by Rawlins and Sumner, 1848, 4$^{1/4}$in. high, 6oz. (Christie's) $638

CLARET JUGS

Gorham Sterling and two-color cut glass claret jug, ovoid body with green and ruby cutting, 10½in. high.
(Skinner Inc.) $2,640

A pair of Victorian pear-shaped claret jugs, by Stephen Smith and William Nicholson, 1858 and 1859, 13½in. high, 71oz.
(Christie's) $3,799

A German tapering cut glass claret jug with plain mount, and slightly-domed hinged cover, 14¼in.
(Christie's) $1,008

A Frederick Elkington silver barrel-shaped claret jug designed by Dr. Christopher Dresser, London 1866, 17.5cm. high, 20.25oz.
(Christie's) $1,672

A pair of Victorian silver-gilt mounted clear glass claret jugs, each on circular slightly spreading foot, by John Figg, 1865, 16½in. high.
(Christie's) $9,677

A crested silver-mounted claret-jug, the flattened oviform body engraved with a crest within an oval cartouche flanked by scantily draped nymphs, London, 1891, 22.5cm. high.
(Christie's) $2,139

A late Victorian clear glass claret jug, of baluster form with diamond facet cut decoration, Birmingham 1893, by Heath & Middleton, 20cm. high.
(Spencer's) $516

A pair of Victorian vase-shaped claret jugs, one engraved with the 'Triumphe of Venus', the other with a 'Sacrifice to Pan', by Roberts and Belk, Sheffield, 1866, 13¾in. high, 43 oz.
(Christie's) $4,400

Continental silver claret jug, 19th century, probably French, mermaid handle and conch finial, apparently unmarked, 12in. high, approximately 33 troy oz.
(Skinner Inc.) $2,090

A pear shaped coffee pot by
Eliza Godfrey, London with
richly chased rocaille
decoration, 27.5cm. high,
1040gr., 1758/9.
(Finarte)　　　　　$2,352

E. E. J. & W. Barnard, a
naturalistic coffee pot, melon
paneled, with foliage entwined
root spout and handle, 8¹/₂in.,
London 1841, 25oz.
(Woolley & Wallis)　　$1,287

A small cylindrical coffee pot,
decorated in relief with
chinoiserie motifs and with a Fo
dog finial, London 1850, 16.5cm.
high.
(Finarte)　　　　　$997

A Belgian pear-shaped coffee
pot, with fluted curved spout,
detachable hinged domed cover
with scroll thumbpiece and
flower finial, by Jacques-
Hermann Le Vieu, Mons, 1753,
11³/₄in. high, gross 1,180 grs.
(Christie's)　　　　$21,120

A rare silver coffee biggin,
maker's mark of Garrett Eoff,
New York, circa 1820, with a
scroll spout chased with
acanthus and a carved wood
handle, 9¹/₂in. high, 32 oz.
10 dwt.
(Christie's)　　　　$3,080

A silver coffee pot by Joyce R.
Himsworth, the tapering
cylindrical body applied with
bands of plaited rope decoration
and wirework motifs, Sheffield
hallmarks for 1926, 23cm. high,
840 grams gross.
(Christie's)　　　　$1,436

George II silver coffee pot by
Thomas Farren, London, 1736,
with cast faceted swan neck
spout, 8³/₄in. high, gross weight
24oz.
(Butterfield & Butterfield)
　　　　　　　　$3,575

A Swedish 19th century fluted
baluster coffee pot with a rising
curved spout, and engraved with
rococo scrolling foliage, 8¹/₂in.,
17oz.
(Christie's)　　　　$965

A German plain pear-shaped
coffee-jug, with a molded drop
to the short curved spout, by
Martin Friedrich Muller, Berlin,
1735–45, 11¹/₂in. high, gross
1056grs.
(Christie's)　　　　$13,371

CREAM JUGS

A George III cow creamer, engraved with hair along the ridge of back, the cover chased with flowers and applied with a fly, 9.5cm. high overall, by John Schuppe, 1767, 4 ozs.
(Phillips) $12,474

A silver cream jug, maker's mark of William Seal, Philadelphia, circa 1815, 6¹/₈in. high, 8oz. 10dwt.
(Christie's) $770

A George IV cream jug, 3in. high, banded to belly with everted gadrooned border and florally-chased reeded strap handle, London, 1829, by Robert Hennell, 3.5 oz.
(Bonhams) $165

A George III cream jug of helmet shape with gadroon border, scroll handle and pedestal foot, by Charles Clark, 1765, 9cm.
(Lawrence Fine Art) $463

A rare George II cast boat-shaped cream jug, the body cast and chased with goats, a cow, bull's masks, shells, scrolls and foliage, by Louis Hamon, 1738, 5¹/₄in. high, 17oz.
(Christie's) $16,017

A fine George II pear-shaped cream jug, on three female mask and claw-and-ball feet, chased with two shaped-oval panels, one enclosing goats, the other cows and a milkmaid, by William Cripps, 1749, 5¹/₄in. high, 9oz.
(Christie's) $21,669

A silver cream jug, maker's mark of Daniel Rogers, Ipswich, Massachusetts, circa 1780, 4¹/₄in. high, 4oz. 10dwt.
(Christie's) $1,540

An Irish George III cream jug, with cut away borders and wide lips banded to belly, Dublin, circa 1770, 6 oz.
(Bonhams) $659

A fine George II cast cream jug, decorated with cows and a milk maid in naturalistic surroundings, by Elias Cachart, London 1740, 7¹/₂oz., 5in.
(Tennants) $7,068

CRUETS

A fine early Victorian oil and vinegar cruet, by Robert Hennell, London 1840, 18.5 oz. weighable silver.
(Woolley & Wallis)
$3,386

A Regency part-fluted rounded square eight-bottle cruet on scrolling foliate feet, Thomas Robins, London 1814, 8³/₄in., 35oz.
(Christie's)
$1,098

A Regency part-fluted rounded square cruet frame on foliate feet and with egg and dart border, Paul Storr , London, 1818, 10³/₄in., 35.50oz. free.
(Christie's)
$7,009

An early George III cruet, the cinquefoil frame with central handle and engraved with a coat of arms on a rococo tablet, maker's mark *ID*, 1763, 23cm., frame 15.5oz.
(Lawrence Fine Art)
$2,124

A George III oblong egg cruet, on four shell and vine feet, fitted with six egg cups, each with shell and gadrooned everted rim, by Philip Rundell, 1818, 8in. long, 28oz.
(Christie's)
$2,970

Russian silver and glass mustard set by Nichols and Plinke, St. Petersburg, 1843, the frame with threaded octagonal holder for two glass mustard jars supported by four vertical supports, 6in. high, 16oz. 14dwts.
(Butterfield & Butterfield)
$1,100

A George IV cruet and stand, fitted with four cut glass vinaigrette bottles, a mustard jar and two pepperette bottles, one mustard spoon, by Jonathan Hayne, 1822.
(Lawrence)
$1,137

A Hukin and Heath four-piece electroplated cruet, designed by Dr. Christopher Dresser, with patent registration marks for 1879, 13cm. high.
(Christie's)
$1,287

A late George III seven bottle cruet, the bombé boat shaped gallery repoussé and chased with scrolling foliage, raised upon four tapering flared feet, London 1866, by Hyam Hyams.
(Spencer's)
$466

CUPS

John S. Hunt, a fine Victorian stag's head stirrup cup, with gilt interior, 6in., London 1846, 19oz.
(Woolley & Wallis)
$6,762

Theodore B. Starr Sterling repoussé loving cup, 10¼in. high, approximately 82 troy oz.
(Skinner Inc.)
$4,675

Silver caudle cup, Jeremiah Dummer, Boston, (1645–1718), engraved *N*ˢ*M* at base and marked *I.D.* in heart cartouche, approx. wt. 6 troy oz.
(Skinner)
$2,090

A large Victorian two-handled trophy cup, 10½ in. high, the sides engraved with diaper-worked panels and chased with 'C'-scrolls, ferns and other foliage, London, 1849, by Samuel Hayne and Dudley Carter, 31 ozs.
(Bonhams)
$1,089

Silver presentation cup, Nicholas J. Bogert (fl. 1801–1830), New York City, the octagonal body engraved *This Goblet was Presented to the Guards by 1st Lieut. W. Bruen as a Prize to be shot for Jan 8th 1845*, 4in. high, 6 troy oz.
(Skinner)
$1,045

Important Sterling silver trophy, 19th century, by Tiffany, cast handles in the form of angels holding children, either side with applied full, two-dimensional figures of women in diaphanous clothing, 24.8 troy oz.
(Eldred's)
$3,300

A George III rare Irish Provincial two-handled cup, the campana-shaped body chased with a foliate festooned classical frieze, by Daniel McCarthy, Cork, circa 1760, 14oz.
(Phillips)
$950

A Charles I shallow wine cup, the hexafoil bowl chased with stylized shells each within shaped-oval surround, 1640, maker's mark *GM*, a bird below, 2¼in. high.
(Christie's)
$13,200

A late 18th century two-handled cup with a domed pedestal foot and reeded handles, the campana shaped body decorated with bands of horizontal convex fluting, 14cm. tall, circa 1780.
(Phillips)
$276

Paul Storr, a George III entrée dish and cover, of plain circular form, the base-dish with a finely applied border of scallop and oak leaf motifs with gadrooning, 20.5cm. high overall, 1810, 61oz. (Phillips) $12,096

A Hukin & Heath electroplated double bon-bon dish designed by Dr. Christopher Dresser, each oval basket with inverted rim, with loop handle, circa 1881, 14cm. high. (Christie's) $827

A silver butter dish and cover, maker's mark of Bigelow, Kennard & Co., Boston, circa 1880, in the Persian taste, eleborately repoussé with foliate scrolls and fluting, 8in. wide, 16½ oz. (Christie's) $880

A late Victorian shaped-circular dish, the broad waved border chased with acorns and oak leaves, by Gilbert Marks, 1898, Britannia standard, 16³/₄in. diameter, 56oz. (Christie's) $9,051

A William IV circular butter dish, formed as a pail with swing handle, engraved with cypher, crest and Garter Motto, by Robert Garrard, 1834, 4³/₄in. diameter, 11oz. (Christie's) $3,960

A Spanish silver-gilt shaped-circular dish, chased with birds, flowers and foliage, with raised molded border, late 17th century, possibly Palencia, 17³/₄in. diameter, 1,098 grs. (Christie's) $2,640

A parcel-gilt silver covered butter dish, maker's mark of Tiffany & Co., New York, 1881–1891, the spot-hammered surface applied with silver-gilt leaves and thistles, 5⁷/₈in. diameter, 15 oz. 10 dwt. (Christie's) $2,860

A Japanese pierced silver dish mounted with a central Shibayama panel, signed, decorated with a vase of flowers on a table, 12¹/₄in. diameter. (Bearne's) $2,383

A Louis XVI shaped-oval shaving dish, with detachable neck-notch and reeded borders, engraved with a coat-of-arms, by Jean-Antoine Gallemant, Paris, 1780–81, 13in. wide, 820 grs. (Christie's) $4,576

EWERS

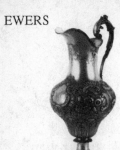

Silver ewer, Robert and William Wilson (active 1825–1846), Philadelphia, baluster form with foliate and acanthus decoration, 45 troy oz.
(Skinner Inc.) **$1,400**

Italian silver ewer, 20th century, helmet form with relief vine design, 9¼in. high, approximately 16 troy oz.
(Skinner) **$1,045**

A George III wine ewer, 12½in. high, with beaded borders and leaf mounted wooden scroll handle, London, 1773, by Daniel Smith and Robert Sharp, 30 oz.
(Bonhams) **$3,874**

An Italian fluted baluster ewer on a shaped circular domed foot, applied with a cast double scroll handle, Venice or Padua, 7¼in., 13.25oz.
(Christie's S. Ken) **$1,877**

A Victorian parcel-gilt ewer, the vase-shaped body repoussé and chased with putti, hops and acanthus foliage, by Elkington & Co., Birmingham, 1864, in fitted wood case, 12in. high, 51oz.
(Christie's) **$7,643**

A Spanish plain cylindrical ewer, the spout cast with a bearded mask, scrolls and foliage, 17th century, marked only *REISS*, 7¾in. high, 825grs.
(Christie's) **$19,800**

A Victorian wine ewer, 12in. high, with scrolling borders and leaf-chased scrolling side handle on domed, circular base, London, 1856, by William Hattersley or William Hewit, 26.5oz. (Bonhams) **$1,555**

A George III plain baluster wine ewer, the domed cover with flame finial and scroll handle, engraved with a crest, by Jacob Marsh, 1773, 11½in. high, 30oz.
(Christie's) **$1,009**

An American silver ewer, Bailey & Co., Philadelphia, circa 1850, chased with chinoiserie buildings, a boat and birds, 64oz. 10dwt., height 19in.
(Sotheby's) **$5,750**

FRAMES

An Edward VII shaped square photograph frame, chased and pierced with figs amongst scrolls and foliate festoons, 10in. high, London 1902.
(Bearne's) $770

A Liberty and Co. silver photograph frame, the top and base decorated with band of mistletoe, stamped maker's mark *L & Co.* and Birmingham hallmarks for 1892, 21.3cm. high. (Christie's) $1,593

An Art Nouveau silver shaped oval photograph frame with easel support, John and William Deakin, Birmingham 1904, 12in. high. (Christie's S. Ken)
$465

A William Hutton and Sons silver and enamel picture frame, with repoussé entrelac decoration, the top corners decorated with blue-green enamel, London hallmarks for 1903, 19.3cm. high.
(Christie's) $2,987

A silver repoussé picture frame of shaped rectangular form, decorated in relief with a stylized foliate pattern, Chester hallmarks, 32.7cm. high.
(Christie's) $1,600

An Art Nouveau silver photograph frame, the shaped square frame with floral repoussé decoration, one corner with drape motif, Birmingham hallmarks for 1904, 15.8cm. high.
(Christie's) $1,991

A William Hutton & Sons Art Nouveau silver and enamel photograph frame, decorated with stylised honesty and green and blue enamelling, 1904, 22.3cm. high. (Christie's London) $4,100

A decorative Edwardian photograph frame, in the Art Nouveau style with ivy on a wood back, 1901, 24.8cm. high x 21.5cm. wide.
(Phillips) $6,036

A Victorian heart-shaped photograph frame, decorated with cherubs faces amongst scrolling flowers and foliage, 7½in. high, William Comyns, London 1897.
(Bearne's) $578

433

GOBLETS

American silver goblet with chased decoration, cast vintage design base, unmarked, 8in. high, 11.2 troy oz.
(Eldred's) $303

A pair of George III gilt-lined goblets on beaded rising circular bases, Hester Bateman, London 1779, 6¹/₂in., 14.25oz.
(Christie's) $1,390

A George III goblet, cylindrical body with half fluted decoration, on circular pedestal foot, by Samuel Hennell, 1816, 16.5cm., 11oz.
(Lawrence Fine Art) $561

A Norwegian goblet, on octagonal foot and with cylindrical stem chased and engraved with scallop shells and stylized foliage, by Johannes Johannesen Reimers, Bergen, circa 1680, 4in. high.
(Christie's) $3,871

A pair of George III goblets, each on a circular bead edge stem foot, 5.65in., one maker Charles Wright, London 1788, the other maker Stephen Adams, London 1808, 14oz.
(Woolley & Wallis) $1,129

A mid Victorian small goblet by Roberts & Briggs, the baluster bowl repoussé with lozenge shaped panels on a matt ground, London 1865, 150 grams, 13cm. high.
(Spencer's) $318

Fine antique American coin silver goblet, mid-19th century, with chased hunting decoration, marked *Pure Coin, Boston*, 8in. high, 11 troy oz.
(Eldred's) $715

William Grundy, a good pair of ovoid goblets, gilt lined with flared feet, 6¹/₄in., London 1776, 17oz.
(Woolley & Wallis) $2,038

Paul Storr silver-gilt goblet, 4³/₄in. high, with an applied frieze of Classical females linked by floral swags, London, 1814, 5.5 oz.
(Bonhams) $3,487

INKSTANDS

A Victorian inkstand, with central taper holder and two cut ruby overlaid glass bottles, by Yapp and Woodward, Birmingham, 1850, 19cm., weight of taper holder and base 10 oz.
(Lawrence Fine Art) $889

A Scottish silver-mounted oak desk stand, of shaped oblong form, carved with thistles and foliage, maker's mark C.D., Inverness, hallmark Edinburgh, 1908, 12¹/₂in. wide.
(Christie's) $531

A silver inkwell, maker's mark of Shiebler & Co., New York, circa 1900, elaborately repoussé with scrolls and rocaille, the fitted silver-mounted glass bottles with fluted swirls, 10in. long, 19 oz. 10 dwt.
(Christie's) $3,080

A late Victorian ink stand, with beaded border and foliate engraved rim, the floriform stamped central panel supporting a diamond and slice cut globular glass ink well, 15.5cm. diameter.
(Spencer's) $313

An Old Sheffield plate globe inkstand on a reeded rising circular foot, applied with paterae and drapery swags, 8¹/₂in. overall.
(Christie's S. Ken) $710

A Victorian oblong inkstand, surmounted by two pierced octagonal inkwells, each with hinged cover, and a similar hexagonal central wafer box, by Joseph Angell, 1855, 14¹/₄in. long, 92oz.
(Christie's) $5,760

A large two-handled oblong treasury inkstand, with three internal inkwells labeled *RED*, *WRITING* and *COPYING*, engraved with the Prince of Wales crest, by Elkington and Co. Ltd., Birmingham, 1903, 12in. long, 117oz.
(Christie's) $8,228

An unusual Continental inkstand on a rising oval base, the inkwell itself finely-modeled and chased as the head of a wild boar resting on scrolling oak leaves, Berthold Muller, London 1910, 7in., 41 oz.
(Christie's S. Ken) $3,483

A good George VI silver mounted heavy clear glass inkwell, the silver mount with hinged and swivelling watch cover, Birmingham 1945, possibly by J. Grinsell & Sons, 11.5cm. square.
(Spencer's) $928

A rare Elizabeth I silver-gilt mounted tiger-ware jug, winged demi-cherub thumbpiece, 1561, maker's mark *GW*, 6½in. high. (Christie's)　　$19,860

A highly unusual milk jug, by Charles Fox, 4⅞in. high, the body chased with hare coursing scenes, London, 1830, 12.5oz. (Bonhams)　　$3,477

A George II pear shaped beer jug with cast scroll handle and lip, maker Fuller White, London 1753, 23oz., 8¼in. high. (Tennants)　　$3,888

A silver covered hot-milk jug, maker's mark of Tiffany & Co., New York, 1891–1902, the spot-hammered surface etched with foliage and thistles, 7in. high, 20 oz. 10 dwt. (Christie's)　　$3,300

A large Tiffany and Co. japanesque jug, the copper baluster body applied with three Sterling silver fish, stamped *Tiffany and Co.*, 21.5cm. high over frog. (Spencer's)　　$18,205

A late George III jug by Edward Edwards, with everted gadrooned rim and hinged flat domed cover, with polished treen handle, London 1817, 737gm. gross. (Spencer's)　　$662

An Edward VII large beer jug with reed strap handle, London 1903, 24oz., maker Goldsmith & Co., London. (Russell Baldwin & Bright)　　$709

A 19th century French silver colored metal hot water jug, the hinged gadrooned cover with applied pomegranate finial, Paris mark, 17cm. high. (Spencer's)　　$774

E. E. J. & W. Barnard, a naturalistic milk jug, melon paneled with foliage entwined root spout, rim and handle, London 1837, 7½oz. (Woolley & Wallis)　　$627

436

MUGS

Joseph Angell, a George IV mug, campana shape repoussé with dancing maidens, London 1830, 8³/₄oz.
(Woolley & Wallis) $676

Rare solid silver shaving mug, circular shaped on a stepped base with beaded edges, Birmingham 1905, 3¹/₂in. tall, 6oz.
(G. A. Key) $405

A pint mug with molded lip and foot, the scroll handle of tapering semi-circular section, by Langlands and Robertson, Newcastle, 1778, 10oz., 5in. high.
(Tennants) $707

A George III baluster pint mug with leaf-capped double scroll handle, W.T., London 1776, 5¹/₂in., 12.75oz.
(Christie's) $1,011

A Victorian mug, 5³/₈in. high, the fluted campana-shaped body chased with floral clusters, London, 1840, by Rawlins and Sumner, 10 ozs.
(Bonhams) $622

A silver mug, maker's mark of Tiffany & Co., New York, 1875–1891, baluster form on spreading rim foot, elaborately repoussé with flowers, 6in. high, 18 oz.
(Christie's) $2,200

A fine early Victorian campana shape half pint mug, chased and embossed with a cow and sheep in pastoral landscape, 5¹/₄in., John Evans II, London 1839, 6.5 oz.
(Woolley & Wallis) $851

Silver mug, George Hanners, Boston, circa 1740, tapering cylindrical form with molded mid-band and base band, scroll handle, 10 troy oz.
(Skinner Inc.) $5,500

A Victorian Aesthetic Movement mug, the body finely engraved with Japanese style swallows, foliage, half-circular and geometric patterns, 10cm. high, Edward Charles Brown, 1879, 6 ozs. (Phillips) $604

MUSTARDS

A Victorian gilt-lined pear-shaped mustard pot on floral and foliate feet, Henry Holland, London 1852, 3¹/₂in.
(Christie's) $645

A George III mustard pot, with bands of bright cut decoration, domed cover, by Crispin Fuller, 1792 (with a salt spoon of 1808), 9cm.
(Lawrence Fine Art) $1,197

A Victorian drum mustard pot with green glass liner with star-cut base, Reily and Storer, London 1847, 3¹/₄in.
(Christie's) $679

A French vase-shaped mustard pot, the bowl chased with a band of foliage and with double serpent scroll handle, Lille, circa 1755, maker's mark *I.B.H.*, 5¹/₄in., 274grs.
(Christie's) $5,634

A George IV gilt-lined part-fluted compressed vase-shaped mustard pot on a spreading circular foot, Philip Rundell, London 1822, 3³/₄in., 9.25oz.
(Christie's) $1,782

A Victorian barrel-shaped mustard pot realistically decorated with simulated staves and hoops and with an engraved bung hole, George Fox, London 1864, 3¹/₄in. high.
(Christie's) $540

An unusual Victorian mustard pot, 3¹/₂in. high, the flat hinged cover engraved with a crest and with an applied frog thumbpiece, London, 1850, by Charles and George Fox, 7 ozs.
(Bonhams) $1,323

A C.R. Ashbee hammered silver mustard pot, set with three amber cabochons, original clear glass liner, stamped *C R A* with London hallmarks for 1900, 6.5cm. high, 100 grams. gross.
(Christie's) $1,707

A George III mustard pot, 3³/₄in. high, with beaded borders and scroll handle, the hinged domed cover with urn finial, detachable blue glass liner, London, 1786, by Thomas Shepherd.
(Bonhams) $1,751

PITCHERS

Sterling silver water pitcher by Durgin, pedestal base, circa 1913, monogrammed, 28.4 troy oz.
(Eldred's) $468

Whiting Sterling and mixed metal water pitcher, 1881, bird and floral decoration, 8¹/₂in. high, approximately 33 troy oz.
(Skinner) $4,125

A silver water pitcher, maker's mark of John W. Forbes, New York, circa 1830, with foliate scroll handle and gadrooned rim, 12in. high, 31 oz. 10 dwt.
(Christie's) $1,540

Mexican silver water pitcher by William Spratling, Taxco, circa 1931–1945, fitted with a carved wooden handle with an abstracted bird mask design, 6⁵/₈in. high, 19oz., all in.
(Butterfield & Butterfield) $3,025

American silver hand wrought water pitcher by Herbert Taylor for Arthur Stone, Gardner, Massachusetts, circa 1935, with mild harp thumbrest, helmet brim spout, 40oz. 4dwts.
(Butterfield & Butterfield) $1,320

A silver water pitcher, maker's mark of Whiting Mfg. & Co., circa 1885, elaborately repoussé with flowers on a matted ground, 7¹/₈in. high, 23 oz. 10 dwt.
(Christie's) $1,870

American Arts and Crafts hand beaten silver pitcher by LeBolt, Chicago, Illinois, circa 1915–1920, applied with cypher monogram on the side, 8¹/₄in. high, 22oz. 6dwts.
(Butterfield & Butterfield) $1,540

An American silver and other metals 'Japanese style' water pitcher, Tiffany & Co., New York, circa 1875–80, 26oz. 15dwt. gross, height 7³/₄in.
(Sotheby's) $42,550

Georg Jensen Sterling water pitcher, 1922, marks of Copenhagen, Jensen, London import mark of 1922, 9in. high, approximately 18 troy oz.
(Skinner) $1,980

A set of twelve William IV shaped-circular soup plates, by William Eaton, 1832, 9³/₄in. diameter, 255oz.
(Christie's) $10,709

Set of eight J. E. Caldwell Sterling dinner plates, reticulated borders and engraved interiors, 12in., approximately 204 troy oz.
(Skinner) $6,050

Set of five Black, Starr & Frost Sterling plates, neoclassical design, approximately 107 troy oz.
(Skinner) $1,210

A set of twelve silver dinner plates, maker's mark of Howard & Co., New York, dated 1907, the center engraved with a coat-of-arms and crest, 10in. diameter, 292 oz.
(Christie's) $6,600

A parcel-gilt silver wheat-pattern serving plate and cake knife, maker's mark of Gorham Mfg. Co., Providence, 1871, the rim applied and chased with gilt wheat sheaves amid foliage, 10¹/₄in. diameter, 22 oz. 10 dwt.
(Christie's) $2,860

Twelve George III shaped circular dinner plates, with molded gadrooned borders engraved with two coats-of-arms and a Ducal coronet, by Andrew Fogelberg, 1773, 9¹/₂in. diameter, 203oz.
(Christie's) $18,497

German silver Pidyon Haben plate, mid 19th century, in the late 17th century style, the oval dish embossed and chased, struck with pseudo-Augsburg and other marks, 13³/₄in. wide, 18oz. 10dwts.
(Butterfield & Butterfield) $4,125

Eight American octagonal dessert plates, each with fluted shaped border, by Black Starr & Frost, stamped Sterling, 817, 7in. wide, 54oz.
(Christie's) $567

Twelve American Sterling service plates by International Silver Co., Meriden, Connecticut, Trianon, 10¹/₂in. diameter, 234oz.
(Butterfield & Butterfield) $3,850

SALTS

A rare trencher salt, maker's mark of Richard Conyers, Boston, circa 1700, with gadrooned rim and foot rim, 2¹/₈in. high, 1 oz. 10 dwt.
(Christie's) $18,700

A pair of salts by Tiffany & Co., New York, 1870–1875, with a die-rolled guilloche border and three cast ram's-head feet, 3in. diam, 4 oz.
(Christie's) $780

A Guild of Handicraft lidded hammered silver salt dish, set with a cabochon amethyst, with green Powell glass liner, with London hallmarks for 1904, 5.5cm. high, 50 grams. gross.
(Christie's) $598

A fine and rare pair of silver salt cellars, maker's mark of Simeon Coley, New York, 1767–1769, on four scroll feet with scallop-shell knees and stepped pad feet, 3¹/₄in. wide, 6 oz.
(Christie's) $3,080

A set of four George III large circular salt cellars, each on dished circular stand with three bracket feet chased with anthemion ornament, by Benjamin and James Smith, 1810, 4¹/₂in. diameter, 74oz.
(Christie's) $19,785

A pair of French shaped-oval trencher salts, each on scroll base and with quatrefoil rims, Arles, 1750, 130 grs.
(Christie's) $2,112

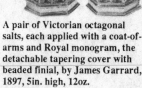

A pair of Victorian salt cellars, each on cast simulated coral and seaweed base, by John Mortimer and John S. Hunt, 1845, 3³/₄in. wide, 22oz.
(Christie's) $6,930

A George III good set of four cauldron salts, the bellied circular bodies finely chased with sprays of flowers and leaves, by Thomas Holland II, 1808, 34 ozs.
(Phillips) $5,090

A pair of Victorian octagonal salts, each applied with a coat-of-arms and Royal monogram, the detachable tapering cover with beaded finial, by James Garrard, 1897, 5in. high, 12oz.
(Christie's) $5,940

SAUCEBOATS

Danish Sterling sauceboat, Georg Jensen, Copenhagen, circa 1925–1930, plain long oval vessel with twisted flat wire handle, 6½in. high, 14oz. 8 dwts. (Butterfield & Butterfield)

$1,760

One of a pair of George III sauce boats on shell and hoof feet, maker's initials *W.F.*, London 1766, 7½in., 18.50oz. (Christie's)

(Two) $1,205

A silver-gilt mounted agate sauceboat, Charles Rawlings & William Summers, London, 1848, the handle formed as a wriggling snake, 6¼in. long. (Sotheby's) $1,364

Pair of French silver sauce boats, late 19th century, helmet form with mythical beast handle, 8⅜in. high, approximately 52 troy oz. (Skinner Inc.) $4,950

A pair of silver sauce boats, maker's mark of Marquand & Co., New York, 1833–1839, 9½in. long, 34oz. (Christie's) $3,080

A pair of George III Irish plain shaped-oval sauceboats, each on cast spreading foot and with leaf-capped scroll handle, by Robert Calderwood, Dublin, circa 1760, 8in. long, 33oz. (Christie's) $12,870

A pair of plain helmet-shaped sauce boats, each on rectangular base with reeded borders and scroll handles, by Hawkesworth Eyre & Co. Ltd., 1911, weight 20oz. (Christie's) $1,180

Swedish silver sauceboat, Bengt Fredrik Tellander, Jonkoping, early 19th century, with applied classical medallions on the sides, 5¾in. high, 5oz. 12 dwts. (Butterfield & Butterfield) $715

A pair of George II shaped-oval sauceboats, each with quilted double-scroll handle and gadrooned rim, by William Cripps, 1750, 8¼in. long, 29oz. (Christie's) $7,399

SILVER

A Queen Anne small tapering tankard with scroll handle and spreading foot, maker Thomas Holland, London 1709, 6oz., 3¹/₂in. high.
(Tennants) $1,053

A Swedish gilt-lined lidded tankard in the 17th century taste, on ball feet, 8¹/₂in.
(Christie's) $1,477

A silver tankard, maker's mark of William Cowell, Sr. or Jr., Boston, 1725–1740, the scroll handle with molded drop, 7⁷/₈in. high, 29oz.
(Christie's) $7,700

A Queen Anne plain tapering cylindrical tankard, with scroll handle, hinged domed cover and bifurcated thumbpiece, by Seth Lofthouse, 1705, 7¹/₄in. high, 27oz.
(Christie's) $5,940

A Hukin & Heath electroplated tankard designed by Dr. Christopher Dresser, tapering cylindrical form with ebonized bar handle, 21.5cm. high.
(Christie's) $748

A George III plain tapering cylindrical tankard, the body with applied rib and with scroll handle, hinged domed cover and corkscrew thumbpiece, by Charles Wright, 1772, 7³/₄in. high, 24oz.
(Christie's) $3,762

A fine silver tankard, maker's mark of John Moulinar, New York, circa 1750, applied with a band of cut-card leaves above the moulded foot rim, 7¹/₄in. long, 35oz.
(Christie's) $38,500

A George II plain tankard and cover, with scroll handle and domed cover with openwork thumbpiece, by Francis Spilsbury, 1741, 7¹/₂in. high, 28 oz.
(Christie's) $4,576

A Charles II plain tapering cylindrical tankard, the handle pricked with initials, the body later engraved with a coat-of-arms within plume mantling, by John Sutton, 1672, 6in. high, 22oz. (Christie's) $9,422

TEA CADDIES

A tea caddy, the hammered body chased and embossed with tulips, signed *Gilbert Marks 1898*, 4³/₄in., London 1897, 10oz. (Woolley & Wallis) $2,241

A pair of George II oblong tea caddies, each chased with bands of scrolls, foliage and rocaille ornament and engraved with initials, by William Soloman, 1758, 4¹/₂in. high, gross 46oz. (Christie's) $8,291

A silver tea caddy, maker's mark of Tiffany & Co., New York, 1891–1902, elaborately repoussé with flowers on a matted ground, 4¹/₂in. high, 7 oz. 10 dwt. (Christie's) $935

A Queen Anne octagonal baluster tea caddy and cover, the detachable cover with shaped finial, the base engraved with initials, by Ebenezer Roe, 1711, 4³/₄ in. high, 6oz. (Christie's) $3,366

Two George II and George III oblong tea caddies, engraved with a foliage and trelliswork design, the covers with similar scroll borders, one by Edward Wakelin, circa 1755, the other by J. Langford and J. Sebille, 1764, 28oz. (Christie's) $6,930

A George III oblong tea caddy, the sides and cover finely engraved with ribbon ornament, festoons of husks and foliage, 1772, maker's mark *I.L.*, 4¹/₂in. high, 6oz. (Christie's) $3,185

A Victorian tea caddy in Indian taste, the engraved borders including a band of figures, animals and fish, by Richard Sibley, 1867, 9.5cm., 8.5oz. (Lawrence Fine Art) $734

A pair of silver-gilt tea caddies, rectangular, die-struck, with amorini and leafage, by Gorham, circa 1890, 14.5cm., 18oz. (Phillips) $1,328

A silver tea caddy, maker's mark of Tiffany & Co., New York, 1879–1891, the shoulder and slip on cap chased with scrolls, 8¹/₈in. high, 9 oz. (Christie's) $1,320

TEA KETTLES

An American silver Japanese-style tea kettle on stand, Gorham Mfg. Co., Providence, RI, 1883, 57oz., height 12in. (Sotheby's) $1,380

George V silver kettle on stand, Hunt and Roskell Ltd., London, 1933–34, stand with shell feet, 13in. high, 44 troy oz. (Skinner Inc.) $880

A late 19th century spirit kettle, richly chased allover à rocaille, part ivory handle, Vienna, 34.5cm., 1710gr. (Finarte) $2,352

A German 19th century spiral-fluted compressed pear-shaped swing-handled tea kettle with fluted rising curved spout, Friedlander, 16in., 56.25oz. gross. (Christie's S. Ken) $1,220

A silver kettle on stand, maker's mark of *Gorham Mfg. Co., Providence, 1885–1895*, the sides elaborately repoussé and chased with flowers on a matted ground, 12in. high, gross weight 66oz. (Christie's) $1,430

A good George I tea kettle-on-stand, 12in. high, compressed pear-shape with faceted spout, fully hallmarked for London, 1723, by Thomas Farrer, 70 ozs. all in. (Bonhams) $30,000

An imposing silver plate kettle on stand of later Georgian design with bright cut motifs, supported on Greek inspired base, 18in. high. (Locke & England) $416

A Victorian plain tapering tea kettle with rising curved spout, scroll handle and flattened rising hinged cover, Hunt and Roskell, London 1869, 12³/₄in., 46oz. (Christie's S. Ken) $1,316

Russian tea kettle and stand, bone inlaid swing handle and finial, St. Petersburg 1759, 1700gr. (Galerie Koller Zürich) $13,108

TEA POTS

E. E. J. & W. Barnard, a
naturalistic tea pot, melon
paneled with foliate entwined
root spout and handle, London
1837, 24oz.
(Woolley & Wallis) $1,188

A silver teapot, maker's mark of
Gerardus Boyce, New York,
circa 1830, 7⅞in. high, gross
weight 21oz.
(Christie's) $1,045

A George III oval teapot on
matching stand, the pot of
straight sided oval section,
6¾in. long, Andrew Fogelberg,
London 1799, 578 gms, 18.5 oz.
(Bearne's) $2,118

Silver teapot, Joseph Lownes,
Philadelphia, circa 1800,
engraved with foliate monogram
on circular pedestal foot with
square base, 11in. high, 26 troy
oz.
(Skinner Inc.) $2,310

A George I plain octagonal
teapot, on narrow rim foot and
with curved spout, hinged
domed cover and baluster finial,
by Joseph Clare, 1715, 6in. high,
gross 14oz.
(Christie's) $19,800

An electroplated teapot on
stand, the design attributed to
Dr. Christopher Dresser, the
circular cover with cylindrical
ebonized finial, on tripod stand,
with spirit burner, 19.7cm. high.
(Christie's) $748

George III silver teapot and
matching stand, London, 1801,
with incurvate shoulder and
domed hinged lid fitted with an
ivory finial, 6¾in. high, 17oz.
14 dwts.
(Butterfield & Butterfield)
                        $1,430

An early Victorian teapot,
chased and repoussé with
flowerheads, acanthus leaves
and rococo scrolls, with cast and
applied flower knop, London
1853, maker's mark W.M., 497
grammes gross.
(Spencer's) $635

George IV Scottish silver teapot
by John McKay, Edinburgh,
1827, with a knopped leaf-
wrapped berry finial, the body
chased in repoussé with rocaille,
scrolls, flowers and a scroll
framed cartouche, 27oz. 10dwts.
(Butterfield & Butterfield)
                         $770

TOAST RACKS

A George III oval six-division toast rack, the base with reeded rim, London 1792, by Peter and Ann Bateman.
(Greenslade Hunt) **$614**

A George III toast tray, 10in. long, the oval body with moulded border and scroll end grips, the four triple hooped bars detachable, London 1785, possibly by John Tweedie, 7oz.
(Bonhams) **$550**

A rare silver toast rack, maker's mark of A. E. Warner, Baltimore, 1818, 8³/₄in. long, 7oz. 10dwt.
(Christie's) **$6,600**

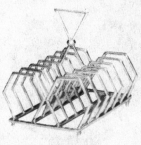

A James Dixon & Sons electroplated toast rack designed by Dr. Christopher Dresser, with seven triangular supports, on four spike feet and with raised vertical handles, 13.5cm. high.
(Christie's) **$3,287**

A Guild of Handicraft silver toast rack, on bun feet, with repoussé decoration of stylized fish and cabochon turquoises, London hallmarks for 1904, 12.5cm. high, 230 grams.
(Christie's) **$2,560**

A rare James Dixon & Sons electroplated toast rack designed by Dr. Christopher Dresser, on four pin feet supporting seven parallel hexagonal sections, 16.7cm. long.
(Christie's) **$5,907**

A rare James Dixon & Sons electroplated toast rack, designed by Dr. Christopher Dresser, divisions with lunette shaped designs, central loop handle, 8.5cm. high.
(Christie's) **$7,832**

A Hukin & Heath electroplated toast rack designed by Dr. Christopher Dresser, on pad feet, the arch base with seven supports, 14cm. high.
(Christie's) **$630**

An Edwardian novelty five bar toast rack by Heath & Middleton, the wire work rack forming the letters 'Toast', Birmingham 1906, 94 grammes, 12.5cm. wide.
(Spencer's) **$282**

TRAYS & SALVERS

A fine silver chrysanthemum-pattern tea tray, maker's mark of Tiffany & Co., New York, 1902–1907, with cast chrysanthemum border, 29in. long, 270 oz. 10 dwt.
(Christie's) $22,000

A Danish shaped-circular salver, with foliage border and the center engraved with a paterae, Copenhagen, circa 1740, maker's mark illegible, assaymaster Peter Nicolai von Haven, 11½in. diameter, 831grs.
(Christie's) $3,291

A George IV two handled tray, with gadroon, shell and foliate border and leafy scroll handles, by William Bateman I, 1826, 66cm., approximately 114oz.
(Lawrence Fine Art)
                                $4,826

A George II silver-gilt shaped-circular salver, the border cast and chased with Bacchanalian masks and applied with trailing vines, by Charles Frederick Kandler, 1738, 13½in. diameter, 50 oz.
(Christie's) $4,576

A pair of William IV shaped rectangular snuffers trays, with gadroon, acanthus and foliate edging, 9¾in. long, maker's mark *W.E.* possibly that of William Eaton, London 1830, 798 gms, 25.6 oz.
(Bearne's) $1,579

A fine silver and mixed-metal salver, maker's mark of Tiffany & Co., New York, circa 1880, the spot-hammered surface inlaid with three butterflies of copper, gold, platinum, and brass, 11in. diameter, 26 oz. 10 dwt.
(Christie's) $13,200

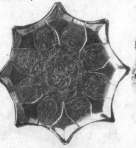

An American silver rectangular tray, Gorham Mfg. Co., Providence, RI, 1899, Martelé, .950 standard, 42oz. 10dwt., length 15in.
(Sotheby's) $6,325

Mixed metal salver in the Persian taste by Tiffany & Co., New York, New York, circa 1880, of shaped octagonal form, 12in. wide, 26oz. 14 dwts.
(Butterfield & Butterfield)
                                $9,350

An Edwardian dressing table tray, with stamped and pierced scroll and flower work folded border, Birmingham 1907, 284 grammes, 12in. wide.
(Spencer's) $448

A George IV silver-gilt two-handled campana-shaped wine cooler, collar and liner, by Paul Storr 1825, 11½in. high, 157oz. (Christie's) $19,861

Fine silver plated champagne bucket, 20th century, with applied vintage decoration, engraved inscription, 11½in. high. (Eldred's) $743

Edwardian silver wine cooler, Edward Barnard & Sons, Ltd., London, 1901-02, 7¾in. high, approx. 29 troy oz. (Skinner) $1,210

American Sterling Arts and Crafts wine cooler by Shreve & Co., San Francisco, California, circa 1909–1922, with pair bracket handles at sides, overall peened finish, 8½in. high, 45oz. 12dwts. (Butterfield & Butterfield) $2,475

A Victorian two-handled campana-shaped champagne cooler, the rockwork and scroll base on three shell and scroll feet, by John Hunt and Robert Roskell, 1865, 16½in. high, 214oz. (Christie's) $10,557

Art Nouveau Sterling wine cooler by Mauser Mfg. Co., New York, circa 1900–1910, with outwardly tapering sides rising to an irregular pierced lip applied with grape clusters and leaves, 10in. high, 72oz. 9 dwts. (Butterfield & Butterfield) $2,000

An American silver wine cooler, Gorham Mfg. Co., Providence, RI, 1906, derived from the Florentine pattern, 104oz., 12⅜in. high. (Sotheby's) $7,150

An Indian silver wine cooler of urn shape, the body decorated with various wild animals, stamped on base *CKC & Sons, Silver, Bangalore*, 100oz., 14in. diameter. (Peter Francis) $860

A Victorian two-handled campana-shaped wine cooler, on spreading circular foot and with dolphin and scroll handles, by Benjamin Smith, 1840, 11½in. high, 74 oz. (Christie's) $7,040

Good white jade snuff bottle, late 19th century, carved as a ripe melon enclosed by leafy fruiting melon vines and a rat.
(Butterfield & Butterfield)
$660

A glass overlay bottle, carved through a layer of red glass to the snowstorm ground, hefengdi, with a frog on a lotus spray to one face, 19th century.
(Christie's)
$2,027

A green glass snuff bottle of flattened ovoid form carved in relief with gourds issuing from a leafy branch, stopper, 19th century.
(Christie's)
$1,921

Mongolian silver-mounted jade snuff bottle, of pale green tone mottling to white with dark brown striations.
(Butterfield & Butterfield)
$495

A fine and rare Yangzhou-school glass overlay snuff bottle of spade shape, carved with three rams beside a tree below the moon, 18th/19th century.
(Christie's)
$12,236

An inside-painted glass snuff bottle of rounded rectangular shape, painted with small figures in a sampan below trees before a mountainous backdrop.
(Christie's)
$4,545

An agate snuff bottle, the ocher inclusions carved to the front to form five monkeys in different postures staring at a bee, circa 1800.
(Christie's)
$3,841

A metal and enameled snuff bottle of Meiping form, the body incised with scrolling foliage, 19th century.
(Bonhams)
$224

A glass overlay snuff bottle each face carved through layers of black and red to a white ground with a horse tethered to a pine tree, 19th century.
(Christie's)
$4,268

An extremely rare Imperial porcelain snuff bottle, moulded in relief and decorated in famille rose enamels with a continuous landscape scene.
(Christie's) $17,772

Good Peking glass overlay snuff bottle, the milky-white body overlaid in rose, purple and lavender.
(Butterfield & Butterfield) $6,600

A glass snuff bottle, 19th century, the clear body with spots of pale caramel tone beneath others of dark chocolate color imitating tortoiseshell, stopper.
(Christie's) $1,998

A four-color glass overlay snuff bottle, 19th century, carved with overlay of tones of orange, yellow, lime-green and blue to depict butterflies in flight, stopper.
(Christie's) $5,627

An unusual Beijing glass snuff bottle, late Qing dynasty, naturalistically molded as a lychee with characteristic bosses and leaves issuing from below the neck.
(Christie's) $1,926

A fine agate snuff bottle, 18th/19th century, cleverly carved to emphasise the honey-colored banding as an oblong melon with smaller fruit growing from a vine on each side, stopper.
(Christie's) $2,221

A fine agate snuff bottle, 19th century, relief carved with a tethered horse beneath a tree, the stone of rich honey tone, stopper.
(Christie's) $7,243

A glass snuff bottle, 19th century, the bubble-suffused glass body with layers of amber and ocher spots imitating realgar.
(Christie's) $888

A small glass snuff bottle, 19th century, the opaque glass body with a mottled run of yellow, brown, white and blue spots, stopper.
(Christie's) $1,185

A Staffordshire enamel circular box, the cover modeled in relief, the base decorated with floral sprigs and gilt scrollwork, 4.5cm. (Phillips) $1,594

A Victorian oblong snuff-box, the center engraved with two huntsmen in a landscape, the sides chased with flowers and scrolls and with engine-turned base, by Nathaniel Mills, Birmingham, 1849, 4½in. wide, 10oz. (Christie's) $2,073

A Mennecy silver-mounted snuff-box and cover naturalistically modeled as an apple and colored in shades of yellow and purple with some dark blemishes, circa 1755, 6.5cm. diameter. (Christie's) $1,387

A Berlin gilt-metal-mounted rectangular snuff-box, the interior of the cover finely stippled in colors with a lady at her dressing table trimming her pigtail accompanied by a gallant, circa 1780, 8.5cm. wide. (Christie's) $5,513

A Meissen gold-mounted waisted rectangular Purpurmalerei snuff-box painted in the style of Watteau with gallants and companions in idyllic landscapes, circa 1750, 7.5cm. wide. (Christie's) $8,109

A George III octagonal two-colored gold and purpurine presentation table snuff-box, the cover set with an enamel miniature of John Iggulden with white hair and sideburns, by William Grimaldi, signed and dated *1816*, 4¼in. long. (Christie's) $15,576

A fine gilt lined snuff box, engraved *The passengers on The Falcon beg Capt. John Adams to accept this small token in admiration of his Seamanship on the passage to Port Sydney. 21st day of May 1829.* (Woolley & Wallis) $38,700

A Mennecy snuff-box as a seated man crouched on a mound base with his arms and legs crossed, circa 1750, 5.5cm. high. (Christie's) $1,091

A cartouche-shaped piqué blond tortoiseshell snuff-box, the cover piqué posé with a couple dancing within an elaborate strapwork and scroll border, circa 1740, 3¼in. wide. (Christie's) $3,894

A Regency oval vari-colored gold and hardstone snuff-box, the cover set with a panel of mottled brown agate, by Alexander James Strachan, London, 1817, 3½in. long. (Christie's) $7,920

A Staffordshire enamel masonic snuff box, the cover painted with masonic insignia divided by a flower spray, 5.5cm. wide. (Phillips) $1,190

A Napoleon III shaped-rectangular gold snuff-box, the cover chased with War Trophies and foliage in four-color gold surrounding the initial N, circa 1855, 3³⁄₈in. wide. (Christie's) $24,640

A Continental oblong vari-colored gold and enamel presentation snuff-box, the cover with an oval miniature of Marshal Bernadotte, in the manner of Autissier, circa 1820, 3½in. wide. (Christie's) $8,567

An attractive Staffordshire enamel casket-shaped box with hinged cover, painted in colors with vignettes of figures in landscapes, 7cm. (Phillips) $359

A fine late 17th/early 18th century oval gilt-lined snuff box, the lid engraved with many emblems purporting to relate to the Stuart monarchy and the Jacobite cause, possibly Lawrence Coles, circa 1697, 3¹⁄₈in. (Christie's S. Ken) $8,857

A French porcelain snuff box and cover with silver mounts, probably St. Cloud, painted with birds, flowers and foliage, 8.2cm. wide, 18th century. (Bearne's) $845

A South Staffordshire enamel snuff-box formed as a finch, the hinged cover painted with parrot pecking grapes, with gilt-metal mount, circa 1765, 2³⁄₈in. long. (Christie's) $3,520

A good 18th century copper-gilt snuff box of cartouche shape chased with a courting couple, by James Ferguson, 7cm. wide, circa 1745. (Phillips) $704

SPECTACLES

A pair of brass framed Chinese spectacles, with folding sides and quartz lenses. **$375**

A rare pair of 'Nuremburg' single wire round rim nose-spectacles, with 'Martins Margins' tortoiseshell visual inserts, frames 17th century, visuals later circa 1758. (Christie's) **$5,181**

An 18th century pair of steel ring side spectacles with tinted lenses in a leather case, 5in. long. **$364**

A rare pair of 'Nuremburg' single wire, round rim nose-spectacles, in flat-edged grooved copper wire with chamois leather fitted cover, German 17th century. (Christie's) **$8,203**

A fine pair of 'Nuremburg' single wire round rim nose spectacles, in flat edged grooved copper wire, with *NUREMBURG* raised in relief on flat arched bridge, German, mid 17th century, 15mm. diameter lens. (Christie's) **$9,499**

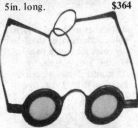

A pair of iron Martins Margins, arched bridge, folding sides with large ring ends, inserted horn vissuals, 1 inch diameter lens, English circa 1760. (Christie's) **$604**

A pair of 'Nuremburg' single wire round rim nose spectacles, with arched bridge in grooved copper wire, German, late 17th century, 4in. wide. (Christie's) **$864**

A rare pair of 'Nuremburg' grooved single wire copper nose spectacles in fitted compartment located in front cover of book, Arndt, Johann., *Sechs Bucher vom Wahren Christentum* Erfurt 1753. (Christie's) **$19,088**

A rare pair of Chinese lacquered frame spectacles, brass cased folding bridge with clasp and ear threads, possibly 18th century, 4½in. wide. (Christie's) **$1,295**

A pair of silver oval lens spectacles with segmental bridge, in fitted silver mounted tortoiseshell case, 5½in. long. (Christie's) **$243**

A pair of silver green tint D end spectacles, with segmental bridge, and folding sides with pad ends. (Christie's) **$260**

A pair of silver round lens spectacles, arched bridge, in brown dyed shagreen case, late 18th century, 5⅛in. long. (Christie's) **$281**

454

A pair of silver and tortoiseshell Martins Margins, with round lens, tortoiseshell inserts inscribed *12*, makers initials stamped *I S*.
(Christie's) **$711**

A rare pair of late 18th century steel double 'D' end spectacles, with segmental bridge, folding side panels, in wood case.
(Christie's) **$322**

A pair of white metal spectacles, probably Swedish, first quarter 19th century, with oval lens, C-bridge, hinged temples with teardrop ends.
(Bonham's) **$61**

A fine pair of Martins Margins, with round lens, arched bridge, horn inserts, circa 1760, in pressed leather covered case.
(Christie's) **$593**

A rare pair of Chevalier binocular spectacles, silver plated frame, with tortoiseshell body tube covers, with maker's plaque *Chevallier a Paris*, circa 1807, 4³/₄in. wide.
(Christie's) **$6,776**

A pair of double glass spectacles, probably English, first quarter 19th century, with steel frames and folding temples with tear-shaped ends.
(Bonham's) **$153**

A pair of 'Nuremberg' single wire round rim nose-spectacles, in flat edged grooved copper wire, with leather nose grips, circa 1700, 1³/₄in. high.
(Christie's) **$3,557**

A rare pair of leather 'Nuremberg' nose spectacles, with impressed decorated arched bridge, flat glass, round lens, early 17th century, 3³/₄in. wide.
(Christie's) **$6,268**

A rare pair of Ayscough-type rivet nose spectacles, with silver folding bridge stamped with makers mark *SS*, with tortoiseshell frames, 2³/₄in. wide.
(Christie's) **$2,033**

A pair of 'Martins Margins' spectacles, probably English, circa 1800, with steel frames, horn lens holders and 2cm diameter lens.
(Bonham's) **$260**

A pair of blued steel spectacles, with round lens, with manuscript memorandum in ink *These spectacles belonged to the Duke of Wellington*.
(Christie's) **$1,271**

A pair of 'Nuremberg' single wire round lens nose spectacles, with arched bridge in grooved gilded copper wire, German, late 17th century.
(Christie's) **$1,440**

A Brewster-pattern hand-held stereoscope with painted floral decoration, green painted pattern and gilt design.
(Christie's) $1,040

A nickel-body Votra stereo viewer.
(Christie's) $782

A hand-held stereoscope with dividing eyepieces, hinged lid and inset maker's label *London Stereoscopic Company, 313 Oxford St.*
(Christie's) $229

A wood-body stereo-graphoscope, with rising magnifier, removable collapsable viewing shade with ground glass screen and photograph holder inset into graphoscope top.
(Christie's) $426

A wood-body patent reflecting stereoscope with screw focusing eyepiece section, hinged lid with label *Chappuis' patent.*
(Christie's) $1,314

A coin operated musical clock and stereo viewer by Henri Vidoudez, St. Croix, the walnut table viewer with Swiss cylinder music works and 57-tone comb, 50cm. high, circa 1900.
(Auction Team Köln) $5,787

Keystone View Co., London, three hand-held Holmes-pattern stereoscopes with a large quantity of stereocards.
(Christie's) $653

An American Stereoscopic Co. Brewster pattern hand held stereoscope with gilt tooled leather covered body.
(Christie's S. Ken) $305

A wooden stereo graphoscope and photograph viewer with white metal decoration and five stereocards. (Christie's S. Ken) $202

A burr walnut Brewster pattern stereoscope with rack and pinion focusing, shaped lens hood mounted on hinged lens section.
(Christie's S. Ken) $337

A wood-body stereoscopic Kromaz color viewer with brass fittings, stereoscopic slide holder, inset label *Barnard & Gowenlock's Kromax.*
(Christie's) $963

A wood-body hand-held Brewster-pattern stereoscope with hinged top, ground glass screen and a pair of focusing eyepieces.
(Christie's) $171

Gaumont, Paris, a 45 x 107mm. mahogany bodied table stereoscope with internal mechanism and slide holders. (Christie's S. Ken) $598

A Jules Richard 'Le Taxiphote' stereoscope, French, circa 1910, the mahogany body with dividing and focusing eyepieces, nine trays of glass diapositives, 49cm high.
(Bonham's) $337

ICA, Dresden, a 45 x 107mm. wood-body automatic stereoscope with a pair of focusing viewing lenses.
(Christie's) $457

Gaumont, Paris, a metal-body table-top automatic 45 x 107mm. stereoscope with dividing eyepieces and internal slide magazine.
(Christie's) $312

A Brewster-pattern hand-held stereoscope with Japanese lacquer-work decoration depicting flying storks and trees.
(Christie's S. Ken.) $726

A mahogany body Kinora viewer with metal eyeshade, hand-crank mechanism and fourteen reels.
(Christie's) $1,059

A late 19th-century brass transit telescope, by Troughton & Simms, the 1³/₄ inch diameter telescope with lens hood and dust cap, 20¹/₄in. wide. (Christie's) $1,891

A rare brass circumferentor signed *G. ADAMS*, with four detachable sighting vanes, twin rotating verniers, compass box divided 10°–360°, late 18th century, 14¹/₂in. wide. (Christie's) $1,648

A rare early 19th-century lacquered brass transit telescopic surveyor's compass, the telescope with bubble level and cross wire adjustors, 10in. wide. (Christie's) $1,786

A rare early 19th-century miniature equatorial surveying telescope, signed on the base plate W & S Jones, the telescope with twin pin-hole sights and draw-tube focusing, 9¹/₂in. high. (Christie's) $4,622

A fine 19th century lacquered brass 'double telescope' surveying level, signed on the silvered dial *Pistor and Martins BERLIN*, 10¹/₄in. high. (Christie's S. Ken) $6,425

An exceptionally rare 19th-century oxidized, lacquered brass and silvered equatorial/azimuth sextant, signed on the latitude ring *Patent Applied for by Wm. A. Burt*, 12⁵/₈in. high. (Christie's) $14,707

A 19th-century surveyor's compass, signed on the silvered dial *W. & L. E. Gurley, Troy, N.Y.*, the blued-iron needle with jeweled cap and pivot, 6¹/₂in. high. (Christie's) $546

A 19th-century lacquered brass surveyor's cross, signed on the silvered compass dial *W & T Gilbert London*, in mahogany case, 4³/₄in. wide. (Christie's) $840

A late 19th century brass transit, by Cary, the telescope with 'V' and bead sights, the axis with vertical circle divided in four quadrants, 19¹/₂in. high. (Christie's S. Ken) $2,703

458

An Anglo-Indian ivory and tortoiseshell table-cabinet, enclosing a fitted interior of nine various-sized hardwood-lined drawers, late 17th century, possibly Dutch or Portuguese Colonial, 15in. wide.
(Christie's) **$4,897**

An Italian ebony and bone-inlaid table cabinet of canted inverted breakfront outline inlaid overall with scrolling foliage, flowerheads and grotesque masks, 36in. wide, late 19th century, probably Milanese. (Christie's S. Ken) **$5,320**

A 19th century Continental painted casket, 11in. wide, with pierced brass gallery.
(Dreweatt Neate) **$5,850**

A Japanese lacquer cabinet decorated with birds in a mountainous landscape, applied throughout with engraved brass corner mounts, hinges and escutcheons, 36in. wide.
(Bearne's) **$1,204**

A gold, silver and mother-of-pearl-inlaid brown tortoiseshell table-cabinet inlaid overall with foliate scrolls, first half 19th century, probably English, $23^{1}/_{2}$in. wide.
(Christie's) **$12,870**

Fine jewelry chest in rosewood with mother-of-pearl inlaid bird and flower decoration, circa 1840, 15in. long.
(Eldred's) **$935**

A French 'Sèvres' porcelain and gilt-bronze table casket, Napoléon III, Paris, circa 1865, of rectangular form, the deep lid set with a plaque of cupids and a young maiden, the canted corners with porcelain columns, 50cm. wide.
(Sotheby's) **$21,715**

A William and Mary oyster olivewood veneered table cabinet, the rectangular top, sides and pair of doors geometrically inlaid with boxwood lines, 1ft. 8in. wide.
(Phillips) **$1,988**

A 19th century Anglo-Indian padouk veneered and ivory inlaid table cabinet, inlaid all-over with a foliate design and checker strung and crossbanded, 12in. wide.
(Christie's S. Ken)
$3,103

A 17th century Flemish verdure tapestry, possibly woven in Oudenarde, with a pair of swans swimming on a pond in the left hand corner of a wooded landscape, 8ft. 6in. x 14ft. 2in.
(Phillips) $20,670

A Flemish Old Testament tapestry, circa 1600, probably Enghien, perhaps from the Story of Eliezur and Rebecca, 10ft. 6in. x 12ft. 9in.
(Sotheby's) $19,544

Aubusson mythological tapestry, late 17th century, the rectangular panel with a mythological scene in a formal garden with a fountain before a pergola screen, a group to its left composed of four figures, a woman wearing a floral garland and classical style clothing standing with arms outstretched, 13ft. 7in. x 9ft. 8in.
(Butterfield & Butterfield) $22,000

Brussels baroque tapestry: Marcus Aurelius reprimanding Faustina, circa 1670, woven in tones of reds, blues and beige, 10ft. 10in. x 11ft. 10in.
(Butterfield & Butterfield) $13,200

An 18th century Flemish verdure tapestry, depicting a characteristic woodland scene with a waterfall running into a stream, 6ft. 10in. x 8ft. 7in.
(Phillips) $9,014

An 18th century Flemish tapestry, probably Brussels, depicting a hawking scene with a group of three ladies, watching a falconer with a falcon on his hand, 10ft. 6in. x 11ft.
(Phillips) $10,335

Flemish baroque verdure tapestry, depicting a fortified town in middle distance in a wooded landscape including flowering plants and exotic birds and animals by a stream, 6ft. 6in. x 9ft. 11in.
(Butterfield & Butterfield) $4,950

A 19th century Flemish verdure tapestry, a landscape filled with tall trees with a peacock in the right forefront in shades of blue, biscuit, sepia and dark brown, 10ft. 6in. x 14ft. 10in.
(Phillips) $17,490

A Brussels tapestry, woven in silks and wools with a battle scene in a pass, with a prophet and attendants on a rocky outcrop above, early 18th century, 140 x 151in.
(Christie's) $23,418

A mid-Victorian Windsor tapestry, from the series of eight The Merry Wives of Windsor, woven in wools and silks depicting the legend of Slender and Anne Page, 76$^{1}/_{2}$ x 87$^{1}/_{2}$in.
(Christie's) $10,626

Flemish verdure tapestry of Diana and Actaeon, 19th century, the goddess striding with a staff in her hand and looking over at Actaeon as he emerges from bushes holding a dog by its collar, 6ft. 4$^{1}/_{2}$in. x 5ft. $^{1}/_{2}$in.
(Butterfield & Butterfield) $3,575

A Brussels tapestry woven in silks and wools with Moses in a basket before Pharaoh's daughter, in an exotic wooded landscape with buildings beyond, early 18th century, 140 x 150in.
(Christie's) $21,747

A Victorian papier mâché tea caddy, circa 1850, by Jennings and Bettridge, inlaid with mother-of-pearl, 6¹/₂in. wide. (John Nicholson) $335

An early 19th century tea caddy in the form of a house with two dormer windows and chimney, the interior with two lidded compartments, 17cm. high. (Phillips) $950

A Regency rosewood-veneered and multiple banded tea caddy, of rectangular form, having lion-mask handles and paw feet, the interior adapted with a metal liner, 30cm. wide. (Phillips) $460

A Federal inlaid mahogany tea-caddy, New York, 1790–1810, the rectangular hinged top with rounded recessed corners with inlaid fluting centering an inlaid conch, 6in. wide. (Christie's) $1,650

A George III white metal-mounted ivory and tortoiseshell tea-caddy with decagonal hinged top with handle enclosing a well, 4¹/₂in. wide. (Christie's) $1,881

An early Victorian tortoiseshell veneered and mother-of-pearl inlaid tea caddy of oblong form, the lid and front panel decorated with trailing thistle and flower motifs, 16.5cm. wide. (Phillips) $900

An inlaid maple tea-caddy, American, possibly mid-Atlantic, 1780-1800, the rectangular hinged lid with line-inlaid and crossbanded edges centering an inlaid conch, 7¹/₂in. wide. (Christie's) $345

A George III amaranth, rosewood and marquetry tea-caddy of rectangular shape with stepped top surmounted by an ormolu Classical urn within a spotted circle of friendship, the interior fitted circa 1820, 13¹/₂in. wide. (Christie's) $32,912

A good William IV papier-mâché tea caddy, of rectangular form, the front of arc en arbalette section, with splayed apron, the lid painted with a spray of summer flowers, 12¹/₂in. wide. (Phillips) $884

A Queen Anne walnut tea-caddy inlaid overall with geometric fruitwood banding, the hinged stepped rectangular top enclosing an interior with two divisions, 10³/₄in. wide. (Christie's)   **$1,602**

A Regency mother-of-pearl inlaid brown tortoiseshell tea-caddy, attributed to W. H. Tooke, inlaid overall with chinoiserie pagodas and stylized foliage, 8in. wide. (Christie's)   **$1,495**

A mahogany veneered miniature sideboard tea chest, inlaid brass stringing with a fitted interior, 13in. wide. (Woolley & Wallis)   **$1,265**

An enamel tea caddy, late 19th century, on turquoise ground, with fluted cut corners and circular lid, painted with landscape and strolling couple, some repair, 11cm. (Lawrence Fine Art)
                                 $1,158

A Chinese rectangular silver-mounted mother-of-pearl tea-caddy case, the walls and cover carved and engraved with animals, birds and butterflies, the mounts English, circa 1760, 7in. long. (Christie's)   **$2,167**

A Regency tortoiseshell tea-caddy, with domed octagonal top, the sides carved with blind Gothic arcading and quatrefoils, on ivory bun feet, 6¹/₄in. high. (Christie's)   **$2,826**

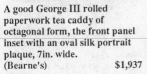

A good George III rolled paperwork tea caddy of octagonal form, the front panel inset with an oval silk portrait plaque, 7in. wide. (Bearne's)   **$1,937**

A George III sycamore and inlaid tea caddy of rectangular form with canted corners, the oval inlaid panels within foliate surrounds, 20cm. wide. (Phillips)   **$637**

A George III mahogany veneered tea caddy, inlaid satinwood and floral marquetry with canted corners, 4¹/₂in. high. (Woolley & Wallis)   **$500**

A Chinese Export gilt-mounted ivory and green-stained tortoiseshell tea-caddy, carved in low relief with chinoiserie landscapes, 8¹/₂in. wide. (Christie's) $2,991

A George III mahogany tea caddy, circa 1790, inlaid with harewood medallions and tulip banding, 4³/₄in. high. (John Nicholson) $437

Patriotic inlaid mahogany box, dated *1864*, 9¹/₄in. wide. (Skinner) $2,090

A mid-19th century rectangular three division tea caddy, veneered in scarlet tortoiseshell and inlaid with brass en premier et contre-partie, 12in. wide. (Christie's) $1,025

A Regency amboyna wood tea caddy, early 19th century, the sarcophagus shape with domed hinged lid inlaid with brass motifs and with a brass stepped rim, 15in. wide. (Christie's) $2,300

An early 19th century serpentine front tortoiseshell veneered tea caddy, opening to reveal two lidded zinc lined compartments, 20cm. wide. (Spencer's) $410

An early 19th century navette shaped giltwood and paper scroll tea caddy, with brass swing handle to the cover, 7³/₄in. wide. (Christie's) $1,361

A Regency ormolu-mounted penwork and painted tea-caddy of sarcophagus form, with hinged domed lid decorated with a chinoiserie pastoral scene, 7¹/₄in. wide. (Christie's) $1,681

A late Regency tortoiseshell veneered and ivory strung tea caddy, the canted lid inset with a silver plaque, the bowed sides with cast loop handles, 31cm. wide. (Phillips) $1,749

Large early 19th century figured walnut tea caddy with sarcophagus formed lid, ring handles and squat circular feet, 15 x 9in. (G. A. Key) $536

A good Regency penwork tea caddy, extensively decorated with neo-classical figures and motifs, 1815, 33cm. wide. (Phillips) $1,335

Late 17th/early 18th century Continental tortoiseshell and mother-of-pearl mounted box, 18¼in. wide. (Lawrence Fine Art) $4,500

A Tunbridgeware domed tea caddy inlaid with a view of Dover Priory within a mosaic border, fitted interior, 9³/₄in. wide.
(Bearne's) $602

A George III tortoiseshell veneered tea caddy, 8in. wide.
(Dreweatt Neate) $1,131

A good Regency tortoiseshell tea caddy with rising top, two division interior, breakfront on small wooden feet, 7³/₄in. wide.
(John Nicholson) $1,385

Shaped Tunbridge Ware double caddy.
(Derek Roberts Antiques)
                              $1,300

An early Victorian tortoiseshell veneered rectangular bow fronted tea chest, on copper ball feet, 8in. wide.
(Woolley & Wallis) $1,137

Regency mahogany tea caddy, central inlaid conch shell decoration, 7¹/₂in. long.
(Peter Wilson) $120

A Regency rosewood and brass inlaid tea caddy, of sarcophagus form, the interior fitted with three lidded canisters, all raised on bun feet, 33cm. wide.
(Phillips) $972

A Regency penwork tea caddy, decorated overall with chinoiserie scenes, the coffered hinged lid with Greek-key frieze, the sides with brass lion-mask handles, 12¹/₂in. wide.
(Christie's) $2,178

Fine Victorian walnut dome lidded tea caddy, inlaid with Tunbridgeware decoration, interior of two small boxes and a glass mixing bowl, 12in. wide.
(G. A. Key) $536

A Regency mother-of-pearl inlaid brown tortoiseshell tea-caddy, by W. H. Tooke with bow-fronted hinged rectangular top, 8in. wide.
(Christie's) $1,143

A George IV mahogany tea caddy, circa 1820, crossbanded with satinwood, inlaid roundel top on four brass ball feet, 5in. high.
(John Nicholson) $292

A George III satinwood, tulipwood crossbanded and boxwood outlined rectangular three-division tea caddy, on gilt paw feet, 9in. wide.
(Christie's S. Ken) $332

A large blonde mohair Steiff, German, circa 1908, with large black boot button eyes, wide apart ears, 27¹/₂in. high.
(Bonhams) $2,190

A rare 'Dicky' Steiff white plush covered teddy bear, with orange and black glass eyes, short plush covered muzzle, 12in. high, 1930.
(Christie's) $5,940

A pale golden plush covered teddy bear, with clear and black glass eyes, black stitched nose, smiling mouth and claws, 16in. high.
(Christie's) $412

Elliot, a unique blue plush covered teddy bear by Steiff, with black boot button eyes, pronounced cut snout, black horizontally stitched nose, black stitched mouth and claws, 13in. tall, circa 1908.
(Christie's) $76,354

'The Dancing Bears': a rare joined couple, the white plush lady-bear with elongated limbs, dancing with a golden plush covered gentleman-bear with elongated limbs, 12in. high, both with Steiff buttons in ears, circa 1910.
(Christie's) $6,500

A Steiff humped teddy bear with original gray eyes, long muzzle and covered in blond mohair, with growl and original pads, lacks button, circa 1925, 50cm. high.
(Auction Team Köln)
     $1,080

A rare early Steiff rod jointed silver plush teddy bear, German, circa 1904–5, the button removed, with long snout and black boot button eyes, standing 41cm. to top of ears.
(Sotheby's) $3,657

A rare and early Steiff golden plush covered teddy bear, with black shoe-button eyes, pronounced snout, remains of sealing-wax nose, 19in. high, 1905.
(Christie's) $6,395

A Steiff dark cinnamon plush teddy bear, German, 1920's, with button in ear and remains of red label, together with a Steiff bear, German, circa 1960, 29in. high.
(Sotheby's) $3,498

A large golden plush covered teddy bear with elongated limbs, boot button eyes, wide apart ears, felt pads, and Steiff button in ear, 1906–08, 28in. high.
(Christie's) $6,500

A Schuco tumbling teddy bear, with pale golden plush covered metal face, body and limbs, 4³/₄in. high.
(Christie's) $634

A Steiff dual plush petsy bear, German, circa 1928, with button in ear, blue glass eyes and center seam with blonde stitched snout, 16in. high.
(Sotheby's) $6,646

A Steiff honey golden plush covered teddy bear, with black boot button eyes, black stitched mouth and claws, swivel head, elongated jointed limbs, 12in. high, 1908–10.
(Christie's) $1,980

A rare rod-jointed Steiff blonde plush teddy bear, German, circa 1904–5, the long snout with remains of black stitching, black boot button eyes, 41cm. standing.
(Sotheby's) $2,194

A fine Steiff pale golden plush covered teddy bear, with large deep set black boot button eyes, black stitched nose, mouth and claws, swivel head, felt pads and hump, 28in. tall, circa 1910.
(Christie's) $9,841

An early 20th century Steiff Excelsior filled mid-brown colored plush teddy bear, with black boot button eyes, 60cm. tall.
(Spencer's) $2,331

A Steiff golden plush covered teddy bear, with large black boot button eyes, pronounced snout, black stitched nose, 23¹/₂in. high, circa 1910.
(Christie's) $3,467

A Steiff golden plush covered center seam teddy bear, with boot button eyes, stitched nose and claws, hump and button in ear, 16in. high, circa 1906.
(Christie's) $1,800

A Bell Telephone Mfg. Comp., Antwerp, desk telephone, circa 1930. (Auction Team Koeln) $75

A Praezisions Telephone, the first model by Siemens & Halske after Bell's patent, with wooden earpiece and leather covered stem, circa 1880. (Auction Team Koeln) $2,600

A line dial Le Parisien desk telephone by Unis France, with bakelite casing and handle, circa 1930. (Auction Team Koeln) $45

A highly decorative L.M. Ericsson & Co. desk telephone, circa 1910. (Auction Team Koeln) $1,100

A Norwegian wall telephone, with decorative cast iron back plate, and simulated intarsia tin 'desk' surface, by Aktieselskabet Elektrisk Bureau Kristiania, Oslo, circa 1890. (Auction Team Koeln) $1,700

A German Reichspost OB 05 telephone with crank, by Rudolf Krueger, 1907. (Auction Team Koeln) $225

A Western Electric magneto telephone with japanned finish, splayed feet and Bell Telephone Mfg. Co. handset, circa 1906. (Christie's) $817

A desk top coin telephone by Merk of Munich, with key, 1938. (Auction Team Koeln) $75

A French desk telephone by Ch. Ventroux Paris, wooden base and stand, receiver and extra receiver marked P. Jacquesson Paris, circa 1920. (Auction Team Koeln) $300

An American Candlestick desk telephone by Stromberg-Carlson, circa 1920. (Auction Team Koeln) **$375**

An early/hand Stanley telephone, with mahogany hand piece, by General Electric Co, London, circa 1880. (Auction Team Koeln) **$600**

Ericsson Skeleton desk telephone with megohmmeter, circa 1910. (Auction Team Köln) **$630**

An oak cased Ericsson Telephones Ltd Magneto telephone. (Spencer's) **$441**

A decorative Tax table telephone with magneto, by L M Ericsson, circa 1900. (Auction Team Koeln) **$1,125**

An early patented plated American desk telephone by the Western Electric Company, of candlestick form, 1904. (Auction Team Köln) **$293**

An OB wall telephone by Siedle & Soehne, Schwenningen, with wooden housing and with crank, circa 1910. (Auction Team Koeln) **$225**

A red PO type 232 telephone, English, mid 20th century. (Bonhams) **$428**

The Praezisions telephone, the first telephone by Siemens & Halske after Bell's patent (1876), with wooden ear piece and leather covered handle, circa 1880. (Auction Team Koeln) **$2,250**

A late 18th-century lacquered brass 2 inch reflecting telescope, signed on the back plate *Made by GEO ADAMS*, the leather covered 15in. long body tube, with speculum mirrors.
(Christie's) **$3,152**

An early 19th century brass 2½in. reflecting telescope, with turned support and folding tripod stand in a fitted mahogany box.
(Phillips) **$962**

An 8½-inch reflecting telescope, with painted steel tube, 76¼in. long, brass eyepiece and viewer, thought to be by George Calver, Chelmsford, Essex.
(Tennants) **$850**

A brass reflecting telescope by Nairne & Blunt, with terrestrial eyepiece, on folding tripod stand, late 18th century, 25½in. length of body tube.
(Christie's New York) **$1,540**

A rare late 18th century lacquered brass miniature refracting telescope, signed *Dollond, London*, the 1¼ inch lens covered with a screw-on dust cap.
(Christie's S. Ken) **$3,089**

A 3 inch reflecting telescope, signed on the back plate *JAMES SHORT LONDON*, on alt-azimuth mounting with column support, with inswept cabriole legs, 21in. wide.
(Christie's) **$3,362**

A fine late 18th century lacquered brass reflecting telescope, unsigned, with tapered pillar over detachable folding tripod, in fitted mahogany case, 15¼in. wide.
(Christie's) **$2,728**

A good late 18th century brass 4in. Gregorian reflecting telescope, signed Mackenzie, 15 Cheapside, London, sighting telescope and dust cap, body tube 61cm. long.
(Phillips) **$1,253**

An early 19th-century lacquered brass 4¾ inch reflecting telescope, unsigned, the 30¾in. long body tube with speculum mirrors and screw-rod focusing, 33¾in. wide.
(Christie's) **$3,992**

French terracotta bust of a young woman, Charles Eugene Breton, dated 1916, smiling with long tresses bound at the back, 22in. high.
(Skinner Inc.) $675

One of two Cretan terracotta oil jars, of bulbous form, each with three carved handles and waisted decoration, 19th century, 43¼in. high.
(Christie's)   (Two) $913

A 19th century French terra-cotta group of a Bacchante, in the manner of Clodion, an infant satyr at her side, 15½in. high. (Christie's S. Ken)
    $1,100

Hellenistic terracotta figure of Dionysus, circa 300 B.C., depicted as the god of the vine, with long curly hair and beard and wearing a wreath of leaves on his head, 7¾in. high.
(Butterfield & Butterfield) $3,025

A large pair of Italian terracotta busts of the rivers Reno and Zena shown as a god and goddess, by Andrea Ferreri, signed and dated, circa 1704, 35¾ and 37½in. high. (Christie's) $22,770

An English terracotta group of a grayhound bitch with three puppies, by Joseph Gott, on black marble circular socle, first half 19th century, 5⅜in. high. (Christie's) $715

A 19th century French terra cotta bust of Rouget de l'Isle, by David d'Angers, signed and dated *David 1835,* 45.5cm. high. (Christie's London)
    $13,300

A French terracotta group of 'Le Fleuve', after Jean-Jacques Caffiére, the bearded river-god shown seated, his left leg over an urn flowing with water, 19th century, 23½in. high.
(Christie's) $2,810

A terracotta bust of an Art Nouveau maiden, with long flowing hair, embellished with large trailing poppies in a green patination, 42cm. high.
(Phillips) $750

A Syro-Hittite terracotta jar, the body decorated with multiple stylized figures, Syria, circa 2000–1500 B.C., 3³/₄in.
(Bonhams) $1,061

A pair of French terracotta figures, by Gossin Frères, Paris, each in 18th century costume, each on a circular naturalistic base, signed, late 19th century.
(Christie's) $13,282

A Hellenistic terracotta female head with an ornate crown of rosettes, circa 2nd-1st century B.C., 4in.
(Bonhams) $522

A glazed terracotta oil jar, of baluster form, with two handles, and two others similar, 46in. high.
(Christie's) $2,718

A Continental painted terracotta group of three boys, German, circa 1900, made in Germany, 11³/₄in. high.
(Sotheby's) $1,925

An 18th century French terracotta portrait bust of a boy, his hair fastened en queue, signed *LP* on the reverse, 40cm. high.
(Phillips) $1,413

A terracotta bas relief of St. Anthony of Padua with the Infant Christ and angels, attributed to Massimiliano Soldani Benzi, 34.5 x 25cm., late 17th/early 18th century.
(Finarte) $5,338

A pair of eighteenth century glazed terracotta figures, each in two sections, with detail picked out in purple, in the form of a smiling bewigged footman with neckerchief, late 18th century, probably Italian, 64¹/₂in. high.
(Christie's) $96,000

A fine and rare modeled terra cotta newsboy architectural plaque, H. A. Lewis, South Boston, Massachusetts, 1883–1887, modeled in the half round with the figure of a running newsboy, 61in. wide.
(Sotheby's) $14,300

A terracotta copy of the Sleeping satyr, called the Barberini Faun, probably 19th century, 90cm. high. (Kunsthaus am Museum) **$6,811**

A pair of terracotta garden ornaments in the form of seated greyhounds, each wearing a studded collar, 33in. high, 19th century.
(Bearne's) **$7,144**

George Goudray 'Les Nenuphars', painted terracotta bust of a girl in Art Nouveau style, with incised signature, 23in. high.
(Lawrences) **$1,728**

A French terracotta bust of **Diana, modeled and cast by Albert-Ernest Carrier-Belleuse,** her head crowned by a crescent moon and star and star, signed *A. CARRIER*, second half 19th century, 24³/₄in. high without socle.
(Christie's) **$12,705**

Two Liberty & Co. terracotta jardinières, designed by Mrs. F. G. Watts, after Archibald Knox.
(Bonhams) **$1,495**

A Wiener Werkstätte terracotta bowl and cover, the circular cover surmounted by a stylized hunter and dog, covered in a running ink-blue glaze, with impressed *WW* monogram, 22.6cm. high.
(Christie's) **$804**

'Lisetta', an Ernst Wahliss terracotta plaque molded in relief with a profile bust of a young woman surrounded by a garland of flowers, 41cm. high.
(Christie's) **$334**

A pair of Watcombe Torquay terracotta portrait busts of Princess Louise and the Marquis of Lorne, circa 1871, 12½in. and 12¼in. high.
(Christie's) **$219**

Portrait medallion of Benjamin Franklin, signed and dated *J. B. Nini 1770*, terracotta, 142mm. diameter.
(Skinner) **$825**

A Shahsevan Sumak cradle, North Persia, each of the four sides comprising a central band in indigo blue, containing characteristic hexagonal motifs, 3ft. 2in. long.
(Phillips) $708

A needlework purse, worked in the shape of a frog, the front and back embroidered in green and brown shades of silk, 1¹/₂in. long, early 17th century.
(Christie's S. Ken) $2,972

A Queen Victoria souvenir beadwork purse, the gilt clasp marked *Victoria June 28th, 1838* with floral beadwork.
(Woolley & Wallis) $144

'Daffodil', a Morris & Co. curtain, designed by J.H. Dearle, printed cotton with braid border, repeating pattern of daffodils and wild flowers between waved stylized vines, 45 x 181cm.
(Christie's) $689

A mid-17th century embroidered cushion worked in silk and metal threads on ivory satin silk ground, having a small tassel at each corner, English, 26.5cm. x 31cm., circa 1660.
(Phillips) $1,112

A William Morris & Company embroidered wool portière designed by Henry Dearle, circa 1910, the central rectangular reserve embroidered with a flowering tree and song birds, 244 x 180.5cm.
(Christie's) $71,610

Beauvais tapestry pillow, 18th century, with one rounded side, sewn in shades of ocher, brown tan, various shades of green and blue, crimson and burgundy, 19 x 18¹/₂in.
(Butterfield & Butterfield) $1,100

A late 18th century chair back cover with colorful crewel work embroidery of a tree with bird and stylized peonies, roses and other flowers, 97cm. x 59cm.
(Phillips) $930

A mid-17th century needlework picture, the ivory satin silk ground worked in silk threads, showing Charles II and Catherine of Braganza, 29.5cm. x 26cm., circa 1660.
(Phillips) $1,112

A shield-shaped needlework purse, embroidered in colored silks and silver gilt threads, one side with a stag, the other with a unicorn, 4in. long, Continental, mid 18th century.
(Christie's) **$1,123**

A fine whitework picture depicting Judith presenting the head of Holofernes, embroidered with seed pearls, first half of 17th century, 5 x 3½in.
(Christie's) **$8,277**

An oval needlework picture, embroidered in colored silks, with a young girl holding a parrot and a bird cage, 13 x 12in., framed and glazed, early 18th century.
(Christie's) **$1,123**

Pieced worsted spread, America, 19th century, pink and olive patches arranged in a zig-zag pattern heightened with feather and parallel line quilting, 86 x 98in.
(Skinner) **$935**

A beadwork picture worked in many colored beads, with a lady and gentleman in a landscape, their hair of metal thread, 10 x 13in., English, mid 17th century.
(Christie's) **$2,763**

A shield shaped needlework purse of yellow silk, one side with the monogram CVI? possibly for the Emperor Charles VI, 4½in., Continental, circa 1740.
(Christie's) **$1,468**

Quilted chintz pocket, America, circa 1825, block printed plum tree and pheasant pattern in madder, blue and drab, 14in. long.
(Skinner) **$880**

A needlework casket, worked in colored silks against an ivory silk ground, depicting the story of Joseph, 5½in. x 14in. x 10in., with key and wooden case, English, 1660.
(Christie's S. Ken) **$159,225**

A rare needlework purse, with Tudor roses and thistles and fleurs-de-lys, crowns and crossed-swords and the initials *J.R.VIII*, very early 18th century.
(Christie's) **$1,815**

A Victorian beaded bag, with draw string top and tassel to the base, circa 1860.
(Woolley & Wallis) $134

A post war screen-printed linen panel by A. Fumeron, depicting a young girl playing a cello, 125 x 157cm.
(Christie's) $234

A needlework purse worked in green silk and gold thread in eye stitch with the initials *P.C.S.* and hearts, late 17th/early 18th century.
(Christie's) $998

A needlework picture, worked in colored silks and gilt threads, with the bust of Charles I within a raised work frame, 15 x 11in., English, late 17th century.
(Christie's) $2,649

Crewel embroidered linen pocket, America, late 18th century, worked in shades of yellow, green, blue and bound with variously printed cotton fabrics, 16¼in. long.
(Skinner) $990

Appliquéd and pieced table rug, England, initialed and dated *E.B. 1858* worked in red, blue, yellow, cream and brown wool patches, 66in. square.
(Skinner) $880

A rare early 18th century tapestry embroidery in the form of a card table top with projecting corner sections, 25 x 31in., glazed and framed.
(Locke & England) $3,440

A needlework picture, embroidered in colored silks, gilt and silver gilt threads, with a lady and gentleman standing in front of a castle, 7 x 10in., English, circa 1660.
(Christie's) $3,799

A petit point embroidered portrait of William and Mary, English, early 18th century, worked in predominantly blue and scarlet wools and silks, 14 x 10in.
(Sotheby's) $954

An oxidized brass theodolite signed *W. & L. Gurley, Troy N.Y.*, with graduated bubble level, rack-and-pinion focusing, in fitted mahogany case, 11¼in. high.
(Christie's) $547

A brass theodolite by OTTO FENNELL SOHNE CASSELL No. 19813 with telescope, graduated bubble levels, the enclosed scale with micrometer adjustment.
(Christie's S. Ken) $425

A late 19th century brass miniature theodolite by Troughton & Simms, with telescope, with twin verniers and magnifiers in mahogany case, 13¹/₂in. wide.
(Christie's) $684

An oxidized brass transit, signed on the silvered compass dial *W. & L. E. Gurley, Troy, N.Y.*, and further engraved *F W Lincoln Jr. & Co., Agents, Boston, Mass.*, in fitted mahogany case, 13¹/₂in. wide.
(Christie's) $1,051

A rare late 19th century lacquered brass transit theodolite indistinctly signed on the horizontal circle *Brunner freres a Paris* further engraved *Depot del a guerre*, the 8 inch vertical circle with silvered scale.
(Christie's) $8,525

A fine brass surveying theodolite, signed on the silvered dial *Troughton & Simms London*, the telescope with graduated bubble level, rack-and-pinion focusing, 13³/₄in. high.
(Christie's) $2,387

A fine lacquered brass transit theodolite, signed *Thomas Jones Charing Cross London*, the telescope with right angle eyepiece on sliding plate, early 19th century, 17¹/₄in. high.
(Christie's) $9,544

A late 19th century oxidized and lacquered brass transit theodolite, signed on the silvered compass dial *Stanley, Gt. Turnstile, Holborn, LONDON*, 13¹/₂in. wide.
(Christie's S. Ken) $1,448

A Stanley transit theodolite, the telescope with rack and pinion focusing, mounted in trunnion, with silver inset verticals and horizontal circles of degrees, 13in. high.
(Henry Spencer) $797

A mid Victorian black and gilt japanned tole purdonium, with shovel, 12½in. wide. (Christie's) **$750**

A Regency black and gilt tole tray with raised pierced rim, later painted with Napoleon observing the field of battle, 30in. x 22in. (Christie's) **$2,772**

A very fine and unusual paint decorated tinware apple tray, probably Connecticut, early 19th century, 11½in. wide. (Sotheby's) **$6,325**

A very fine paint decorated tinware canister attributed to the Filley Family, Connecticut, early 19th century, 8⅜in. high. (Sotheby's) **$4,945**

A pair of early 19th century japanned metal chestnut urns and covers, each body with twin lion mask ring handles, decorated with gilt heightened sprays of flowers, 30cm. high. (Phillips) **$1,660**

A paint decorated tinware tea caddy, Pennsylvania, early 19th century, the oval form with fitted circular lid, 4¼in. high. (Sotheby's) **$1,035**

A tin birdcage, New England, mid 19th century, the cylindrical form with tubular bars and shaped conical top suspended from a tin ring, 26in. high. (Sotheby's) **$288**

Painted Tin Trade sign, America, 19th century, painted ocher and green (paint loss). 8in. high. **$1,369**

Tole decorated tea dispenser, 19th century, advertising *Van Dyke*, 27½in. high. (Eldred's) **$154**

One of a pair of yellow and gilt-painted tole verrieres of oval shape, each painted with chinoiserie scenes, with waved rim and looped handles, 12½in. wide. (Christie's) (Two) $1,693

Paint decorated shaped tin tray, Continental, 19th century, salmon reserve centering a portrait medallion of a Hessian officer, 20½ x 16in. (Skinner Inc.) $330

Empire tin-lined zinc baignoire, circa 1820, with rounded tapering and slightly arched ends, 5ft. 4in. wide. (Butterfield & Butterfield) $1,100

A fine paint decorated tinware gooseneck coffee pot, Pennsylvania, early 19th century, decorated with large stylized floral rondels in red, green and yellow, 10½in. high. (Sotheby's) $5,750

A set of three japanned metal cylindrical tea canisters, the fronts decorated with armorials, 17in. high. (Christie's) $1,650

Rare pair of painted and decorated tin wall sconces, New England, circa 1830, each with crimped circular crest, 13½in. high. (Skinner Inc.) $1,800

A Regency painted tole jardiniere, decorated throughout with palmettes, a musical trophy and a vignette enclosing classical ruins against a green ground, 11in. high. (Christie's) $5,175

A fine paint decorated tinware deed box, Connecticut, early 19th century, painted with brilliantly colored red, yellow and green blossoms and buds, 10in. wide. (Sotheby's) $3,738

A Regency painted tole pitcher, early 19th century, with swelling vessel and bold handle decorated with chinoiserie vignettes. 9¼in high. (Christie's) $1,035

A RYNA 87 two slice folding toaster with original electric flex, unused, circa 1952. (Auction Team Köln) $39

An Estate Electric Toaster No. 177, 4 slice toaster with simultaneous turning mechanism, 1925. (Auction Team Köln) $208

A Meriden Mod. 60 decorative plated toaster with 2-slice tip mechanism, circa 1925. (Auction Team Köln) $77

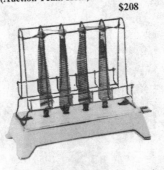

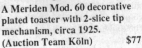

An early American Simplex T211 toaster with simple folding mechanism and heavy black enameled cast base, plated casing with wooden handle, 1909. (Auction Team Köln) $131

An early American General Electric D12 ceramic toaster with two-sided toasting fork, white ceramic base with gold decoration, original flex with metal plug, circa 1910. (Auction Team Köln) $772

An early Universal toaster No. E 945 by Landers, Frary & Clark, New Britain CT, with warming rack attachment, plated, circa 1918. (Auction Team Köln) $169

A chromium Hotpoint Mod. 129 T41 2-slice toaster with simultaneous tip mechanism, by General Electric, Bridgeport CT, 1929. (Auction Team Köln) $69

The first electric toaster, the Eclipse, with ceramic handle and base, patented 1893. (Auction Team Koeln) $2,200

A Hotpoint Model 115 T 1 plated toaster with two-sided tip mechanism, by the Edison Electric Appliance Co. Inc., New York, circa 1919. (Auction Team Köln) $69

Elem 4-slice swivel toaster. (Auction Team Köln) **$144**

The Universal E 947 toaster, with two-sided horizontal turning facility and turned wood handles. (Auction Team Köln) **$92**

Universal E 942 single slice push-in toaster, with keep-warm facility. (Auction Team Köln) **$105**

A Torrid 2-slice toaster by Frank Wolcott Mfg. Co., Hartford, CT, with unusual key operated swing mechanism. (Auction Team Köln) **$228**

Universal E 9410 heart shaped push-button toaster with unusual flip mechanism, circa 1929. (Auction Team Köln) **$850**

American Auto Toastmaker Model 73, with spring mechanism and timer with bell, in decorative case, by Sears Roebuck, Chicago. (Auction Team Köln) **$157**

Prometheus nickel plated 2-slice folding toaster, German, circa 1925. (Auction Team Köln) **$157**

Gold Seal Electric nickel plated toaster with vertical turning mechanism. (Auction Team Köln) **$294**

Universal D-12 porcelain mounted toaster with low wire basket, circa 1910. (Auction Team Köln) **$653**

A Hess lithographed tinplate crank-operated flywheel-drive four-seat rear-entrance tonneau, with composition driver and pierced artillery wheel, circa 1908, 11in. long.
(Christie's) $895

A Märklin hand-painted kitchen, circa 1900, featuring a sideboard, sink, shelves, pots, pans and elaborate cookstove, 37in. wide.
(Christie's) $9,900

A German ocean liner with three stacks, having single mast and painted red and black with a tan deck, 11in. long.
(Butterfield & Butterfield) $413

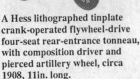

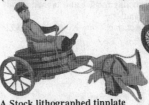

A Günthermann lithographed tinplate spring-motor four-seat open tourer, with chauffeur, crank-handle spring-wind and four opening doors, circa 1912, 11½in. long.
(Christie's) $1,025

A Stock lithographed tinplate spring-motor 'Paddy's Pride', with original box lid, 8in. long.
(Christie's) $746

Compagnie Industrielle du Jouet, clockwork P2 Alfa Romeo racing car finished in red, treaded tires, 52cm., with key.
(Phillips) $2,872

Lehmann Uho car with driver having lithographed plate mounted on hood marked with cities around the world, 7½in. long.
(Butterfield & Butterfield) $715

A rare and unusual tinplate castle, probably German, featuring steps leading to spires, towers, turrets and tiled courtyards, 31in. high.
(Christie's) $4,400

A large Tippco lithographed tinplate clockwork sixteen-seat charabanc with folded tinplate hood, with driver, 1920's, 18in. long.
(Christie's) $2,610

A French bicycle racing game, circa 1920, in fitted box which opens to reveal circular race course with four cyclists, 18 x 18in.
(Christie's) $2,420

An early Günthermann tinplate keywind hook and ladder fire truck, circa 1910, hand-painted in red and yellow, with four original firemen, 14in. long overall.
(Christie's) $4,620

An unusual Märklin pond, circa 1900, the circular base molded and painted to resemble a grassy slope with boat and cupola at center, 16in. wide.
(Christie's) $1,760

482

A fine oversized early Märklin tin-plate horsedrawn hansom cab, the cast lead white and black horse on wheels, 28in. long overall.
(Christie's) $18,700

A Märklin painted tinplate swimming bath, with operating diving-board and ladder, circa 1900, 17in. long, 14½in. wide overall.
(Christie's) $871

A magnificent early French tinplate horse-drawn open double decker tram, circa 1890, pulled by a pair of brown metal horses in livery, 42in. long overall.
(Christie's) $71,500

A rare Märklin clockwork painted camouflaged tinplate anti-aircraft half track, with steering and rubber front tires, circa 1938, 8in. long.
(Christie's) $348

An "Automatic Rower" keywind oarsman toy, circa 1915, constructed of wood with a jointed cloth dressed sailor having a composition body and celluloid face, 23in. long.
(Christie's) $3,520

A Meier penny toy lithographed tinplate three-funnel battleship 'Emden', 5¼in. long.
(Christie's) $597

Triang painted and lithographed tinplate clockwork Captain George Eyston's Magic Midget, finished in green and white rubber tires, in original box, circa 1935, 15in. long.
(Christie's S. Ken) $1,128

A French painted cast metal and steel single-seater military biplane, finished in khaki with French markings, circa 1917, 12in. long.
(Christie's) $447

A Lineol painted tinplate farm wagon, finished in gray, with painted composition driver and two-oxen team, on wheeled bases, circa 1934, 15in. long.
(Christie's) $653

A Nomura battery operated electrically lit tinplate Cadillac, with forward and reverse action, in original box, circa 1952.
(Christie's) $1,492

A Carette tinplate four-passenger keywind open tourer, circa 1910, lithographed in red, gold and black, and all four original passengers, 8½in. long.
(Christie's) $5,060

A German painted tinplate clockwork billiards player, the brown table with circular feed action, circa 1910, 11in. long.
(Christie's) $559

A Carette painted and lithographed tinplate four-light landaulette, with chauffeur, opening doors, handbrake, start/stop lever and luggage rack, circa 1911, 13in. long. (Christie's) **$2,424**

A Lehmann lithographed and painted tinplate EPL No. 640 Zig-Zag, rocking boat in rolling wheel. (Christie's) **$746**

A Distler lithographed tinplate clockwork motorcyclist, with belt-driven rear wheel and oscillating steering action, 1920's, $7^{1}/2$in. long. (Christie's) **$1,715**

A tinplate cooking range and accessories, German, circa 1900, the body finished in black with brass handrail and embossed brass doors, 11in. high. (Sotheby's) **$833**

A Märklin tinplate 'Aeropal" hand or steam operated lighthouse roundabout, circa 1909, with stairways and many flags aloft, 19in. high. (Christie's) **$22,000**

A Lehmann painted tinplate and fabric 'Dancing Sailor' with 'Brandenburg' cap tally, with swaying action, in original box. (Christie's) **$736**

A splendid Märklin tinplate hand-painted castle with revolving moat, finished in tones of tan and green, with red and blue accents, 13in. high. (Christie's) **$3,520**

A Märklin Third Series painted tinplate clockwork Ship of the Line, with twin masts, single main funnel and six gun turrets, circa 1930, 14in. long. (Christie's) **$2,610**

A German steam-jet powered painted tinplate two-tier carousel, fitted with seats and painted composition horses and figures, circa 1910, 15in. high. (Christie's) **$2,904**

A Distler lithographed tinplate electrically-lit clockwork fire brigade turntable ladder truck, with driver and five seated crew, 1930's, 14½in. long.
(Christie's) $485

A Lehmann lithographed tinplate flywheel-drive EPL No. 723 'Kadi', two Chinamen with tea chest, 7in. long.
(Christie's) $895

A large Bing tinplate keywind transitional open phaeton, circa 1902, hand-painted in yellow with maroon piping, 13¾in. long.
(Christie's) $24,200

A Müller and Kadeder painted tinplate wind-up roundabout, with four painted cream-color canoes with painted figures of children and paper propellers, 11½in. high.
(Christie's) $2,640

A rare Bing hand-enameled tinplate clockwork 'Brake' four-seat motor car, black mudguards, plated wheels, rubber tires and mechanism operating eccentric steering, circa 1902, 10in. long.
(Christie's) $7,458

A Lehmann lithographed tinplate EPL No. 590 autobus, with original price label and tags for securing string handle, in original box with pencil inscription *Motor Buss*.
(Christie's) $3,356

A Bing painted and lithographed tinplate Continental windmill, in original A W Gamage box, circa 1912.
(Christie's) $354

A painted and carved wooden rocking horse, English, 1910, the well carved horse with remains of original paintwork, 52in. long.
(Sotheby's) $787

A Lehmann 'Adam' porter featuring a man in a blue jacket and red print trousers pushing an orange suitcase, 8in. high.
(Butterfield & Butterfield)
$935

A Louis Vuitton upright trunk covered in LV fabric and bound in brass, the lid opening to reveal a top compartment with tray, 25 x 16 x 45¹/₂in. (Christie's) $8,516

Brass and wood bound Louis Vuitton trunk with fitted interior, 44¹/₂in. high. (Eldred's) $2,750

A Louis Vuitton shoe case, covered in LV fabric and bound in leather and brass, divided into eight shoe compartments, 24 x 14 x 8in. (Christie's) $1,553

A Louis Vuitton suitcase covered in LV fabric with travel stickers, bound in brass, the interior fitted with a tray, 24 x 15 x 8¹/₂in. (Christie's) $595

A Louis Vuitton Jubilee wardrobe trunk, covered in LV fabric, bound in brass and wood, with key commemorating Louis Vuitton London's Jubilee 1885–1935, 22 x 22 x 44in. (Christie's) $2,225

A brown pigskin leather dressing case with foul weather cover, the interior fitted with silver gilt (London 1929) mounted tortoiseshell topped flasks, hairbrushes and manicure set. (Christie's) $869

A gentleman's green leather dressing case, completely fitted with four silver-topped (London 1907) flasks, 20 x 14 x 7in. (Christie's) $750

A Louis Vuitton shoe secretaire, fitted with thirty shoe boxes with lids, two large drawers top and bottom and tray, 112 x 64 x 40cm. (Onslow's) $11,470

A brown crocodile leather dressing case, the interior completely lined in matching crocodile leather, 26 x 16 x 8in. (Christie's) $525

A fine tan leather hat box by The Our Boys Clothing Company Oxford Street, with red velvet lining.
(Onslow's) $197

A Louis Vuitton shaped motor car trunk, covered in black material, interior with three matching fitted suitcases, 85 x 65 x 50cm.
(Onslow's) $6,265

A fine large leather Gladstone bag, with key and straps, initialed M.W.H., little used, with foul weather cover.
(Onslow's) $358

A Louis Vuitton Johnny Walker whisky traveling drinks case, fitted for one bottle of whisky, two bottles of mineral water, one packet of cheese biscuits, two glasses and ice container.
(Onslow's) $3,580

A Louis Vuitton gentleman's cabin trunk, bound in brass and leather with leather carrying handle, on castors, 91 x 53 x 56cm.
(Onslow's) $1,486

A Louis Vuitton special order tan pigskin gentleman's fitted dressing case, accessories include silver tooth brush, soap and talc containers, 54 x 32cm., circa 1930.
(Onslow's) $4,475

A Louis Vuitton "Sac Chauffeur", the two circular halves covered in black material, the lower section watertight, 89cm diameter, circa 1905, designed to fit inside spare tires.
(Onslow's) $5,370

A Garrison black fabric covered picnic service for six persons, complete with yellow and gold crockery, 56 x 40 x 30cm.
(Onslow's) $716

A matching white hide suitcase and hat box by John Pound, with chromium-plated locks and foul weather covers, the suitcase 56 x 36cm.
(Onslow's) $501

A fine mahogany cutlery tray, possibly Thomas and/or John Seymour, Boston, Massachusetts, circa 1805, the sides with dividers cyma-shaped, width 10½in.
(Sotheby's) $5,750

A late George III mahogany booktray with carrying handle and galleried sides, 17in. wide.
(Christie's London) $600

A William IV rosewood double-sided book-tray of rectangular shape with spindle-filled central divide, on ribbed bun feet, 16½in. wide.
(Christie's) $3,678

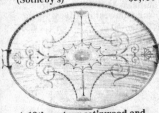

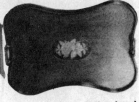

A 19th century satinwood and marquetry oval tray, 24in. wide.
(Dreweatt Neate) $819

A mid-Georgian brass-inlaid padoukwood tray in the style of John Channon with rectangular top, the gallery pierced with ovals, 18¾in. wide.
(Christie's) $8,712

Edwardian mahogany bordered tray with attached brass handles with marquetry motif to center, 20 x 13in.
(G. A. Key) $119

Victorian papier mâché tray on later stand, with scalloped rim, painted with a central flower-filled urn, a peacock perched on a branch to one side, 32in. wide.
(Butterfield & Butterfield) $1,760

A Japanese silver colored metal and Shibayama tray, the central gold lacquered panel inlaid in mother of pearl, 25.5cm. wide.
(Spencer's) $3,663

A Gallé marquetry tray on stand, inlaid in various fruitwoods with five sailing boats, on carved trestle ends, 78cm. high.
(Christie's) $1,637

A late 18th/early 19th century oval tray, the burr yew plateau with satinwood fan patera and tulipwood crossbanded edge, 28¼in. wide.
(Christie's) $650

Victorian black lacquered papier mâché tray, mid 19th century, stamped *Jennens & Bettridge*, centered by a floral design, 31in. wide.
(Skinner Inc.) $1,430

A Liberty 'Tudric' tray designed by Archibald Knox, of bowed rectangular section cast in relief with foliate roundels, 19¼in. wide.
(Christie's) $712

A 19th century mahogany wine tray, with six square divisions, 10¾in. long. (Christie's) **$600**

A George III mahogany and yew wood tray of oval brass-bound form with raised shaped handles, 21¾in. wide. (Bearne's) **$1,204**

A mid-Georgian mahogany bottle-stand with arched carrying-handle and four divisions, on ogee bracket feet. (Christie's) **$11,682**

A Regency rectangular papier mâché tray by Clay, King St., Covent Garden, decorated in red, green and gold, 30 x 22in. (Bearne's) **$2,471**

Cantonese enameled tray, depicting a village and shipping scene, circa 1750, approximately 12 x 8in. (G. A. Key) **$596**

Fisher-Strand inlaid Art Nouveau tray, Germany, circa 1900, rectangular tray with bronze handles and brass stylized inlay, 13¾in. long. (Skinner) **$330**

Good Regency papier mâché painted tray, circa 1815, painted with the Battle of Trafalgar, with five warships, including Admiral Nelson's VICTORY, 29½in. wide. (Butterfield & Butterfield) **$3,300**

A Russian porcelain oval tray based on a design by Sergei V. Chekhonin with the silhouette in red of a sailor of the Baltic Fleet, circa 1921, 17¾in. wide. (Christie's) **$2,225**

A George III inlaid mahogany serving-tray, probably English, 1780-1800, centering an oval reserve engraved and shaded with a shell on a green ground, 28¼in. wide. (Christie's) **$1,500**

A mid 19th century tole oval tray, painted flowers and clouds, gilt foliage sprays to the serpentine border, 25in. (Woolley & Wallis) **$864**

A George III brass-bound mahogany oval tray with scrolled handles and gadrooned lip, previously with castors, the brass probably later, 27½ x 19¾in. (Christie's) **$6,090**

A Victorian black papier mâché tray of shaped rounded rectangular form, centered by a copy of the famous work, after Landseer. (Spencer's) **$512**

A rosewood work box, circa 1840, the top decorated with a fine panel depicting the state apartments at Windsor Castle, 11½in. wide.
(Sotheby's) $2,557

A rosewood dressing table companion, circa 1850, the top fitted with compartments, three lidded and four with associated scent bottles, on bun feet, 12¾in. wide.
(Sotheby's) $2,046

A rosewood tea caddy of sarcophagus shape, circa 1845, the top inlaid with floral panel, floral and geometrical bandings, all sides with broad floral bandings, 12½in. wide.
(Sotheby's) $546

An unusual rosewood stationery box, circa 1845, the angled hinged top inlaid with the Prince of Wales' feathers and royal supporters and *Ich Dien*, 8in. wide.
(Sotheby's) $1,500

Miniature cabinet of cube design with six drawers by Thomas Barton.
(Derek Roberts Antiques) $2,500

A coromandel tea caddy, circa 1850, of rectangular form, with a cube pattern top and floral mosaic inlaid sides, 5½in. wide.
(Sotheby's) $409

A coromandel jewel cabinet, circa 1860, the hinged top with a scene of Tonbridge Castle enclosing compartments, on bun feet, 10in. wide.
(Sotheby's) $818

A fine rosewood writing slope, circa 1860, the top inlaid with a panel depicting Hever Castle, with floral bandings and parquetry panel, 12in. wide.
(Sotheby's) $2,302

A fine rosewood tea caddy, circa 1860, the top inlaid with Battle Abbey Gatehouse flanked by oval medallions inlaid with geometrical designs, 14½in. wide.
(Sotheby's) $2,216

A rosewood box, circa 1860, the top decorated with a floral panel depicting a lily and nasturtiums surrounded by a broad rose banding, 10½in. wide. (Sotheby's) $682

A rosewood tea caddy, circa 1840, the hinged lid with a sycamore-reserved scene of Muckross Abbey, the three division interior lacking blending bowl, on bun feet, 12in. wide. (Sotheby's) $682

A rosewood work box, circa 1850, inlaid throughout with floral borders, the lined interior with a removable tray, 12in. wide. (Sotheby's) $938

A bird's-eye maple jewel cabinet, circa 1850, the floral inlaid hinged lid above a fitted interior, on bun feet, 8¾in. wide. (Sotheby's) $716

A fine coromandel box, circa 1870, the top with a fine inlaid view of Battle Abbey Gatehouse and floral bandings, 9½in. wide. (Sotheby's) $2,216

An adjustable bookstand, circa 1860, veneered in stained ash on one face and rosewood on the back, incorporating two mosaic panels of flowers, 10in. wide. (Sotheby's) $767

A stained ash box, circa 1870, the top decorated with a fine view of The Parade (Pantiles, Tunbridge Wells), 9½in. wide. (Sotheby's) $2,131

A late Victorian burr walnut, satinwood and Tunbridge ware table cabinet, the top with a view of Windsor Castle, with squat bun feet, 14½in. high. (Christie's S. Ken) $1,706

A coromandel stationery box, circa 1850, the domed top with a scene of Tonbridge Abbey, the lined interior with divisions and concave sides, 9¾in. wide. (Sotheby's) $938

A North's typewriter with original metal case, a rare over-strike machine with reverse type bar arrangement, 1892. (Auction Team Koeln) $5,250

A very rare Salter No. 5 improved model of the English type bar typewriter, with three row circular keyboard, 1892. (Auction Team Koeln) $4,125

An Emerson No. 3 typewriter with unusual type bar arrangement, 1907. (Auction Team Koeln) $900

An early Daugherty US type bar typewriter, with open type basket, 1890. (Auction Team Koeln) $1,800

An unusual Burnett American typewriter with slanting type basket and streamlined shape, one of only four models known, 1907. (Auction Team Koeln) $9,000

American Chicago cylinder type machine, 1898. (Auction Team Koeln) $600

A Sholes & Glidden typewriter with blue and gold line decoration and rare fully detachable hood, 1873. (Auction Team Koeln) $6,750

A Moya Visible No. 2 typewriter with oxidized top-plate and mahogany case. (Christie's) $2,082

An American Postal No. 7 typewriter, produced only in limited numbers as a prototype, with wooden case and instructions, 1908. (Auktion Team Köln) $3,477

A rare Diskret code typewriter with control arm and sliding second scale for printing coded texts, by Friedr. Rehmann, Karlsruhe, 1899.
(Auktion Team Köln)
$3,766

A rare Morris index typewriter, American, circa 1885.
(Auction Team Koeln)
$22,000

A rare Bar-Lock Model 1b typewriter by Columbia Type Writer Co New York with highly ornate cast iron type basket.
(Auction Team Koeln)
$5,250

A rare 'The Pocket Typewriter, Swan Arcade, Bradford', with name and characters on circular white enamel dial, 10cm. long, circa 1887.
(Phillips)
$1,900

A rare Munson typewriter, the three row keyboard with octagonal keys, horizontal type-sleeve and wide ribbon,
(Phillips)
$1,500

An early Hammond typewriter, in oak case, 13^{1}/2in. wide.
(Anderson & Garland)
$165

American Index pointer typewriter with semi-circular control scale, 1893. (Auction Team Koeln)
$600

An Active typewriter with sliding typewheel, steel frame and leatherette case.
(Christie's)
$521

A rare Fitch typewriter with downstroke action and plate of the Fitch Typewriter Company Ltd., London.
(Christie's S. Ken)
$6,089

A fine Italian violoncello by Carlo Tononi labeled *Carlo Tononi Bolognese/Fece in Venetia l'A 1730.* (Christie's)

$240,240

A violoncello by Bernard Simon Fendt, London, circa 1830, in black hard carrying case. (Phillips)

$22,230

A fine Italian violin by Camillo Camilli labeled *Camillo Camilli/Fecit in Mantova/Anno 1742.* (Christie's)

$74,360

A fine violin by Antonius & Hieronymus Fr. Amati bearing the maker's label *Cremonen Andreae Fil. F 1621.* (Phillips)

$141,200

A fine Italian violin by Guiseppe Rocca labeled *Joseph Antonius Rocca/fecit Taurini/anno Domini 18,* the one-piece back of handsome medium curl. (Christie's)

$111,540

A fine French violin labeled *Jean Baptiste Vuillaume à Paris/Rue Croix des Petits Champs* and numbered *1912* and signed on the inside back. (Christie's)

$53,130

An interesting violoncello by a maker not recorded, bearing the label: *Made by Smith Sycamore Street Sheffield* and dated *1789.* (Phillips)

$7,524

A violin by Giovanni Battista Rogeri bearing the label *Jo. Bap. Rogerius Bon: Nicolai Amati de Cremona Alumnus Brixiae fecit Anno Domini 1695.* (Phillips)

$40,595

A fine Italian violin by Giovanni Pressenda labeled *Joannes Franciscus Pressenda q. Raphael/fecit Taurini anno Domini 1837*. (Christie's)

$102,245

A fine violin by Jean Baptiste Vuillaume in Paris, circa 1840, bearing his original undated label. (Phillips)

$60,600

A Hardangerfele violin circa 19th century Swedish, bearing a repair label. (Phillips)

$1,252

An Italian violin by Giovanni Battista Guadagnini labeled *Joannes Baptista filius Laurentji Gua/dagnini fecit Placentiae 174?*. (Christie's)

$164,472

A fine Italian violin, circa 1720, labeled *Gia. Bapt. Grancino*, the scroll by another contemporary maker, l.o.b. 13⁷/₈in., in case with two bows. (Christie's)

$57,032

An important violin by Antonio Stradivari labeled *Antonio Stradivari Cremonensis/Faciebat Anno 1720*. (Christie's)

$1,776,940

A fine composite violin, the back, ribs and scroll by Giuseppe Guarneri, filius Andrea, labeled *Joseph Guarnerius*. (Christie's)

$55,440

An important and rare, small size violin by *Antonius & Hieronymus Fr Amati Cremonen, Andreae Fil. F 1588*. (Phillips)

$89,000

A gentleman's rectangular Swiss gold wristwatch by Longines, the signed movement numbered 3739388, 30 x 25mm.
(Phillips) $756

An 18 carat gold perpetual calendar wristwatch with moonphases and chronograph, signed *Patek Phillipe & Co., Geneve, No. 863178*, circa 1944.
(Christie's) $108,625

Dunhill, an 18ct. white gold, diamond and emerald-set petrol burning lighter with watch inset to the hinged front cover, 43 x 38mm.
(Christie's) $5,518

A fine enameled gold verge watch, the case signed *Huaud le Puisne fecit*, the purpose made movement signed *Hoendshker, Dresden*, finely painted with "Roman Charity" after Simon Vouet, 40mm. diameter.
(Christie's) $38,500

Rolex, a rare pink gold Oyster anti-magnetic triple calendar chronograph wristwatch, tonneau case, silvered dial with outer date ring and central date hand, dot five-minute divisions, apertures for day and month.
(Christie's) $24,633

Eterna, a gold and enamel keyless hunter pocketwatch, the front cover with a painted portrait of a seated Maharajah with guilloche background, matt gilt dial with Arabic numerals, 49mm. diameter.
(Christie's) $1,584

Patek Philippe & Co., Genève, a fine steel chronograph wristwatch, circular case with scalloped bezel, two-tone silvered dial with baton and Arabic numerals.
(Christie's) $13,196

Minerva, a silver keyless masonic openface pocketwatch, a silver shield-shaped case engraved with masonic symbols, the signed movement jeweled to the center.
(Christie's) $1,885

A gold steel Rolex Oyster Perpetual chronometer bubble-back wristwatch with gold bezel, the pink dial with Arabic quarter-hour marks, 30mm. diameter.
(Christie's S. Ken) $1,568

A Swiss gold circular Rolex wristwatch, the signed white dial marked in ¹/₅th seconds, with Arabic numerals and red sweep seconds, 29mm. diameter.
(Phillips) $1,080

Rolex, an unusual gilt masonic keyless pocketwatch, in triangular case with masonic symbols in relief, signed mother of pearl dial.
(Christie's) $2,913

A white metal keyless open-face Mickey Mouse pocket watch by Ingersoll in plain case, the white dial with Arabic numerals, 49mm. diameter.
(Christie's S. Ken) $885

Rolex, a stainless steel Cosmograph chronograph wristwatch, the black bezel calibrated in units per hour, the brushed steel dial with raised baton numerals, and subsidiary seconds, 37mm. diameter.
(Christie's) $4,455

A gold quarter repeating automata verge pocketwatch, black enamel dial-plate with central white enamel dial, two vari-colored gold jacquemarts apparently striking on two bells, 53mm. diameter.
(Christie's) $5,630

Cartier, an 18ct. gold Santos automatic calendar wristwatch, the octagonal bezel secured by eight screws, the white dial with Roman numerals and secret signature at VII, 30mm. diameter.
(Christie's) $4,455

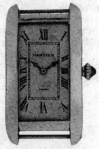

Eberhard, a late 1920's gold single button chronograph wristwatch, sweep center seconds operated by a single button in the band, signed movement jeweled to the center.
(Christie's) $1,713

A Swiss gold curved rectangular wristwatch by Cartier, the signed dial with Roman numerals, the numbered case also marked 1326, with cabochon winder.
(Phillips) $6,480

Patek Philippe, Genève, a gold automatic wristwatch, made for the company IOS, case with integral gold mesh bracelet, movement signed, with gold rotor, 35mm. diameter.
(Christie's) $3,343

Copper touring-car weathervane, America, circa 1910, missing one headlight, 31in. long. (Skinner) $1,430

Steam locomotive sheet metal weathervane, America, late 19th century, 64in. long, wear to paint decoration. (Skinner) $2,310

A fine and rare gilded copper peacock weathervane, attributed to A. L. Jewell, Waltham, Massachusetts, third quarter 19th century, the elegant swell-bodied figure of a stylized peacock with repoussé tail and wrought iron legs, 39in. long. (Sotheby's) $9,350

A silhouette sheet iron weathervane, American, 19th century, depicting a horse with cut ears, full tail, and raised foreleg and a standing groom holding his reins, 28³/₄in. long. (Christie's) $1,870

A molded sheet copper flying dove weathervane, American, late 19th/early 20th century, the boxy stylized silhouette of a flying dove with wings raised and tail extended, overall length 22¹/₂in. (Sotheby's) $770

A fine and rare molded and gilt copper weathervane attributed to A.L. Jewell & Co., Waltham, Massachusetts, circa 1870, the galloping shell-bodied centaur, with drawn bow and arrow and shaped head and beard, 39in. long. (Christie's) $33,000

Molded copper and zinc weather vane, stamped *A L Jewell & Co Waltham, Mass* 1852–1861, in the form of Ethan Allen, (bullet holes, imperfections), 42in. long. (Skinner Inc.) $4,400

A carved and painted pine flying Canada goose, possibly Maritime Provinces, early 20th century, in the style of Ira Hudson, length 40in. (Sotheby's) $2,750

Paint decorated sheet metal pig weather vane, America, 19th century, 42in. long. (Skinner) $2,070

Molded copper stag weather vane, attributed to Harris & Co., Boston, 19th century, with fine verdigris surface, (bullet holes), 31in. long. (Skinner Inc.) $4,675

An unusual molded and painted copper horse and sulky weathervane, probably New York, third quarter 19th century, repaired bullet holes, 45in. wide. (Sotheby's) $11,000

An amusing carved and painted pine and sheet copper horned cow weathervane, American, late 19th/early 20th century, 33½in. long. (Sotheby's) $2,530

A rare and important carved and gilded pine large rooster weathervane, Maine, late 18th century, the striking and impressive full-bodied figure with prominent comb, beak, wattle and strong feather and tail detail, 28in. high. (Sotheby's) $66,000

A molded copper and zinc ram weathervane, attributed to L. W. Cushing & Company, Waltham, Massachusetts, third quarter 19th century, length 34¼in. (Sotheby's) $6,600

A molded copper weathervane, American, late 19th/early 20th century, modeled in the form of a shooting star continuing to a serrated and fluted banner mounted on a spire, 41in. long. (Christie's) $7,150

Carved and painted trumpeting angel weathervane, America, 19th century, the figure of a woman with trumpet painted white, black, pink and blue-green, 33¼in. wide. (Skinner Inc.) $2,200

WHISKY

Oban Whisky, circa 1890, Registered J. Walter Higgin, Oban Distillery, Oban, N.B, three-piece molded glass bottle.
(Christie's) $2,525

Logans Extra Age, circa 1940, by appointment to His Majesty The King, screw cap, lead capsule embossed *Laird O'Logan De Luxe*.
(Christie's) $377

Dallas Dhu, 64-year-old, distilled 16th April 1921, debonded 1st July 1985 from cask No. 296, bottled by Dallas Dhu Distillery.
(Christie's) $8,580

Chivas Regal, 25-year-old, early 20th century, shoulder label reads *Purveyors to His Majesty King George V and to Her Majesty Queen Alexandra*, imported by Fred L. Meyers & Son, The Sugar Wharf, Kingston, Jamaica.
(Christie's) $2,826

Heather Dew, circa 1930, blended and bottled by Mitchell Brothers Ltd., Glasgow, imported by Foreign Vintages Incorporated, New York, glazed stoneware flagon reads *The Greybeard, Federal Law Forbids Sale or Re-Use Of This Bottle*.
(Christie's) $283

Buchanan's Finest Old Liqueur Scotch Whisky, circa 1925, Buchanan's Liqueur, By Appointment, Distillers to His Majesty The King, James Buchanan & Co. Ltd., Glasgow and London.
(Christie's) $673

Young's Directors Special, circa 1925, Edward Young & Co. Limited, Glasgow, London and Liverpool, Quality First Since 1797, Regd. Trade Mark.
(Christie's) $367

Dalmore, circa 1900, remains of sample label still distinguishable, distilled by McKenzie Brothers, Dalmore Distillery, Ross-shire, sample drawn June 190?.
(Christie's) $440

Dalintober, 40-year-old, distilled 1868, bottled 1908, accompanied by tie on neck label (see illustration). Lead capsule slightly damaged.
(Christie's) $4,934

500

House of Lords Fine Old Scotch Whisky, 1899, *'Lion Brand', Special Quality*, Stephen W. Young & Co., Bonnington, Edinburgh.
(Christie's) $1,806

Scotch Whisky P.S.2., mid 19th century, circular flask embossed *Hay & Son Ltd Scotch P.S.2 Whiskey, Registered*, three-piece molded glass bottle.
(Christie's) $612

Long John Special Reserve, 1925, bottle bears British Analytical Control Certificate dated September 1925.
(Christie's) $429

The Glenlivet, 1937, distilled 12th May 1937 for the Coronation of H.M. King George VI and bottled by the distillery in the year of Coronation of H.M Queen Elizabeth II.
(Christie's) $1,973

Heirloom Finest Scotch Whisky, circa 1860–1900, bottled by Rutherford & Kay, Edinburgh, London and Birmingham, three-piece molded glass bottle, driven cork, embossed lead capsule, unlabeled.
(Christie's) $2,512

Strathmill Fine Old Scotch Whisky, circa 1910, *By Appointment to H.M. King George V*, bottled and guaranteed by W. & A. Gilbey Ltd., driven cork, wax capsule.
(Christie's) $3,925

Kings Quality Rare Old Blended Special Liqueur, circa 1940, *By Appointment, Purveyors to the Royal Household during three reigns*, J. G. Thomson & Co. Ltd., Leith.
(Christie's) $408

Haig Dimple, circa 1940, bottle embossed *Federal Law Forbids Sale or Re-Use of This Bottle* around shoulder, Haig & Haig, Edinburgh, Scotland.
(Christie's) $1,683

John O'Groats Scots Liqueur Whisky, circa 1920, Registered Trade Mark, Produced and bottled by The Drambuie Liqueur Company, Edinburgh, Scotland.
(Christie's) $765

Fine Victorian walnut sewing box with Tunbridgeware crossbanding.
(G. A. Key) $169

A Regency horn veneered work box of sarcophagus outline, with ribbed sides and gabled top, 11in. wide.
(Christie's S. Ken) $462

Shaker butternut sewing box, the drawers with ebonized diamond escutcheon and turned ivory pull, New England, circa 1820, 7½in. wide. (Robt. W. Skinner Inc.)
$7,750

A Regency octagonal work box finely painted with putti, masks, birds, urns, flowers and foliage, the interior divided into compartments with similarly-decorated covers.
(Bearne's) $512

A South Indian coromandel workbox with waved hinged rectangular top enclosing a fitted interior with two tiers, 19th century, 17½in. wide.
(Christie's) $5,544

A Regency mahogany and foliate inlaid sewing box, the interior with tray, 9¼in. wide.
(Christie's) $867

A late 18th/early 19th century sycamore workbox in the form of a miniature cottage, with central chimney, the compartmented interior with a thimble, 5½in. wide.
(Christie's S. Ken) $1,662

A Regency amarillo, parquetry and penwork sewing box, the coffered rectangular top inlaid with cube-pattern within a triangular-pattern border.
(Christie's) $1,198

An early 19th century blond tortoiseshell veneered work casket, of plain rectangular form, veneered with rectangular panels, the hinged cover opening to reveal a paper and velvet fitted interior, 30cm. wide.
(Spencer's) $459

A fine Regency rosewood traveling writing box, the exterior inlaid with foliate cut-brass and with sunken carrying handles, 19in. wide.
(Bearne's)   **$1,185**

An Anglo-Indian Vizigapatam ivory and sandalwood table-bureau banded overall with scrolling foliate decoration, the sides formerly with carrying-handles, late 18th century, 20½in. wide.
(Christie's)   **$2,449**

A polychrome marquetry and oyster-cut walnut writing-box, the rectangular top with molded edge and inlaid with a flower spray within an oval, the marquetry and oyster-veneers late 17th century, 19¼in. wide.
(Christie's)   **$1,495**

A Regency leather covered and gilt metal molded lady's dressing table compendium, the chamfered, reeded top with a gilt metal plaque inscribed *Eliza B. Swayne, March 5th 1817.*, 12in. wide x 13½in. high.
(Christie's S. Ken)   **$1,646**

A giltmetal-mounted red velvet-covered casket, the fall-flap enclosing two long and four short drawers each mounted with a pierced foliate panel, the sides with carrying handles, early 17th century, 15¾in. wide.
(Christie's)   **$3,432**

A late 18th century North Italian hardwood and ivory inlaid table cabinet, the interior with an arrangement of nine drawers, the doors with caryatid putti, 10½in. wide.
(Christie's)   **$1,266**

A George III rectangular gold-mounted shagreen writing set, the hinged cover and front wall applied with a cagework of putti, birds and scrolls, circa 1770, 2½in. wide.
(Christie's)   **$3,520**

An unusual mid Victorian rosewood and mother of pearl inlaid traveling box, with ring handles to sides and raised on tapering bun feet, 26cm. wide.
(Phillips)   **$660**

An 18th century German lacquered table writing desk, the panels decorated with chinoiseries, the sloping fall enclosing two pairs of drawers flanking three compartments above a long drawer, 46cm. wide.
(Phillips)   **$1,352**

A fine George III inlaid satinwood lap desk, circa 1795, the rectangular hinged top centering an oval reserve inlaid with a conch and beetle, 20in. wide.
(Sotheby's) **$2,750**

Regency rosewood and brass inlaid lap desk, circa 1815, inlaid with star, crescent and leaf design, 21¹/₂in. wide.
(Skinner Inc.) **$1,800**

Small Victorian figured walnut lap desk, brass bound and having fitted interior, 11in. wide.
(G. A. Key) **$294**

A late 17th/early 18th century Indo-Colonial hardwood and ivory inlaid traveling writing cabinet, the fall front, top and sides decorated all over with a profusion of arabesque scrolls, 1ft. 3in. wide.
(Phillips) **$1,908**

A late Victorian ormolu-mounted figured-walnut writing-case by Asprey, the interior with hinged blue velvet-lined slope enclosing satinwood wells and with Berry's Patent ink and light boxes, 14in. wide.
(Christie's) **$4,057**

A Victorian coromandel writing slope, the interior in unused state with tooled green velvet and glass ink bottles with engraved gilded coves.
(Locke & England) **$896**

A German neo-classic ormolu-mounted mahogany writing box, late 18th century, attributed to David Roentgen, 10¹/₂in. wide.
(Christie's) **$15,525**

A late Victorian oak stationery cabinet and combined writing slope with fitted interior and fall front, 14in. wide.
(David Dockree) **$300**

A Victorian coromandel and foliate-cut brass-mounted traveling writing box, the inset jasperware plaquettes with raised classical figure subjects, the interior compartmented and with fittings, 14in. wide.
(Christie's S. Ken) **$1,773**

INDEX

INDEX

INDEX

INDEX